Psychology for Professional Groups

D0714738

Psychology for Occupational Therapists

Psychology for Professional Groups

Series Editors: Antony J. Chapman and Anthony Gale

Psychology for Professional Groups is a new series of major textbooks published with the British Psychological Society. Each is edited by a teacher with expertise in the application of psychology to professional practice and covers the key topics in the training syllabus. The editors have drawn upon a series of specially commissioned topic chapters prepared by leading psychologists and have set them within the context of their various professions. A tutor manual is available for each text and includes practical exercises and projects, further reading and general guidance for the tutor. Each textbook shows in a fresh, original and authoritative way how psychology may be applied in a variety of professional settings, and how practitioners may improve their skills and gain a deeper understanding of themselves. There is also a general tutorial text incorporating the complete set of specialist chapters and their associated teaching materials.

Other titles:
Psychology and Management. Cary L. Cooper
Psychology for Social Workers. Martin Herbert
Psychology for Teachers. David Fontana
Psychology and Medicine. David Griffiths
Psychology for Physiotherapists. E. N. Dunkin
Psychology for Careers Counselling. Ruth Holdsworth
Psychology for Speech Therapists. Harry Purser
Psychology for Nurses and Health Visitors. John Hall
Psychology and People: A tutorial text. Antony J. Chapman and Anthony Gale

Psychology for Occupational Therapists

Fay Fransella

First published 1982 by THE BRITISH PSYCHOLOGICAL SOCIETY
and THE MACMILLAN PRESS LTD.

Distributed by The Macmillan Press Ltd, London and
Basingstoke. Associated companies and representatives
throughout the world.

ISBN 0 333 31859 5 (hard cover)
ISBN 0 333 31883 8 (paper cover)

Printed in Great Britain by Wheatons of Exeter

Note: throughout these texts, the masculine pronouns have
been used for succinctness and are intended to refer to both
females and males.

The conclusions drawn and opinions expressed are those of
the authors. They should not be taken to represent the
views of the publishers.

Contents

Foreword

This book is one of a series, the principal aims of which are to illustrate how psychology can be applied in particular professional contexts, how it can improve the skills of practitioners, and how it can increase the practitioners' and students' understanding of themselves.

Psychology is taught to many groups of students and is now integrated within prescribed syllabuses for an increasing number of professions. The existing texts which teachers have been obliged to recommend are typically designed for broad and disparate purposes, and consequently they fail to reflect the special needs of students in professional training. The starting point for the series was the systematic distillation of views expressed in professional journals by those psychologists whose teaching specialisms relate to the applications of psychology. It soon became apparent that many fundamental topics were common to a number of syllabuses and courses; yet in general introductory textbooks these topics tend to be embedded amongst much superfluous material. Therefore, from within the British Psychological Society, we invited experienced teachers and authorities in their field to write review chapters on key topics. Forty-seven chapters covering 23 topics were then available for selection by the series' Volume Editors. The Volume Editors are also psychologists and they have had many years of involvement with their respective professions. In preparing their books, they have consulted formally with colleagues in those professions. Each of their books has its own combination of the specially-prepared chapters, set in the context of the specific professional practice.

Because psychology is only one component of the various training curricula, and because students generally have limited access to learned journals and specialist texts, our contributors to the series have restricted their use of references, while at the same time providing short lists of annotated readings. In addition, they have provided review questions to help students organize their learning and prepare for examinations. Further teaching materials, in the form of additional references, projects, exercises and class notes, are available in Tutor Manuals prepared for each book. A comprehensive tutorial text ('Psychology and People'), prepared by the Series Editors, combines in a single volume all the key topics, together with their associated teaching materials.

It is intended that new titles will be added to the series and that existing titles will be revised in the light of changing requirements. Evaluative and constructive comments, bearing on any aspect of the series, are most welcome and should be addressed to us at the BPS in Leicester.

In devising and developing the series we have had the good fortune to benefit from the advice and support of Dr Halla Beloff, Professor Philip Levy, Mr Allan Sakne and Mr John Winckler. A great burden has been borne by Mrs Gail Sheffield, who with skill, tact and courtesy, has managed the production of the series: to her and her colleagues at the BPS headquarters and at the Macmillan Press, we express our thanks.

Antony J. Chapman
UWIST, Cardiff

Anthony Gale
University of Southampton

May 1982

Introduction
Fay Fransella

The subject matter of this volume

This volume aims to provide you, an occupational therapist, with psychological knowledge which will increase understanding of yourself and of others and thus enhance your professional skills. The chapters are divided up in terms of some of the important roles you play, or will play, in the full knowledge that there are others some may think of equal or greater importance. The number of very diverse roles you are called upon to play necessitates a relatively large number of chapters. Even so, these cover only a small portion of the whole discipline of psychology. Because the nature of your work involves your being in close contact with individuals over a prolonged period of time, the topics chosen are mainly from the personal and interpersonal areas in psychology.

Everything we do can, in some senses, be seen as an experiment. In your training, you will experiment with new knowledge: you will like some and reject some. But you will also, in a very real way, experiment with the sort of person you are and, by the end of your training, you will have created a new person.

In order to do this in a useful way, you will have to increase your knowledge of your present self. For example, you will have to develop your resources to be able to help the young and the aged and infirm, either with colleagues in a hospital or by yourself in the community. You will have to develop a high level of patience and compassion as you watch other people struggle with daily living and with death or those whose disruptive behaviour seems at times designed to try the patience of a saint. You will have to decide before the end of training whether you prefer to work mainly with a psychiatric or a physically handicapped population, and you will need to be ready to adjust perhaps to working on your own after training, which not only means coping with loneliness but also being self-reliant. The first chapter by Bannister deals with ways of, and issues involved in, increasing knowledge of the self.

As you come to know yourself more, so you will want to increase your knowledge of others. One way to do this is to see them in terms of some theoretical framework. We all have our own personal theories about people, and theories of personality simply offer you explicit statements of your otherwise implicit understandings. Another reason for studying how psychologists have tried to explain human personality is that you will be working alongside medical or other colleagues who themselves work within a particular framework. For instance, if you decide to specialize in psychiatric work, many of the psychiatrists will conduct their individual and group therapy along psychodynamic lines: that is, they use the ideas of Freud or Jung. If you are asked to participate in such a group, it is important to understand the psychological language being spoken. There are no rights and wrongs about the theories discussed in chapter 2; the one you finally decide upon as best for you is a personal decision.

So much for you as a person. The text moves on next to aspects of psychology that relate to a person's interactions with others. The first two chapters in the section deal with the development of the child, both in terms of personal abilities and in relation to society. It is of value to know what behaviours are usual in children at certain ages and how these change with time. This is particularly relevant for those who go to work in the community or those specializing in work with young children. Sometimes, socialization does not progress satisfactorily and disruptions in the mother-child relationship occur. Some very influential work was carried out in the early 1960s with young monkeys who were isolated from their mothers early in life. The young monkeys were studied, and an attempt was made to understand the effects this isolation had on their later development. You will find very few animal studies cited in this volume, although they are not uncommon in psychology as a whole. These studies are described partly because of the light they throw on the development of abnormal behaviour, but also because it gives you the opportunity to consider the extent to which it is reasonable to draw comparisons between animals and humans, and to generalize findings from animal studies to humans.

Other aspects of development that are discussed include the effect of our social class on the language we develop, the nature and role of play, and the development of our sexual identity. We are not concerned in the study of language with the accents we have, or the English or French that we speak, but with the extent to which our patterns of thought may be influenced by the social class environment in which we develop. You will notice that here, and at several other points in this book, there are apparent diversions into the role our gender plays in our lives. Since the majority of occupational therapists are female, I believe it is useful for you to know what psychology has to say about such matters as sex-role stereotyping, fear of success, and so forth. It will be important for your understanding of the problems facing some of your female patients and for your own understanding of the blocks and prejudices which you may encounter as you climb up the career ladder. For instance, it is no idle question to ask yourself 'Why are there so few women in top jobs?'

For those who choose to work in the community or in geriatric and psycho-geriatric hospital wards it is very necessary to have some ideas about the nature of the social problems relating to ageing. You will also sometimes find yourself, as a professional or private person, having to face the dying and the bereaved. Such experiences call for special skills from us all.

Interviewing forms an essential part of the occupational therapist's working life, be it with relatives, an old person, or someone psychologically disturbed. Although much of our social interaction is dominated by words, much is communicated non-verbally. It is very helpful to know about some of these non-verbal cues when trying to gain insight into what another is trying to convey. This also extends into a discussion of training in social skills, a form of work in which occupational therapists are increasingly involved. All this is described in Argyle's chapter.

The last chapter in the section dealing with interactions with others is about the ways in which we can describe those whom society says are 'disturbed'. You will quickly realize, if you have not done so already, that our ways of categorizing people to a large extent determine how we interact with them.

Above all else, the occupational therapist is a teacher. Part III therefore contains information on motivation, conditioning and the learning of skills. Up to this point terms like 'reinforcement' have been used without much detailed information: for instance, when talking about social skills training. Both classical and instrumental conditioning are outlined here, in order to clarify what has gone before and to set the stage for Beech's chapter on behaviour therapy and behaviour modification. For many, your work will involve encouraging a patient to carry out some physical movement which causes pain, so Part III ends with a chapter aimed at increasing your understanding of the complexities of the experience of pain.

How do you know that what occupational therapists do is of any use? That may sound an odd question, but it is obviously an important one if the answer were to be 'NO use'. Research is something occupational therapists are increasingly concerning themselves with and for this you need a knowledge of scientific method (chapter 13). Occupational therapists also often feel it necessary to assess the memory, intelligence or attitudes of their patients. This is far more difficult than at first appears. You will find some of the issues involved in psychological measurement, and the difficulties inherent in it, discussed in chapter 14.

If you intend to advance in your career, you will soon find it necessary to develop the skills of a manager. You may have to organize a district service, ensure that the cash returns match the expenditure on materials, and so forth. The chapters on institutions and organizations will help you understand, and hence be in a better position to grapple with, the complexities of management.

Lastly, there is the vexed question of the occupational therapist as a psychological therapist, whether acting as counsellor, behaviour therapist or in the more complex role of psychotherapist. Whether you are visiting people in their homes or trying to help people with their problems, in groups or individually, you need to know some of the ways in which others before you have tried to be of help to their fellow humans. It is with accounts of this complex and fascinating work that this volume ends.

The subject matter of psychology in historical perspective

In order to be able to grasp fully the issues involved in all aspects of psychological enquiry, it is useful to have a conceptual framework. For instance, you will be reading about urges, reinforcements, constructs, self-actualization, scientific method, and much else besides. Without a framework, these may seem like isolated categories with nothing to weld them together to make up the discipline of psychology.

It is true that there is no single agreed approach to the study and understanding of human (and animal) behaviour. But, as with so many other things, if you consider the problem from a relatively high level of abstraction, some of the apparent disorganization within the subject becomes comprehensible.

One way of looking at a problem is to see how it got there in the first place. This as much applies to a personal problem in yourself or a client as it does to a discipline like psychology. For instance, knowing that Pavlov's dogs became 'neurotic' because they failed to be able to distinguish between a circle and an ellipse, having been conditioned to respond to the former and not to respond to the latter, makes their otherwise extraordinary behaviour understandable. If you can understand someone's problem from a biographical perspective you may be able to help them to find ways of solving it. It is a historical perspective which I hope will help provide you with a way of unifying the various concepts used in the different chapters to come. A great deal is about the nature of knowledge.

For want of somewhere better to start, we find Plato (427 BC–347 BC) arguing that we all have within us a part, or soul, which existed in a previous world of Being. This Being is perfect and, because we receive a part of it at birth, we have innate knowledge about the nature of things. But we immediately forget it at birth, so in life we have to look inside ourselves in order to attain a glimpse of this knowledge; and we can do this by using the method of dialectical reasoning which the character of Socrates made famous.

Aristotle (384 BC–322 BC) said something to the contrary. He said that knowledge comes largely from the senses, and by no means from our intellect alone. We come to know things by observation of external events. He was not arguing that we could not reason intellectually, but rather that

this was of secondary importance to reasoning demonstra-
tively. In formulating the principle of demonstrable reasoning, Aristotle was paving the way for our present-day
concern with empirical research. Facts must be demonstrated
and not solely reasoned about in the mind. Aristotle was a
biologist, and so for him we are natural beings, a part of
nature, and must be studied as such.

The centuries went by with little change as far as we
are concerned here until the sixteenth century, when Galileo
and Descartes appeared. Galileo (1564-1642) brought mathematics into scientific study. He felt that without this
skill we could not decipher the knowledge which nature possesses. It was Descartes (1586-1650) who split us clearly
into two parts: one part mechanical body and the other
'incorporeal, that is to say mind or soul which we may
define as a substance which thinks'.

Newton (1642-1727) then developed Galileo's approach
to experiments into the form of scientific method that is
recognizable today (see chapter 13). Newton saw the entire
universe as a perfect machine which is governed by precise
laws. And it is these laws which can be discovered by experimentation. At this same time, Locke (1632-1704) was
saying that he accepted Descartes' dualism, but saw the
mind, as well as the body, as working on the principle of
mechanics: mental mechanics as opposed to material mechanics. Locke also introduced a term which is often used today, that of the mind being a 'tabula rasa': a blank sheet
upon which external events imprint themselves through
our senses. Here we have the defining characteristics of
'Empiricism'.

From these ideas came the eventual development of
Watson's behaviourism, a model stressing both the passive
nature of the organism and the necessity to study it scientifically by experimentation. In 1913 Watson said:

> Psychology as the behaviorist views it is a purely
> objective experimental branch of natural science. Its
> theoretical goal is the prediction and control of be-
> havior. Introspection forms no essential part of its
> methods, nor is the scientific value of its data depen-
> dent upon the readiness with which they lend themselves
> to interpretation in terms of consciousness. The be-
> haviorist, in his efforts to get a unitary scheme of
> animal response, recognises no dividing line between
> man and brute.

Going back now to the eighteenth century, we find
that Kant (1724-1804) was proposing an alternative to the
strictly mechanistic scientific approach to the study of
the universe and Man. He argued that we can never be in a
position to perceive reality directly (the noumena); all we
can see is what has been sifted through our 'mind's eye'
(the phenomena). We are seen by Kant as acting rather than
reacting. By reasoning we create mental 'categories' through

which we sift experience, and in this way our minds bring
something to our experience and act upon it. You will see
how clearly such ideas are reflected in the thinking of
Kelly and his psychology of personal constructs (constructs
through which we actively peer at life and so place our
interpretations upon it). In chapter 1 you will see how
Bannister represents this Kantian point of view in psychology. But, in fact, the whole humanistic movement in this
century can be said to have followed the path laid down by
Kant. This can particularly be seen in the theories and
therapies of such people as Kelly, Rogers and Maslow.

Along the opposite, behaviourist path, with the model
of the person as reactor to external events, come Pavlov
and Skinner with their theories relating to learning, conditioning and behaviour therapy (see chapters 10 and 18).
Psychologists argue fiercely about the rights and wrongs of
each approach.

A second argument stems from the idea, inherent in
psychological thought since Aristotle's time, that human
beings are part of nature. If this is so, then the subject
matter of psychology must include its physical underpinnings. The argument about such physical REDUCTIONISM
rests on the assumption that one set of abstractions
(psychology) will ultimately have to be reduced to another
set (such as physiology or chemistry) in order for the
phenomena to be adequately explained, because the latter
abstractions are in some way more 'basic'. Bannister takes
a totally non-physicalistic stand in his chapter, and
elsewhere discusses reductionism as follows:

> Perhaps the key to misconceptions in this type of re-
> ductionism is the notion that problems (or phenomena
> or areas of study) exist somehow independently of the
> sciences which define them. A chemical 'problem' is one
> which is stated IN CHEMICAL TERMS and a psychological
> problem is so because it represents alternative lines of
> implication for a group of psychological concepts (this
> is why it is a problem). As such it cannot be solved in
> non-psychological terms. What may happen is that some
> other problem involving similar operational definitions
> is set up in other (e.g. neurophysiological) terms. This
> can be solved in such neurophysiological terms but the
> psychologically defined problem has not thereby been
> 'transcended' or 'reduced', it remains to be solved in
> its own terms (Bannister, 1970).

In addition to the problem of languages, there is the
question 'Is it really true that physiological constructs
are more basic than psychological ones?' Some say 'yes' and
some say 'no'. For example, in a recent book you will find
Eysenck talking about a bio-social model and strongly supporting reductionism, as does Miller (1980).

A third argument centres round whether or not Newtonian
scientific method is appropriate to the study of persons.
The Newtonian view assumes that there is an objective

reality 'out there' to be studied; it assumes that ultimately we will have all the pieces of the jig-saw puzzle and so come to understand the nature of nature; it assumes that we can observe events without their being changed by the very act of our observing them; and it aims to predict events. But physics had a revolution earlier this century with the arrival of quantum mechanics. This new physics does not assume that there is an objective reality 'out there'; it does assume that we cannot observe something without changing it; and it claims only to correlate experience correctly. According to quantum mechanics, it is not possible, even in principle, to know enough about the present to make a complete prediction about the future. This is not because of the enormity of the task, or the poverty of measuring instruments, but because of the fact that we can only choose certain aspects to study and to come to know. In his fascinating book, 'The Dancing Wu-Li Masters', Gary Zukav (1979) gives the following example:

> The mind-expanding discovery of quantum mechanics is that Newtonian physics does not apply to subatomic phenomena. In the subatomic realm, we cannot know both the position and the momentum of a particle with absolute precision. We can know both, approximately, but the more we know about one, the less we know about the other. We can know either of them precisely, but in that case, we can know nothing about the other.

These three arguments (humanism versus behaviourism, reductionism or no reductionism, and whether we can know reality or we cannot) are currently very lively within psychology, for it is not simply academic 'truth' that is at stake. Psychologists are people, as are scientists. Einstein said: 'The state of mind which enables a man to do work of this kind is akin to that of the religious worshipper or lover. The daily effort comes ... straight from the heart.'
Agnew and Pike (1969) put it poetically:

> The rejection of a theory once accepted is like the rejection of a girl friend once loved - it takes more than a bit of negative evidence. In fact, the rest of the community can shake their collective heads in amazement at your blindness, your utter failure to recognize the glaring array of differences between your picture of the world, or the girl, and the data.

References

Agnew, N.M. and Pike, S.W. (1969)
The Science Game. Englewood Cliffs, NJ: Prentice-Hall.
Bannister, D. (1970)
Comment on H.J. Eysenck's 'Explanation and the concept of personality.' In R. Borger and F. Cioffi (eds), Explanation in the Behavioural Sciences. Cambridge: Cambridge University Press.

Eysenck, H.J. (1980)
   The bio-social model of man and the unification of
   psychology. In A.J. Chapman and D.M. Jones (eds),
   Models of Man. Leicester: The British Psychological
   Society.
Miller, E. (1980)
   Neuropsychology and the relationship between brain and
   behaviour. In A.J. Chapman and D.M. Jones (eds),
   Models of Man. Leicester: The British Psychological
   Society.
Watson, J.B. (1913)
   Psychology as the behaviorist sees it. Psychological
   Review, 20, 158-177.
Zukav, G. (1979)
   The Dancing Wu-Li Masters. New York: Hutchinson.

Acknowledgements

I wish to acknowledge the help of several people who have
been particularly concerned with this volume. These include
two occupational therapists: Anne Murdoch, who was a great
help in selecting the chapter topics, and Gina Selby, who
provided several of the examples. There was also the encouragement and interest expressed by the Series Editors,
but particularly by Tony Gale who gave me most skilful
guidance when the going got tough. Lastly, there was Jane
Farrer who spent a great deal of time and energy in getting
the manuscript into its final stage.

Part one

The Occupational Therapist as a Person

1

Knowledge of self

D. Bannister

What is self?

Definition is a social undertaking. As a community we negotiate the meaning of words. This makes 'self' a peculiarly difficult term to define, since much of the meaning we attach to it derives from essentially private experiences of a kind which are difficult to communicate about and agree upon. Nevertheless, we can try to abstract from our private experience of self qualities which can constitute a working definition. Such an attempt was made by Bannister and Fransella (1980) in the following terms.

Each of us entertains a notion of our own separateness from others and relies on the essential privacy of our own consciousness

Consider differences between the way in which you communicate with yourself and the way in which you communicate with others. To communicate with others involves externalizing (and thereby blurring) your experience into forms of speech, arm waving, gift giving, sulking, writing and so on. Yet communicating with yourself is so easy that it seems not to merit the word communication: it is more like instant recognition. Additionally, communicating with specific others involves the risk of being overheard, spied upon or having your messages intercepted and this contrasts with our internal communications which are secret and safeguarded. Most importantly, we experience our internal communications as the origin and starting point of things. We believe that it is out of them that we construct communications with others. We know this when we tell a lie because we are aware of the difference between our experienced internal communication and the special distortions given it before transmission.

We entertain a notion of the integrity and completeness of our own experience in that we believe all parts of it to be relatable because we are, in some vital sense, the experience itself

We extend the notion of me into the notion of my world. We think of events as more or less relevant to us. We distinguish between what concerns and what does not concern us. In this way we can use the phrase 'my situation' to indicate the boundaries of our important experience and the ways in which the various parts of it relate to make up a personal world.

We entertain the notion of our own continuity over time; we possess our biography and we live in relation to it

We live along a time line. We believe that we are essentially the 'same' person now that we were five minutes ago or five years ago. We accept that our circumstances may have changed in this or that respect, but we have a feeling of continuity, we possess a 'life'. We extend this to imagine a continuing future life. We can see our history in a variety of ways, but how we see it, the way in which we interpret it, is a central part of our character.

We entertain a notion of ourselves as causes; we have purposes, we intend, we accept a partial responsibility for the consequences of our actions

Just as we believe that we possess our life, so we think of ourselves as making 'choices' and as being identified by our choices. Even those psychologists who (in their professional writing) describe humankind as wholly determined, and persons as entirely the products of their environments, talk personally in terms of their own intentions and purposive acts and are prepared to accept responsibility, when challenged, for the choices they have made.

We work towards a notion of other persons by analogy with ourselves; we assume a comparability of subjective experience

If we accept for the moment the personal construct theory argument (Kelly, 1955, 1969) and think not simply of 'self' but of the bipolar construct of self versus others, then this draws our attention to the way in which we can only define self by distinguishing it from and comparing it to others. Yet this distinction between self and others also implies that others can be seen in the same terms, as 'persons' or as 'selves'. Our working assumption is that the rest of humankind have experiences which are somehow comparable with, although not the same as, our own and thereby we reasonably assume that they experience themselves as 'selves'.

We reflect, we are conscious, we are aware of self

Everything that has been said so far is by way of reflecting, standing back and viewing self. We both experience and reflect upon our experience, summarize it, comment on it and analyse it. This capacity to reflect is both the source of our commentary on self and a central part of the experience of being a 'self'. Psychologists sometimes, rather quaintly, talk of 'consciousness' as a problem. They see consciousness as a mystery which might best be dealt with by ignoring it and regarding people as mechanisms without awareness. This seems curious when we reflect that, were it not for this problematical consciousness, there would be no psychology to have problems to argue about. Psychology itself is a direct expression of consciousness. Mead (1925) elaborated this point in terms of the difference between 'I' and 'me', referring to the 'I' who acts and the 'me' who reflects upon the action and can go on to reflect upon the 'me' reflecting on the action.

Do we or do we not know ourselves?

The question 'do you know yourself?' seems to call forth a categorical 'yes' by way of answer. We know, in complete and sometimes painful detail, what has happened to us, what we have to contend with and what our thoughts and feelings are. We can reasonably claim to sit inside ourselves and know what is going on.

Yet we all have kinds of experience which cast doubt on the idea that we completely know ourselves. A basic test (in science and personal life) of whether you understand someone is your ability to predict accurately what they will do in a given situation. Yet most of us come across situations where we fail to predict our own behaviour; we find ourselves surprised by it and see ourselves behaving in a way we would not have expected to behave if we were the sort of person we thought we were.

We also sense that not all aspects of ourselves are equally accessible to us. There is nothing very mysterious in the notion of a hidden storehouse. We can confirm it very simply by reference to what we can readily draw from it. If I ask you to think about what kind of clothes you wore when you were around 14 years old you can probably bring some kind of image to mind. That raises the obvious question: where was that knowledge of yourself a minute ago, before I asked you the question? We are accustomed to having a vast knowledge of ourselves which is not consciously in front of us all the time. It is stored. It is not a great step to add to that picture the possibility that some parts of the 'store' of your past may not be so easily brought to the surface. We can then go one stage further and argue that although parts of your past are not easily brought to the surface they may nevertheless influence the present ways in which you feel and behave.

The best known picture of this kind of process is the Freudian portrait of the unconscious. Freud portrayed the self as divided. He saw it as made up of an id, the source of our primitive sexual and aggressive drives; a super-ego, our learned morality, our inhibitions; and an ego, our conscious self, struggling to maintain some kind of balance between the driving force of the id and the controlling force of the super-ego. Freud argued that the id is entirely unconscious and a great deal of the super-ego is also unconscious, and that only very special strategies such as those used in psychoanalytic therapy can give access to the contents of these unconscious areas of self. We do not have to accept Freud's particular thesis in order to accept the idea of different levels of awareness, but it may well be that

13

the enormous popularity of Freudian theory is due to the fact that it depicts what most of us feel is a 'probable' state of affairs; namely, that we have much more going on in us than we can readily be aware of or name.

Indeed, if we examine our everyday experience then we may well conclude that we are continually becoming aware of aspects of ourselves previously hidden from us.

A great deal of psychotherapy, education and personal and interpersonal soul-searching is dedicated to bringing to the surface hitherto unrecognized consistencies in our lives.

How do we know ourselves?

There is evidence that getting to know ourselves is a developmental process: it is something we learn in the same way that we learn to walk, talk and relate to others. In one study (Bannister and Agnew, 1977), groups of children were tape-recorded answering a variety of questions about their school, home, favourite games and so forth. These tape-recordings were transcribed and re-recorded in different voices so as to exclude circumstantial clues (names, occupations of parents and so forth) as to the identity of the children. Four months after the original recording the same children were asked to identify their own statements, to point out which statements were definitely not theirs and to give reasons for their choice. The children's ability to recognize their own statements increased steadily with age, and the strategies they used to pick out their own answers changed and became more complex. Thus, at the age of five, children relied heavily on their (often inaccurate) memory or used simple clues such as whether they themselves undertook the kinds of activity mentioned in the statement; 'That boy says he plays football and I play football so I must have said that'. By the age of nine, they were using more psychologically complex methods to identify which statements they had made and which statements they had not made. For example, one boy picked out the statement 'I want to be a soldier when I grow up' as definitely not his because 'I don't think I could ever kill a human being so I wouldn't say I wanted to be a soldier'. This is clearly a psychological inference of a fairly elaborate kind.

Underlying our notions about ourselves and other people are personal psychological theories which roughly parallel those put forward in formal psychology. A common kind of theory is what would be called in formal psychology a 'trait theory'. Trait theories hinge on the argument that there are, in each of us, enduring characteristics which differentiate us from others, who have more or less of these characteristics. The notion that we or someone else is 'bad-tempered' is closely akin to the notion in formal psychology that some people are constitutionally 'introverted' or 'authoritarian' and so forth. The problem with trait descriptions is that they are not explanatory. They are a kind of tautology which says that a person behaves in a bad-tempered way because he is a bad-tempered kind of person. Such approaches tend to distract our attention from what is going on between us and other people by firmly lodging 'causes' in either us or the other person. If I say that I am angry with you because I am 'a bad-tempered person' that relieves me of the need to understand what is going on specifically between you and me that is making me angry.

Environmental and learning theories in psychology have their equivalents in our everyday arguments about our own nature. The fundamental assertion of stimulus-response psychology, that a person can be seen as reacting to his environment in terms of previously learnt patterns of response, is mirrored in our own talk when we offer as grounds for our actions that it is all 'due to the way I was brought up' or 'there was nothing else I could do in the circumstances'. Those theories and approaches in formal psychology which treat the person as a mechanism echo the kinds of explanation which we offer for our own behaviour when we are most eager to excuse it, to deny our respon-sibility for it and to argue that we cannot be expected to change.

Any theory or attempt to explain how we come to be what we are and how we change involves us in the question of what kind of evidence we use. Kelly (1955) argued that we derive our picture of ourselves through the picture which we have of other people's picture of us. He was arguing here that the central evidence we use in understanding ourselves is other people's reactions to us, both what they say of us and the implications of their behaviour towards us. He was not saying that we simply take other people's views of us as gospel. Obviously this would be impossible because people have very varying and often very disparate reactions to us. He argued that we filter others' views of us through our view of them. If someone you consider excessively rash and impulsive says that you are a conventional mouse, you might be inclined to dismiss their estimate on the grounds that they see everyone who is not perpetually swinging from the chandelier as being a conventional mouse. However, if someone you consider very docile and timid says that you are a conventional mouse, then this has quite different implica-tions. You do not come to understand yourself simply by contemplating your own navel or even by analysing your own history. You build up a continuous and changing picture of yourself out of your interaction with other people.

Do we change ourselves?

That we change in small ways seems obvious enough. Looking at ourselves or others we readily notice changes in pre-ferred style of dress, taste in films or food, changes in interests and hobbies, the gaining of new skills and the rusting of old and so forth.

Whether we change in large ways as well as small involves us in the question of how we define 'large' and 'small' change. Kelly (1955) hypothesized that each of us has a 'theory' about ourselves, about other people, and about the nature of the world, a theory which he referred to as our personal construct system. Constructs are our ways of discriminating our world. For many of them we have overt labels such as nice-nasty, ugly-beautiful, cheap-expensive, north-south, trustworthy-untrustworthy and so forth. He also distinguished between superordinate and subordinate constructs. Superordinate constructs are those which govern large areas of our life and which refer to matters of central concern to us, while subordinate constructs govern the minor detail of our lives.

If we take constructs about 'change in dress' at a subordinate level then we refer simply to our tendency to switch from sober to bright colours, from wide lapels to narrow lapels and so forth. If we look at such changes superordinately then we can make more far-reaching distinctions. For example, we might see ourselves as having made many subordinate changes in dress while not changing superordinately because we have always 'followed fashion'. Thus at this level of abstraction there is no change because the multitude of our minor changes are always governed and controlled by our refusal to make a major change: that is, to dress independently of fashion.

Psychologists differ greatly in their view of how much change takes place in people and how it takes place. Trait psychologists tend to set up the notion of fixed personality characteristics which remain with people all their lives, which are measurable and which will predict their behaviour to a fair degree in any given situation. The evidence for this view has been much attacked (e.g. Mischel, 1968). Direct examination of personal experience suggests that Kelly (1955) may have been right in referring to 'man as a form of motion and not a static object that is occasionally kicked into movement'.

Psychological measurement, to date, suggests that people change their character, if only slowly, and have complex natures so that behaviour is not easily predictable from one situation to another. Psychologists have also tended to argue that where change takes place it is often unconscious and unchosen by the person. The issue of whether we choose change or whether change is something that happens to us is clearly complex. One way of viewing it might be to argue that we can and do choose to change ourselves, but that often we are less aware of the direction which chosen change may eventually take.

A person in a semi-skilled job may decide to go to night-school classes or undertake other forms of training in order to qualify themselves for what they regard as more challenging kinds of work. They might be successful in gaining qualifications and entering a new field. Up to this point they can reasonably claim to have chosen their direction of personal change and to have carried through that change in terms of their original proposal. However, the long-term effect may be that they acquire new kinds of responsibility, contacts with different kinds of people, new values and a life style which, in total, will involve personal changes not clearly envisaged at the time they went to their first evening class.

On the issue of how we go about changing ourselves, Radley (1974) speculated that change, particularly self-chosen change, may have three stages to it. Initially, if we are going to change, we must be able to envisage some goal; we must have a kind of picture of what we will be like when we have changed. He argued that if we have only a vague picture or no picture at all then we cannot change; we need to be able to 'see' the changed us in the distance. He went on to argue that when we have the picture then we can enact the role of a person like that. That is to say, we do not at heart believe that we are such a person but we can behave as if we were such a person, rather like an actor playing a role on stage or someone trying out a new style. (This may relate to the old adage that adolescence is the time when we 'try out' personalities to see which is a good fit.) He argued that if we enact in a committed and vigorous way for long enough then, at some mysterious point, we become what we are enacting and it is much more true to say that we are that person than that we are our former selves. This is very much a psychological explanation, in that it is about what is psychologically true, rather than what is formally and officially true. Thus the student who qualifies and becomes a teacher may officially, in terms of pay packet and title, be 'a teacher'. Yet, in Radley's terms, the person may still psychologically be 'a student' who is enacting the role of teacher, who is putting on a teaching style and carrying out the duties of a teacher but who still, in his heart of hearts, sees himself as a student. Later, there may come a point at which he becomes, in the psychological sense, a teacher.

However, we are also aware that there is much that is problematic and threatening about change. The set expectations of others about us may have an imprisoning effect and restrict our capacity to change. People have a picture of us and may attempt to enforce that picture. They may resist change in us because it seems to them unnatural, and it would make us less predictable. Phrases such as 'you are acting out of character', or 'that is not the true you', or 'those are not really your ideas' all reflect the difficulty people find and the resistance they manifest to change in us. Often the pressure of others' expectations is so great that we can only achieve change by keeping it secret until the change has gone so far that we can confront the dismay of others.

This is not to argue that we are simply moulded and brainwashed by our society and our family so that we are merely puppets dancing to tunes played by others. We are clearly influenced by others and everything, the language we speak, the clothes we wear, our values, ideas and feelings, is derived from and elaborated in terms of our relationships with other people and our society. But the more conscious we become of how this happens, the more likely we are to become critical of and the less likely automatically to accept what we are taught (formally and informally), and the more we may independently explore what we wish to make of ourselves as persons.

Equally, when we attempt to change we may find the process personally threatening. We may lose sight of the fact that change is inevitably a form of evolution: that is to say, we change from something to something and thereby there is continuity as well as change. If we lose faith in our own continuity we may be overwhelmed by a fear of some kind of catastrophic break, a fear of becoming something unpredictable to ourselves, of falling into chaos. Whether or not we are entirely happy with ourselves, at least we are something we are familiar with, and quite often we stay as we are because we would sooner suffer the devil we know than the unknown devil of a changed us. Fransella (1972) explored the way in which stutterers who seem to be on the verge of being cured of their stutter often suddenly relapse. She argued that stutterers know full well how to live as 'stutterers'; they understand how people react and relate to them as 'stutterers'. Nearing cure they are overwhelmed with the fear of the unknown, the strangeness of being 'a fluent speaker'.

Monitoring of self

One of the marked features of our culture is that it does not demand (or even suggest) that we formally monitor our lives or that we record our personal history in the way in which a society records its history. True, a few keep diaries, and practices such as re-reading old letters from other people give us glimpses into our past attitudes and feelings. For the most part, our understanding of our past is based on our often erratic memory of it. Moreover, our memory is likely to be erratic, not just because we forget past incidents and ideas but because we may actively 're-write' our history so as to emphasize our consistency and make our past compatible with our present.

Psychologists have tended to ignore the importance of personal history. The vast majority of psychological tests designed to assess the person cut in at a given point in time; they are essentially cross-sectional and pay little heed to the evolution of the person. It would be a very unusual psychology course that used biography or autobiography as material for its students to ponder. There are exceptions to this here-and-now preoccupation. In child psychology great emphasis is laid on the notion of 'development' and a great deal of the research and argument in child psychology is about how children acquire skills over a period, how they are gradually influenced by social customs and how life within the family, over a period of years, affects a child's self-value. Additionally, clinical psychologists involved in psychotherapy and counselling very often find themselves engaged in a joint search with their clients through the immediate and distant past in order to understand present problems and concerns. This does not necessarily argue that a person is simply the end product of their past. We need to understand and acknowledge our past, not in order to repeat it but in order either to use it or to be free of it. As Kelly (1969) put it, 'you are not the victim of your autobiography but you may become the victim of the way you interpret your autobiography'.

Obstacles to self-knowledge and self-change

To try and understand oneself is not simply an interesting pastime, it is a necessity of life. In order to plan our future and to make choices we have to be able to anticipate our behaviour in future situations. This makes self-knowledge a practical guide, not a self-indulgence. Sometimes the situations with which we are confronted are of a defined and clear kind so that we can anticipate and predict our behaviour with reasonable certainty. If someone asks you if you can undertake task X (keep a set of accounts, drive a car, translate a letter from German and so forth) then it is not difficult to assess your skills and experience and work out whether you can undertake the task or not. Often the choice or the undertaking is of a more complex and less defined nature. Can you stand up in conflict with a powerful authority figure? Can you make a success of your marriage to this or that person? Can you live by yourself when you have been used to living with a family? The stranger the country we are entering the more threatening the prospect becomes; the more we realize that some degree of self-change may be involved, the more we must rely upon our understanding of our own character and potential.

In such circumstances we are acutely aware of the dangers of change and may take refuge in a rigid and inflexible notion of what we are. Kelly (1955, 1969) referred to this tendency as 'hostility'. He defined hostility as 'the continued effort to extort validational evidence in favor of a type of social prediction which has already been recognized as a failure'. We cannot lightly abandon our theory of what we are, since the abandonment of such a theory may plunge us into chaos. Thus we see someone destroy a close relationship in order to 'prove' that they are independent or we see teachers 'proving' that their pupils are stupid in order to verify that they themselves are clever.

Closely connected to this definition of hostility is Kelly's definition of guilt as 'the awareness of dislodgement of self from one's core role structure'. Core constructs are those which govern a person's maintenance processes; they are those constructs in terms of which identity is established and the self is pictured and understood. Your core role structure is what you understand yourself to be.

It is in a situation in which you fail to anticipate your own behaviour that you experience guilt. Defined in this way guilt comes not from a violation of some social code but from a violation of your own personal picture of what you are.

There are traditional ways of exploring the issue of 'what am I like?' We can meditate upon ourselves, ask others how they see us, or review our history. Psychologists have devised numerous tests for assessing 'personality', though in so far as these are of any use they seem to be designed to give the psychologist ideas about the other person rather than to give the people ideas about themselves. Two relatively recent attempts to provide people with ways of exploring their own 'personality' are offered by McFall (in Bannister and Fransella, 1980) and Mair (1970).

McFall offers a simple elaboration on the idea of talking to oneself. His work indicated that if people associate freely into a tape-recorder and listen to their own free flow then, given that they erase it afterwards so that there is no possible audience other than themselves at that time, they may learn something of the themes, conflicts and issues that concern them; themes that are 'edited out' of most conversation and which are only fleetingly glimpsed in our thinking. Mair experimented with formalized, written conversation. Chosen partners wrote psychological descriptions of each other (and predictions of the other's description) and then compared and discussed the meaning and the evidence underlying their written impressions.

Although we have formal ways of exploring how we see and how we are seen by others (the encounter group), and informal ways (the party), it can be argued that there is something of a taboo in our society on direct expression of our views of each other. It may be that we fear to criticize lest we be criticized, or it may be that we are embarrassed by the whole idea of the kind of confrontation involved in telling each other about impressions which are being created. Certainly if you contemplate how much you know about the way you are seen by others, you may be struck by the limitations of your knowledge, even on quite simple issues. How clear are you as to how your voice tone is experienced by other people? How often do you try and convey to someone your feelings and thoughts about them in such an oblique and roundabout way that there is a fair chance that they will not grasp the import of what you are saying?

Psychologists are only very slowly seeing it as any part of their task to offer ways to people in which they may explore themselves and explore the effect they have on others.

Role and person

Social psychologists have made much use of the concept of 'role'. Just as an actor plays a particular role in a drama it can be argued that each of us has a number of roles in our family, in work groups, in our society. We have consistent ways of speaking, dressing and behaving which reflect our response to the expectations of the group around us. Thus within a family or small social group we may have

inherited and developed the role of 'clown' or 'hardheaded
practical person' or 'sympathizer'. Jobs often carry
implicit role specifications with them so that we perceive
different psychological requirements in the role of teacher
from the role of student or the role of manager from the
role of worker. We are surprised by the randy parson, the
sensitive soldier, the shy showbusiness person. Society also
prescribes very broad and pervasive roles for us as men or
women, young or old, working-class or middle-class and so
forth. It is not that every word of our scripts is pre-
written for us, but the broad boundaries and characteristics
of behaviour appropriate to each role are fairly well
understood. These social roles can and do conflict with
personal inclinations and one way of defining maturity would
be to look on it as the process whereby we give increasing
expression to what we personally are, even where this
conflicts with standard social expectations.

Kelly chose to define role in a more strictly personal
sense in his sociality corollary which reads: 'to the extent
that one person construes the construction processes of
another he may play a role in a social process involving the
other person'. He is here emphasizing the degree to which,
when we relate to another person, we relate in terms of our
picture of the other person's picture of us. Role then
becomes not a life style worked out by our culture and
waiting for us to step into, but the on-going process
whereby we try to imagine and understand how other people
see the world and continuously to relate our own conception
to theirs.

The paradox of self-knowing

We reasonably assume that our knowledge of something does
not alter the 'thing' itself. If I come to know that Guatemala produces zinc or that the angle of incidence of a light
ray equals its angle of reflection, then this new knowledge
of mine does not, of itself, affect Guatemala or light.
However, it alters me in that I have become 'knowing' and
not 'ignorant' of these things. More pointedly, if I come to
know something of myself then I am changed, to a greater
or lesser degree, by that knowledge. Any realization by a
person of the motives and attitudes underlying their
behaviour has the potential to alter that behaviour.

Put another way, a person is the sum of their understanding of their world and themselves. Changes in what we
know of ourselves and the way in which we come to know it
are changes in the kind of person we are.

This paradox of self-knowledge presents a perpetual
problem to psychologists. An experimental psychologist may
condition a person to blink their eye when a buzzer is
pressed, simply by pairing the buzzer sound with a puff of
air to the person's eyelid until the blink becomes a response to the sound of the buzzer on its own. But if the
person becomes aware of the nature of the conditioning process and resents being its 'victim' then conditioning may

cease, or at least take much longer. Knowledge of what is going on within that person and between the person and the psychologist has altered the person and invalidated the psychologist's predictions. Experimental psychologists seek to evade the consequences of this state of affairs by striving to keep the subject in ignorance of the nature of the experimental process or by using what they assume to be naturally ignorant subjects: for example, rats. But relying on a precariously maintained ignorance in the experimental subject creates only a mythical certainty in science. Psychotherapists, on the other hand, generally work on the basis that the more the person (subject, patient, client) comes to know of themselves, the nearer they will come to solving, at least in part, their personal problems.

This self-changing property of self-knowledge may be a pitfall for a simple-minded science of psychology. It may also be the very basis of living, for us as persons.

References

Bannister, D. and Agnew, J. (1977)
The Child's Construing of Self. In A.W. Landfield (ed.), Nebraska Symposium on Motivation 1976. Nebraska: University of Nebraska Press.
Bannister, D. and Fransella, F. (1980)
Inquiring Man (2nd edn). Harmondsworth: Penguin.
Fransella, F. (1972)
Personal Change and Reconstruction. London: Academic Press.
Kelly, G.A. (1955)
The Psychology of Personal Constructs, Volumes I and II. New York: Norton.
Kelly, G.A. (1969)
Clinical Psychology and Personality: The selected papers of George Kelly (ed. B.A. Maher). New York: Wiley.
Mair, J.M.M. (1970)
Experimenting with individuals. British Journal of Medical Psychology, 43, 245-256.
Mead, G.H. (1925)
The genesis of the self and social control. International Journal of Ethics, 35, 251-273.
Mischel, W. (1968)
Personality and Assessment. New York: Wiley.
Radley, A.R. (1974)
The effect of role enactment on construct alternatives. British Journal of Medical Psychology, 47, 313-320.

Questions

1. Examine the way in which a person's idea of 'self' is affected by the nature of their work.
2. Discuss the nature of sex differences in ideas about 'self'.
3. Describe some way in which you have increased your knowledge of yourself.

4. How do parents influence their children's ideas about 'self'?
5. To what extent is our picture of our self influenced by our physical state and appearance?
6. We come to understand ourselves through our relationship with others. Discuss.
7. Examine the way in which social customs inhibit our revealing of 'self'.
8. People are born with a fixed character which they cannot alter. Discuss.
9. 'He is not himself today.' What triggers off this kind of comment, and does it say more about the speaker than the person of whom it is said?
10. Your job enables you to express yourself. Your job prevents you being yourself. Discuss.

Annotated reading

Axline, V.M. (1971) Dibs: In search of self. Harmondsworth: Penguin.
> A finely written description of a withdrawn and disturbed child who in the process of psychotherapy comes vividly to life. It casts light on our early struggles to achieve the idea of being a 'self'.

Bannister, D. and Fransella, F. (1980) Inquiring Man: The psychology of personal constructs. Harmondsworth: Penguin.
> The second edition of a book which sets out the way Kelly sees each of us as developing a complex personal view of our world. The book describes two decades of psychological research based on the theory and relates it to problems such as psychological breakdown, prejudice, child development and personal relationships.

Bott, M. and Bowskill, D. (1980) The Do-It-Yourself Mind Book. London: Wildwood House.
> A lightly written but shrewd book on the ways in which we can tackle serious personal and emotional problems without recourse to formal psychiatry.

Fransella, F. (1975) Need to Change? London: Methuen.
> A brief description of the formal and informal ways in which 'self' is explored and change attempted.

Rogers, C.R. (1961) On Becoming a Person. Boston: Houghton-Mifflin.
> Sets out the idea of 'self-actualization' and describes the ways in which we might avoid either limiting ourselves or being socially limited, and come to be what Rogers calls a fully functioning person.

2

The person in personality
Fay Fransella

What is personality?

In the previous chapter, Bannister mentioned various types of personality theory, particularly trait theories and those represented by Freud and Kelly. The present chapter focusses attention more directly on these three differing approaches. But first it is necessary to decide what is meant by 'personality'.

One of the most important things to keep in mind about 'personality' is that it does not exist. It is not a 'thing' sitting there waiting to be discovered. It is all in the mind. It is a concept, like intelligence, which some people find useful in coming to an understanding of others.

When considering someone's 'personality' we may talk about the consistencies in his behaviour and say 'he is aggressive', meaning he can be predicted to be aggressive in certain situations. This would be a TRAIT theory, such as that proposed by Eysenck or Cattell. At other times we take some general characteristic of a person and then use this as a label of his total personality. Examples of such TYPE theories can be seen in Jung's typology of extraversion and introversion.

Others focus more on the motivational aspects of personality. Freud focusses as much on how we are influenced by unconscious processes as on how our personality is structured. Maslow likewise emphasizes the motivational aspects that make us what we are (see chapter 11). Some theorists focus not on personality structure, nor on process, but on the person as a whole. Rogers, for instance, sees the concept of self as being at the very heart of all our experience, and hence our interaction with the world. Kelly emphasizes our attempts to interpret the events confronting us and how we may become increasingly effective in anticipating what will be the consequences of our acts.

It is interesting to note that the more recent theories, like those of Rogers, Maslow and Kelly, are theories that very much deal with the person as a person trying to interact with the world, rather than our being viewed from outside as a type, or a bundle of traits, or under the control of our psychodynamics.

You may now see what a diverse subject the study of personality is. Of course, if the study of the person were the central issue in psychology, there would be no need for a chapter specifically written about 'personality' for it would be the subject matter of psychology itself. However, psychology did not evolve in this way.

Which theory is most likely to be right? One cannot even ask that question because the study of personality is the study of a concept. It is neither true nor false, but is best judged on the basis of its usefulness in increasing our understanding of ourselves as human beings. A good theory leads to new insights and to the asking of questions about ourselves. It should, in the scientific sense, generate hypotheses which are brittle enough to be tested. The more these turn out to be valid the more valuable is the theory. But any theory must be ultimately expendable so as to make room for another which gives an even better explanation of the presently available facts and which, in its turn, generates new ideas, testable hypotheses and so forth. So knowledge advances.

What is the definition of personality?

There is not one. The definition depends entirely upon one's theory. And, even then, few theorists attempt the task. For them, the theory itself is the definition.

The differing emphases

However, there are some underlying issues which may make your enquiry into the nature of personality more organized. One thing to do is to look at where the theorist places most emphasis. What is the model of the person being proposed? For instance, one theory may emphasize a person's social nature; another discuss us in terms of free will versus determinism; another focus on our instinctual nature, or the uniqueness of our nature; and yet another on our similarities to others. For example, a theory that focusses on unconscious processes and instincts and is deterministic would see the person as someone who is driven rather than driving, irrational rather than rational and so forth. Conversely, a theory that emphasizes consciousness and free will may well see the person as someone who drives rather than is driven, as someone who reasons, who chooses, who decides his own fate, and as someone who is responsible for his own actions. Thus we see that the different views of what psychology is and how to describe people (discussed in the Introduction) have a strong influence upon each theorist's model of the person.

Theories that focus on our uniqueness are often said to be unscientific because 'the person' cannot be studied objectively: critics point out that all the data must be biassed. These objectors usually prefer the type of theory that tries to categorize people; they like to emphasize the similarities between people as well as the differences, and to be sympathetic towards objective and standardized methods of assessment and to favour a rigorous empirical approach to the study of personality.

Some dimensions of personality theories

To help make sense of all the theories, you might look to see how each theory deals with a number of issues. What is the relative importance given to conscious and unconscious experience; or to free will and determinism? Does the author favour studying the individual or strive to establish laws governing groups of individuals? Is the person considered to be mainly a rational or an irrational being? To what extent can each of us be truly known to others or even know ourselves? Are we to be studied as a total, unified being or as an amalgam of a number of discrete characteristics that can be studied separately? These are just some of the questions you can ask of a theory of personality.

Why these theories?

Throughout this volume you will come across various approaches to human understanding; for instance, in chapter 1 Bannister leans heavily on the psychology of Kelly. Freud's theory comes into the chapters on child development and the work of Eysenck and Cattell are relevant to the development and use of questionnaires covered in chapter 14 on psychometrics. These theorists are therefore covered here in some detail to enable you to grasp the full implications of what is discussed elsewhere.

The work of Rogers and Maslow could also have been included here, but it was felt that these theorists are adequately covered in other chapters such as that on counselling (for Rogers) and on motivation (for Maslow).

Lastly, the theory of Jung has been included. You will be hard put to find him mentioned elsewhere in this volume. You will not find many among your fellow workers or friends who have much knowledge of Jung's ideas. If you talk of extraverts and introverts they are more likely to think you are talking about Eysenck than Jung. So why include him? Because interest in his concepts of the collective unconscious and archetypes is very much on the increase. Perhaps it is because, as some would say, we, in modern society, have lost our way and need to search for a soul and for the meaning of life. Jung's psychology is thus included because of its possible usefulness to you as a person rather than you as an occupational therapist.

All the theories written about in this chapter also have particular relevance for you as a psychological therapist. Just as you will find it useful to have some theoretical framework within which to understand your fellows in daily life, so it is useful, if not essential, to have one which will help you to help those in trouble. Thus you will find these theories extended in the last section (chapters 17-19) to give explanations of, and ways of helping, those in psychological distress.

Some personality theories

Sigmund Freud 1856-1939

Freud was born in 1856 in Austria and died in London in 1939. It would be difficult to start with any other theorist in a discussion of personality, partly because his was the first comprehensive theory to be developed, but also because his views have had such a profound effect on our culture. He is acknowledged as one of the intellectual giants of this century.

Freud qualified first in medicine and did some research but never intended to practise. His interest in the clinical aspects of neurology led him to specialize in the treatment of nervous conditions. At this time he was particularly excited by Charcot's use of hypnosis as a treatment method, and this greatly influenced his later thinking.

Throughout his life Freud is said to have been constantly troubled by periods of depression and, following the death of his father in 1878, he started a self-analysis. He continued with this for the rest of his life, devoting the last half hour of each day to the task. From this self-analysis stemmed the therapy of psychoanalysis and his life-long attempts to understand the workings of the human mind, particularly the unconscious mind.

There is no one theory of psychoanalysis and Freud never proposed a single unified theory of personality. Rather, his understanding of personality function came through the practice of psychoanalysis, and his views on both developed with the years. It is probably true to say that the whole of psychoanalysis is concerned with personality; so, to understand Freud's view of personality, we have to look at the development of psychoanalysis.

Freud's first psychological observations concerned the hysterical symptoms he observed in his young neurotic patients. He thought that these symptoms had meaning, but that some active process kept it out of the patient's conscious awareness. Hysterical symptoms were thus seen as expressions of some traumatic experience, often of sexual seduction, during childhood. The emotion 'attached' to this experience constantly seeks some channel by which it can be discharged. Since it cannot be discharged by being brought to conscious awareness, it is 'got rid of' in the form of a physical symptom. Although this was an early affect-trauma explanation of neurosis in young people, the fact that the personality has to find a way of coping with strong emotion, and will have characteristic ways of dealing with it, remains a part of modern psychoanalytic theory.

In 1900 Freud's most influential book, 'The Interpretation of Dreams', was published. He says that: 'the theory of dreams ... occupies a special place in the history of psychoanalysis and marks a turning point; it was with it that analysis took the step from being a psychotherapeutic procedure to being a depth psychology' (Freud, 1965a).

Rather surprisingly, it was in this masterpiece that he developed a clear model of the mind. In it he crystallized the important idea that unconscious mental material could be forcibly held out of consciousness. He distinguished between two types of thinking. One is the system of the Unconscious which represents the older, more basic, thought processes

striving for gratification. It is characterized by PRIMARY
PROCESS THINKING which is guided by the PLEASURE
PRINCIPLE. Unfortunately, behaviour guided only by the
pleasure principle very quickly brings us into conflict with
others. This realization brings a pause between the thought
and the action which allows the REALITY PRINCIPLE, char-
acterizing SECONDARY PROCESS THINKING, to come into
existence. With the development of the system Conscious,
immediate gratification can be delayed for the sake of
future rewards. Although the reality principle becomes more
and more dominant as we develop, it never totally supersedes
the pleasure principle. Our conscious selves can never fully
triumph since there are always unconscious forces striving
to gain immediate gratification.

In between the systems Conscious and Unconscious, there
is the Preconscious. Thoughts here are momentarily out of
consciousness, but are not actively being kept out or RE-
PRESSED. In dreaming, our wishes and impulses are disguised
in the Preconscious and so are permitted to achieve their
goals within awareness. Freud first thought that all dreams
were wish-fulfilments. While we sleep, secondary process
thinking sleeps also, allowing primary thinking to take
over. However, these primary thoughts are so threatening
that they cannot be tolerated, even in sleep. So the Preconscious has the task of coding the wishes into an acceptable guise. Thus, each dream has two aspects: the latent
content contains the wishes originating in the Unconscious,
which are striving for expression and result in the dream;
and the 'manifest content', which is the actual dream we
experience. An analysis of the dream symbols transforms them
and so exposes the latent content. Dream analysis forms an
important part of the therapeutic process.

Freud now developed his ideas of the stages of development associated with the need to bring our sexual drives
under control. This is discussed more fully at the beginning
of Foss's chapter (see pp. 45-46).

In his early work Freud described two classes of instinct: the libidinal or sexual instincts, associated with
the pleasure principle and preservation of the species, and
the self-preservation instincts, associated with the reality
principle. But later he reformulated this because such
things as sadism and masochism contradicted the pleasure
principle. He preferred to think in terms of sexual or life
instincts and aggressive or death instincts. Every human
action has a component of each and, if the aggressive component is not controlled, behaviour will be egotistical and
antisocial. Freud said:

> What we have come to see about the sexual instincts
> applies equally and perhaps still more to the other
> ones, the aggressive instincts. It is they above all
> that make human communal life difficult and threaten its
> survival. Restriction of the individual's aggressiveness
> is the first and perhaps the severest sacrifice which
> society requires of him (Freud, 1965b).

So we have here clearly spelt out the view of the person as an energy system. At certain times during development this energy gets dammed up and, in finding its outlets, provides us with our present-day personality. Sexuality was, for Freud, an extremely troublesome thing and was something potentially dangerous. Far from the popular belief that he was advocating sexual licence, Freud was saying that the sexual nature of the human was not to be taken lightly.

Eventually, Freud chose to use the words ID and EGO instead of talking about the conscious and unconscious aspects of the mind. The id is the 'dark, unaccessible part of our personality' and is the reservoir of psychic energy or the instincts. Only after these have been dealt with by the ego can the impulses derived from the id be expressed. The ego is concerned with our everyday life in the external world. However, not only has the ego to deal with the demands of the id, it must also pay heed to the third part of the structure of personality: the SUPER-EGO or the conscience.

Freud said relatively little about the ego. He seemed to regard it as a rather weak structure, having to serve three masters: id, super-ego and reality. But at the end of his life he began to give it more attention and so have subsequent psychoanalytic theorists. In recent years it has been the particular focus of interest in object-relationship theory. Personality is seen as being dominated by personal relationships. As time goes on we develop a picture of ourselves (a self-representation) which we relate to an internal model of other people (object-representations). Personality is dominated by our attempts to achieve organized self-object relationships, and our adult life consists of attempts to restructure some of our important early relationships.

In summary, Freud's views on personality come directly from the procedure of psychoanalysis. He never wrote a theory of personality as such. If taken in historical perspective, the various accounts of the psychoanalytic view are comprehensible even though Freud sometimes changed his views quite radically.

Freud's is a theory in which determinism plays a considerable part. Not only is our adult behaviour largely laid down in the early years of life, but it is determined by forces outside our awareness, making it irrational. Also, even though Freud did not consider our personality to be greatly influenced by our genetic make-up, he retained physical concepts, for instance, by translating physical energy into the libido.

Psychoanalytic theory has been criticized for being unscientific and untestable, although some attempts have been made to redress the balance in recent years. But, even were these views proved to be true, to be unscientific does not necessarily make a theory of no value. Freud produced ideas that have profoundly affected our living and thinking and they continue to be influential. For this reason, if for no other, an acquaintance with the theory is of value. This is particularly so for those working in a psychiatric context since, if any model of personality is used at all, it is likely to be based on Freud's ideas. His influence on psychiatry and the treatment of mental illness is discussed later in this book (chapters 9 and 19).

Carl Gustav Jung 1875-1961

Opinions vary greatly about the importance of Jung as a theorist and practitioner. Some see him as a great and imaginative thinker, others as a mystic and romantic who has made little contribution to our understanding of ourselves. Hughes has written that Jung's wisdom 'was of no profit to him: he was unable to express what he had learned in any unambiguous form ... and his writings are a trial to anyone who attempts to discover in them a logical sequence of ideas' (Hughes, 1958). Freud's writings were also disconnected, his ideas changing over the years, but he attracted a number of interpreters of his work who presented them to us in a relatively clear form.

A certain amount of the hostility to Jung comes from the Freudians themselves and they like to keep alive the animosity that existed between him and Freud before the final rift occurred. Although respecting Freud's contribution to psychology, Jung was especially critical of his ideas of the sexual nature of dreams and neuroses.

The bitterness that grew between the two men can be glimpsed from one of the series of letters that passed between them.

18 December 1921

Dear Professor Freud,

May I say a few words to you in earnest? I admit the ambivalence of my feelings towards you, but am inclined to take an honest and absolutely straightforward view of the situation. If you doubt my word, so much the worse for you. I would, however, point out that your technique of treating your pupils like patients is a blunder. In that way you produce either slavish sons or impudent puppies (Adler-Stekel and the whole insolent gang now throwing their weight about in Vienna). I am objective enough to see through your little trick. You go around sniffing out all the symptomatic actions in your vicinity, thus reducing everyone to the level of sons and daughters who blushingly admit the existence of their faults. Meanwhile you remain on top as the father, sitting pretty. For sheer obsequiousness nobody dares to pluck the prophet by the beard and inquire for once what you would say to a patient with a tendency to analyse the analyst instead of himself. You would certainly ask him: 'Who's got the neurosis?'

You see, my dear Professor, so long as you hand out this stuff I don't give a damn for my symptomatic actions: they shrink to nothing in comparison with the formidable beam in my brother Freud's eye (McGuire, 1974).

When Jung finally broke with Freud he resigned from the International Psychoanalytic Society and founded his own school in Zurich which later came to be called Analytical Psychology. For him, a person's psyche is a whole, a totality, a unity in which the individual parts are co-ordinated into an integrated system. Jung sees us as being all alike in that our lives are influenced by unconscious forces. But he differed from Freud in arguing that not all thoughts in the unconscious are necessarily of a sexual nature. All sorts of memories of childhood can be repressed and these cluster with their emotions to form complexes.

Jung called these troublesome, but not necessarily sexual, repressed experiences the PERSONAL UNCONSCIOUS. Although complexes can cause neurosis, he thought that there must be more to it. People kept having dreams and fantasies about things that they could never have experienced and so could not have repressed. Jung thus developed the concept of the COLLECTIVE UNCONSCIOUS.

Jung (1956) explained this very vital part of his theory thus:

> There are present in every individual, besides his personal memories, the great 'primordial' images, as Jacob Burkhardt once aptly called them, the inherited powers of human imagination as it was from time immemorial ... I have called these images or motifs 'archetypes', also 'dominants' of the unconscious ... The primordial images are the most ancient and the most universal 'thought-forms' of humanity. They are as much feelings as thoughts; indeed, they lead their own independent life rather in the manner of part-souls.

The ARCHETYPES are the basic units of the collective unconscious. They provide 'A kind of readiness to produce over and over again the same or similar mystical ideas'. They can be thought of as inherited predispositions to respond to situations and events in an organized but unconscious manner. Jung explains: 'It seems to me that their origins can only be explained by assuming them to be deposits of the constantly repeated experiences of humanity'.

Jung described a large number of archetypes, but some are more important and better known than others.

The PERSONA is our social or public mask. It is the 'I' which interacts with the world and which results from our social class, religious beliefs, occupation and so forth. 'The persona ... is only a mask for the collective psyche, a mask that feigns individuality and tries to make others and oneself believe that one is individual, whereas, one is simply playing a part in which the collective psyche speaks.' The SHADOW is the part of ourselves that we try to hide from our own sight and the sight of others. These are our personal devils.

The ANIMA and ANIMUS are among the best known of Jung's concepts. These are our idealized versions of the opposite sex and the potential source of our creative inspiration and insight. They are really distorted versions of our mothers, fathers, brothers, sisters and so on. If we are dominated by this archetype, our whole personality is affected. The man dominated by his anima is nervous, irritable and cries a lot. The woman dominated by her animus is stubborn, argumentative and aggressive.

The HERO archetype is just that: the universal hero myth. Heroes have miraculous but humble births (Moses and Christ) and provide early proof of their superhuman powers (young David slew Goliath; the infant Hercules slew serpents). The hero rises rapidly to power, wins over evil, and dies through betrayal or making a heroic sacrifice. If we become aware of this archetype it can guide us and serve as a model during difficult periods of development.

The SELF is obviously the most central of the archetypes. This primordial image makes us long for wholeness and unification within ourselves.

Jung's concepts of archetypes and the collective unconscious are controversial, but the many myths that exist give them at least face validity. It can be argued that Freud based his Oedipal complex and dream symbolism on some such notion since he certainly felt that little boys universally loved their mothers and were jealous of their fathers. But Jung found no evidence for an 'Oedipal' archetype. He believed it natural for a child to admire and respect the parent of the opposite sex.

The collective unconscious is the larger part of the unconscious and it is not repressed. It is something we inherit and are born with. In general terms we can say that, for Freud, the unconscious contains repressed material and it is potentially dangerous and antisocial. For Jung it is potentially helpful and mostly not repressed. It is the most powerful and dominant force in our lives, the source of both madness and creativity. It is something we must all come to terms with and come to understand to the best of our ability. As with Freud, the key to the unconscious is dream analysis.

JUNG'S TYPOLOGY. Psychic energy or libido is generated by the tensions set up between our conscious and unconscious, and within the structure of the mind itself, and between other parts of the psyche. In his 'Psychological Types' (1933), Jung describes how our thinking (attitudes or basic habits of the mind) is structured in terms of the balance between INTROVERSION and EXTRAVERSION. Introverts concern themselves primarily with internal events and extraverts pay more heed to external events. One of Jung's most important principles concerns the balance between these two attitudes of the mind; when one is highly developed in consciousness, the other develops proportionately in the unconscious.

These two superordinate types or categories or attitudes of the mind work in conjunction with four fundamental functions divided into rational and irrational components.

Irrational functions are SENSATION and INTUITION; the rational ones are THINKING and FEELING. Personal preference for one of these determines aspects of personality. For example, those preferring intuition are creative and original, filtering information through the unconscious; those who prefer thinking are logical and try to decide whether information is right or wrong. Everyone has all the attitudes and functions and the various combinations produce eight personality types.

Thinking extraverts like fixed rules and think in a positive and dogmatic way (some say that Jung had Freud in mind here); feeling extraverts are conservative, respectful of authority and are very emotional; sensation extraverts are pleasure-seeking, easy-going and sociable; whereas, in contrast to these, intuitive introverts are eccentric, daydreamers and very much absorbed in their own thoughts: Jung himself might fit into this category.

Our individual personalities thus come from three sources; from our persona, from our distinctive pattern of the structure of the mind and from the degree to which we become aware of the unconscious. The more aware of it we are, the more mature and creative we are and the more personal balance we have.

Personality traits

Traits are those characteristics or styles of behaviour that are evident in a large number of widely differing situations. The process whereby we come to attribute a trait to someone in everyday life goes something like this. First we look at an act of behaviour and say, for example, 'He is acting aggressively'; then we transfer the quality from the act to the person, so it comes to describe the reactive nature of the individual: the adverb 'aggressively' becomes the adjective 'aggressive' and is used to describe the person ('He is an aggressive person'); and finally, having decided that the quality belongs to the individual rather than to the action, we refer to the quality as a thing; that is, it becomes a noun and we say there is a trait of aggression. Traits are not necessarily theoretically related to any structural aspect of the individual. However, for some theorists, they are. For example, Eysenck sees traits as related to central nervous activity.

Eysenck and Cattell are particularly well-known figures in psychology, both having developed trait theories of personality based upon the statistical procedure of factor analysis. In general terms Kelly compares factor analysis with what you and I strive to achieve in daily life:

> One of the popular prescriptions for science is Occam's Razor or the so-called law of parsimony. It is the rather unimaginative notion that the simpler of two explanations is always the better as long as it covers the facts at hand ... But simple explanations are not necessarily the most fertile ones ... One of man's most

pressing psychological problems is to understand his circumstances in variety as well as in depth - most of all to understand himself and his fellow man in variety and in depth.

One way to be aware of greater variety is to conjure up more constructs. But the number of constructs needed does not increase in direct ratio to the number of events to be distinguished. So what we have is a minimax problem; how to discriminate meaningfully the greatest variety of events with the least number of constructs. Since constructs are not only hard to come by but are difficult to keep in mind after you get them it becomes psychologically strategic to devise a system which will do the most with the least (Kelly, 1969).

This system of factor analysis results in the differences to be found between Cattell and Eysenck concerning the number of constructs needed to describe personality most fully.

Hans J. Eysenck 1916–present
Eysenck began his research in the 1940s when working with psychiatric patients. In his first study psychiatrists rated each of 700 patients on a set of scales. These ratings were then factor analysed and two factors were found which described most of the data. One was NEUROTICISM (N), which is to do with having little energy, worrying, moodiness and general nervousness and is associated with general symptoms of anxiety. The other was the EXTRAVERSION-INTROVERSION (E) dimension, to do with sociability, friendliness, enjoyment of excitement, talkativeness, impulsiveness, activity and spontaneity. As Kline (1981) says: 'The extravert is stimulus-hungry and expressive. The introvert is the opposite of this: aloof and inhibited.' More recently a third dimension of psychoticism-superego (P) has been identified. Eysenck speculates on how these three dimensions are related to properties of the nervous system. In 1967 he said extraversion is related to differences in activity of the reticular formation, neuroticism to activity of the autonomic nervous system, and in 1980) related psychoticism to hormonal secretion, particularly that to do with masculinity.

His theory has been applied to explain many aspects of our human functioning; for instance, psychopathic and criminal behaviour (1977), and how people differing on these trait dimensions respond to drugs and alcohol. Previous work suggests that our position on the E scale is related to how susceptible we are to classical conditioning. Those who are high on extraversion have low arousal levels, and are therefore not readily conditioned and so are slow to learn the rules of society. This, in turn, makes them more vulnerable to temptation of an antisocial nature. Kline, however, concludes his summary of Eysenck's work by saying:

Although this implies that criminality is biologically determined, it does not ignore the obvious social determinants of crime since the conditioning by which the conscience is or is not acquired is clearly a social matter. It must be noted that this theory of crime is far from complete. ... not all criminals are extra-verted; is there any evidence that conditionability is a unitary trait? Is the notion of crime a single homo-geneous concept? Do not some criminals learn only too well - delinquent or criminal mores? All these questions render the theory less than entirely convincing. Never-theless, the theoretical and practical power of the theory is impressive (Kline, 1981).

Raymond B. Cattell 1905-present

Cattell's attempt to define personality by a set of dimen-sions started from a far wider base than did Eysenck's. He searched through a dictionary for all words describing be-haviour and, having removed all synonyms, had subjects rated on all the remaining. Work since then has elaborated and defined more precisely the various factors that emerged. The factors can be grouped into various types. There are 16 tem-peramental factors which form the basis of the best known of Cattell's questionnaires: the 16 PF. There are also second-order factors, derived by factor analysing the cor-relations (see chapter 14) between these 16 primary factors. Other groups of factors are to do with mood, motivation and strength of interest. It is your score on each of these factors that describes your personality and relates to your behaviour.

There are some substantial similarities between the factors found by Cattell and Eysenck, since Cattell finds second-order factors of both extraversion (exvia) and neuroticism (anxiety). But Eysenck does not seem to find Cattell's first-order or primary factors. This may well be because they use different statistical procedures. Kline comments:

> Thus despite appearances, there is good agreement be-tween Cattell and Eysenck that N and E or Anxiety and Exvia are the two largest personality dimensions. Their point of difference lies in the importance attributed to primary factors. Cattell finds them stable and useful, Eysenck does not. The differences in results are due in part to technical factor-analytic methods (Kline, 1981).

In Eysenck and Cattell we see trait theory in its most elaborate form.

George Kelly 1905-1966

Kelly's introduction to psychology came about largely by chance. He had studied physics and mathematics at university and planned to spend the rest of his life as an engineer. However, the university deemed it necessary for all such students to take a course or two in 'human' subjects. He

chose psychology and found himself caught up in the rising
tide of behaviourism (see chapter 10). He found the S   R
behaviourist approach to the understanding of human beings
quite incomprehensible but felt that, if he waited, someone
would start talking about the 'arrow-in-between'. But they
never did.

So long did he wait for the revelation that he took a
degree in psychology, specializing in its more physiological
side. Still attempting to come to some understanding of the
person, he waded through volumes of Freud, but found there
little that was of value for him, except the notion of
'interpretation'. He found that students who were sent to
him with personal problems were sometimes helped by being
given an interpretation of their predicament, always providing it gave them a new perspective on their old problem.

And so he started his theorizing which culminated in the
publication of his two volumes 'The Psychology of Personal
Constructs' in 1955. In the climate of thought existing at
the time, Kelly realized that some would not easily accept
what he was proposing. So, in the Preface of Volume 1, he
wrote:

TO WHOM IT MAY CONCERN

It is only fair to warn the reader about what may be in
store for him. In the first place, he is likely to find
missing most of the familiar landmarks of psychology
books. For example, the term 'learning', so honorably
embedded in most psychological texts, scarcely appears
at all. That is wholly intentional; we are for throwing
it overboard altogether. There is no ego, no emotion,
no motivation, no reinforcement, no drive, no unconscious, no need. There are some words with brand-new
psychological definitions, words like 'foci of convenience', 'preemption', 'propositionally', 'fixed-role
therapy', 'creativity cycle', 'transitive diagnosis',
and the 'credulous approach'. 'Anxiety' is defined in a
special systematic way. 'Role', 'guilt' and 'hostility'
carry definitions altogether unexpected by many; and
to make heresy complete, there is no extensive bibliography. Unfortunately, all this will make for periods
of strange, and perhaps uncomfortable reading. Yet, inevitably, a different approach calls for a different
lexicon; and, under its influence, many old terms are
unhitched from their familiar meanings.

To whom are we speaking? In general, we think the
reader who takes us seriously will be an adventuresome
soul who is not one bit afraid of thinking unorthodox
thoughts about people, who dares peer out at the world
through the eyes of strangers, who has not invested
beyond his means in either ideas or vocabulary, and who
is looking for an ad interim, rather than an ultimate,
set of psychological insights (Kelly, 1955).

It is the elimination of emotion that has caused most controversy. Kelly refused to segment us into a 'mind' and a 'body'. He argued that we are a totality, indivisible. So emotion is linked to an awareness of various types of change in our construing or of our inability to construe an event. The place of emotion within Kelly's theoretical framework is described more fully in Bannister (1977).

THE MODEL OF THE PERSON. Kelly had found that the behaviourist way of looking at the person 'as if' you and I were responders to stimuli resulted in a dehumanized model of the person; likewise he had found that looking at us 'as if' we were a piece of flotsam drifting with the tide of instinctual urges, as Freud would have it, too vague to lead to understanding. This 'as if' philosophy led him to ask what might happen if he looked at us 'as if' we were all scientists, in full charge of ourselves, sitting in our own driving seats. Thus was born his model of the 'person-as-scientist'. No models come out of a vacuum, and both Kelly's model and his theory are based on his philosophy of 'constructive alternativism'.

THE PHILOSOPHY AND BASIC THEORY. The psychology of personal constructs is not solely a theory of personality as some have labelled it, but a grandiose attempt to sketch out a framework which might encompass the whole complexity of the person.

The theory's Fundamental Postulate and the 11 Corollaries that elaborate it, together with the model of Man Kelly presents, all stem directly from his philosophy of CONSTRUCTIVE ALTERNATIVISM. This states that 'all of our present interpretations of the universe are subject to revision or replacement'. Events are real and not just figments of the imagination, but they do not reveal themselves directly for us to see. Events are construed. In our attempts to understand and interpret as much of the life milling around us as possible, we develop an organized system of these constructions. By facing the world with our own personal set of such constructions we give the world meaning and ourselves a sense of continuity of personal experience. Kelly comments on the inventive nature of the person as follows:

> Whatever nature may be, or however the quest for truth will turn out in the end, the events we face today are subject to as great a variety of construction as our wits will enable us to contrive. This is not to say that one construction is as good as any other nor is it to deny that at some infinite point in time human vision will behold reality out to the utmost reaches of existence. But it does remind us that all our present perceptions are open to question and reconsideration, and it does broadly suggest that even the most obvious

occurrences of everyday life might appear utterly trans-
formed if we were inventive enough to construe them
differently (Kelly, 1970a).

The 11 Corollaries describe how we, as individuals,
develop a system of bi-polar construct dimensions, each
based on perceived similarities and differences within the
sea of events with which we are continually confronted.
Having construed, say, that cats are similar in that they
sit and purr when stroked and are thereby different from
dogs who stand and wag their tails when patted, we predict
that such events will recur when we pat or stroke each
animal. Our prediction also includes a negative clause: we
probably predict that the cat will not stand and wag its
tail when stroked and that the dog will not sit and purr
when patted. In this sequence of events, the patting and the
stroking (that is, the behaviour) is the way we test the
prediction: it becomes the independent rather than the dependent variable.

Construing involved in interpersonal relations is, of
course, far more complex. Some men are known to construe
women as unpredictable drivers. They therefore predict that
being behind a woman driver is a dangerous undertaking. To
test this prediction the man has to act: he has to carry
out the act of driving behind a woman driver. For Kelly,
behaviour is the experiment. It is by behaving that we test
out the predictions derived from the hypotheses resulting
from a construction. In his article 'Behaviour is an Experiment', Kelly says:

> Instead of being a problem of threatening proportions,
> requiring the utmost explanation and control to keep man
> out of trouble, behaviour presents itself as man's prin-
> cipal instrument of inquiry. Without it his questions
> are acdemic and he gets nowhere. When it is prescribed
> for him he runs around in dogmatic circles. But when he
> uses it boldly to ask questions, a flood of unexpected
> answers rises to tax his utmost capacity to understand.
> It is true that in most of psychology's inquiries
> some patently desirable behaviour is sought as an answer
> to the question posed. But the quest always proves to
> be elusive. In the restless and wonderful world of
> humanistic endeavour, behaviour, however it may once
> have been intended as the embodiment of a conclusive
> answer, inevitably transforms itself into a further
> question - a question so compellingly posed by its
> enactment that, willy nilly, the actor finds that he
> has launched another experiment. Behaviour is indeed a
> question posed in such a way as to commit man to the
> role and obligations of an experimenter (Kelly, 1970b).

So the act of driving can be a man's test of the hypothesis that women drivers do odd things. If the woman drives
impeccably, his prediction is invalidated. It is such invalidation of our construing that can bring about change.

This man may say to himself that the sample was too small and that he must test his hypothesis again. He may say that the woman was having an 'off day' and that he was correct all the time. He may even reconstrue and consider the hypothesis that only some women are erratic drivers. On the other hand, he may attempt to 'make' the woman drive erratically. He may drive bumper to bumper, speed past her on the wrong side, or cut across her bows or hoot loudly and angrily.

In this latter case he would be extorting validational evidence for a social prediction that had already proved itself a failure. This is how Kelly defines HOSTILITY. This man may have too much invested in his behavioural experiment to allow it to fail. Construct systems are organized in a hierarchical fashion so that the invalidation of a prediction at one level can have personally unacceptable implications at a more superordinate level. If he were forced to acknowledge that, in general, women were as good as men at driving cars, he might find himself forced to consider the notion that women were equal in other areas of social functioning, and so his core construing of himself as a male 'superior' being would be at risk. In psychotherapy such hostility is common; clients may demonstrate that the therapist does not 'understand' by designing behavioural experiments to show that their symptoms are still as bad as ever; therapists may keep clients overlong in therapy to 'prove' they are successful as therapists.

The driving example can be used to make two more theoretical points. In order for people to drive in relative safety on crowded roads there has to be some commonality of construing. Thus, even though each person has a construct system that is unique (no two people construe events in identical ways), similarities do exist to some extent. Psychotherapy would be impossible if no similarity in construing existed between patient and therapist; everyday conversation could not take place if we had no understanding of the word symbols which others use.

But similarity alone is not sufficient for understanding. Most drivers do not behave as the man in my example. Most attempt to predict what the drivers around them are going to do. Kelly argued that when we attempt to understand (construe) the construction processes of another, we are playing a social role in relation to that other person. Having worked out what we think another may be thinking, we test that hypothesis by behaving and looking to see whether the other reacts as we expect. It is only the attempt to construe the constructions of another that results in a role relationship, not the extent to which the interpretations are correct.

As you will see, Kelly's theory is not just about personality, but about psychology as a whole. How we construe (make discriminations between) events in our world is directly related to how we behave, what we think, and what we feel. Our behaviour is the means whereby we test out our construing and which is modified in the light of the outcomes we observe. Some constructs have no verbal labels attached to them and so are not available to conscious awareness. In the attempt to stand in others' shoes and peer at the world through their eyes lies our understanding of them as persons.

Kelly's theory invites you to look on any theory about you and I 'as if' it were true. 'Does it increase your understanding?' 'Does it lead us to ask different questions?' 'Is it useful?' In some sense it can be said to be a theory about theories: yours as well as the psychologists'.

A general point

Whether you are persuaded by what you have read that you are an incipient Freudian, Jungian, Eysenckian or Kellyan, remember that these are only a very small, if important, sample of personality theories available. They provide you with some insights into the range of thoughts psychologists have had when trying to understand human beings.

References

Bannister, D. (1977)
The logic of passion. In D. Bannister (ed.), New Perspectives in Personal Construct Theory. London: Academic Press.

Eysenck, H.J. (1967)
The Biological Bases of Personality. Springfield, Ill.: C. C. Thomas.

Eysenck, H.J. (1977)
Crime and Punishment. London: Routledge & Kegan Paul.

Eysenck, H.J. (1980)
The bio-social model of man and the unification of psychology. In A.J. Chapman and D.M. Jones (eds), Models of Man. Leicester: The British Psychological Society.

Freud, S. (1965a)
The Interpretation of Dreams. New York: Avon Books.

Freud, S. (1965b)
New Introductory Lectures. New York: Norton.

Hughes, H.S. (1958)
Consciousness and Society. New York: Random House.

Jung, C.G. (1933)
Psychological Types. New York: Harcourt Brace Jovanovich.

Jung, C.G. (1956)
Two Essays on Analytical Psychology. New York: Meridian Books.

Kelly, G.A. (1955)
The Psychology of Personal Constructs. New York: Norton.

Kelly, G.A. (1969)
The strategy of psychological research. In B. Maher (ed.), Clinical Psychology and Personality. New York: Krieger.

Kelly, G.A. (1970a)

A brief introduction to personal construct theory. In D. Bannister (ed.), Perspectives in Personal Construct Theory. London: Academic Press.

Kelly, G.A. (1970b)

Behaviour is an experiment. In D. Bannister (ed.), Perspectives in Personal Construct Theory. London: Academic Press.

Kline, P. (1981)

The work of Cattell and Eysenck. In F. Fransella (ed.), Personality: Theory, measurement and research. London: Methuen.

McGuire, W. (ed.) (1974)

The Freud/Jung Letters: The correspondence between Sigmund Freud and C.G. Jung. London: Routledge & Kegan Paul.

Questions

1. Distinguish between factor analytic, psychodynamic and humanistic approaches to the description of people.
2. Explain the terms 'introversion' and 'extraversion' as used by two different personality theorists.
3. Which theory of personality appeals to you most? Give reasons for your choice.
4. Discuss some of the ways in which theorists have dealt with the observation that we do not always behave in a logical fashion.
5. What is 'personality'? Outline some of the basic features of human nature which have to be explained.
6. 'There are no facts about personality, only theories.' Discuss this statement.
7. Discuss the importance of constitutional factors in our personality.
8. What is meant by the terms 'free will' and 'determinism'? Discuss how some personality theorists deal with them.
9. What are the 'defence mechanisms'? Describe how any one theorist suggests 'normal' people employ these in everyday life.
10. There is an essential 'me' inside each one of us struggling to get out. Discuss this statement in the context of any two theories of personality.
11. Write a description of a dream you have had recently. Discuss this from a Kellyan, Jungian and Freudian standpoint. Say which helps you understand your dream best.
12. You are confronted by a patient, described by the nursing staff as 'difficult'. Discuss ways in which your understanding of different approaches to personality may help you in your first interview with this patient.
13. Write an account of some of the personal difficulties you have encountered in your time as a student from a personal construct psychology point of view.

Annotated reading

General texts

Fransella, F. (ed.) (1981) Personality: Theory, measurement and research. London: Methuen.

> This covers the theories of Freud, Eysenck, Cattell and Kelly in greater detail, and provides an account of the research and measuring instruments (projective techniques, questionnaires, and repertory grid technique) which are associated with them.

Hjelle, L.A. and Ziegler, D.J. (1976) Personality. New York: McGraw-Hill.

> This is a wide-ranging text giving clear general accounts of the theories of Freud, Erikson, Murray, Skinner, Allport, Kelly, Maslow and Rogers.

Specific texts

RAYMOND CATTELL

Cattell, R.B. and Kline, P. (1977) The Scientific Analysis of Personality and Motivation. London: Academic Press.

> A detailed account of Cattell's rather complex theory.

HANS EYSENCK

Eysenck, H.J. and Eysenck, S.B.G. (1969) Personality Structure and Measurement. London: Routledge & Kegan Paul.

> A standard text on Eysenck's theory.

SIGMUND FREUD

Wollheim, R. (1975) Freud. Glasgow: Fontana.

> A paperback which looks at Freud the man and his ideas. These Fontana books are usually worth buying.

CARL JUNG

Storr, A. (1973) Jung. Glasgow: Fontana.

> Like the Freud paperback, this is an easy read, and gives a clear picture of Jung's ideas.

GEORGE KELLY

Bannister, D. and Fransella, F. (1980) Inquiring Man (2nd edn). Harmondsworth: Penguin.

> This presents an account of Kelly's ideas and some of the ways in which people have used them.

Part two
The Occupational Therapist Interacting with Others

3

Abilities and behaviour in childhood and adolescence
B. M. Foss

Opening remarks
FAY FRANSELLA

The first two chapters in this section deal with development in the child: first in terms mainly of its process and, second, from the standpoint of its relation to the demands and needs of society.

Whether you will work in the community, in a subnormality hospital, or in a children's ward in a general hospital, these two chapters will guide you in your struggle to gain some insight into a child's world-view.

In this chapter Foss first discusses the process of perceptual development. You may see certain similarities here between the points he raises and the ideas on construing discussed in chapters 1 and 2. For instance, Foss states: 'Probably from birth, infants are able ... to categorize various colours; so they probably have a category for 'red moving objects'. If you substitute the word 'construe' for 'categorize', you will have linked the efforts of the infant to make sense of its world with the theoretical system of Kelly's psychology of personal constructs.

Piaget used very similar ideas, and following Foss's contribution I elaborate on these and discuss their particular relevance to the work of the occupational therapist (pp. 59-65). Like Freud, Piaget talks of development in terms of stages. As indicated in chapter 2, ideas on successive stages of development marked the second major elaboration in Freud's thinking. The idea was that our lives are determined by basic sexual drives and that these must come to be mastered, more or less, in order for us to conform to social demands. These drives develop throughout childhood in a sequence of stages that are the same for everyone. These psychosexual stages are defined by that part of the body which gives the most erotic gratification at a particular age. First there is the ORAL stage, from birth up to 18 months, in which sexual drive or libidinal tension is released through stimulation of the mouth, lips and tongue. In the second year of life, the focus of erotic sensation is the anus. In the ANAL stage, urination and defecation are primary concerns. At the beginning of the third year, the child's genitalia become the main source of gratification. After this PHALLIC stage, the child, at about five years of age, starts the latency period when sexual activity is minimal. This goes on until adolescence when the sex drive becomes powerful again. Now the child is ready to enter the final stage of psychosexual development: the GENITAL stage.

At each stage there may be some residual sexual energy when the child moves on. Such fixations are unconscious and result from either excessive gratification or undue frustration at that time. These fixations Freud saw as giving individuality to a person's personality style. For instance, an 'orally-dependent' person is said to be one who has been frustrated at the oral stage; constantly longing for support and showing itself in passivity, low self-esteem, and oral activities such as nail-biting, smoking, and so forth. Too much oral gratification in early childhood results in an 'orally-aggressive' person: one who characteristically is confident, sarcastic (verbally aggressive) and quarrelsome.

Freud thought fixations at the anal stage, due to severe toilet training, led to the 'anal character'. Such a person is excessively orderly, neat and tidy, mean, obstinate and overly concerned about the functioning of the bowels. On the other hand, children who have a very easy time during toilet training are generous, slovenly and uncaring about themselves, ignore rules and are careless generally. Fixations at the phallic stage, Freud thought, may lead to a person being noisy, inconsiderate, egotistical and so on.

Schaffer comments in chapter 4 that Freud's ideas about the relationship between experiences at the different stages of development and later personality characteristics have not been borne out by research. This is so. At best, the studies yield equivocal results.

This illustrates nicely the conflict that sometimes arises between scientific and non-scientific observation. Popper, one of the leading philosophers of science, put the point this way:

> 'clinical observations' which analysts naively believe confirm their theory cannot do this any more than the daily confirmations which astrologers find in their practice. And as for Freud's epic of the Ego, the Superego, and the Id, no substantially stronger claim to scientific status can be made for it than Homer's collected stories from Olympus. These theories describe some facts, but in the manner of myths. They contain most interesting psychological suggestions but not in a testable form (Popper, 1972).

However, he argues that such myths are very important and, indeed, form the foundation of science. Nearly all scientific theories originated in such myths. He says:

> I thus felt that if a theory is found to be non-scientific, or 'metaphysical' (as we might say), it is not hereby found to be unimportant, or insignificant, or 'meaningless', or 'nonsensical'. But it cannot claim to be backed by empirical evidence in the scientific sense – although it may easily be in some generic sense, the 'result of observation' (Popper, 1972).

It is thus true to say that many of Freud's ideas have not stood the test of scientific investigation, but this may just mean no one has found a way of translating them from myth to scientific 'fact'.

If you are interested in an evaluation of some of the scientific evidence about Freud's stages of development and the oral, anal character, you will find a recent short survey in Fonagy (1981).

Foss makes several references to psychological differences between boys and girls and the development of these differences, and I therefore consider SEX-TYPING at the end of this chapter. It is important for you to be aware of those aspects of psychology which deal with the development of sexual identity and sex roles not only because you are a member of a predominantly female profession, but also because it will help you to develop a deeper understanding of the needs and problems of your female patients, child or adult. Is the little girl's unruly rebellion really a fight against the demands of her parents that she play with dolls, when she dearly wants to have a go with her brother's train? Is the little girl sullen and resentful because nothing she does is ever quite accepted by her parents because, after all, she is not the son for whom they longed? If you are in charge of a play group, bear in mind that the toys available for play have sexual connotations not only in terms of Freudian symbolism. See for yourself what toys the children play with if left to themselves. Look carefully at the main characters in the book you read to the children. Ask the girls what they think of the fact that the boy is so often the hero, up and doing the exciting things. Are they aware of this?

Both Foss and Schaffer talk about the process of socialization of the child. In this process, Freud saw the superego playing a major role along with the mechanism of IDEN-TIFICATION. The little boy takes his father as an ideal: 'This behaviour has nothing to do with a passive or female attitude toward his father (and towards males in general); it is on the contrary typically masculine. It fits in very well with the Oedipus complex for which it helps prepare the way' (Freud, 1960). Around the time he starts to identify with his father, the boy also develops a sexual desire for his mother. The Oedipal crisis is at hand.

The conflict between desire to please his father and incestuous longings for his mother reaches a peak around five years of age. At some point in time, perhaps in relation to masturbation, he interprets some words or actions as a threat by his father to castrate him. To avoid castration and to retain his father's love, the child 'identifies with the aggressor'. He gives up desiring his mother and concentrates on being like his father.

Having dealt with or repressed his sexual impulses, the small boy now has to deal with his aggression. To do this he internalizes the rules of his parents and of society. Instead of being punished by a parent, the child comes to punish himself by feeling guilty. Thus aggression felt against the restrictive behaviour of parents is internalized and turned against the child within the child's own mind.

Freud has little time for women. His attempts to translate the Oedipus complex for boys into the Electra complex for girls were not very successful. For Freud, the little girl is envious of the little boy: she wants a penis like he has, feels she has been castrated and blames her mother for this. Needless to say, her mother has been a bit careless too. So the girl is seen as developing PENIS ENVY and a MASCULINITY COMPLEX which she never overcomes. It is hardly surprising that many feminists regard Freud as the archetypal sexist who set back the clock of women's equality many decades.

Freud looms large because there is hardly a chapter in this volume that does not mention his ideas in some context, but this simply indicates the all-pervasiveness of his influence and should not be taken as an indication of his prominence in modern-day psychology as a whole. As an indication of the breadth of the psychological spectrum, I have also chosen to elaborate on the work of Harlow mentioned in Foss's chapter in relation to play. This research used rhesus monkeys as subjects. It may seem strange to talk about animals in the context of human development, but Harlow's work has been carried out over a number of years and has had a considerable influence on our thinking about social development. It is also useful because it gives you the opportunity to consider the important issue concerning the degree to which one should generalize research findings from animal studies to human behaviour. Some say one should not. Perhaps animal research should only be used to give us cause to question some of our existing assumptions about human processes. Maybe it is valuable in giving us new ideas, or in leading us to ask new questions, or old questions in new ways. Animal research certainly offers us opportunities to investigate problems in a way which would be unethical with human subjects. Harlow's work should be seen in this light and it is up to you to consider whether the results give you any further insight into human beings. I have chosen to focus on the development of social behaviour and attachment in the monkeys and so it comes at the end of Schaffer's chapter.

Schaffer comments that socialization should not be seen 'as a long drawn-out battle ... between wilful young children and irritated parents'. Quite clearly there can also be much mutual love and sensitivity. As a lay person without any knowledge of the findings of psychologists, you might be forgiven, on entering a strange household, for immediately having a negative reaction on hearing that the mother goes out to work. There is, in fact, evidence to the contrary. But, of course, unpleasant things do happen. Children do get separated from their parents, parents do separate from each other and mothers, particularly, do ill-treat their children. Psychologists look at all these aspects of life and you will feel a more confident person if you are familiar with some of their findings before you enter into a strange family setting in your professional role.

The last point I want to make concerns social class which is touched on by Schaffer in relation to birth abnormalities. Although things are changing, the majority of occupational therapists were brought up in middle-class environments. For this reason I have included a discussion of Bernstein's pioneering work on language and social class (p. 82). This does not concern itself with vocabulary or local accent, but with the relationship between thought process and language usage. Like Piaget, Bernstein has his critics and their criticisms may prove to be valid. However, like Piaget, Bernstein has offered us a new dimension in our attempts to understand others; with Piaget it is the suggestion that the child may think in ways that are fundamentally different from the adult, with Bernstein it is the idea that verbal communication may be fundamentally different between two social classes.

These next two chapters are of obvious relevance if you are going to work with children in an institutional setting or in the home. But the information they give will put you in a position of gaining a better understanding of, and insight into, the problems and pleasures of your adult patients, for everyone has a personal biography.

Childhood
B. M. FOSS

Early development
Even at birth the differences between infants are very great, and the range of abilities and behaviour which can be called normal is large at all ages.

Apart from sleeping (80 per cent of the time), the newborn seems to spend most of his time eating, excreting or crying. There are several kinds of cry which most mothers can distinguish from each other and which can be analysed using spectographs (which break up the sound into its frequency components). The birth cry appears to be unique. Then there is a basic cry, sometimes called a hunger cry, which is the common pattern. The pain cry, which may be elicited on the first day (for instance, when a blood sample is taken), is characterized by an initial yell followed by several seconds of silence during which the baby maintains expiration and which finally gives way to a gasp and loud sobbing, which in its turn reverts to a basic cry. There is also a frustration cry which is rather like a diminished version of the pain cry. Many mothers have also recognized a different kind of cry which starts at, say, the fourth week. It seems to be a sham cry in the sense that it is caused by no specific need, but seems simply to be a way of calling for attention. Presumably this kind of cry develops into the distress which older children show when separated from their mothers.

What things does the infant attend to? Can it recognize its mother's face and voice, or are these learnt gradually over a period of time? Until recently it was believed that

recognition of faces and voices did not occur until the
infant was several months old, but it now looks as though
infants become competent in this way very much earlier, as
many mothers already suspected. At least, what they can do
is distinguish between different voices and faces probably
as early as the third week of life, and it is likely that
they can tell difference in smell between different people
as early as the second week of life, and there is some evidence that even at this age infants are particularly attracted to representations of the human face. This is a topic
on which there is a conflict of evidence. What is clear,
though, is that most babies have a great deal of opportunity
to get to know faces, in that mothers play face-to-face
games with their babies from the very first days of life;
indeed, where they are allowed to be with the baby from
birth they will tend to play these games immediately. By the
time the baby is three weeks old it gets 'turned off' if,
when face to face with an adult, the adult fails to react to
the baby's changes in facial expression.

Perception

What seems vital for later perceptual learning is some kind
of interaction between the child and the environment. In
describing what happens it is useful to think in terms of
perceptual categories. Probably from birth, infants are
able to categorize movements and discriminate them from lack
of movement and also to categorize various colours; so they
probably have a category for 'red moving objects'. If later
in life an infant reaches out to touch such objects, a red
moving object which is a flame may be encountered, and as
a result of touching it the infant's behaviour will have
an outcome which is different from that when other kinds
of objects are touched. In such a way the infant learns to
discriminate a special sub-category of red moving objects.
Movements of all kinds - eye movements, head movements, and
body movements, and all kinds of interaction with the environment - seem to be important for the development of new
perceptions, and this leads to the possibility that perceptual development will be affected by the child's interests
(in the wider sense; that is, matters of concern): the child
is more likely to attend to and interact with those aspects
of the environment which are relevant to those interests.
One can see evidence for this kind of effect in the many
cross-cultural studies that show, for instance, that Eskimos
have many categories for snow. Similarly, small boys may
have many categories for motor cars. It will be seen that
the psychological idea of a percept is not very different
from a concept. One's perception of a dog is not only affected by the sight of the dog, but also knowing what it
sounds like, or what it feels like to be patted, or to be
bitten by, and what it smells like; and if one happens to be
a dog fancier one's perception of the dog will involve very
much finer discriminations than those made by other people.

Perception, then, is affected not only by the present state of affairs - the stimuli from the environment, and the perceiver's attention, and motivation and emotional state - but also by the perceiver's whole previous history, and this leads to the possibility that different kinds of people have rather different perceptions. The members of a gang will perceive that gang's symbols (haircut and clothing, favourite music, favourite drink, etc.) quite differently from the way they would be perceived by a member of an opposing gang.

Skills

It is only about halfway through the first year of life that a child begins to show good evidence for integrating its movements with its perception by being able to get hold of objects in an obviously intentional way. The gradual development from these early stages through walking and various kinds of play activity to complex skills involved in sports, for instance, are well documented. It may be useful to have a model of the way in which such skills are acquired, and one such model is to regard the skill as built up of a hierarchy of lower-order habits. For instance, a child learning to write must have first learnt to hold a pencil (there is an innate grasping reflex but the child will have to relinquish this method of grasping for one using finger and thumb opposition), will have had to learn to move the pencil across the paper hard enough to leave a mark but not break the paper, will have had to learn to match shapes, to move from left to right across the page, to distinguish between mirror image letters, and so on. Many of these habits can be learnt only in a fairly definite sequence because one will depend on the acquisition of previous habits. Eventually the child will have a whole hierarchy of writing and drawing habits, and at some stage these will have to be integrated with other hierarchies of talking and hearing habits if the child is to become an ordinary literate person. The establishment of these hierarchies depends obviously on having the necessary sensory and motor abilities. They also depend on practice (one cannot learn to drive a car just by reading a book), the knowledge of results (otherwise movements will not become perfected) and on having the motivation to continue learning. One of the characteristics of these skill hierarchies is that the lower-order habits become automatic, and the skilled person does not have to think about them at all but can concentrate on the 'higher' aspects of what is being done. Such a model helps to throw light on some of the reasons why children may fail to develop skills necessary for everyday life. For instance, some sensory or motor abilities may be deficient, an essential lower-order habit may be missing, there may have been difficulty in integrating one or more hierarchies, or there may have been inadequate motivation.

Solving problems

Investigation of problem-solving has been one of the main ways in which psychologists have studied thinking. A main impetus in the study of the development of this kind of ability has been the work of the Swiss psychologist Jean Piaget. He based an elaborate theory on the way in which children develop concepts of number, space, relationships, etc., and claimed that the thinking of a child develops through a series of definite stages, rather as in the development of a skill hierarchy. His results and his theory have been called into question, and although many psychologists do not agree with his theoretical formulation, many of his empirical results have been replicated in a variety of cultures. There has, though, been a tendency to show that some of the problems which Piaget posed can be solved by children at a slightly earlier age given a different method of presenting the problem, and it turns out that sometimes the child fails to solve a problem for reasons other than those given by Piaget. For instance, the child's short-term memory may be inadequate for the storage of information necessary to solve the problem. One of the most interesting class of problems used by Piaget is concerned with what he called conservation. For instance, in testing a child's ability to show conservation of volume, the child is faced with two identical beakers filled with equal amounts of, say, lemonade. If the child agrees that there is an equal amount in each beaker the lemonade from one is then poured into a tall thin glass. The child who has not acquired the concept of conservation will choose the lemonade in the tall thin glass in preference because it will appear greater in quantity. According to Piaget, it is only in middle childhood that children acquire conservation concepts, and it is only when they are, say, 11 or 12 that full logical thinking is possible.

One major concern of psychologists has been to determine how important language is in the development of a child's thinking abilities. Perhaps it is because educationists themselves are rather verbal people that many believe language to be the most important single thing. However, there is some contrary evidence. For instance, deaf mutes who have very little vocabulary or syntax may nevertheless be rather competent in dealing with a whole range of problems varying from those found in ordinary intelligence tests to complicated problems in logic. Of all the tests which have been tried, it happens to be that conservation problems are those which seem most affected by lack of adequate language. In dealing with questions of this kind it is important to realize that there are several kinds of thinking and of intelligence. For instance, when a very broad range of intelligence tests are analysed by a technique such as a factor analysis (which is essentially a way of classifying tests), it usually turns out that there are two broad groups of tests: those involving language and those which do not, but may depend more, for instance, on

being able to manipulate space and pattern. There are also
large individual differences between people in this matter.
Some seem to use language very much more in ordinary thinking, and there is some evidence across cultures that on
the whole girls are better at language skills and boys are
better at spatial skills. There is one kind of problem whose
solution seems to depend on developmental stages and which
may hold the key to some of the changes which occur with
age. If young children are given a series of objects varying
in colour, size and shape, and asked to sort them, they may
do so by their colour or their shape or their size, but
having sorted by one method they will be unable to see that
there is a second or third method of sorting them, and it is
only when they are considerably older that they can see from
the start that there is an ambiguity about how sorting
should be done.

Play

Play in animals and humans is usually easy to recognize
but not so easy to define. Most play does have the property
of appearing to be 'not for real', but there are difficult
borderline cases. For instance, when children are playing
together with toys there may be frequent episodes where
there is competition for toys or for territory, and this may
involve aggression which certainly appears real. Play at
first tends to be solitary even when other children are
there. There may be 'parallel play' in which children pursue
the same tasks though with no obvious co-operation. Fully co-
operative play is not seen much before children are three or
four years old. In most cultures it seems that there are sex
differences in typical play. Boys tend to play more with
boys and girls with girls, and boys show much more of what
has come to be called 'rough and tumble play'. This is the
sort of play where there is a lot of wrestling and tumbling
about and rolling over, sometimes with open-handed arm
beating, often without contact, and rapid jumping up and
down sometimes with arm slapping, and the whole thing is
often accompanied by laughter. Where there is a largish
group of children, one variant is that there is a great deal
of group running, usually in a circle and often occurring
with a lot of laughter. Chasing is another very common
variant. Another sex difference is observed when children
play with their mothers, in that girls tend to have closer
proximity to the mother than boys do, at least on the
average. When play is solitary, dolls and other playthings
and pets are sometimes made to stand for parents and for
children. Such play is often taken to reveal a child's preoccupations, and play therapy is based on the notion that
emotional preoccupations can be acted out. In older children
a lot of play becomes competitive. The dominance fighting
to establish a 'pecking order', which can be seen in all
social animals, is very evident in children. Some of it may
be symbolic and indirect, especially in girls, where dominance fighting is more likely to be verbal than physical.

Arguments about the functions of play are centuries old, and the theories are on the whole untestable (as are most functional theories). However, there is now a certain amount of evidence from animals and from children regarding the effects of deprivation of play. Harlow's experiments at Wisconsin on the effects of various kinds of upbringing on later behaviour in rhesus monkeys have shown that if small monkeys are deprived of play, especially rough and tumble play, they may become maladroit later at both sexual and social behaviour. It is possible that play has this kind of functional importance for humans also. A more popular theory is that play in humans is essential for cognitive development. Many educationists believe this, and they get theoretical support from Piaget's notion that the growth of understanding depends heavily on a child's actions with respect to the environment. An intervention programme has been reported in which children who appeared to be intellectually backward as a result of malnutrition were given regular structured play sessions with toys, and as a result showed considerable development compared with children not given such a programme.

Reinforcement

This is the notion that behaviour is controlled by its consequences. In the sense in which 'reinforcement' is used by B. F. Skinner, a reinforcing state of affairs is one which, when it follows a response of an animal or human, will reinforce that response so that the probability of that response occurring in similar circumstances in the future will increase. Much of the fundamental work on reinforcement has been done on rats and pigeons but also on a very wide variety of other animals and on humans too, and it is the basis for many of the techniques used in behaviour modification. In a typical experiment a rat learns to press a lever which results in the delivery of a food pellet, and this is reinforcing to the hungry rat. Using such a simple set-up it is possible to investigate the effects of a wide variety of variables on the rate of learning. When the animal has learnt that food is no longer delivered when the lever is pressed (extinction trials) it will go on pressing for a while and then cease; but there may be spontaneous recovery. If the animal has been put on a schedule of reinforcement, in which reinforcement is not given for every response but only now and again, either regularly or irregularly and unpredictably, then the animal tends to be much more persistent in pressing the lever and will go on doing so for much longer when food is no longer delivered at all. In other words, after a schedule of reinforcement, especially if the reinforcement has been irregular, the behaviour is much more 'resistant to extinction'. A rat can also be put very much under the control of the environment, in that if a light is always on during reinforced trials but never on during unreinforced trials the animal will learn quite rapidly to press the lever only when the light is on.

The light is then described as a 'discriminative stimulus'. A wide variety of things may act as reinforcers. For instance, isolated monkeys will press a lever for a view of the monkey colony or for a tape-recording of other monkeys, and these stimuli act as reinforcers. These kinds of experimental results have to be applied to humans with a good deal of caution. It is not clear how human behaviour is modified if individuals know that they are being subjected to a patterning of reinforcement; nor is it clear what the effects are of having language and being able to conceptualize the set-up.

Apart from behaviour modification techniques as used by therapists, the following are some applications which may be made. There is one kind of crying, which was mentioned earlier, whose function seems to be to get attention even though there is nothing physically wrong with the child. Such attention-getting crying may be very persistent, and attempts have been made to extinguish it by not attending to the child when he produces this kind of cry. There are several published papers indicating that this kind of procedure is effective. Getting attention, presumably benign attention, is an important reinforcer for many children. There are reports, for instance, of a child who spent most of his time in a horizontal position and crawling, and as a result obtained a lot of attention which presumably reinforced his crawling behaviour. The teachers were trained to attend to the child only when he approximated standing up and not to attend to him when he was crawling, and as a result the child learnt to produce more normal behaviour. One well-known experiment controlled the smiling of babies by reinforcing them with smiles and pleasant noises whenever they smiled. A comparison was made of babies who had been reinforced at every smile, and those who had been put on a schedule, that is, they had been reinforced only at every fourth smile. As predicted, the babies on the schedule smiled more and the smiling was more resistant to extinction. It is not known, though, how long this kind of learning persisted. One prediction of the theory would be that if a child produced a certain kind of behaviour to obtain affection, then that behaviour would be more persistent if the affection were given capriciously and, for the child, unpredictably. As Skinner himself pointed out, in everyday life most reinforcers are irregular rather than regular. This is particularly true in gambling and it is quite likely that one of the mechanisms at work in the persistent gambler is the direct result of unpredictable reinforcement. Bearing in mind the way in which an animal's behaviour can be controlled by a discriminative stimulus in the environment, one could argue that it would be much easier for a child to learn appropriate behaviour if it were made quite clear in the environment when that behaviour was appropriate and when not. To caricature the situation, if a father wore a tie whenever the child was expected to behave in a fairly orderly fashion, but not to wear a tie during playtime, then it should be much easier for the child to discriminate between those two situations. It must be very difficult for young children to know what is appropriate behaviour in a typical supermarket when everyone else is taking goods off the shelves but they themselves are not allowed to do so.

Imitation

There is some evidence that infants will imitate facial expressions when they are only a few weeks old. For instance, they will put out their tongue apparently imitatively at two or three weeks. However, it may not be true imitation since they will also put out their tongues at a pencil pointed at them at the same age. In the second half of the first year, though, a great deal of facial imitation does go on. Detailed analysis of videotape shows that in most cases it is the mother imitating the infant and not the other way around. A lot of this imitative play seems to be a precursor of language and conversation but it is not yet known how important it is. In the second and third year and later, there is a great deal of imitation, much of it important for 'sex typing'. For instance, a three-year-old girl will spend a great deal of time imitating her mother's activities about the house. There have now been many studies of the extent to which imitation or copying occurs in middle childhood from adults or television. Boys in particular tend to copy aggressive movement, especially if the person they are imitating is a man and more especially if the man appears to be rewarded for what he is doing. It is still very unclear to what extent this sort of behaviour persists as a result of such imitation. It is still also not known in general which people children imitate most.

Freud

Many present-day theories of child development are more or less based on classical psychoanalytic theory, and many people would consider that Freud's main contribution was to focus attention on the first five years of life as being of paramount importance in determining later personality. For Freud the central concept in child development is identification, and he believed that imitation was one of the best behavioural signs that identification existed. He believed that identification with the mother figure occurred very early in life and that later, at about the time the superego develops, identification with the aggressor (the aggressive aspects of either mother or father figure) took place. Freud also suggested that the child passes through stages related to the way in which the libido (instinctual energy) operates. The first stage is the oral stage, in which the child's erotic life (in Freud's rather special meaning) centres on the mouth; this is followed by the anal stage, when life centres on excretion; then the phallic stage in which sexual (but of course pre-pubertal) interests centre on the genitals and the body surface as a whole.

There then follows a latent period during which there is little development until the genital period is reached at adolescence. Mental illness in later life was seen as originating from traumatic experiences occurring during these periods. The situation is complicated for boys by the Oedipus situation in which the five year old sees himself as competing with his father for the love of the mother. Some of these ideas were elaborated by other psychoanalysts by devising personality typologies which were based on infantile experience. For instance, an orally-accepting type of person would be a lover of food and drink, a smoker, fond of words; the phallic type might be a lover of the body beautiful, perhaps an exhibitionist or an admirer of sculpture. Needless to say, it is extremely difficult to test the validity of such speculations.

Adolescence

In the first half of this century adolescence was treated as a period of 'storm and stress', of rebellion, of altruism, and searching for an identity. Some of these characteristics of adolescence now seem to be specific to the cultures in which the originators of the ideas lived, and this is particularly true for the notion that adolescence is a period of storm and stress. From anthropological and other studies, it is clear that in some cultures such a period does not exist. The last few decades have seen major changes occurring in the adolescent world so that many of the old generalizations no longer apply. A few decades ago the situation could be stated in fairly black and white terms: young adolescents were economically dependent; they were sexually capable but not expected to have, or were even legally forbidden from having, intercourse; and their social roles were essentially non-adult. In the course of a decade they were expected to go through a fairly clear series of transitional stages until they inevitably reached the desired position in an adult society in which their economic, sexual and social roles would all have changed utterly. At the present day sexual intercourse is often practised soon after the onset of puberty; many children, including working-class children, have considerably more spending money than their parents had at the same age; and there are now so many sub-cultures all the way from pre-adolescence to adulthood that at any age children can find themselves fully accepted within a culture, as a full member of society.

Biological factors
It is now generally accepted that the onset of puberty occurs earlier as time passes. The results of the onset of puberty on individual children seem to depend very much on what they and their peers expect those effects to be. For instance, there are large differences in the extent of menstrual pain, and those differences vary somewhat between cultures and seem to reflect the expectations within those cultures. Some studies suggest that menarche affects

performance at school, whereas there are other studies giving contrary evidence. Here again much may depend on expectations. It is likely that if an individual reaches puberty long before or long after other children in the peer group, this may have considerable effect on behaviour and attitudes. It may be that ignorance of biological factors is detrimental in individual cases, but no one has yet shown what is the best way to carry out sex education, or indeed yet shown that sex education is a good thing (and it would be extremely difficult to show, since the investigator would have the problem of deciding what sex education is good for).

Social factors

Not many generations ago a person was unlikely to survive if not attached physically to a group of people. The need to belong to a group is still as great, though little is known about the psychological mechanisms involved. Avoidance of loneliness is one powerful drive. In modern Man this need may be satisfied by simply identifying with the group and not necessarily belonging to it physically. A century ago a person's choice of group was limited usually to the family, the immediate neighbourhood, work, church, and perhaps hobbies and sport. Now, especially in cities or where people are mobile, groups are based more on common interests. It is very easy these days for a person to find other people who want to behave in the same way or have common goals. There is a tendency for members of a group to come to look alike, talk alike, make the same choices in food, music, beliefs, etc.; and these tendencies are often seen in an exaggerated form in adolescent groups, especially where the identification with the group is so complete that members see themselves as belonging to that group only and to no other. One very noticeable thing about human groups of all kinds (and this applies to groups at all levels of sophistication) is that they are not only bound together by common likes but also by common dislikes. All groups are against something. Anything which lessens old group allegiances will also make new groupings easier so that one would expect gangs to be especially prevalent in new high-rise housing estates, or with people who have just left school. One idea about adolescence, which seems not to have changed over the centuries, is that there is something called 'adolescent revolt'. It has been observed in many cultures (though not in all) that soon after puberty there tends to be a reaction against the parental ways of life. The idea that there is something primitive and possibly biological about this has been reinforced by many observations of primate societies which show that young males tend to form breakaway groups and also start fighting for dominance within the old group.

Dominance fighting is well accepted as an explanatory concept applied to social animals of all kinds, and some biologists and psychologists see it as a main source of competitiveness in human behaviour. Besides the pressures to belong to a group and to conform to it, there are still these largely competitive tendencies which may take the form of wanting to be unique, and to have a role of one's own within the group. Very often such a role involves being best at something. Being best may involve owning things, being most daring, or beautiful, or cleverest. With small boys, competitiveness may show itself in actual dominance fighting. Psychologists of various kinds have talked a lot about the adolescent need for having an identity. It is possible that that need may be partly and perhaps completely satisfied once the person finds a role within a group, especially if the role and the group are of high esteem.

Attitudes and beliefs

Sociologists and social psychologists use the concept 'reference groups'. Market researchers may want to know how to advertise a certain kind of cosmetic product. If it is intended to be attractive to adolescent girls, they may well use the technique of finding out which reference group is relevant. For instance, they may, using questionnaire techniques, ask questions of the kind designed to find out with whom adolescent girls identify when buying cosmetics. In general, one's reference group is the group of people with whom one identifies with respect to one's attitudes, beliefs and values. Developmental studies show that for young children the home provides the main reference group, but in middle childhood already there is a tendency to adopt values of heroes from stories or from television and this becomes very marked in pre-adolescence. In adolescence there may be a complete change of reference groups as has already been suggested, and if this change is very radical then it may be a source of conflict. The way in which the conflict expresses itself will, of course, vary between individuals, and any of the usual clinical manifestations are possible, such as anxiety, depression, hysterical reactions, aggression, and in some cases an attempt at a rational solution of the conflict. Attitudes towards choice of work will be affected by group pressures in just the same way as all other attitudes. The situation is affected by the fact that in many adolescent sub-cultures all the heroes and heroines are roughly of the same age as members of the sub-culture, and there is no need to look ahead to what is going to happen when one belongs to an older age group. In such cases attitudes towards work are likely to be unrealistic in terms of planning ahead.

Some further aspects of human development
FAY FRANSELLA

Development of intelligence: Jean Piaget 1896–1980

Piaget set himself the task of trying to unravel the stages through which a child's mind passes as it develops. For him the child is not an ignorant, untrained, mini-adult, but a person who sees the world in an entirely different way from adults. Piaget's work may be controversial but it has certainly been influential. Much of his theory is based on incredibly detailed studies of the behaviour of his own three children: Laurent, Lucienne and Jacqueline.

I will outline the basic stages of his theory of intellectual development and mention three of the most important terms that are central to his theorizing. First there is the SCHEMA, which is an organized set of actions. When the child develops the manual skill of picking things up, be they lumps of coal or toothbrushes, this 'picking-up' behaviour is a schema.

To start with, the baby's behaviour is organized by doing. But after about two years these action schemata become internalized and so starts the process of thinking. The term for an internalized schema is an OPERATION. The growth of intellect is concerned with the development of operational thinking.

Last, there is the concept of ADAPTATION. This consists of two parts: accommodation and assimilation. These are reciprocal processes which result in the infant organizing its random actions into schemata, and so becoming increasingly able to adapt to its environment. The schema is a structure which develops by assimilating (or 'feeding on') sensory experience. For instance, when the infant eats a new substance the stomach muscles contract, digestive juices are secreted, and so forth; the stomach is said to have accommodated to a new environmental event, the food, and is now able to assimilate it. In other words, the individual changes in response to environmental events. Once the food is in the stomach the juices, contractions and so forth, deal with it and transform it so that the body can assimilate or make use of it. Adaptation consists both of the modifying of our existing structures in response to environmental demands (accommodation) and also of using these structures to incorporate the new elements of the external world (assimilation). These processes are two sides of the same coin leading to an increasing number of schemata. When they are in balance there is equilibrium.

So much for some of Piaget's basic terms; now for the stages of development. To begin with the baby's behaviour is dominated by sensori-motor activity. This SENSORI-MOTOR stage has, in fact, six sub-stages. First of all, for instance, there is the job of co-ordinating the reflexes and random movements such as sucking and grasping. The baby then starts to repeat actions it has discovered in order to make interesting things continue. But the six-month infant is easy to fool. One of Piaget's most interesting and important observations was that babies have no idea that an object is something that continues to exist when it is out of sight. It is 'out of sight, out of mind' in a very literal sense. It takes some time for the concept of object permanence to develop. The idea that objects remain constant over time and space is clearly crucial for the development of intelligence and the child's ability to adapt to the environment.

By around 24 months, most children have moved on to the next, the PRE-OPERATIONAL, stage. From now until around seven years of age, children are prisoners of their immediate perceptions. To start with, they use pre-concepts rather than concepts. This phase of the pre-operational stage is sometimes called PRE-CONCEPTUAL. For instance, if a girl is given a number of beads that differ in colour and in shape and you ask her to give you four that are alike, she may well hand you first a red square one, then a red round one, then a round blue one and finally a blue tri-angular one. The first two were associated by colour, the next by shape and the last again by colour. Or, if you pre-sent her with a large number of brown beads together with a few white beads and ask whether there are more brown or wooden beads, the three or four year old may say there are more brown beads. A child of this age cannot handle the concept 'wooden beads' and the sub-classes 'brown' and 'white'.

Children next enter the second phase of pre-operational thinking, called the INTUITIVE stage, and there they con-front the problem of conservation. It is in this context that Piaget developed some of his best known experiments in which he studied the development of the concept of conser-vation of such things as quantity, weight, substance and volume. For instance, if water is poured from a short fat jar into a long thin jar, children of five will probably say there is more water in the long thin jar even though they have seen it is the same water that was poured from the short fat jar (reversibility). Equally, if beads are laid out in two rows and clearly paired to show there are equal numbers and then, in clear view of the child, one row of beads is spread out into a longer line, the child will say there are more beads in the longer line (invariance).

By about seven years of age the child is beginning to enter the next stage of development: that of CONCRETE OPERATIONS. But the transition from pre-operational to concrete operational stage does not occur suddenly and may even be spread over a number of years. For instance, child-ren come to understand that substances and quantities remain the same even though they look different. But conservation of other things takes longer. They may not understand the conservation of weight until about the age of nine or ten and the conservation of volume until about eleven or twelve. It is important to remember that these ages are only ap-proximations, and variations within cultures and between cultures are great.

Even with the establishment of vital concepts at the stage of concrete operations, the child has still not deve-loped the ability to think in abstract terms. This does not come until the period of FORMAL OPERATIONS at around eleven or twelve years of age.

Piaget holds to the view that human intelligence deve-lops according to a pre-set biological pattern. He argues that some children move faster than others, but that no child can skip a stage. He also considers, unlike Chomsky, that language lags behind the development of thought. The child learns by doing things, seeing things from different angles, and develops language to describe what has already developed in thought.

There are many critics of Piaget's stage theory. He is criticized in terms of the slackness of his methodology; also for the fact that, with careful instructions, five-year-old children can indeed do the water jug problem; also for seeing the stages as definite and discrete steps. But even these critics never fail to emphasize the major influence that Piaget's ideas have had on our child-rearing practices and on education. In a later chapter (chapter 8), Farr points out that, because of Piaget's brilliant use of interviewing, we have become aware 'just how different the world of the child is from the world of the adult'.

If the community occupational therapist is called upon to visit a disabled mother with a very disruptive child, it is helpful to have an idea about what one can reasonably expect from that child. It may also help her analyse what it is in that situation that is causing the child to be so disruptive. For instance, if very small, the child may think that every time mother has to go into hospital she will never appear again. Or, if the child is older but not yet old enough to have reached the stage of formal operations, the occupational therapist will realize it will be no use trying to persuade the child to conceptualize what is happening to the mother in abstract terms. The child may look old enough to understand, but will not be able to do so. Understanding the stage of thinking the child may have achieved may give the occupational therapist a broader understanding of what it means for the child to behave in a disruptive way.

Sex-typing

One question to which we have to address ourselves is 'To what extent are the differences in behaviour and attitudes between men and women the result of our genetic inheritance, and to what extent are they the result of our blue or pink bootees?' A very large number of studies has been carried out in an attempt to provide an answer to this question.

Some studies have been aimed at identifying the differences in behaviour between the sexes that are thought to originate very early on in life. The general conclusion from these studies must be that there is an astonishing lack of difference. The only consistent general findings are that boys are more prone to be aggressive and girls are more verbally fluent. There are also a few specific ones. For instance, boys appear to have more spontaneous motor activity at birth, predominantly of gross movements, whereas girls have typically finer movements, largely of the face (Korner, 1969). Also, boys may be more susceptible to visual reinforcers, whereas girls appear to respond better to auditory ones (Watson, 1969). Although these differences could well have important implications for future development, they may actually do no more than provide the constitutional soil which allows the differences in the ways adults treat infant boys and girls to flourish; that is, these early differences might not continue in later life if the social environment did not build on them in particular ways.

The picture of how adults behave in relation to sex of infant is as confusing as that about differences between the sexes at birth. There is some evidence suggesting that mothers give more physical stimulation to boys and imitate the vocalizations of girls more. This is a little surprising in that there seems to be no difference between infant boys and girls in actual quantity of early vocalizations. But it is clearly possible that mothers' attention to their daughters' vocalizations contributes to the greater verbal fluency in girls. Even so, these findings have to be considered along with those showing that mothers talk more to first-born children than to subsequent ones, and that educated mothers talk more to their children than do uneducated ones. In other words, as with so many problems in psychology, the picture is a complex one.

In reviewing all the available literature up to 1974, Maccoby and Jacklin conclude that, on the whole, boys and girls are treated markedly the same during pre-school years. But, yet again, exceptions arise to this generalization. Boys are handled more roughly than girls, and parents indicate more concern about girls' physical well-being. Also, boys are physically punished more than girls, so boys seem to receive more aggression at an early age as well as showing it. Which is the cause and which the effect? It is interesting to note that boys whose fathers have died, or have left home before the boys are five years old, show less aggression and participate less in boy-type games, but this is not so if the child is over six years old.

Whatever the psychological differences between boys and girls early in life, these are likely to be widened by the type of toys used in play. Preferences for different types of toy certainly develop increasingly as children grow up. Boys are particularly reluctant to play with dolls as they increase in age from three to eight years, but the change is not nearly so marked in girls, who are quite ready to play with 'boy-toys', such as guns, given a chance. It may well be that parents feel it important to influence boys against dolls but are not so concerned when little girls play with guns.

Experiments have shown that imitation of other children also plays a part. For example, Wolfe (1973) had 60 children between the ages of seven and eleven watch a child of either the same or different sex play with a toy that adults would consider appropriate. When each child had watched the 'model' play with the toy, they were observed for five minutes to see how long it was before they touched the toy and the total time spent playing with it. There were no sex differences on these measures. Nor were there any sex differences when the 'model' played with an inappropriate toy. But both boys and girls played longer with a sex-inappropriate toy when the model was the same sex as themselves. Wolfe suggests that a boy will play with a gun, not because he sees himself as a boy and 'knows' that boys play with guns, but that his behaviour is the result of his having been consistently rewarded for doing so in the past. For instance, loving parents will have given him 'boy-toys' all his young life and clearly reinforce him when he runs round the room shouting 'stick 'em up'.

It seems highly likely that boys and girls learn something about the type of behaviour that is appropriate for them in terms of their sex from the toys they have available for play. But so must they also learn from children's books. In 1973, Jacklin and Mischel analysed 270 children's stories and found several interesting things. For instance, characters in boys' books were almost exclusively male, whereas in girls' books 57 per cent were male and 43 per cent female. In terms of behaviour, boys were portrayed as being more aggressive, indulging more in physical exertion and in solving problems. Girls were more often 'absorbed in fantasy' and in making statements about themselves such as 'I've blue eyes' or 'I'm too stupid'. When adult, men in the stories behaved just as boys did in terms of physical exertion and problem-solving but were not so aggressive, whereas the women were very much more conformist and indulged more in general chat. Men were portrayed more often out of doors and in business, and women more in home or school. Jacklin and Mischel say:

> Sex role stereotyping is pervasive in elementary readers. Girls and women appear less frequently and engage in distinctly different activities than boys and men. Females are rarely main characters in stories: they seldom solve problems or do interesting things. Girls are depicted as fantasizing and talking about themselves. Women are shown as conforming and talking a great deal, though not about themselves. Men, on the other hand, construct and produce things, solve problems, and engage in various kinds of hard work and play (Jacklin and Mischel, 1973).

It does seem likely that this is one important way in which society helps boys and girls come to understand what society thinks is appropriate for them. Many women feel that it is little use trying to change attitudes in adults when such biasses occur in children's books, and that authors' stereotyping of the sexes should change. But this is not to be confused with a suggestion that there should be 'guidelines' for authors. That would be exchanging one form of tyranny for another. The idea is simply that a more equal state of affairs will only exist if adults are made more aware of the implications of the content of children's books so that they may, if they wish, be more selective in what they give little Johnnie and Mary Jane to read.

In his chapter on self-knowledge, Bannister discussed how it may be that we come to have an understanding of ourselves, by developing a self-concept, and how this increases in complexity with age. It is interesting to know that the girls in a study he did with Agnew (1977) were found to have ideas about themselves as persons before boys of a comparable age. If this is so, we can only at present guess at the implications for development of psychological differences between sexes. But, for nearly all of us, some notion of being male or female is central to any notion of ourselves as persons.

The development of this notion of our masculinity or femininity, and our acceptance of it, is likely to depend on more than whether we had pink or blue bootees placed on our tiny feet.

References

Bannister, D. and Agnew, J. (1977)
The child's construing of itself. In A.W. Landfield (ed.), Nebraska Symposium on Motivation 1976. Nebraska: Nebraska University Press.

Fonagy, P. (1981)
Research on psychoanalytic concepts. In F. Fransella (ed.), Personality: Theory, measurement and research. London: Methuen.

Freud, S. (1960)
The Ego and the Id. New York: Norton.

Jacklin, C. and Mischel, J. (1973)
As the twig is bent: sex role stereotyping in early readers. School Psychology Digest, 2, 30-38.

Korner, A.F. (1969)
Neonatal startles, smiles, erections and reflex sucks as related to state, sex and individuality. Child Development, 40, 1039-1053.

Maccoby, E. and Jacklin, C. (1975)
The Psychology of Sex Differences. Oxford: Oxford University Press.

Popper, K. (1972)
Conjectures and Refutations: The growth of scientific knowledge (4th edn). London: Routledge & Kegan Paul.

Watson, J.S. (1969)
Operant conditioning of visual fixation in infants under visual and auditory reinforcement. Developmental Psychology Monographs, 1, 508-516.

Wolfe, T. (1973)
Effects of live modelled sex-inappropriate play behavior in a naturalistic setting. Developmental Psychology, 9, 120-123.

Questions

1. Write short notes on: crying; the development of perception and attention; the development of movement.
2. How do skills develop? Illustrate with examples of your own choosing from early and later childhood.
3. What is reinforcement? How may it operate in controlling behaviour?

4. In what ways does a child's ability to solve problems vary with age?
5. Men and women are born and not made. Discuss this statement with reference to sex roles.
6. How would you classify different kinds of play? What functions may they have?
7. What are the main developmental stages a child passes through according to (i) Piaget, (ii) Freud?
8. Discuss the extent to which development during adolescence is determined by social factors.
9. How do attitudes and beliefs change during childhood and adolescence?
10. Piaget will be known more for his method of enquiry than for his findings. Discuss this statement.

Annotated reading

Boden, M.A. (1979) Piaget. London: Fontana.
    Another interesting book about the man himself as well as his ideas.

Brown, G. and Desforges, C. (1979) Piaget's Theory: A psychological critique. London: Routledge & Kegan Paul.
    A detailed account of Piaget's theory with some criticism of his findings.

Bryant, P. (1974) Perception and Understanding in Young Children. London: Methuen.
    A critic's view.

Bower, T. (1977) Perceptual World of the Child. London: Fontana.

Garvey, C. (1977) Play. London: Fontana.

Donaldson, M. (1978) Children's Minds. London: Fontana.
    These belong to a series of short books on children called 'The Developing Child' and edited by Jerome Bruner, Michael Cole and Barbara Lloyd. The last of these three references is particularly good on cognitive growth and its relevance to education.

Ginsberg, H. and Oper, S. (1969) Piaget's Theory of Intellectual Development: An introduction. Englewood Cliffs, NJ: Prentice-Hall.
    A straightforward explanation and description of Piaget's theory and work.

Hadfield, J.A. (1979) Childhood and Adolescence. Harmondsworth: Penguin.

Sandstrom, C.I. (1968) Psychology of Childhood and Adolescence. Harmondsworth: Penguin.
    These cover both childhood and adolescence. The book by Hadfield is particularly useful for parents. The one

by Sandstrom is a little dated though there is a revised edition from 1979.

Miller, G.A. (1966) Psychology: The science of mental life. Harmondsworth: Penguin (pp. 316-336).
    An excellent brief introduction, with emphasis on Piaget the man.

Turner, J. (1975) Cognitive Development. London: Methuen.

Green, J. (1974) Thinking and Language. London: Methuen.
    These are part of a series called 'Essential Psychology' and are particularly relevant.

Watson, R.I. and Lindgren, H.C. (1979) Psychology of the Child and the Adolescent (4th edn). New York: Collier Macmillan.
    This is an American book, but covers the non-American work well, and is slightly more advanced than the other suggested readings.

4

Social development in early childhood
H. R. Schaffer

Introduction
H. R. SCHAFFER

Psychologists study children for two main reasons. First, they want to find out how a helpless, naïve and totally dependent baby manages in due course to become a competent, knowledgeable adult. They are interested therefore in studying the process of development. The second reason stems from the many social problems associated with childhood. Should we protect children from viewing violence on television? Are children of mothers who go out to work more likely to become delinquent? Does hospitalization in the early years produce later difficulties? How can one mitigate the effects of divorce on children? Why do some parents become baby batterers? Increasingly the psychologist is asked to examine such problems and produce answers useful to society. It is primarily to this aspect of child psychology that we pay attention here.

The child's socialization

How a child develops depends very much on the people around him. From them the child learns the skills and values needed for social living, from the use of knives and forks to knowing the difference between right and wrong. Other people are always around the child, being of influence by means of example and command, and none more so at first than the members of the immediate family. On them depend the initial stages of socialization.

Disadvantaged children and their families
It is, of course, only too apparent that not every family carries out its socializing task with equal effectiveness. By way of illustration, let us look at the way in which intellectual development is shaped by the child's social environment.

At one time it was thought that intelligence is entirely determined by an individual's inborn endowment. There are few who now believe this: it seems rather that the environment in which a child is reared can have a powerful effect on development.

The issue has been much debated in relation to the poor educational achievement of 'disadvantaged' children. These are children who come from the economically and socially

most deprived sectors of the community and who so often
appear to be at a severe disadvantage when first starting
school, because (as it has been put) 'they have learnt not
to learn'. Their failure in the education system, in other
words, is ascribed not so much to some genetic inferiority
as to factors operating in the home, which result in an
inability to make use of whatever intellectual capacities
they have.

A great many schemes have been launched to counter
this situation, especially in the USA. Some of the earlier
efforts, designed to give children some extra training in
basic cognitive skills before school entry, were clearly
inadequate and produced no lasting benefits. This is partly
because the schemes were too brief, partly because they came
too late in the child's life, but partly also because they
left untouched the home situation. Given a conflict of
values about education between home and school it is highly
likely that the home will always win. It is there that the
child has already lived and learned for several years before
ever starting school, and it is therefore significant that
more recent efforts have attempted to involve the parents as
well as the child or even to work solely through the
parents.

There is now little doubt that parents can enhance or
suppress the child's educational potential. One way in which
they apparently do this is by the extent to which they
foster the development of language: a function so necessary
for the expression of intelligence. There are pronounced
social class differences in the style of language mothers
use to communicate with their children; in addition,
however, it has also been shown that mothers from disadvantaged homes engage in face-to-face talking with their
infants less frequently than middle-class mothers. The
poorer child often lives in much noisier surroundings than
the middle-class child in a quiet suburban home, but to
profit from stimulation the young child must be exposed to
it under the personalized conditions that only the to-and-
fro reciprocity of a face-to-face situation provides. It is
in this respect that many lower-class 'socially deprived
children' are at a disadvantage.

Child effects on adults

Let us not now jump to the conclusion that children's
development is totally a matter of what parents do to them.
A child is never just a passive being that one can mould
into whatever shape the adult desires. Even the youngest
babies can already exert an influence on their caretakers
and so help to determine how they behave towards them.

Take an obvious example: babies cry and thereby draw
attention to themselves. It is a sound that can have a most
compelling effect on the adult: we have all heard of the
mother who can sleep through a thunderstorm, but is immediately awoken by her child's whimper in the next room.

Babies, by this powerful signal, can initiate the inter-action: they can thereby influence both the amount and the timing of attention which others provide.

Babies come into the world as individuals. Some are active and restless, others quiet and content; some are highly sensitive, others are emotionally robust and easy-going. The kind of care provided for one is therefore inappropriate for another, and any sensitive mother will therefore find herself compelled to adopt practices suitable for her individual child. A good example is provided by babies' differences in 'cuddliness'. Not all babies love being held and cuddled: some positively hate it and resist such contact by struggling and, unless released, by crying. It has been found that these 'non-cuddlers' tend to be more active and restless generally, and to be intolerant of all types of physical restraint (as seen when they are being dressed or tucked into bed). The mother is accordingly forced to treat her child in a manner that takes into account his 'peculiarity': when frightened or unwell these children cannot be comforted by being held close but have to be offered other forms of stimulation such as bottles, bis-cuits or soothing voices. Each mother must therefore show considerable flexibility in adjusting to the specific requirements of her child.

There is one further, and perhaps unexpected, example one can quote of the way in which parents are influenced by their children. It concerns the phenomenon of baby batter-ing, which has attracted so much attention in recent years. It is by no means a new phenomenon; historically speaking, it is probably as old as the family itself. What is new is public concern that such a thing can happen, and this in turn has given rise to the need for research into such cases. As a result of various investigations it is now widely agreed that violence results from a combination of several factors: the presence of financial, occupational and housing problems facing the family; the parents' emotional immaturity which makes it difficult for them to deal with such problems; their social isolation from potential sources of help such as relatives and neighbours; and, finally, some characteristic of the battered child that singles him out as a likely victim.

It is the last factor that is particularly relevant to us, for it illustrates once again that the way in which parents treat their children is influenced by the children themselves. There is evidence that children most likely to be battered are 'difficult': they are more likely to be sickly, or to have been born prematurely, or to have feeding and sleeping problems. Being more difficult to rear, they make extra demands that the parents are just not able to meet. The child's condition acts on the parent's inadequacy, and so the child, unwittingly, contributes to his own fate.

Mother-child mutuality
It is apparent that children do not start life as psycho-logical nonentities. From the beginning they already have an

individuality that influences the adults around them. Thus a mother's initial task is not to create something out of nothing; it is rather to dovetail her behaviour to that of the child.

Such dovetailing takes many forms. Take our previous example of the non-cuddlers. If the mother herself has a preference for close physical contact with the baby which are then rejected, some mutual readjustment will need to take place. Fortunately, most mothers quickly adjust and find other ways of relating to the child. It is only when they are too inflexible, or interpret the baby's behaviour as rejection, that trouble can arise from a mismatch.

Mutual adjustment is the hallmark of all interpersonal behaviour; it can be found in even the earliest social interactions. The feeding situation provides a good example. Should babies be fed by demand or by a rigid, pre-determined schedule? Advice by doctors and nurses has swung fashion-wise, sometimes stressing the importance of exerting discipline from the very beginning and of not 'giving in', at other times pointing to the free and easy methods of primitive tribes as the 'natural way'. In actual fact each mother and baby, however they may start off, sooner or later work out a pattern which satisfies both partners. On the one hand, there are few mothers who can bear to listen for long to a bawling infant unable as yet to tell the time; on the other hand, one should not under-estimate the ability of even very young babies to adjust to the demands of their environment. An example is provided by an experiment, carried out many years ago, in which two groups of babies were fed during the first ten days of life according to a three-hour and four-hour schedule respectively. Within just a few days after birth each baby had already developed a peak of restlessness just before the accustomed feeding time, and this became particularly obvious when the three-hour group was shifted to a four-hour schedule and so had to wait an extra hour for their feed. In time, however, these babies too became accustomed to the new timetable and showed the restlessness peak at four-hourly intervals. We can see here a form of adaptation to social demands that must represent one of the earliest forms of learning.

Not surprisingly, the major responsibility for mutual adjustment lies initially with the adult. The degree of flexibility one can expect from very young children is limited. Yet the very fact that they are involved in social interactions from the very beginning of life means that they have the opportunity of gradually acquiring the skills necessary to become full partners in such exchanges. Observations of give-and-take games with babies at the end of the first year have made this point. Initially babies know only how to take: they have not learnt that their behaviour is just one part of a sequence, that they need to take turns with others, and that the roles of two participants are interchangeable (one being a giver, the other a taker). Such and other rules of behaviour they will learn in time; rules form the basis for much of social intercourse, and it is through social intercourse that children acquire them in the first place.

Socialization is sometimes portrayed as a long drawn-out battle, as a confrontation between wilful young children and irritated parents that must at all cost be resolved in favour of the latter. Goodness knows such battles occur, yet they are far from telling us everything about the process of socialization. There is a basic mutuality between parent and child without which interaction would not be possible. The sight of the mother's face automatically elicits a smile from the baby; that produces a feeling of delight in the mother and causes her in turn to smile back and to talk or tickle or pick up, in this way calling forth further responses from the baby. A whole chain of interaction is thus started, not infrequently initiated by the baby. Mother and child learn about each other in the course of these interactions, and more often than not mutual adjustment is brought about by a kind of negotiation process in which both partners show some degree of flexibility. On the mother's part, this calls for sensitivity to the particular needs and requirements of her child, an ingredient of parenthood that we return to subsequently; on the child's part, it refers to one of the most essential aspects of social living that he must learn early on.

Some conditions that foster development

If we are to promote the mental health and social integration of children, it is necessary to identify the factors that further, or on the contrary hinder, such an aim. We all have our favourite theories as to why some children do not develop in what we regard as a desirable manner: not enough parental discipline, too much violence on television, the declining influence of religion, the social isolation of today's family, and so on. It is much more difficult, however, to substantiate through objective research that any one factor does play a part. Nevertheless, there are some conclusions to which we can point.

The blood-bond: myth or reality?

Is it essential, or at least desirable, that children should be brought up by their natural parents? Is a woman who conceived and bore a child by that very fact more fitted to care for this child than an unrelated individual?

This is no academic question. Children have been removed by courts of law from the foster parents with whom they had lived nearly all their lives and to whom they had formed deep attachments, in order to restore them to their biological mother from whom they may have been apart since the early days of life, and all because of the 'blood-bond'. Yet such a thing is a complete myth. There is nothing at all to suggest that firm attachments cannot grow between children and unrelated adults who have taken over the parental role. The notion that the biological mother, by virtue of being the biological mother, is uniquely capable of caring for her child is without foundation.

Were it otherwise, the whole institution of adoption would be in jeopardy. Yet there is nothing to suggest that adoptive parents are in any way inferior to natural parents. In a study by Barbara Tizard (to which we refer again), children who had been in care throughout their early years were followed up on leaving care. One group of children was adopted, another returned to their own families. It was found that the latter did less well than the adopted children, both in the initial stages of settling in and in their subsequent progress. The reason lay primarily in the attitudes of the two sets of parents: the adoptive group worked harder at being parents, possibly just because the child was not their own. There have been a good many studies which have examined the effects of adoption, and virtually all stress the high proportion of successful cases to be found. And this despite the difficulties such children may have had to face, such as problems in the pre-adoption phase and the knowledge gained later on of the fact of their adoption. Successful parenting is a matter of particular personality characteristics that need to be identified, not of 'blood'.

Fathers as parents: more myths?
Do children have to be cared for primarily by women? Is there something about females that makes them more suitable for this task than males? What part should fathers play in the child's upbringing?

The answer is simple. There is no 'should' or 'should not'. It is a matter of what each society and each family decides about the division of roles between the parents. There have in fact been marked changes over the last few decades in the extent to which fathers participate in child care. They now do so to a far greater extent than they used to, and this trend is continuing. For instance, with increasing unemployment it is no longer uncommon to find families in which a complete role reversal has taken place: mother, having found a job, goes out to work, leaving her unemployed husband in charge of home and children. Fortunately, there is no evidence to indicate that the biological make-up of men makes them unfit for this task or even necessarily inferior to women in this respect. Parenting is unisex; the reasons for the traditional division of labour (such as the need to breast-feed the child and the importance of using men's greater physical strength for hunting and tilling the fields) are no longer applicable.

Children brought up without a father are more likely to encounter difficulties than those in a complete family. There are various reasons for this. One is that in any single-parent family the remaining parent must cope with a great multiplicity of stresses - financial, occupational, or emotional - and the strain felt by him or (more often) her is very likely to have repercussions for the child too. Again, a fatherless boy has no model to imitate, and the developmental tasks of acquiring sex-appropriate behaviour may be more difficult. And, finally, the child isolated with

his mother and caught up in one all-encompassing relationship does not have the same chance of learning from the
beginning about some of the complexities of the social
world: having two parents helps him to learn at once that
not all people are alike and that he must adapt his own
behaviour according to their different characteristics and
different demands.

Parenthood: full-time or part-time?

Until fairly recently there was a widespread belief among
parents and professional workers that children in the pre-
school period required full-time mothering, and that it was
the duty of mothers to stay with the child night and day,
24 hours on end. Otherwise, it was feared, children's mental
health would suffer.

We can look at this situation from both the mother's and
the child's point of view. As far as mothers are concerned,
a crucial consideration is the recent finding of an extremely high incidence of depression among house-bound
women. With no outlet such as a job, tied to the house by
the presence of several dependant children, a large proportion of mothers (especially among the working class) become
isolated and hence depressed. Mothers, on the other hand,
who do go out to work are far less likely to suffer from
depression, anxiety and feelings of low self-esteem.

As far as the children are concerned, comparisons of
those with mothers at work and those with mothers at home
have not found any differences between them. Far from being
adversely affected, the former may even stand to gain both
intellectually and socially. The intellectual effects stem
from the extra stimulation and extra provision of play
materials that most children in day care obtain: a point of
particular significance for those from disadvantaged backgrounds. And, socially, not only is there no evidence that
the child's attachment to the mother is in some way 'dilu-
ted' by a daily period of being apart, but also the child in
day care has the enormous advantage of coming into contact
with other children. The benefit of such experience for
social development has until quite recently been overlooked;
yet other children, even in the early years, can exercise a
considerable socializing influence, and in addition may
further the child's diversification of social behaviour.
After all, the more children are encouraged to adapt to a
variety of other individuals the more their repertoires of
social skills will grow.

Thus a daily period away from mother may produce good
rather than harm. There is, however, one important proviso,
and this concerns the quality of the substitute care which
the child receives. For one thing, there is a need for consistency: a young child continually being left with different people is likely to become bewildered and upset. And for
another, we have the enormous problem of illegal childminders, looking after an estimated 100,000 children in
Britain. According to recent findings, the quality of care

provided by such childminders is only too frequently of an unsatisfactory nature, being marked by ignorance and neglect that in some cases can be quite appalling. It is only in the officially provided facilities, such as nursery schools, that the care given by trained staff is such that the social and intellectual benefits can be felt.

Sensitive and insensitive parents

A child's development does not take place in a vacuum; it occurs because the people responsible for his care carefully and sensitively provide him with the kind of environment that will foster his growth. They do so not only by such conscious decisions as what toys to buy him for Christmas or which nursery school to send him to, but also quite unconsciously by the manner in which they relate to him.

Take the language which adults use in talking to a child. This is in many ways strikingly different from the language used to address another adult: it has a much more restricted vocabulary, a considerably simplified grammar, and a great deal of repetition. In addition, it is characterized by a slowing down in the rate of speech, a high pitch of voice, and the use of special intonation patterns. Not only mothers but most adults will quite unconsciously adopt this style when confronted by a young child. What is more, the younger the child the more marked is the simplification, repetition, slowing down and all the other characteristics listed. It is as though the adult is making allowance for the child's limited ability to absorb whatever one tells him, thereby showing sensitivity to the abilities and requirements of that particular child.

Such examples of (usually quite unconscious) sensitivity in relating to children are numerous. Watch how a mother hands her baby a rattle to grasp: how carefully she adjusts the manner and speed with which she offers the toy to the still uncertain reaching skills of the child. She shows thereby that she is able to see things from the child's point of view, that she is aware of his requirements and can respond to these appropriately. Sensitivity is an essential part of helping a child to develop. Children brought up in institutions, in which they are all treated the same and where care is never personalized, become developmentally retarded. While most adults show sensitivity to children quite naturally, some parents are unfortunately devoid of this vital part of parenting. Why this is so we still do not know for certain; it does seem, however, that parents who themselves had a deprived childhood and did not themselves experience sensitive care are more likely to show the same attitude to their own children.

Are the early years special?

There is a widespread belief that experience in childhood, and particularly so in the earliest years, has a crucial formulative influence on later personality. Thus the early years are said to be the most important, and special care therefore needs to be taken to protect the child during this period against harmful experiences that might mark him for life. Let us look at the evidence for this belief.

The influence of child-rearing practices

According to Freud, a child's development is marked by a series of phases (oral, anal, genital) during which he is especially sensitive to certain kinds of experience. During the oral phase, for example, the baby is mainly concerned with activities like sucking, chewing, swallowing and biting, and the experiences that matter to him most thus include the manner of his feeding (breast or bottle), the timing of feeding (schedule or demand), the age when he is weaned, and so on. When these experiences are congenial to the child he passes on to the next developmental phase without difficulty; when they are frustrating and stressful, however, he remains 'fixated' at this stage in the sense that, even as an adult, he continues to show characteristics such as dependence and passivity in his personality make-up that distinguish babies at the oral stage. In this way Freud's theory suggests that there are definite links between particular kinds of infantile experiences on the one hand, and adult personality characteristics on the other.

However, this theory has not been borne out. A large number of investigations have compared breast-feeding with bottle-feeding, self-demand with rigidly scheduled regimes, early with later weaning, and other aspects of the child's early experience that could be expected to produce lasting after-effects. No such effects have been found. The sum total of these investigations adds up to the conclusion that specific infant care practices do not produce unvarying traces that may unfailingly be picked up in later life. Whatever their impact at the time, there is no reason to believe that these early experiences mark the child for good or ill for the rest of his life.

And just as well! Were it otherwise we would all be at the mercy of some single event, some specific parental aberration, that we happened to have experienced at some long-distant point in our past. Freud's theory made little allowance for the ameliorating influence of later experience, yet the more we study human development the more apparent it becomes that children, given the opportunity, are able to recuperate from many an early misfortune. Let us consider some other examples that make this point.

Maternal deprivation

In 1951 a report was published by John Bowlby, a British child psychiatrist, pointing to the psychological ill-effects of being deprived of maternal care during the early years. The evidence, Bowlby believed, indicated that a child must be with his mother during the crucial period of the first two or three years if he is to develop the ability to form relationships with other people. Deprived of a relationship with a permanent mother-figure at that time, such an ability will never develop. Thus children in institutions and long-term hospitals, where they are deprived of this necessity, become 'affectionless characters': that is, they are unable ever to form a deep, emotionally meaningful relationship with another person. Having missed out on a vital experience, namely being mothered, the child is mentally crippled for life. And that experience has to happen at a particular time, namely in the first years. No amount of good mothering subsequently can remedy the situation.

There is no doubt about the tremendous influence on the practice of caring for childen that Bowlby's ideas have had. And no wonder, for so many children are thereby implicated. Many thousands of children every year are taken into the care of local authorities; many thousands are admitted to hospital. Anything that can be done to improve the lot of so many children is therefore worth considering, and there is no doubt that in the last two decades a great deal has been done in the UK. Children's institutions have become less impersonal with the introduction of family group systems; there is greater emphasis on fostering children with ordinary families and, most important, far more stress is placed on prevention and keeping children with their own parents. Similarly, the psychological care of children in hospitals has improved greatly during this period. Visiting by parents is nowhere near as restricted as it was at one time; mother-baby units make it possible for parents to stay with their children; and again the emphasis on prevention means that rather more thought is now given to the need to admit the child in the first place.

Anyone who has ever seen a young child separated from his mother and admitted, say, to a strange hospital ward, where he is looked after by strangers and may be subjected to unpleasant procedures like injections, knows the extreme distress that one then finds. It is perhaps difficult for an adult to appreciate the depth of a child's panic when he has just lost his mother: a panic that may continue for days and only be succeeded by a depressive-like picture when the child withdraws into himself from a too painful world. Parents also know only too well about the insecurity which the child shows subsequently on return home, even after quite brief absences, when he dare not let the mother out of sight. There is no doubt about these dramatic short-term effects, and for their sake alone the steps taken to humanize procedures have been well worth while.

Far more problematic, however, is the question of long-term effects: that is, the suggestion that periods of prolonged maternal deprivation in the early years impair the child's capacity to form interpersonal relationships. What evidence we have here suggests that things are not as cut and dried as Bowlby indicated, and to make this point we can do no better than to turn to the report by Barbara Tizard to which we have already referred.

Tizard examined adopted children who had spent all their early lives in institutions, with no opportunity to form any stable attachments to any adult during that period. One might have expected them to be so marked by this experience as to be incapable of forming any emotional relationship to their adoptive parents and to show all the signs of the affectionless character. Yet this proved not to be the case. Nearly all these children developed deep attachments to their adoptive parents, and this included even a child placed as late as seven years of age. They did show some deviant symptoms, such as poor concentration and over-friendliness to strangers, but there was no indication that the inevitable outcome of their earlier upbringing was the 'affectionless character'. We must conclude that children's recuperative powers should not be under-estimated: given a new environment in which they receive very much improved treatment, the outlook can be good. There is no reason to believe that they will be marked for life by earlier misfortunes, just because these occurred early on.

Birth abnormalities and social class
When misfortune takes a 'physical' form, such as some abnormality of the birth process, the outcome is again not necessarily a poor one. Once more, it all depends on the child's subsequent experience.

Take such birth complications as anoxia (the severe shortage of oxygen in the brain) or prematurity. Follow-up studies of children who arrive in the world in such a precarious condition show that, on the basis of the child's condition at birth, it is impossible to predict his subsequent development. Two children coming into the world with the identical kind of pathology may develop along quite different lines. In one case, the child's condition at birth may give rise to a whole sequence of problems that continue and even mount up throughout his life; in the other, the difficulty is surmounted and the child functions normally.

The answer to this paradox lies in the different kinds of social environment in which the children develop. Where these are favourable the effects of the initial handicap may be minimized and in due course be overcome altogether. Where they are unfavourable the deficits remain and may even be amplified. The outcome, that is, depends not so much on the adverse circumstances of the child's birth as on the way in which his family then copes with the problem. And this, it has been found, is very much related to the social class to which the family belongs.

Social class is in many respects a nebulous concept. Nevertheless, it does refer to a set of factors (concerned with education, housing, health and so forth) that usually exert a continuing influence on the child throughout his formative years, and it is therefore not surprising that social and economic status turn out to have a much stronger influence on the course of development than some specific event at birth.

Thus even organic damage, just as the other aspects of a child's early experience, cannot in and of itself account for the particular course which that child's development takes. The irreversible effects of early experience have no doubt been greatly overrated. To believe in such effects is indeed dangerous for two reasons: first, because of the suggestion that during the first few years children are so vulnerable that they are beyond help if they do encounter some unfortunate experience; second, because it leads one to conclude that the latter years of childhood are not as important as the earlier years. All the evidence indicates that neither proposition is true: the effects of early experiences are reversible if need be, and older children may be just as affected by unfortunate circumstances (though possibly different ones) as younger children.

Conclusions

A child's development always occurs in a social context. Right from the beginning he is a member of a particular society, and the hopes and beliefs and expectations of those around him will have a crucial bearing on his psychological growth.

There is still a tremendous amount to be learnt about the nature of the child's development and the way that it is affected by particular features of the environment. But in the meantime we can at least make one negative statement with some very positive implications: development can never be explained in terms of single causes. Thus we have seen that isolated events, however traumatic at the time, do not preclude later influences; that the one relationship with the mother does not account for everything. For that matter, development is not simply a matter of the environment acting on the child, for the child too can act on his environment. Not surprisingly, when confronted with a specific problem such as child abuse, we invariably find that a combination of circumstances needs to be considered if one is to explain it. Simple-minded explanations of the kind, 'juvenile delinquency is due to poverty (or heredity or lack of discipline)' never do justice to such a complex process as a child's development. And, similarly, action taken to prevent or treat which focusses on only single factors is most unlikely to succeed.

Some further aspects of social behaviour
FAY FRANSELLA

Social behaviour in isolated young monkeys
Harlow decided he wanted to carry out further research into how organisms learn and, to do this in the most systematic way, he proposed setting up a monkey breeding colony. But no sooner had he and his wife started on this project than the whole research effort was put in jeopardy: the monkeys kept falling ill. To try and prevent this, the monkeys were taken away from their mothers at birth and reared in individual cages within sight and sound of each other but out of touching range.

Monkeys, as well as humans, seem to require a certain amount of comfort for healthy development, and this was provided. The small monkeys were in cages with artificial or surrogate mothers. These were in the form of wire frames, each fitted with a nipple to provide milk. Each had a doll-like head and was covered with soft terry towelling.

The aim of this isolation appeared to be successful in that the infants grew and developed normally, physically, and appeared to behave in ways similar to monkeys reared with their own mothers. However, when the isolated monkeys were put into a cage with the others of their own kind for the first time, they showed abnormal amounts of aggression. They also showed other abnormal ways of behaving. Some became paralysed with fear when approached by another monkey; some indulged in strange stereotyped behaviour, making odd repetitive gestures which seemed to have no function; some stayed and stared at nothing for hours on end or would freeze into bizarre positions.

These monkeys had been socially isolated from birth. Not only had they been deprived of their mothers, but also of the company of other young monkeys. So Harlow and his colleagues set about conducting a series of experiments to try and understand what was happening. For one group of monkeys he replicated the original conditions; the infants were separated from their mothers at birth and raised in a wire cage within sight and sound of other monkeys, but unable to touch or be touched by them. Some were isolated for three months, some for six months and some for two years. A second group was raised with a mother. Of these, some had their real mothers but never had contact with other infants. A third group of monkeys was raised alone with a surrogate mother. This 'mother' was either plain wire with a cylindrical head or was covered with soft terry towelling. The remaining monkeys were raised with no mother but with four infants to a cage. The results can be seen in figure 1.

The experiments showed that having no physical contact with others of their kind, even though others could be seen and heard, is disastrous for the normal development of infant monkeys. After two years of such treatment, social behaviour is grossly abnormal, after six months there is little disturbance, and after less than three months of isolation any deficiencies in social behaviour can be reversed; so the critical period appears to be somewhere between three and six months of isolation. Of those in the group raised with their own mothers, only those raised with no peers were socially abnormal; particularly was this so in relation to sexual behaviour. It would thus seem that the crucial variable for normal social development in the rhesus monkeys is the presence of other infants rather than the mother.

Yet this proves to be too sweeping a generalization. The mother has been shown to be important if she has been with the infant from birth. Kaufman and Rosenblum (1967) found that infants separated from their mothers at the age of five or six months first showed agitation and then depression, from which they recovered after five or six days. So it would seem that after a period of ATTACHMENT, absence of the mother causes psychological upset and a reduction in normal behaviour. When there has been no mother from birth,

Figure 1

Effects of infant-rearing conditions on later behaviour in rhesus monkeys

EXPERIMENTAL CONDITIONS		BEHAVIOUR			
		NONE	LOW	ALMOST NORMAL	NORMAL
Raised in total isolation	2 years	play defence sex			
	6 months	defence sex	play		
	3 months			defence sex	
Raised with mother	normal mother, no peers	sex	play		defence
	normal mother, peers				play defence sex
Raised with peers	four together				play defence sex
	surrogate raised peers				play defence sex

neither depression nor abnormal social behaviour occurs as long as other young monkeys are present.

Harlow has demonstrated the vital importance of contact comfort for the infant monkey: it likes clinging to something. But a normal mother does more than provide something warm and cuddly for the infant to snuggle up to: she moves about. Mason (1968) has shown the importance of movement by using a 'robot' mother. This is a large mop-like structure attached on the end of a pendulum sitting in a shallow dish, large enough for the young monkey to sit alongside it. From this position the infant monkey can 'make' it swing or move with its own movements. The monkeys raised with robots were much more nearly normal compared with those reared with stationary surrogate mothers.

Although it would seem that early social deprivation produces abnormalities in behaviour that are irreversible after three months or so, this has not always been shown to be the case. For instance, Suomi, Harlow and McKinney (1972) used 'psychiatrist' monkeys to 'treat' the abnormal infants. These psychiatrists were monkeys that showed normal social behaviour although reared with surrogate mothers. They had, in fact, been given just two hours of peer inter- action daily. However, these psychiatrists were three months younger than the total isolates they were to treat. At this age, a psychiatrist's main reaction was to cling. When con- fronted with this other infant, the isolated infant's first response was to huddle into a corner. But the 'psychiatrist' followed and just clung to it. By the end of a year, the isolated monkeys were indistinguishable from the therapists and by the age of two, showed virtually complete recovery.

One firm conclusion that can be drawn from Harlow's work is that the opportunity for social interaction is crucial to normal development in monkeys. Of particular interest is the demonstration that the effects of even severe isolation may be reversible.

There are many parallels that can be drawn between the behaviour of these deprived young monkeys and humans, child or adult; for instance, the sequence of agitation, depres- sion and detachment seen in small children on admission to hospital, or the rhythmic rocking carried out by many se- verely subnormal humans. But care must be taken not to infer the same causative factors as a result of the gen- eralization.

Social class and language development

In 1959, Bernstein put forward the idea that there was a relationship between social class, language and success and failure in the school system. He suggested that working- class children are brought up in a world which uses a 're- stricted' or public code, whereas middle-class children enjoy an environment in which an 'elaborated' or formal code is used. He has developed his ideas over the years and in 1971 wrote 'Class, Codes and Control'.

Bernstein defines the two ways of speaking thus:

> A public language is a form of language use which can be marked off from other forms by the rigidity of its syn- tax and the restricted use of formal possibilities for verbal organization.
>
> A formal language is one in which the formal pos- sibilities and syntax are much less predictable for any one individual and the formal possibilities for sentence organization are used to clarify meaning and make it explicit.

He then goes on to clarify this distinction by giving the example of a working-class and middle-class mother on a bus each talking to their respective child.

```
working-class mother: Hold on tight.
              child: Why?
             mother: Hold on tight.
              child: Why?
             mother: You'll fall.
              child: Why?
             mother: I told you to hold on tight,
                     didn't I?
```

In this exchange Bernstein points out that the 'natural curiosity of the child has been blunted'. This is in contrast to the exchange between a mother and her middle-class child in which there is an emphasis on reason and cause and effect. It is a teaching rather than a power-maintaining situation.

```
mother: Hold on tightly, darling.
 child: Why?
mother: If you don't you will be thrown forward and
        you'll fall.
 child: Why?
mother: Because if the bus suddenly stops you'll jerk
        forward on to the seat in front.
 child: Why?
mother: Now darling, hold on tightly and don't make
        such a fuss.
```

Bernstein outlines many ways in which these two codes differ. The working-class person's sentences are much more predictable after the first few words; they have a less extensive vocabulary; they use shorter, grammatically more simple, sentences and fewer subordinate clauses; and they use phrases involving 'Sympathetic Circularity', such as 'wouldn't I?' and 'know what I mean?', whereas the middle class are more prone to use 'I ...'.

Because of these differences, Bernstein suggests that working-class children experience much more difficulty at school since teachers and books use the middle-class elaborated code which a working-class child does not always understand. In support of this, Whendall (1975) has shown that working-class children have much more difficulty in understanding certain sentence structures than do middle-class children when they start at infant school. However, nursery school education redresses this imbalance and brings the working-class child up to the level of the middle-class child.

These two codes come about through the different types of socialization children experience in the home and with their peers. Children come to perceive themselves and the world around them in different ways. Implicit in Bernstein's theory is the idea that working-class children have a basic cognitive deficit which is far more extensive and important than just the use of different language form. The importance attached to the idea that working-class children are deficient in language use can be seen in the huge sums of government money that the United States poured into schemes to offset this deficit. It is from Bernstein's ideas that the Head Start and Compensatory Education Programmes stemmed.

There have been many supporters of Bernstein's claim: for example, Gahagan and Gahagan (1976) and Hess and Shipman (1972). These latter authors studied 160 negro mothers and their four-year-old children. They analysed the interactions between mother and child when involved on a task. They saw three levels of interaction determined by mother's approach.

MOTHER 1: 'All right, Susan, this board is the place where we put the little toys; first of all you're supposed to learn how to place them according to colour. Can you do that? The things that are all the same colour you put in one section; in the second section you put another group of colours, and in the third section you put the last group of colours. Can you do that? Or would you like to see me do it first?'

MOTHER 2: 'Now I'll take them all off the board; now you put them all back on the board. What are these?' Child: 'A truck.' Mother: 'Alright, just put them right here; put the other ones right here; all right put the other one there.'

MOTHER 3: 'I've got some chairs and cars, do you want to play the game?' 'This is not a wagon. What's this?'

Over 60 per cent of the middle-class children put the objects on the board correctly whereas only 29 per cent of the working-class children did so. Hess and Shipman concluded that what is beginning to emerge is the idea of deprivation of meaning. The working-class child's environment is controlled largely by status rules rather than by attention to the individual characteristics of the specific situation. It is also one in which the child's behaviour is not mediated by verbal cues or by teaching aimed at relating events to one another, and the present to the future.

There are, however, many critics of Bernstein and his ideas (e.g. Labov, 1972; Rosen, 1972). Most protest that working-class speech is not deficient; it is just different.

Rosen criticizes Bernstein's theory on three counts: (i) it is based on an inadequate concept of class and one which lacks theoretical support; (ii) Bernstein presents a stereotyped view of working-class life in general and its language in particular; and (iii) he attributes rare and remarkable intellectual virtues to middle-class speakers, and there is inadequate examination of the way in which their language is affected by their class position.

Labov compared an English youth and an educated black adult's non-standard English in terms of their speech, and concluded that a negro person is less likely to be as verbal with a white middle-class person, but may be highly verbal with a member of his or her own race and class, especially when taboo subjects are being discussed.

Labov was especially critical of Bernstein's view as it applies to the Black culture in the States. When working-class Blacks talk informally with other Blacks, they show a very great range of thought and concept. Labov prefers to think of language differences between the groups as simply different. Labov points out that the teaching programme Operation Head Start was designed to help deprived children speak 'correctly' in the belief that this would automatically lead them to more logical ways of thinking.

Failure of the Head Start programmes is in line with Labov's contention: that is, they failed because their goal was to correct a deficit which simply does not exist. But the notion of cultural deprivation continued to grow during the 1960s. It was the working-class and ethnic groups who were considered to be culturally deprived simply because their cultures were not in accord with the mainstream white, middle-class culture.

However, more recently both Bernstein's views and the idea that the Head Start programmes were total failures have been modified. In 1973, Bernstein made it clear that elaborated codes are not necessarily 'middle class communication procedures', nor do these necessarily put the working-class child at a disadvantage. Whether it is important or not will largely depend on the rigidity of the structure within the school.

Bronfenbrenner has played an important part in trying to salvage something from the various attempts at intervention with the 'disadvantaged child'. He has developed what he has called an 'ecological model' (1977). From an intensive study of all the intervention programmes, he concluded that

> for children from the most deprived groups no strategy
> of intervention is likely to be effective that focusses
> attention solely on the child or on the parent-child
> relationship ... What is called for is intervention at
> the ecological level, measures that will effect radical
> changes in the immediate environment of the family and
> the child.

One of the real problems with most of the attempts to evaluate the American early intervention programmes has been the almost universal emphasis on intellectual growth as the only significant aspect. One of the rare exceptions is Zigler who, in 1973, stressed the importance of motivation and other factors. He pointed out that it is not much use, for example, raising the IQ level of the poor negro children if a large number of them continue to drop out of education prematurely.

It is unlikely that anyone is going to confirm or disconfirm Bernstein's results and ideas to everyone's satisfaction. But he should be considered in the context of focussing people's attention on the importance of language in relation to the ways in which we try to make sense of our worlds, and of having been instrumental in stimulating society to try to do something for some of its disadvantaged members.

References

Bernstein, B. (1959)
A public language: some sociological implications of linguistic form. British Journal of Sociology, 10, 311-326.

Bernstein, B. (1971)
Class, Codes and Control. London: Routledge & Kegan Paul.

Bernstein, B. (1973)
A brief account of the theory of codes. In V. Lee (ed.), Social Relationships and Language. Bletchley: Open University.

Bronfenbrenner, U. (1977)
The Experimental Ecology of Human Development. Cambridge, Mass.: Harvard University Press.

Gahagan, G. and Gahagan, D. (1976)
Talk Reform. London: Routledge & Kegan Paul.

Hess, R. and Shipman, V. (1972)
Early experience and the socialization of the cognitive modes in children. In A. Cashdan and E. Grugeon (eds), Language in Education. London: Routledge & Kegan Paul.

Kaufman, I.C. and Rosenblum, L.A. (1967)
Depression in infant monkeys separated from their mothers. Science, 155, 1030-1031.

Labov, W. (1972)
The logic of nonstandard English. In P.H. Mussen, J.J. Conger and J. Kagan (eds), Basic and Contemporary Issues in Developmental Psychology. New York: Harper & Row.

Mason, W.A. (1968)
Early social deprivation in nonhuman primates: implications for human behavior. In D.C. Glass (ed.), Biology and Behavior: Environmental influences. New York: Rockefeller University Press.

Rosen, H. (1972)
Language and Class: A critical look at the theories of Basil Bernstein. Bristol: The Falling Press.

Suomi, S.J., Harlow, H.F. and McKinney, W.T. (1972)
Monkey psychiatrists. American Journal of Psychiatry, 128, 927-932.

Whendall, K. (1975)
Social Behaviour. London: Methuen.

Zigler, E. (1973)
Project Head Start: success or failure? Children Today, 2, 2-7.

Questions

1. What are the principal controversial issues that have been raised by the study of maternal deprivation?
2. In what way can a child's social experience affect intellectual development?

3. What advice would you give to the mother of a three year old who is considering taking up employment?
4. What is known about the reasons for baby battering? What effects on the child would you expect such treatment to have?
5. What is the role of the father in the family?
6. The parent-child relationship is said to be 'reciprocal'. Explain what is meant and provide examples.
7. What principles ought to guide a child's adoption?
8. Should education begin during the pre-school years? Explain what you mean by 'education' and discuss the settings in which it could take place.
9. How do relationships with other children affect development during the pre-school years?
10. What psychological principles should be taken into account in looking after children in residential care?
11. 'Why use animals in research when we are concerned with the study of humans?' Discuss this question, giving both the pros and cons of the argument.
12. Discuss the contribution that Harry Harlow has made to our understanding of human emotional attachment.
13. Work such as Bernstein's has been influential in psychology, sociology and education, and yet it has now been shown to be either erroneous or a too simplistic view of language. Consider the implications of this.
14. Would you say, from your personal observations, that the concepts of 'elaborated' and 'restricted' codes have face validity? Give examples from your own experience to support your views.

Annotated reading

Bernstein, B. and Henderson, D. (1969) Social class differences in the relevance of language to socialization. In M. Argyle (ed.), Social Encounters. Harmondsworth: Penguin.
   It is always useful to read people in the original as well as others' accounts of what they say.

Booth, T. (1975) Growing up in Society. London: Methuen (Essential Psychology Series).
   A general account of the influences that determine the way in which people grow up together. It takes into account not only the contribution of psychology but of such other social sciences as sociology, anthropology and social history. Its main value lies in the way child development is seen as occurring within the social context of each particular culture.

Bowlby, J. (1965) Child Care and the Growth of Love. Harmondsworth: Penguin.
   A more widely available version of Bowlby's classic report, first published in 1951, concerning the link between maternal deprivation and mental pathology. It should be read in conjunction with Rutter's book (see below).

Clarke, A.M. and Clarke, A.D.B. (1976) Early Experience:
Myth and evidence. London: Open Books.
    A collection of contributions by different authors, all
    concerned with the question of whether early experience
    exerts a disproportionate influence on later develop-
    ment. A wide range of research studies are reviewed,
    and the consensus is against seeing the early years
    as in some sense more important than later stages of
    development.

Dunn, J. (1977) Distress and Comfort. London: Fontana/Open
Books.
    Discusses some of the issues that concern parents during
    the early stages of the child's life, with particular
    reference to the causes and alleviation of distress, but
    places these issues in the wider context of the parent-
    child relationship and its cultural significance.

Harlow, H.F. and Harlow, M.K. (1968) Effects of various
mother-infant relationships on rhesus monkey behaviours. In
B. Foss (ed.), Determinants of Infant Behaviour. London:
Methuen.
    An account that looks specifically at the mother-infant
    relationship.

Harlow, H.F. and Suomi, S.J. (1970) The nature of love -
simplified. American Psychologist, 25, 161-166.
    Again, an original source written in a very clear way.

Kempe, R.S. and Kempe, H. (1978) Child Abuse. London:
Fontana/Open Books.
    An account by the foremost experts on child abuse of the
    state of knowledge regarding all aspects of this vexed
    area: causation, treatment and prevention.

Lewin, R. (1975) Child Alive. London: Temple-Smith.
    Various researchers summarize in brief and popularized
    form what we have learnt about child development in
    recent years. Most contributions deal with young child-
    ren, and the book as a whole emphasizes how psycho-
    logically sophisticated even babies already are.

Rutter, M. (1981) Maternal Deprivation Reassessed (2nd
edn). Harmondsworth: Penguin.
    A systematic review of the evidence on this contro-
    versial topic that has accumulated since Bowlby high-
    lighted its importance. Discusses the various studies
    that have been carried out on the effects, both short-
    and long-term, of early deprivation of maternal care.

Schaffer, H.R. (1971) The Growth of Sociability. Harmondsworth: Penguin.
    A description of work on the earliest stages of social
    development. It shows how sociability in the early years

has been studied, and reviews what we have learnt about
the way in which a child's first social relationships
are formed.

Schaffer, H.R. (1977) Mothering. London: Fontana/Open
Books.
An account of what is involved in being a parent. Brings
together the evidence from recent studies of the mother-
child relationship, and examines different conceptions
of the parent's task. Gives special emphasis to the
theme of mutuality in the relationship.

Tizard, B. (1977) Adoption: A second chance. London: Open
Books.
An account of an important research study on children
in residential care who were subsequently adopted.
Raises some crucial issues regarding the effects of
early experience and the public care of young children.

5

Social behaviour
Michael Argyle

Opening remarks
FAY FRANSELLA

Bannister, in chapter 1, contrasted communication with the
self and communication with others. Whereas he dealt with
the former, Argyle now deals with the latter.

As an occupational therapist you work primarily in a
social context, whether it be in a department, on the wards
or with families. Much of your success in interaction with
others will depend on your ability to interpret correctly
the other's communications. It is a salutary lesson when we
first come to realize that the word 'depressed', for instance, may mean something quite different to the patient
from what it means to you. For you it may mean feeling low
in spirits, lacking in energy, being inefficient and introverted and generally undesirable; whereas for your depressed
patient it may mean being low in spirits, lacking in energy,
being sensitive to others and undemanding and generally
desirable. If that sort of misunderstanding can happen with
words, how much more likely it is to occur when we try to
interpret another's non-verbal signals?

Argyle talks in particular about non-verbal communication, and provides many descriptions and examples which
you will find of great relevance when you try to gain an
understanding of your patient's thoughts and feelings. He
points out how easy it is to make errors when forming impressions of others, which anyone naturally wants to keep
to a minimum. Although there may well be, as Argyle says,
'favourite constructs' which we all use in our culture to
construe others, there is obviously a great deal of individual variation. Likewise, some of us use more construct
dimensions than do others. This notion of cognitive complexity was developed from Kelly's personal construct psychology, and has aroused a considerable amount of academic
interest. From the practical point of view it appears that
those who are more 'complex' in their construing of others
are better able to predict, or successfully interpret, another's behaviour. It is probable that the more differentiation there is between the constructs you use in interpersonal situations the better able you are to grasp others'
viewpoints. The constructs we use are also obviously important when we decide who will be our friends. Duck
(1977) finds that similarity of construing is important in
the formation of friendships, probably because it eases

communication in the first instance. It is therefore likely that you will find those patients with whom you have constructs in common easier to get on with (more likeable?) than those who are dissimilar in their outlook from you. This means that you will have to make greater efforts to understand the construing of these latter patients if you are not going to be seen to favour some over others.

Of great importance in your work as a psychological therapist is the part in this chapter to do with social skills training. It may be useful to try and read this in conjunction with chapter 10 on operant conditioning and chapter 18 on creating change.

Introduction: social behaviour as a skill
MICHAEL ARGYLE

We start by presenting the social skill model of social behaviour, and an account of sequences of social interaction. This model is relevant to our later discussion of social skills and how these can be trained. The chapter then goes on to discuss the elements of social behaviour, both verbal and non-verbal, and emphasize the importance and different functions of non-verbal signals. The receivers of these signals have to decode them, and do so in terms of emotions and impressions of personality; we discuss some of the processes and some of the main errors of person perception. Senders can manipulate the impressions they create by means of 'self-presentation'. The processes of social behaviour, and the skills involved, are quite different in different social situations, and we discuss recent attempts to analyse these situations in terms of their main features, such as rules and goals.

We move on to a number of specific social skills. Research on the processes leading to friendship and love makes it possible to train and advise people who have difficulty with these relationships. Research on persuasion shows how people can be trained to be more assertive. And research on small social groups and leadership of these groups makes it possible to give an account of the most successful skills for handling social groups.

Social competence is defined in terms of the successful attainment of goals, and it can be assessed by a variety of techniques such as self-rating and observation of role-played performance. The most successful method of improving social skills is role-playing, combined with modelling, coaching, videotape-recorder (VTR) playback, and 'homework'. Results of follow-up studies with a variety of populations show that this form of social skills training (SST) is very successful.

Harré and Secord (1972) have argued persuasively that much human social behaviour is the result of conscious planning, often in words, with full regard for the complex meanings of behaviour and the rules of the situations. This is an important correction to earlier social psychological views, which often failed to recognize the complexity of individual planning and the different meanings which may be given to stimuli, for example in laboratory experiments. However, it must be recognized that much social behaviour is not planned in this way: the smaller elements of behaviour and longer automatic sequences are outside conscious awareness, though it is possible to attend, for example, to patterns of gaze, shifts of orientation, or the latent meanings of utterances. The social skills model, in emphasizing the hierarchical structure of social performance, can incorporate both kinds of behaviour.

The social skills model also emphasizes feedback processes. A person driving a car sees at once when it is going in the wrong direction, and takes corrective action with the steering wheel. Social interactors do likewise; if another person is talking too much they interrupt, ask closed questions or no questions, and look less interested in what is being said. Feedback requires perception, looking at and listening to the other person. Skilled performance requires the ability to take the appropriate corrective action referred to as 'translation' in the model: not everyone knows that open-ended questions make people talk more and closed questions make them talk less. And it depends on a number of two-step sequences of social behaviour whereby certain social acts have reliable effects on another. Let us look at social behaviour as a skilled performance similar to motor skills like driving a car (see figure 1).

Figure 1

The motor skill model (from Argyle, 1969)

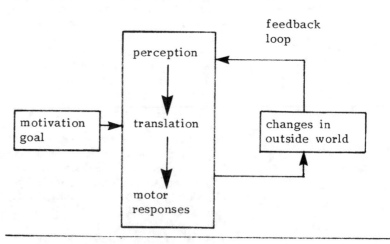

In each case the performer is pursuing certain goals, makes continuous response to feedback, and emits hierarchically-organized motor responses. This model has been heuristically very useful in drawing attention to the importance of feedback, and hence to gaze; it also suggests a number of different ways in which social performances can fail, and suggests the training procedures that may be effective, through analogy with motor skills training (Argyle and Kendon, 1967; Argyle, 1969).

The model emphasizes the motivation, goals and plans of interactors. It is postulated that every interactor is trying to achieve some goal, whether or not there is awareness of that. These goals may be, for example, to be liked by another person, to obtain or convey information, to modify the other's emotional state, and so on. Such goals may be linked to more basic motivational systems. Goals have sub-goals; for example, doctors must diagnose patients before they can be treated. Patterns of response are directed towards goals and sub-goals, and have a hierarchical structure: large units of behaviour are composed of smaller ones, and at the lowest levels these are habitual and automatic.

The role of reinforcement
This is one of the key processes in social skills sequences. When interactor A does what B wants done, B is pleased and sends immediate and spontaneous reinforcements: smile, gaze, approving noises, and so on, and modifies A's behaviour, probably by operant conditioning; for example, modifying the content of subsequent utterances. At the same time A is modifying B's behaviour in exactly the same way. These effects appear to be mainly outside the focus of conscious attention, and take place very rapidly. It follows that anyone who gives strong rewards and punishments in the course of interaction will be able to modify the behaviour of others in the desired direction. In addition, the stronger the rewards that A issues, the more strongly other people will be attracted to A.

The role of gaze in social skills
The social skills model suggests that the monitoring of another's reactions is an essential part of social performance. The other's verbal signals are mainly heard, but non-verbal signals are mainly seen; the exceptions being the non-verbal aspects of speech and touch. It was this implication of the social skills model which directed us towards the study of gaze in social interaction. In dyadic interaction each person looks about 50 per cent of the time, mutual gaze occupies 25 per cent of the time, looking while listening is about twice the level of looking while talking, glances are about three seconds, and mutual glances about one second, with wide variations due to distance, sex combination, and personality (Argyle and Cook, 1976). However, there are several important differences between social behaviour and motor skills.

*   Rules: the moves which interactors may make are governed by rules; they must respond properly to what has gone before. Similarly, rules govern the other's responses and can be used to influence behaviour; for example, questions lead to answers.

* Taking the role of the other: it is important to perceive accurately the reactions of others. It is also
necessary to perceive the perceptions of others; that
is, to take account of their points of view. This
appears to be a cognitive ability which develops with
age (Flavell, 1968), but which may fail to develop
properly. Those who are able to do this have been found
to be more effective at a number of social tasks, and
more altruistic. Meldman (1967) found that psychiatric
patients are more egocentric (that is, talked about
themselves more than controls), and it has been our
experience that socially unskilled patients have great
difficulty in taking the role of the other.
* The independent initiative of the other sequences of
interaction: social situations inevitably contain at
least one other person, who will be pursuing personal
goals and using social skills. How can we analyse the
resulting sequences of behaviour? For a sequence to
constitute an acceptable piece of social behaviour, the
moves must fit together in order. Social psychologists
have by no means discovered all the principles or
'grammar' underlying these sequences, but some of the
principles are known, and can explain common forms of
interaction failure.

Verbal and non-verbal communication

Verbal communication
There are several different kinds of verbal utterance.

* Egocentric speech: this is directed to the self, is
found in infants and has the effect of directing
behaviour.
* Orders, instructions: these are used to influence the
behaviour of others; they can be gently persuasive or
authoritarian.
* Questions: these are intended to elicit verbal information; they can be open-ended or closed, personal or
impersonal.
* Information: may be given in response to a question,
or as part of a lecture or during problem-solving
discussion.

(The last three points are the basic classes of utterance.)

* Informal speech: consists of casual chat, jokes, gossip,
and contains little information, but helps to establish
and sustain social relationships.
* Expression of emotions and interpersonal attitudes: this
is a special kind of information; however, this
information is usually conveyed, and is conveyed more
effectively, non-verbally.
* Performative utterances: these include 'illocutions'
where saying the utterance performs something (voting,
judging, naming, etc.), and 'perlocutions', where a goal

is intended but may not be achieved (persuading, intimidating, etc.).

* Social routines: these include standard sequences like thanking, apologizing, greeting, and so on.
* Latent messages: in these, the more important meaning is made subordinate ('As I was saying to the Prime Minister ...').

There are many category schemes for reducing utterances to a limited number of classes of social acts. One of the best known is that of Bales (1950), who introduced the 12 classes shown in figure 2.

Non-verbal signals accompanying speech
Non-verbal signals play an important part in speech and conversation. They have three main roles:

* completing and elaborating on verbal utterances: utterances are accompanied by vocal emphasis, gestures and facial expressions, which add to the meaning and indicate whether it is a question, intended to be serious or funny, and so on;
* managing synchronizing: this is achieved by head-nods, gaze-shifts, and other signals. For example, to keep the floor a speaker does not look up at the end of an utterance, keeps a hand in mid-gesture, and increases the volume of his speech if the other interrupts;
* sending feedback signals: listeners keep up a continuous, and mainly unwitting, commentary on the speaker's utterances, showing by mouth and eyebrow positions whether they agree, understand, are surprised, and so on (Argyle, 1975).

Other functions of non-verbal communication (NVC)
NVC consists of facial expression, tone of voice, gaze, gestures, postures, physical proximity and appearance. We have already described how NVC is linked with speech; it also functions in several other ways, especially in the communication of emotions and attitudes to other people.

A sender is in a certain state, or possesses some information; this is encoded into a message which is then decoded by a receiver.

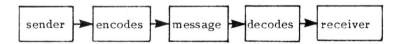

Encoding research is done by putting subjects into some state and studying the non-verbal messages which are emitted. For example Mehrabian (1972), in a role-playing experiment, asked subjects to address a hat-stand, imagining it to be a person. Men who liked the hat-stand looked at it more, did not have hands on hips and stood closer.

Figure 2

The Bales categories (from Bales, 1950)

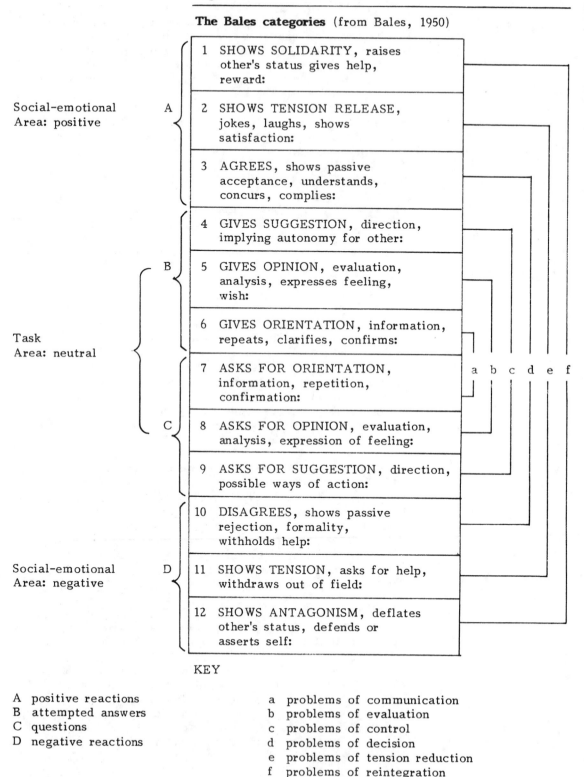

KEY

A positive reactions
B attempted answers
C questions
D negative reactions

a problems of communication
b problems of evaluation
c problems of control
d problems of decision
e problems of tension reduction
f problems of reintegration

Non-verbal signals are often 'unconscious': that is,
they are outside the focus of attention. A few signals are
unconsciously sent and received, like dilated pupils,
signifying sexual attraction, but there are a number of
other possibilities as shown in table 1.

Table 1

Awareness of non-verbal signals

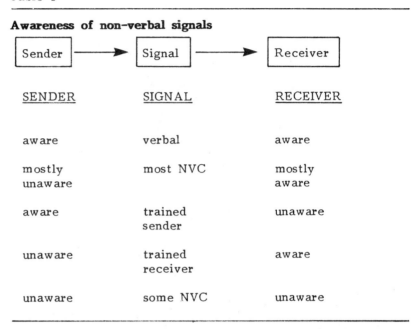

SENDER	SIGNAL	RECEIVER
aware	verbal	aware
mostly unaware	most NVC	mostly aware
aware	trained sender	unaware
unaware	trained receiver	aware
unaware	some NVC	unaware

Strictly speaking pupil dilation is not communication at
all, but only a physiological response. 'Communication' is
usually taken to imply some intention to affect another; one
criterion of successful communication is that it makes a
difference whether the other person is present and in a
position to receive the signal; another is that the signal
is repeated, varied or amplified if it has no immediate
effect. These criteria are independent of conscious intention to communicate, which is often absent.

* Interpersonal attitudes: interactors indicate how much
  they like or dislike one another, and whether they think
  they are more or less important, mainly non-verbally. We
  have compared verbal and non-verbal signals and found
  that non-verbal cues like facial expression and tone of
  voice have far more impact than verbal ones (Argyle,
  Salter, Nicholson, Williams and Burgess, 1970).
* Emotional states: anger, depression, anxiety, joy,
  surprise, fear and disgust/contempt, are also communicated more clearly by non-verbal signals, such as facial
  expression, tone of voice, posture, gestures and gaze.
  Interactors may try to conceal their true emotions, but
  these are often revealed by 'leakage' via cues which are
  difficult to control.

Person perception

In order to respond effectively to the behaviour of others it is necessary to perceive them correctly. The social skills model emphasizes the importance of perception and feedback; to drive a car one must watch the traffic outside and the instruments inside. Such perception involves selecting certain cues, and being able to interpret them correctly. There is evidence of poor person perception in mental patients and other socially unskilled individuals, while professional social skills performers need to be sensitive to special aspects of other people and their behaviour. For selection interviewers and clinical psychologists the appraisal of others is a central part of the job.

We form impressions of other people all the time, mainly in order to predict their future behaviour, and so that we can deal with them effectively. We categorize others in terms of our favourite cognitive constructs, of which the most widely used are:

* extraversion, sociability;
* agreeableness, likeability;
* emotional stability;
* intelligence;
* assertiveness.

There are, however, wide individual differences in the constructs used, and 'complex' people use a larger number of such dimensions. We have found that the constructs used vary greatly with the situation: for example, work-related constructs are not used in purely social situations. We also found that the constructs used vary with the target group, such as children versus psychologists (Argyle, Furnham and Graham, 1981).

A number of widespread errors are made in forming impressions of others which should be particularly avoided by those whose job it is to assess people:

* assuming that a person's behaviour is mainly a product of personality, whereas it may be more a function of situation: at a noisy party, in church, and so on;
* assuming that behaviour is due to the person rather than the person's role; for example, as a hospital nurse, as a patient or as a visitor;
* attaching too much importance to physical cues, like beards, clothes, and physical attractiveness;
* being affected by stereotypes about the characteristics of members of certain races, social classes, etc.

During social interaction it is also necessary to perceive the emotional states of others: for example, to tell if they are depressed or angry. There are wide individual differences in the ability to judge emotions correctly (Davitz, 1964). As we have seen, emotions are mainly conveyed by non-verbal signals, especially by facial expression and tone of voice. The interpretation of emotions is also based on perception of the situation the other person is in. Lalljee at Oxford found that smiles are not necessarily decoded as happy, whereas unhappy faces are usually regarded as authentic.

Similar considerations apply to the perception of interpersonal attitudes, for instance who likes whom, which is also mainly based on non-verbal signals, such as proximity, gaze and facial expression. Again use is made of context to decode these signals: a glance at a stranger may be interpreted as a threat, an appeal for help or a friendly invitation. There are some interesting errors due to pressures towards cognitive consistency: if A likes B, then A thinks that B likes A more than B on average actually does: if A likes both B and C, A assumes that they both like each other more than, on average, they do.

It is necessary to perceive the on-going flow of interaction in order to know what is happening and to participate in it effectively. People seem to agree on the main episodes and sub-episodes of an encounter, but they may produce rather different accounts of why those present behaved as they did. One source of variation, and indeed error, is that people attribute the causes of others' behaviour to their personality ('He fell over because he is clumsy'), but their own behaviour to the situation ('I fell over because it was slippery'), whereas both factors operate in each case (Jones and Nisbett, 1972). Interpretations also depend on the ideas and knowledge an individual possesses: just as an expert on cars could understand better why a car was behaving in a peculiar way, so also can an expert on social behaviour understand why patterns of social behaviour occur.

Situations, their rules and other features

We know that people behave very differently in different situations; in order to predict behaviour, or to advise people on social skills in specific situations, it is necessary to analyse the situations in question. This can be done in terms of a number of fundamental features.

Goals

In all situations there are certain goals which are commonly obtainable. It is often fairly obvious what these are, but socially inadequate people may simply not know what parties are for, for example, or may think that the purpose of a selection interview is vocational guidance.

We have studied the main goals in a number of common situations, by asking samples of people to rate the importance of various goals, and then carrying out factor analysis. The main goals are usually:

* social acceptance, etc.;
* food, drink and other bodily needs;
* task goals specific to the situation.

We have also studied the relations between goals, within and between persons, in terms of conflict and instrumentality.

This makes it possible to study the 'goal structure' of situations.

Rules
All situations have rules about what may or may not be done in them. Socially inexperienced people are often ignorant or mistaken about the rules. It would obviously be impossible to play a game without knowing the rules and the same applies to social situations.

We have studied the rules of a number of everyday situations. There appear to be several universal rules; to be polite, friendly, and not embarrass people. There are also rules which are specific to situations, or groups of situations, and these can be interpreted as functional, since they enable situational goals to be met. For example, when seeing the doctor one should be clean and tell the truth; when going to a party one should dress smartly and keep to cheerful topics of conversation.

Special skills
Many social situations require special social skills, as in the case of various kinds of public speaking and interviewing, but also such everyday situations as dates and parties. A person with little experience of a particular situation may find that he lacks the special skills needed for it (cf. Argyle et al, 1981).

Repertoire of elements
Every situation defines certain moves as relevant. For example, at a seminar it is relevant to show slides, make long speeches, draw on the blackboard, etc. If moves appropriate to a cricket match or a Scottish ball were made, they would be ignored or regarded as totally bizarre. We have found 65-90 main elements used in several situations, like going to the doctor. We have also found that the semiotic structure varies between situations: we found that questions about work and about private life were sharply contrasted in an office situation, but not on a date.

Roles
Every situation has a limited number of roles: for example, a classroom has the roles of teacher, pupil, janitor, and school inspector. These roles carry different degrees of power, and the occupant has goals peculiar to that role.

Cognitive structure
We found that the members of a research group classified each other in terms of the concepts extraverted and enjoyable companion for social occasions, but in terms of dominant, creative and supportive for seminars. There are also concepts related to the task, such as 'amendment', 'straw vote' and 'nem con', for committee meetings.

Environmental setting and pieces
Most situations involve special environmental settings and

props. Cricket needs bat, ball, stumps, and so on; a seminar requires a blackboard, slide projector and lecture notes.

How do persons fit into situations, conceived in this way? To begin with, there are certain pervasive aspects of persons, corresponding to the 20 per cent or so of person variance found in P x S (personality and situation) studies. This consists of scores on general dimensions like intelligence, extraversion, neuroticism and so on. In addition, persons have dispositions to behave in certain ways in classes of situations; this corresponds to the 50 per cent or so of the P x S variance in relation to dimensions of situations like formal-informal, and friendly-hostile. Third, there are more specific reactions to particular situations; for example, behaviour in social psychology seminars depends partly on knowledge of social psychology, and attitudes to different schools of thought in it. Taken together these three factors may predict performance in, and also avoidance of, certain situations - because of lack of skill, anxiety, etc. - and this will be the main expectation in such cases.

Friendship

This is one of the most important social relationships: failure in it is a source of great distress, and so it is one of the main areas of social skills training. The conditions under which people come to like one another have been the object of extensive research, and are now well understood.

There are several stages of friendship: (i) coming into contact with the other, through proximity at work or elsewhere; (ii) increasing attachment as a result of reinforcement and discovery of similarity; (iii) increasing self-disclosure and commitment; and, sometimes, (iv) dissolution of the relationship. Friendship is the dominant relationship for adolescents and the unmarried; friends engage in characteristic activities, such as talking, eating, drinking, joint leisure, but not, usually, working.

Frequency of interaction

The more two people meet, the more polarized their attitudes to one another become, but usually they like one another more. Frequent interaction can come about from living in adjacent rooms or houses, working in the same office, belonging to the same club, and so on. So interaction leads to liking, and liking leads to more interaction. Only certain kinds of interaction lead to liking. In particular, people should be of similar status. Belonging to a co-operative group, especially under crisis conditions, is particularly effective, as Sherif's robbers' cave experiment (Sherif, Harvey, White, Hood and Sherif, 1961) and research on inter-racial attitudes have shown.

Reinforcement

The next general principle governing liking is the extent to which one person satisfies the needs of another. This was shown in a study by Jennings of 400 girls in a reformatory (1950). She found that the popular girls helped and protected others, encouraged, cheered them up, made them feel accepted and wanted, controlled their own moods so as not to inflict anxiety or depression on others, were able to establish rapport quickly, won the confidence of a wide variety of other personalities, and were concerned with the feelings and needs of others. The unpopular girls on the other hand were dominating, aggressive, boastful, demanded attention, and tried to get others to do things for them. This pattern has been generally interpreted in terms of the popular girls providing rewards and minimizing costs, while the unpopular girls tried to get rewards for themselves, and incurred costs for others. It is not necessary for the other person to be the actual source of rewards: Lott and Lott (1960) found that children who were given model cars by the experimenter liked the other children in the experiment more, and several studies have shown that people are liked more in a pleasant environmental setting.

Being liked is a powerful reward, so if A likes B, B will usually like A. This is particularly important for those who have a great need to be liked, such as individuals with low self-esteem. It is signalled, as discussed above, primarily by non-verbal signals.

Similarity

People like others who are similar to themselves, in certain respects. They like those with similar attitudes, beliefs and values, who have a similar regional and social class background, who have similar jobs or leisure interests, but they need not have similar personalities. Again there is a cyclical process, since similarity leads to liking and liking leads to similarity, but effects of similarity on liking have been shown experimentally.

Physical attractiveness

Physical attractiveness (p.a.) is an important source of both same-sex and opposite sex liking, especially in the early stages. Walster, Aronson, Abrahams and Rottmann (1966) arranged a 'computer dance' at which couples were paired at random: the best prediction of how much each person liked their partner was the latter's p.a. as rated by the experimenter. Part of the explanation lies in the 'p.a. stereotype'. Dion, Berscheid and Walster (1972) found that attractive people were believed to have desirable characteristics of many other kinds. However, people do not seek out the most attractive friends and mates, but compromise by seeking those similar to themselves in attractiveness.

Self-disclosure

This is a signal for intimacy, like bodily contact, because it indicates trust in the other. Self-disclosure can be measured on a scale (1-5) with items like:

What are your favourite forms of erotic play and sexual lovemaking? (scale value 2.56)

What are the circumstances under which you become depressed and when your feelings are hurt? (3.51)

What are your hobbies, how do you best like to spend your spare time? (4.98) (Jourard, 1971).

As people get to know each other better, self-disclosure slowly increases, and is reciprocated, up to a limit.

Commitment
This is a state of mind, an intention to stay in a relationship, and abandon others. This involves a degree of dependence on the other person and trusting them not to leave the relationship. The less committed has the more power.

Social skills training
The most common complaint of those who seek SST is difficulty in making friends. Some of them say they have never had a friend in their lives. What advice can we offer, on the basis of research on friendship?

* As we showed earlier, social relations are negotiated mainly by non-verbal signals. Clients for SST who cannot make friends are usually found to be very inexpressive, in face and voice.
* Rewardingness is most important. The same clients usually appear to be very unrewarding, and are not really interested in other people.
* Frequent interaction with those of similar interests and attitudes can be found in clubs for professional or leisure activities, in political and religious groups, and so on.
* Physical attractiveness is easier to change than is social behaviour.
* Certain social skills may need to be acquired, such as inviting others to suitable social events, and engaging in self-disclosure at the right speed.

The meaning and assessment of social competence

By social competence we mean the ability, the possession of the necessary skills, to produce the desired effects on other people in social situations. These desired effects may be to persuade the others to buy, to learn, to recover from neurosis, to like or admire the actor, and so on. These results are not necessarily in the public interest: skills may be used for social or antisocial purposes. And there is no evidence that social competence is a general factor: a person may be better at one task than another, for example, parties or committees. SST for students and other more or less normal populations has been directed to the skills of dating, making friends and being assertive. SST for mental patients has been aimed at correcting failures of social competence, and also at relieving subjective distress, such as social anxiety.

To find out who needs training, and in what areas, a detailed descriptive assessment is needed. We want to know, for example, which situations individual trainees find difficult (formal situations, conflicts, meeting strangers, etc.), and which situations they are inadequate in, even though they do not report them as difficult. And we want to find out what individuals are doing wrong: failure to produce the right non-verbal signals, low rewardingness, lack of certain social skills, and so on.

Social competence is easier to define and agree upon in the case of professional social skills: an effective thera-pist cures more patients, an effective teacher teaches better, an effective salesperson sells more. When we look more closely, it is not quite so simple: examination marks may be one index of a teacher's effectiveness, but usually more is meant than just this. Salespersons should not simply sell a lot of goods, they should make the customers feel they would like to go to that shop again. So a combination of different skills is required and an overall assessment of effectiveness may involve the combination of a number of different measures or ratings. The range of competence is quite large: the best salesmen and saleswomen regularly sell four times as much as some others behind the same counter; some supervisors of working groups produce twice as much output as others, or have 20-25 per cent of the labour turnover and absenteeism rates (Argyle, 1972).

For everyday social skills it is more difficult to give the criteria of success; lack of competence is easier to spot: failure to make friends, or opposite sex friends, quarrelling and failing to sustain co-operative relation-ships, finding a number of situations difficult or a source of anxiety, and so on.

Methods of social skills training

Role-playing with coaching
This is now the most widely-used method of SST. There are four stages:

* instruction;
* role-playing with other trainees or other role partners for five to eight minutes;
* feedback and coaching, in the form of oral comments from the trainer;
* repeated role-playing.

A typical laboratory set-up is shown in figure 3. This also shows the use of an ear-microphone for instruction while role-playing is taking place. In the case of patients, mere practice does no good: there must be coaching as well.

For an individual or group of patients or other trainees a series of topics, skills or situations is chosen, and introduced by means of short scenarios. Role partners who can be briefed to present carefully graded degrees of difficulty are used.

It is usual for trainers to be generally encouraging, and also rewarding for specific aspects of behaviour, though there is little experimental evidence for the value of such reinforcement. It is common to combine role-playing with modelling and video-playback, both of which are discussed below. Follow-up studies have found that role-playing combined with coaching is successful with many kinds of mental patients, and that it is one of the most successful forms of SST for these groups.

Role-playing usually starts with 'modelling', in which a film is shown or a demonstration given of how to perform the skill being taught. The feedback session usually includes videotape-playback and most studies have found that this is advantageous (Bailey and Sowder, 1970). While it often makes trainees self-conscious at first, this wears off after the second session. Skills acquired in the laboratory or class must be transferred to the outside world. This is usually achieved by 'homework': trainees are encouraged to try out the new skills several times before the next session. Most

Figure 3

A social skills training laboratory

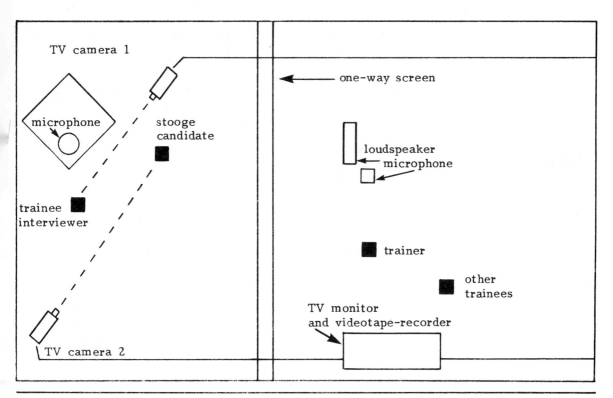

trainers take people in groups which provides a source of role partners, but patients may need individual sessions as well for individual problems.

Other methods of training

TRAINING ON THE JOB: this is a widely used traditional method. Some people improve through experience but others do not, and some learn the wrong things. The situation can be improved if there is a trainer who regularly sees the trainee in action, and is able to hold feedback sessions at which errors are pointed out and better skills suggested. In practice this method does not appear to work very well, for example with trainee teachers (see Argyle, 1969).

GROUP METHODS: these, especially T-groups (T standing for training), are intended to enhance sensitivity and social skills. Follow-up studies have consistently found that 30-40 per cent of trainees are improved by group methods, but up to 10 per cent are worse, sometimes needing psychological assistance (e.g. Lieberman, Yalom and Miles, 1973). It has been argued that group methods are useful for those who are resistant to being trained.

EDUCATIONAL METHODS: these, such as lectures and films, can increase knowledge, but to master social skills it is necessary to try them out, as is the case with motor skills. Educational methods can be a useful supplement to role-playing methods.

Areas of application of SST

NEUROTIC PATIENTS: role-playing and the more specialized methods described above have been found to be slightly more effective than psychotherapy, desensitization, or other alternative treatments, but not much (Trower, Bryant and Argyle, 1978). Only one study so far has found really substantial differences: Maxwell (1976), in a study of adults reporting social difficulties and seeking treatment for them, in New Zealand, insisted on homework between training sessions. However, SST does produce more improvement in social skills and reduction of social anxiety. A few patients can be cured by SST alone, but most have other problems as well, and may require other forms of treatment in addition.

PSYCHOTIC PATIENTS: these have been treated in the USA by assertiveness training and other forms of role-playing. Follow-up studies have shown greater improvement in social behaviour than from alternative treatments. The most striking results have been obtained with intensive clinical studies of one to four patients, using a 'multiple baseline' design: one symptom is worked on at a time over a total of 20-30 sessions. It is not clear from these follow-up studies to what extent the general condition of patients has been improved, or how well they have been able to function outside the hospital (Hersen and Bellack, 1976). It has been argued by one practitioner that SST is more suitable than psychotherapy for working-class patients in view of their poor verbal skills (Goldstein, 1973).

Other therapeutic uses of SST

ALCOHOLICS have been given SST to improve their assertiveness, for example in refusing drinks, and to enable them
to deal better with situations which they find stressful and
make them drink. Similar treatment has been given to drug
addicts. In both cases treatment has been fairly successful,
though the effects have not always been long-lasting; SST is
often included in more comprehensive packages.

DELINQUENTS AND PRISONERS have often been given
SST with some success, especially in the case of aggressive
and sex offenders. SST can also increase their degree of
internal control.

TEACHERS, MANAGERS, DOCTORS, etc.: SST is
increasingly being included in the training of those whose
work involves dealing with people. The most extensive
application so far has been in the training of teachers by
'micro-teaching'. They are instructed in one of the component skills of teaching, such as the use of different
kinds of question, explanation or the use of examples; they
then teach five to six children for 10-15 minutes, followed
by a feedback session and 're-teaching'. Follow-up studies
show that this is far more effective than a similar amount
of teaching practice, and it is much more effective in era-
dicating bad habits (Brown, 1975). In addition to role-
playing, more elaborate forms of simulation are used, for
example to train people for administrative positions.
Training on the job is a valuable addition or alternative,
provided that trainers really do their job.

NORMAL ADULTS: students have received a certain
amount of SST, especially in North American universities,
and follow-up studies have shown that they can be successfully trained in assertiveness (Rich and Schroeder, 1976),
dating behaviour (Curran, 1977), and to reduce anxiety at
performing in public (Paul, 1966). Although many normal
adults apart from students have social behaviour difficulties, very little training is available unless they seek
psychiatric help. It would be very desirable for SST to be
more widely available, for example in community centres.

SCHOOLCHILDREN: a number of attempts have been
made to introduce SST into schools, though there are no
follow-up studies on its effectiveness. However, there have
been a number of successful follow-up studies of training
schemes for children who are withdrawn and unpopular or
aggressive, using the usual role-playing methods (Rinn and
Markle, 1979).

Conclusion

In this chapter we have given an account of those aspects of
social psychology which are most relevant to the work of
teachers, social workers and others, both in understanding
the behaviour of their clients and also in helping them with
their own performance. We have used various models of social
behaviour, such as the social skills model and the model of
social behaviour as a game. Some of the phenomena described
cannot be fully accounted for in terms of these models: for

example, the design of sequences of interaction. A number o
practical implications have been described; in particular,
discussion of the skills which have been demonstrated to
be the most effective in a number of situations, and the
methods of SST which have been found to have most impact.
should be emphasized that much of this research is quite new
and it is expected that a great deal more will be found out
on these topics in the years to come.

References

Argyle, M. (1969)
Social Interaction. London: Methuen.
Argyle, M. (1972)
The Social Psychology of Work. London: Allen Lane and
Penguin Books.
Argyle, M. (1975)
Bodily Communication. London: Methuen.
Argyle, M. and Cook, M. (1976)
Gaze and Mutual Gaze. London: Cambridge University
Press.
Argyle, M., Furnham, A. and Graham, J.A. (1981)
Social situations. London: Cambridge University Press.
Argyle, M. and Kendon, A. (1967)
The experimental analysis of social performance. In L.
Berkowitz (ed.), Advances in Experimental Social
Psychology, Volume 3. New York: Academic Press.
**Argyle, M., Salter V., Nicholson, H., Williams, M. and
Burgess, P.** (1970)
The communication of inferior and superior attitudes by
verbal and non-verbal signals. British Journal of Social
and Clinical Psychology, 9, 221-231.
Bailey, K.G. and Sowder, W.T. (1970)
Audiotape and videotape self-confrontation in
psychotherapy. Psychological Bulletin, 74, 127-137.
Bales, R.F. (1950)
Interaction Process Analysis. Cambridge, Mass.: Addison-
Wesley.
Brown, G.A. (1975)
Microteaching. London: Methuen.
Curran, J.P. (1977)
Skills training as an approach to the treatment of
heterosexual-social anxiety. Psychological Bulletin, 84,
140-157.
Davitz, J.R. (1964)
The Communication of Emotional Meaning. New York:
McGraw-Hill.
Dion, K., Berscheid, E. and Walster, E. (1972)
What is beautiful is good. Journal of Personality and
Social Psychology, 24, 285-290.
Duck, S.W. (1977)
Inquiry, hypothesis and the quest for validation:
personal construct systems in the development of
acquaintance. In S.W. Duck (ed.), Theory and Practice in
Interpersonal Attraction. London: Academic Press.

Flavell, J.H. (1968)
The Development of Role-taking and Communication Skills in Children. New York: Wiley.

Goldstein, A.J. (1973)
Structured Learning Therapy: Toward a psychotherapy for the poor. New York: Academic Press.

Harré, R. and Secord, P. (1972)
The Explanation of Social Behaviour. Oxford: Blackwell.

Hersen, M. and Bellack, A.S. (1976)
Social skills training for chronic psychiatric patients: rationale, research findings, and future directions. Comprehensive Psychiatry, 17, 559-580.

Jennings, H.H. (1950)
Leadership and Isolation. New York: Longmans Green.

Jones, E.E. and Nisbett, R.E. (1972)
The actor and the observer: divergent perceptions of the causes of behavior. In E.E. Jones, D. Kanouse, H. Kelley, R.E. Nisbett, S. Valins and B. Weiner (eds), Attribution: Perceiving the causes of behavior. Morristown, NJ: General Learning Press.

Jourard, S.M. (1971)
Self Disclosure. New York: Wiley Interscience.

Lieberman, M.A., Yalom, I.D. and Miles, M.R. (1973)
Encounter Groups: First facts. New York: Basic Books.

Lott, A.J. and Lott, B.E. (1960)
The formation of positive attitudes towards group members. Journal of Abnormal and Social Psychology, 61, 297-300.

Maxwell, G.M. (1976)
An evolution of social skills training. (Unpublished, University of Otago, Dunedin, New Zealand.)

Mehrabian, A. (1972)
Nonverbal Communication. New York: Aldine-Atherton.

Meldman, M.J. (1967)
Verbal behaviour analysis of self-hyperattentionism. Diseases of the Nervous System, 28, 469-473.

Paul, G.L. (1966)
Insight v. Desensitization in Psychotherapy. Stanford, Ca: Stanford University Press.

Rich, A.R. and Schroeder, H.E. (1976)
Research issues in assertiveness training. Psychological Bulletin, 83, 1081-1096.

Rinn, R.C. and Markle, A. (1979)
Modification of social skill deficits in children. In A.S. Bellack and M. Hersen (eds), Research and Practice in Social Skills Training. New York: Plenum.

Sherif, M., Harvey, O.J., White, B.J., Hood, W.R. and Sherif, C. (1961)
Intergroup Conflict and Cooperation: The Robbers' Cave experiment. Norman, Oklahoma: The University of Oklahoma Book Exchange.

Trower, P., Bryant, B. and Argyle, M. (1978)
Social Skills and Mental Health. London: Methuen.

Walster, E., Aronson, E., Abrahams, D. and Rottmann, L.
(1966)
Importance of physical attractiveness in dating
behavior. Journal of Personality and Social Psychology,
5, 508-516.

Questions

1. Is it useful to look at social behaviour as a kind of
   skill?
2. What do bad conversationalists do wrong?
3. What information is conveyed by non-verbal communication and in what ways do non-verbal signals supplement
   verbal ones?
4. How is the perception of other people different from the
   perception of other physical objects?
5. What information about a social situation would a
   newcomer to it need to know?
6. Do we like other people primarily because they are
   rewarding?
7. Why do some people have difficulty in making friends?
8. What criticisms have been made of experiments in social
   psychology? What other methods are available?
9. Does social behaviour take the same form in other
   cultures?
10. Are there fundamental differences between social
    behaviour in families, work-groups and groups of
    friends?

Annotated reading

Argyle, M. (1978) The Psychology of Interpersonal Behaviour
(3rd edn). Harmondsworth: Penguin.
Covers the field of the chapter, and related topics at
Penguin level.

Argyle, M. and Trower, P. (1979). Person to Person. London:
Harper & Row.
A more popular account of the area covered by the
chapter, with numerous coloured illustrations.

Argyle, M. (1975). Bodily Communication. London: Methuen.
Covers the field of non-verbal communication in more
detail, with some illustrations.

Berscheid, E. and Walster, E.H. (1978). Interpersonal
Attraction (2nd edn). Reading, Mass.: Addison-Wesley.
A very readable account of research in this area.

Bower, S.A. and Bower, G.H. (1976). Asserting Yourself.
Reading, Mass.: Addison-Wesley.
An interesting and practical book about assertiveness,
with examples and exercises.

Cook, M. (1979). Perceiving Others. London: Methuen.
A clear account of basic processes in person perception.

Goffman, E. (1956). The Presentation of Self in Everyday Life. Edinburgh: Edinburgh University Press.
A famous and highly entertaining account of self-presentation.

Trower, P., Bryant, B. and Argyle, M. (1978). Social Skills and Mental Health. London: Methuen.
An account of social skills training with neurotics, with full details of procedures.

6

Ageing and social problems
Peter G. Coleman

Opening remarks
FAY FRANSELLA

What more telling example can there be of Bannister's third part of the definition of the self (p. 12) that 'We entertain the notion of our own continuity over time; we possess our biography and we live in relation to it', than the geriatric patient's poem cited by Peter Coleman on p. 116? Unless you are able to look past the label 'geriatric' you will fail to communicate with the old person, let alone understand him or her.

It is almost inevitable that you will spend some of your time with geriatric patients either in the community or in hospital. Many people are helped in dealing with a group of people who are some psychological distance from them by having had personal experiences with that group. Many of you will have an ageing grandparent in, or closely associated with, your family. If this has been a rewarding experience you will be in a good position to generalize those feelings to your geriatric strangers and come to a quicker understanding of their needs. If it was a negative experience, if the grandparent was 'difficult' or played one family member off against the other, then you have to be careful not to transfer these feelings on to your geriatric patients. Bear in mind also what was said about the formation of friendships in the last chapter. Friendships are likely to be formed where there are shared constructs. You may be in your early twenties or younger, so it is likely that you will have relatively few constructs that are similar to those of old people. That just means you have to work harder to see things as they do.

Perhaps the most common barrier to understanding between the young and the ageing is 'threat'. Old people very often are threatening to the young. Threat comes in the realization that you yourself will be like this person if you continue to live that long. You too will be dependent on an occupational therapist for satisfaction of some of your psychological needs, and on the nurses for some of your care and personal hygiene; you too may suffer the shame of being incontinent and having to be treated like a child. It is not surprising that some people cannot bear being in the presence of old people or else cope with the threat by seeing that old person as a child, or as less than human, or as someone who has to be kept clean and as physically healthy as possible until they die.

If old age is threatening to some, it is probably not a gross over-generalization to say that every one of us is threatened by death. It is a 'hang-up' which we all have to overcome if we want to be of help to those who are themselves dying. As Simpson has said:

> Death is a very badly kept secret. I have over four hundred books on my shelves and thousands of articles on file, all announcing that ours is a Death-denying Society, and congratulating themselves on breaching that Denial ... Exploitation of the theme in books, audiotapes and cinema - often in very shoddy products - has become frequent. Death Kitsch is upon us, and the Death 'n Dying T-shirt seems imminent (1979).

Those of you who choose to work with those suffering from a terminal illness will naturally find Carr's chapter 7 invaluable, but I believe that we can all benefit by working on the threats that death has for us personally. If you have the very natural reaction of 'I don't want to think about it', then consider whether this is really so and see whether you think you will be in a better position to help your patients who may be facing death, or who may just have escaped as a result of an accident, by facing up to some of the issues that are important for you personally.

Carr also talks about the human response to bereavement. Many of you will have your own personal experiences to call upon here also, whether you are helping a relative cope with the knowledge of the death of someone who was your patient, or whether the bereaved person is your patient. Carr's point about the ephemeral nature of the so-called stages of bereavement cannot be emphasized enough. And this goes for all 'stage' theories. The stages that have been described, whether it be in personality or intellectual development, or reactions of children entering hospital or response to bereavement, may well be similarly described by many people. But, and it is a big but, descriptions can all too easily become prescriptions: that is, 'many people seem to go through these stages' is changed to 'people should go through these stages', and if they do not then something is wrong with them. And, if something is wrong in a medical setting, this often means some intervention to 'make' the stages happen.

Of all the chapters in this book, these two are likely to be the most challenging to you. Because of that, or in spite of that, I believe you will find them both useful and interesting.

What is it to be old?
PETER G. COLEMAN

The study of ageing and problems associated with it are now recognized as important. This is not surprising, for older people have become the major clients of the health and social services. They also have a lot of free time at their disposal. If there is to be an expansion in adult education and opportunities for creative leisure activities, the benefits should go especially to retired people.

What is surprising is that it has taken so long for the social sciences to pay attention to ageing and old age. So many young professionals are called on to devote their attention to the needs of people at the other end of the life span, yet they are likely to have received little in the way of stimulating material about the distinctive psychological features of old age.

Professional people do nevertheless have to be introduced to the subject of ageing, and it is interesting to note how that introduction has come to take on certain standard forms over the last ten years. There are two very popular, almost obligatory it seems, ways to begin talking or writing about ageing. The first way is to present the demographic data about the increasing numbers of elderly people in the population; the second way is to discuss the negative attitudes people have about working with the elderly.

The common introduction to ageing
In important respects old age as we know it today is a relatively modern phenomenon. Though there may have been individual societies in the past where a comparably large part of the population was old, it is clear that there has been a dramatic change in developed countries since the turn of the century. At that time in Britain those over the age of 65 constituted one in 20 of the population; today they constitute one in seven.

In recent years much more use is being made of the statistic 'over the age of 75', since it has become clear that this is the group in the population which makes the largest demands on the health and social services. This has highlighted the worrying news for service planners in a time of economic constraints that, while the total number of those over 65 will not increase very much in the coming years, the population of those over 75 has already passed 5 per cent of the total population and will reach 6 per cent by the end of the 1980s.

However, expressing concern simply at the number of elderly people in the population is misleading. Why after all should it be a problem that 15 per cent rather than, say, 10 per cent or 5 per cent of the population is over the age of 65, or that 6 per cent rather than 4 per cent or 2 per cent is over the age of 75? A lot of the issues have to do with economics. The state must find the means to continue paying adequate and perhaps even improved pensions, and to provide welfare services to larger numbers of people.

Yet perhaps the more fundamental issues are the availability and willingness of people, whether relatives, neighbours, professionals or volunteers, to give assistance to large numbers of disabled people in the population. For ageing, as any introduction to the subject makes abundantly clear, is associated with an increasing likelihood of developing chronic disability.

Global estimates of disability in daily living (in getting around the house and providing for oneself) indicate that the need for assistance is present in 15-20 per cent of the age group 65-74, rising to 35-40 per cent in the 75-84 age group and to over 60 per cent in those above 85. If one adds on the number of people living in institutions (hospitals and old people's homes), which is about 4-5 per cent of the total elderly population, one can conclude that about 30 per cent, or nearly one in three, of all people over the age of 65 are disabled and in need of help.

A typical introduction to ageing then goes on to present further numerical data on the social position of the elderly. Almost one-third of people over 65 have been found to live alone and large numbers are lonely. Many live in poor housing, lack basic amenities and so on.

The need for a life-span perspective
Large numbers of elderly people, large numbers of disabled elderly people, and large numbers of elderly people live in deprived circumstances; such is a typical introduction to old age. But there are vitally important perspectives missing. No wonder indeed that we should be concerned with attitudes, with finding enough people prepared to work with the elderly, enough geriatricians, enough nurses, enough social workers and so on, when the only image we present of old age is a negative one. If the only perspective we emphasize is one of endless problems, often insoluble because of irremediable physical and mental deterioration, we cannot expect many people to have the courage to become involved.

Old people are people like the rest of us. What is special about them is not that they may be mentally deteriorated, disabled or isolated. The majority, after all, is none of these things and many people reach the end of their lives without suffering any disadvantages. What is special about old people is that they have lived a long time. They have had all the kinds of experience we have had and many, many more. They are moving towards the end of life it is true, but it is every bit as important how one ends one's life as how one begins it.

The perspective on ageing that is needed is one which takes into account the whole life span. The discovery any student of old age has to make is not only that old people have a long life history behind them but that their present lives, their needs and wishes, cannot be understood without an appreciation of that life history.

If we really talk to old people all this will become evident. But how often do we do this? A most eloquent testimony of our neglect is a poem (88 lines long) that was found in the hospital locker of a geriatric patient. (It can be found in full, quoted in the preface of the Open University Text, Carver, V. and Liddiard, P., 1978, 'An Ageing Population', Hodder & Stoughton.)

What do you see nurses
  What do you see?
Are you thinking
  When you are looking at me
A crabbit old woman
  Not very wise,
Uncertain of habit
  With far-away eyes
. . . .
Then open your eyes nurse,
  You're not looking at me.

The writer emphasizes the continuity between her identity as
an old person and her identities at previous stages in the
life cycle. She is still the small child of ten with a large
family around her, still the 16 year old full of hopes and
expectations, still the bride she was at 20 and the young
woman of 30 with her children growing up fast. At 40 her
children are leaving home, and she and her husband are on
their own again. But then there are grandchildren for her to
take an interest in. Years pass and she has lost her husband
and must learn to live alone. She is all of these people.
But the nurse does not see them.

**Psychological changes
with age**

It is only proper to admit at the outset that the main activity of psychologists interested in ageing, with some exceptions, has not been of a life span perspective. Their
work has mainly been concerned with trying to establish what
psychological changes, usually changes of deterioration,
occur with advancing age, with understanding the bases of
such changes and finding ways of compensating for them.
These are obviously important questions.

Cognitive deterioration
It would be wishful thinking to deny that there is any
deterioration with age. Physical ageing is a fact which is
easy to observe, though it may occur at different rates in
different people. Performance in everyday tasks in which we
have to use our cognitive ability to register things we see
or hear, remember them and think about them also deteriorates. Absent-mindedness is one of the most common complaints
of older people in everyday life.

    In more recent cross-sectional studies of the perform-
ance of different age groups on experimental tasks, psychologists have tried their best to control for obvious factors
which might produce differences in their own right, like
education, illness, sensory impairment and willingness to
carry out the tasks in question. Of course, certain question
marks remain over differences in attitude and perceived
role: for instance, whether older people see the purpose of
such tasks in the same way as younger people. Nevertheless,
certain conclusions can be drawn about the abilities which
seem to change the most as one grows older. In the first

place, older people take much longer to carry out tasks and this is not only because their limb movements are slower. In tasks in which they have to divide their attention ('try to do two things at once'), decline with age is very marked and is already evident in those over 30. Ability to remember things we have seen or heard declines, as does the ability to hold associations in mind.

However, in some older people decline is not evident at all. Particular experiences, for example particular occupational backgrounds, may develop certain abilities in an individual to such an extent that they remain well developed throughout old age. Retired telephone operators who have no difficulty in dividing attention between a number of messages are a case in point. The prominence of so many older people in public life where they reap the fruit of years of experience in political dealings is also an obvious illustration. Moreover, it seems to be true that in some old people deterioration does not, in fact, occur. There are studies which indicate that the cognitive ability of a sizeable minority of elderly people, perhaps as many as one in ten, cannot be distinguished from that of younger people.

This, then, is evidence that age itself is not the important thing. Indeed it seems better to view age simply as a vector along which to measure the things that happen to people. Some things that happen with age are universal. They occur at different times, but they are unavoidable. These things we can, if we like, describe as 'age' changes. But a lot of the things we associate with old age are not due to ageing processes and are not universal. There is a great variation in the extent to which people are hit by physical and social losses as they grow old. Some people are fortunate, some people are unfortunate.

From the point of view of cognitive ability, the most unlucky are those people who suffer from the various forms of dementia or brain diseases which lead to a progressive deterioration in mental functioning. But health is by no means the only extrinsic factor influencing mental state in old age. A lot of research has been done recently on the psychological effects of such brain-washing treatments as isolation and sensory deprivation. Disorientation and confusion are common results. Yet we are often slow to recognize that old people may be living in circumstances where by any ordinary standards they are extremely isolated and deprived of stimulation. No one calls to see them, to engage them, to remind them of their names, roles and relationships. Disorientation in time and space, and confusion about identity and relationship with others, can be a natural result. From our own experience we know how time can lose meaning after one has been ill in bed for a day or two, away from the normal daily routine.

Other social and psychological factors play a role too. Motivation to recover or maintain abilities is obviously a crucial factor, and a number of studies have shown that amount of education remains one of the major factors in cognitive ability and performance throughout life.

Personality and life style

Scientific work on personality and style of life in old age does not match the amount that has been done on cognitive functioning. The evidence we do have, however, relates both to change and stability.

One clear finding from research is that introversion or interiority increases with age. This means that as people grow old they become more preoccupied with their own selves, their own thoughts and feelings and less with the outside world. This change is only relative, of course, but it is evident both from responses to questionnaires and also from projective tests, where people are asked to describe or react to stimuli they are presented with, such as pictures of family and social situations.

The term disengagement has been used to describe such a change in orientation; a decreased concern with interacting with others and being involved in the outside world and an increased satisfaction with one's own world of memories and immediate surroundings. However, critics have been quick to point out the dangers of exaggerating the extent to which disengagement is a 'natural' development in old age. Most of the decreased interaction and involvement of older people is forced upon them by undesired physical and social changes: disability, bereavement, loss of occupational roles and so on. Moreover, there is also clear evidence that old people are happier when there is a good deal of continuity between their past and present activities.

Indeed, in contrast to any change in personality that may occur, the stability that people show in their characteristics and style of life over a period of time is far more striking. Longitudinal studies show that people continue to enjoy the same interests and activities. When striking negative changes occur in a person's interests or familiar mode of activities, or ways of coping with life in old age, for no obvious reason, this is often a sign of psychiatric illness, especially depression.

Some of the most valuable studies on personality in old age are, in fact, those which have shown how important it is to take into reckoning a person's life style, for instance in explaining why people react differently to changes and losses such as retirement, bereavement and living alone, or a move to a residential home. Any research finding about old people usually has to be qualified by a reference to life style. This is mentioned again when talking about adjustment to relocation.

Growth and development

Though deterioration has been the main perspective of psychological research on ageing up to now, it is not the only one. Certainly in literature old age has been treated much more generously. The works of Nobel prize winners, such as Patrick White ('The Eye of the Storm', 1973), Saul Bellow ('Mr Sammler's Planet', 1969) and Ernest Hemingway ('The Old Man and the Sea', 1952), present vivid and compelling pictures of old age that, like King Lear, have to do with deterioration and change but also with growth in understanding and the values of existence.

Indeed, a characteristic theme in literature is of old age as a time of questioning; of one's own achievements, of the meaning of one's life, of the values one lived by and of what is of lasting value. It is as if an old person, freed from the strait-jacket of society, suffering losses in his ability to function and in his social position - perhaps indeed precisely because of them - is, somehow, let free to question life. Psychologists have only begun tentatively to approach these issues, but there is a lot in writers like Jung to consider.

Adaptation to loss in old age

From what has already been said it should be clear that old age is a time of great inequality. It is a time when losses occur, loss of physical and mental abilities, loss of people who were close to one, loss of roles and loss of activities. These losses are not inevitable; they do not occur in the same degree to everyone; but adapting to loss is a characteristic feature of old age.

Attitudes to health and well-being

Severe disability is one of the major losses of old age and its central importance in shaping the rest of an individual's life is one of the most common findings to emerge from investigations on social aspects of ageing. People who are disabled have more problems in maintaining their desired styles of life and are more dissatisfied than people who are not disabled. This is not surprising.

What is more surprising, or at least not logically to be expected, is the fact that, in general, levels of well-being do not decline with age. This is despite the fact that the incidence and severity of disability tend to increase with age and have a great influence on well-being. The key to understanding this comes from studies on subjective health.

The clear evidence from both longitudinal and cross-sectional studies is that whereas objective health and physical functioning of elderly people tend to deteriorate with age, the same is not true in regard to how they feel about their health. The most likely explanation has to do with expectations. People expect to become somewhat more disabled with old age. If they do, they accept it. But if their physical functioning remains stable they may in fact experience this as a bonus and feel better as a result. Only if their health deteriorates beyond the expected norm are they likely to feel badly about it.

This argument applies strictly only to feeling well, but it has a wider implication for well-being generally and for reactions to other losses in old age. Expectation is a very

important aspect of reaction to loss. It is what people
expect and what people find normal that determines how they
react to things and how satisfied they feel with their situation. This kind of consideration also leads one to reflect
how different things could be if old people's expectations
changed. This is in fact not so unlikely. Future generations
of elderly people may be far less accepting of lower standards of health and also, for instance, of income. They may
expect things to be a good deal better for them. And if
things are not going to be better they are going to be less
happy as a result.

Adjustment to relocation

Another misfortune often following from disability is that
people can find themselves being obliged to move, sometimes
quite unexpectedly and against their will, to different
environments, particularly institutional settings, where
they often have to remain for the rest of their lives.
Though this is usually done to them 'for their own good'
(they are judged incapable of looking after themselves in
their own homes), the end result may be much worse than
leaving them alone: for instance, further deterioration and
loss of interest in life.

There has been growing realization of the extent to
which environmental changes can contribute to physical
illness and psychiatric disorders. Even where it is voluntarily undertaken and has otherwise favourable effects,
there are indications that rehousing can undermine a person's health. There is also a great deal of variation
between individuals in their reactions, so it is important
to discover which factors might predict the ability to
adjust easily to new surroundings.

Among psychological factors cognitive ability is clearly
crucial. There appear to be two major reasons why cogni-
tively impaired old people react worse to relocation. In the
first place, their lack of ability to anticipate and prepare
means that they experience more stress on making the move.
Second, because of their poor short-term memory and orientation abilities it may take them a long while to understand
their new surroundings.

Personality is important too. We are not sufficiently
sensitive to the fact that the institutional environments we
provide may be fine for one kind of elderly person but not
for another. American studies have shown the importance, for
instance, of rebellious and aggressive traits, as opposed to
passive and compliant ones, in predicting survival and lack
of deterioration after relocation to institutional settings.
Vital as well, of course, are attitudinal factors concerned
with what a move means to the persons concerned, whether
they want to go, and how they see their own future in a new
setting.

Self-esteem and its sources: the lynchpin of adjustment?

Disability and environmental change have been picked out for consideration as two of the negative changes associated with old age. There are others, of course. Bereavement requires a major adjustment which seems to follow certain definite stages. Grieving is a normal, healthy part of the process, and the support and understanding of those around in allowing bereaved people to express themselves may be very important to it. Loss of occupational role with retirement is another big change. Indeed, adjustment to it is often thought of in the same terms as adjustment to the old age role itself. Most people make good adaptations, but not all, and retirement can be a major precipitating factor in the onset of late life depression.

Then again, a very significant loss for many people as they grow older is that of income: they must adapt to making do with less. There has been almost no psychological investigation of this kind of adaptation. From what one can see it would seem that a lot of old people positively take pride in stretching their money. This, of course, may also have a lot to do with their experience of deprivation in the past.

Naturally, in all these adaptations much depends on the characteristics of the individual person involved, and one is led to ask whether there are any general ways in which one can conceptualize how a person adapts to the various losses and changes that occur with old age. Some authors talk in terms of the individual possessing particular qualities: for instance, 'coping ability'. But the most valuable index of adjustment in old age is that of self-esteem.

Maintenance of positive attitudes to oneself seems to be one of the key issues in old age. An especially important component of self-image is a sense of being in control of one's own life. Development in childhood and adulthood is associated with an increasing sense of effectiveness and of impact on the external world. In old age this sense may well be taken away.

Intrinsic to this conception of self-identity is the notion that it must have roots outside itself. Therefore, if individuals are to maintain self-esteem they have a continuing need of sources from which they can define acceptable self-images. For some people these sources can exist in past relationships and achievements or in an inner conviction about the kind of person one is, but in the main they depend on the present external circumstances of their lives; their roles in the family, in relation to other people, in work and in other activities.

When these circumstances change, as they often do in old age, individuals may have to find alternative sources to maintain positive views of themselves. Here again it is vital to understand a person's life history. A person whose sense of self has been based on one particular kind of source, for instance relationships with close family members, is going to suffer especially if such family contacts are lost through death.

One way to investigate sources of self-esteem is to ask people directly what makes them say that they feel useful or

feel useless, for instance. Not surprisingly, lack of infirmity and contact with other people including the family
emerge as the major sources of self-esteem. Especially in
disabled people, being able to do things for oneself, and in
particular to get around, appear to be key factors; also
being a source of help and encouragement to others is very
important.

In this context it is worth putting in a good word for
residential care and other types of grouped housing schemes.
In a previous part of this section it was noted that a move
to an institutional setting can be damaging for certain
types of individual, but a good institutional setting can
also be of great benefit to certain people. This is possible when sources of self-esteem are likely to be
strengthened rather than weakened by the move.

For instance, some people could be said to be 'living
independently in the community'. But in reality they may be
extremely isolated and totally dependent on the services
being brought to them. Once they have moved to a genuine
communal setting the burden of infirmity and consciousness
of being alone can be diminished. Precisely because they are
better able to cope for themselves in the new environment
and to be of importance to others, they may gain a new lease
of life.

Helping old people

Not all the loss and trauma of old age can be countered from
an individual's own resources. The modern welfare state
provides a range of services for the elderly; housing,
health and social services. These are, of course, limited,
subject to decisions about what level of services the
country can 'afford'. We do not know what a perfect service
for the elderly would be like, but we certainly do know that
what we provide at present falls a long way short of it.

However, the achievement of the present level of services needs to be respected if we are to develop further,
and it is important that people in the various caring
professions who carry out these services remember their
responsiblities. One of the real dangers is taking the
operation of a service for granted and applying it automatically or mindlessly. The people on the receiving end then
cease to be considered as individuals.

A key element in any work with elderly people is the
individual assessment, and it is here that the psychological
perspective has a vital role. We need a good assessment not
only of people's physical condition and capabilities and of
their social situations, but also of their individual needs,
their abilities and interests, which should include a good
picture of how they used to be.

Besides helping in assessment, psychology can also play
a role in the actual provision of therapeutic interventions
both to old people themselves and to those around them.
Applied psychology should be able to show the best way: for
example, to help recover abilities that seem to be lost or
to mend social relationships that have become tense.

Maintenance of interests, activities and functioning

One of the most tragic images we have of old age is that of an old person with shoulders sunk, sitting collapsed in a chair, totally uninvolved in the world around. In a previous section the question of 'disengagement' in old age was raised, and let us repeat the point made there that, although some decline in activity may be an intrinsic part of growing old, most of such decline is the result of physical disability and environmental trauma.

When there is a dramatic decline in a person's activities for no obvious reason, we need to alert ourselves to the possibility that the person may be depressed. Loss of well-established habits and activities and lack of interest or anxiety about trying to regain them may be symptoms of the kind of depression which will respond to treatment, even though the person may not admit to having depressed feelings. But, of course, there also has to be some activity and interests for the person to go back to. Particularly if someone is disabled there may be few possibilities available, and the person is then likely to decline again. It is also quite clear that prolonged inactivity has deleterious effects both on physical and psychological functioning. Skills that are not exercised tend to atrophy.

In recent years a lot of new initiatives have been taken in geriatric hospitals in providing opportunities for patients to engage in different types of activity, arts and crafts, music discussion and so on. Generally, staff report improvements in elderly people who do take part in such activities, which can be seen in their personal appearance, in their physical and mental functioning and in their contact with others.

An even greater challenge is offered by people who are mentally deteriorated. In the first place it is very important to distinguish elderly people who really have irretrievable brain disease from those who only appear to have because they are depressed. Indeed, it may be symptomatic of someone's depression that he thinks his brain is rotting. It may be no easy matter to distinguish this, because it is difficult to motivate someone who is depressed actually to demonstrate his abilities. With the right treatment and support depressed people can be encouraged to regain their old abilities.

However, elderly people who clearly are deteriorating mentally should not be abandoned to their fate. Tests have shown that such people, given encouragement and help, can still acquire and retain new information and maintain skills. But the effort needed from outside is great. A good example is the use of so-called 'reality orientation', where people around the elderly person, either informally throughout the day or in concentrated formal classes, systematically try to help remind the person of time, place and season, of names of people, of objects, and of activities and so on.

Psychologists have a lot to do applying findings from the study of learning and memory to help old people. The trouble at present is that such people are often left alone, and this only exacerbates their condition. Dementia is a progressive illness, but what happens between its onset and death is important. If in the future we find medical means of slowing down its progress, it will become an even more urgent matter to find means as well to allow people to maintain their optimum potentialities in the time that remains left to them.

Family relationships

Another vital issue is the relationship between disabled elderly people and their families. Many more of such people are supported by their families than live in institutions for the elderly. For instance, in the case of severe dementia, there are four to five times as many suffering from such a condition living in the community as live in residential homes or hospitals. Yet often families who are doing the caring get pitifully little in the way of support services.

If they become overburdened by the stress of their involvement, both they and their elderly relatives suffer. The old person's mental condition may well be aggravated by tired and irritable relatives, and if there is a breakdown in care and there is no alternative but to take the old person into an institution, the family members are likely to suffer greatly from feelings of guilt. They often want to care for a relative until that person dies, but need help in carrying it out.

It is an important principle to accept that work with families is an integral part of work with elderly people. Family ties after all usually form a substantial part of an individual's identity. If those ties are damaged, so is the person's identity. The physical and mental deterioration that affects many people as they grow older and their ensuing state of dependency can put a strain on many relationships. Men, for instance, usually do not expect to outlive their wives. They can encounter great problems if they find instead that they have to spend their old age looking after a physically or mentally deteriorated wife, especially if in the past it was their wives who ran the household. Children too often find difficulty in taking over responsibility for ailing parents.

The actual symptoms, particularly of mental disturbance in old age, can be very disturbing. In some forms of dementia (probably dependent on the part of the brain that has been affected) the behavioural changes that can occur, caricaturing the person's old personality, increasing aggression or leading to a loss in standards of cleanliness, can be very painful for relatives to bear. It may be difficult for them to accept that the patient is not simply being difficult or unreasonable.

Families need counselling about the nature of the illness and, in the case of dementia, of its progressive nature, and preferably, too, promise of continued practical support. Group meetings held for relatives of different patients by doctors, social workers or other professionals can also be useful in allowing relatives to share common experiences and problems. Groups for the bereaved, particularly husbands or wives, can also play their part. The last years of their lives may have revolved around the care of a sick spouse and they must now find new meaning in life.

The future

In discussing ageing and social problems it may seem strange to end with a note about the future. But from what has been said it should be obvious that great improvements need to take place, both in society's provision for the elderly and in the attitudes of each and every one of us to the elderly people we live among.

For most people old age is not a particularly unhappy time, though for some it is. In part that may be, as we have suggested, because old people have low expectations. They quietly accept a society that treats them meanly and as somehow less important. In the future that may all change. We may see new generations of elderly people, foreshadowed in today's Grey Panthers in America, who will mobilize their potential power as a numerically important part of the electorate and pressurize society to give them a better deal.

On the other hand, old people may continue to remain on the sidelines. They may refuse to see their own material and other interests as being of central importance to society, in which case the rest of the population must see they are not forgotten.

The most important changes indeed are the attitudinal ones. We must recognize that old people are ourselves. They are our future selves. There is a continuity in life both between their past and present and between our present and future.

Old people remain the same people they were. Indeed, if we really want to know about a person's needs and wants and how they could be satisfied, the best introduction would be to let them tell us about their life history. Whatever new steps are taken in the future must follow on from this and make sense in relation to it.

Better provision would follow from such a recognition. If we really respected people's individuality we would provide them with choice about the circumstances and activities with which they end their days, not just enforce certain standard solutions. In short, we must allow people to grow old in ways that suit them, perhaps to explore new avenues of development in order to make the most of the years that remain. Also, when we consider those who need our help, who suffer in old age and perhaps are dependent upon us, we should not forget these wider perspectives.

Reference

Simpson, M.A. (1979)
The Facts of Death. Englewood Cliffs, NJ: Prentice-Hall.

Bibliography

Birren, J.E. and Schaie, K.W. (eds) (1977)
Handbook of the Psychology of Ageing. London: Van Nostrand Reinhold.
Brearley, C.P. (1975)
Social Work, Ageing and Society. London: Routledge & Kegan Paul.
Bromley, D.B. (1974)
The Psychology of Human Ageing (2nd edn). Harmondswor Penguin.
Carver, V. and Liddiard, P. (eds) (1978)
An Ageing Population (Open University text). Sevenoaks: Hodder & Stoughton.
Chown, S.M. (ed.) (1972)
Human Ageing. Harmondsworth: Penguin.
Dibner, A.S. (1975)
The psychology of normal aging. In M.G. Spencer and C.J. Dorr (eds), Understanding Aging: A multi-disciplinary approach. New York: Appleton-Century-Crofts.
Gray, B. and Isaacs, B. (1979)
Care of the Elderly Mentally Infirm. London: Tavistock.
Kastenbaum, R. (1979)
Growing Old - Years of Fulfilment. London: Harper & Row.
Kimmel, D.C. (1974)
Adulthood and Ageing. An interdisciplinary developmental view. Chichester: Wiley.
Miller, E. (1977)
Abnormal Ageing. The psychology of senile and presenile dementia. Chichester: Wiley.
Neugarten, B. and associates (1964)
Personality in Middle and Later Life. New York: Atherton Press.

Questions

1. Discuss the view that old people do not differ from young people except in the number of years they have lived.
2. What factors influence mental performance in old age? What evidence do we have on their relative importance?
3. How important is a knowledge of life style or personality type to understanding how people react to change and stress in old age?
4. Are the changes we observe in old people's behaviour related more to the physical and social losses they incur or more to intrinsic processes of ageing?
5. Do old people show genuine developmental changes as well as changes of deterioration?

6. Analyse the relationship between well-being and health in old age with particular regard to increasing occurrence of disease and disability.
7. Discuss the role of 'expectations' in adaptation to loss in old age.
8. What behavioural and other psychological techniques are there available to help people to recover interests and customary activities that they may have lost in old age?
9. 'Social and psychological factors are more responsible for mental deterioration in old age than are physical disorders of the brain.' Discuss.
10. 'Too many of our views on the psychology of ageing are restricted by the limits of our own society.' Discuss the value of a cross-cultural approach to the psychology of ageing.
11. 'Ageing' is a process; it is growing old that is the problem, not being old. Discuss this statement both from your own observations and from your reading of the psychological literature.
12. Discuss findings showing a relationship between memory and ageing. What implications have these findings for your work with the ageing person?
13. What is the day-to-day importance of the slowing of reaction times for the ageing person?

Annotated reading

Brearley, C.P. (1975) Social Work, Ageing and Society. London: Routledge & Kegan Paul.
  A book written for social workers, bringing together a wide range of material from medicine, psychology and sociology.

Bromley, D.B. (1974) The Psychology of Human Ageing (2nd edn). Harmondsworth: Penguin.
  Written by a British psychologist, it gives a very thorough coverage of subjects such as changes in performance and cognitive skills with age, and is good on the methodological issues involved in doing research on ageing.

Carver, V. and Liddiard, P. (eds) (1978) An Ageing Population (Open University Text). Sevenoaks: Hodder & Stoughton.
  A collection of readings for the Open University course. The papers have been drawn from a variety of sources to provide a multidisciplinary perspective on the needs and circumstances of the elderly.

Gray, B. and Isaacs, B. (1979) Care of the Elderly Mentally Infirm. London: Tavistock.
  A specialized book on the elderly mentally infirm also intended for social workers, written jointly by a geriatrician and a social worker.

Kastenbaum, R. (1979) Growing Old - Years of Fulfilment. London: Harper & Row.

A short introduction to the subject written by an American psychologist. He presents a balanced approach to old age, giving due weight to positive perspectives. The book is also attractively illustrated.

7

Dying and bereavement
A. T. Carr

If you had been born at the beginning of this century, your life expectancy at birth would have been 44 years if you were male or 48 years if you were female. If you were born today, your initial life expectancy would be 70 years or 76 years respectively. These figures reflect an ageing of the population that has occurred in all western industrial societies over the past 80 years. Although we all will die, most of us will do so at a relatively advanced age. Although we all will be bereaved, most of us will not suffer this until we are young adults or until we are in our middle years.

The fatal conditions of the present day, once hidden by the mass diseases, are those associated with longevity. In 1978, almost 590,000 people died in England and Wales and 85 per cent of these deaths were attributable to only three categories of illness: diseases of the circulatory system (heart and blood circulation), neoplasms (cancer) and diseases of the respiratory system (OPCS, 1979). Also, more than two people in every three now die in institutions of one form or another.

In the absence of any radical changes of events, the vast majority of us will die aged 65 years or over, in an institution of some sort and as a result of a disease of our circulatory system, or respiratory system, or of cancer. This underlines an important feature of dying and death at the present time: they have become unfamiliar events that take place in unfamiliar surroundings, watched over by unfamiliar people. We all know that we will die and that we may be bereaved, yet we have very little relevant experience upon which to develop our construing or anticipation of these events and states.

Telling

The majority of fatally ill people realize, at some point, that they will not recover, even if they have not been informed of the nature of their illness. However, it would appear that only about half of all fatally ill people appreciate their condition before significant changes in health force the conclusion 'I am dying'. This is almost certainly an under-estimate: there will be some people who know that they will not recover but who do not communicate this.

Although about one-half of terminally ill people appear to appreciate the seriousness of their illness, this awareness is usually achieved independently, informally and indirectly. No more than 15 per cent of terminally ill cancer patients are told of their prognosis either by their general practitioner or by a hospital doctor (Cartwright, Hockey and Anderson, 1973). This contrasts markedly with the experiences of their close relatives. Almost 90 per cent of the close relatives of terminally ill patients are aware that the patient's illness is terminal and most of them are informed of this by a general practitioner or by a hospital doctor. There are several implications of these data, the two most obvious being that fatally ill people and their principal carers often do not share the same information about the illness, and that doctors usually are unwilling to tell patients when they have a disease that will kill them. Perhaps the most serious consequence is that one or more of the familial participants has to cope with the demands of this most stressful period without adequate support.

It is remarkable how little emphasis is placed upon the wishes of the patient. Most people, including doctors, whether they are young or old, ill or well, say they would want to know if they had a fatal illness or that they are glad they do know. Several studies have examined this issue and the results are consistent in showing that more than 70 per cent of all the samples used say they would want to be informed if they had a terminal disease. It is clear that most people say they would want to be informed of the seriousness of their illness and most doctors say that they would want to be told; yet the majority of fatally ill patients are not told. Also, the existence of a real threat to life does not reduce the very high proportion of people who want to know if they have a fatal illness.

In general, learning that one has a fatal illness is followed by a period of disquiet, even grief, although the emotional response may be concealed from others. It is worth noting that some patients do not 'hear' or at least appear not to remember, what they have been told regarding their prognosis. Although it has been proposed that the defence mechanism of denial is a ubiquitous response to learning of a fatal prognosis (Kubler-Ross, 1969), there are other more mundane possibilities. The first is the use of terminology that may have very precise meanings for a professional but which may mean nothing, or something very different, to the patient. To inform a patient of 'malignant lymphoma' or 'secondary metastases' may not constitute communication. Even when the words that are used are understood reasonably well, they may not convey what was intended. For some individuals, the knowledge of their impending death will be extremely distressing; in such cases the person may be quite unable to accept what is plain to everybody else. They may become distraught as their bodies show increasing signs of impending death while they continue to deny that they are dying. Such extreme responses, as a terminal illness progresses, correspond to denial as elucidated by Kubler-Ross (1969). However, it would be inappropriate to regard as denial a person's failure to comprehend or to recall initial statements about prognosis. Quite apart from the communication problems mentioned above, if people have no prior suspicions that their conditions may be terminal it is probable that they will be unable to accept a fatal diagnosis. It is not that they refuse to accept such information but they are unable to accept it. It demands a radical revision of their view of the world and such a major psychological adjustment takes time. Initially, such news is not disbelieved, but on the other hand, it cannot be fitted into a person's perception of the world: it cannot be accommodated. The revised view of the world will need to be tested, amended and confirmed in the light of further information. The person will seek such information in what people say, how they behave and how his body feels. It is only when the revised view of the world 'fits', in the sense that it is not violated by new observations or new information, that the person is able fully to accommodate the 'truths' that have been offered. Individuals who have prior suspicions about the seriousness of their illnesses have already constructed, at least in part, a view of their world that includes themselves as dying individuals.

Our aim must be to maintain dignity, to alleviate suffering and to help people live as fully as possible for as long as they are able: they should be told what they are prepared to hear at a time when they are prepared to listen. The same principle might be kept in mind when dealing with relatives. There are indications that those who are told with care show improved family relationships, less tension and less desperation during their terminal illnesses than those who are not (Gerle, Lunden and Sandblow, 1960). Helping a person towards fuller awareness of, and adjustment to, a fatal prognosis is the beginning of a communication process which is itself an integral part of caring for the terminally ill.

Terminality and dying

The two words terminality and dying are being used to draw a distinction that can have important implications for the way in which fatally ill people are managed and treated. The main implication is that of regarding someone as terminally ill, but nevertheless as living and with some valuable life remaining, rather than regarding the person as dying with all the negative attitudes this provokes. Once illnesses have been diagnosed as terminal we need to regard patients as living and possibly living more intensely than the rest of us, until they clearly are dying. Terminality, then, begins when a terminal diagnosis is made but dying starts later, usually when death is much closer and when individuals are prepared to relinquish their biological life in the absence of valuable, functional life.

Sources of distress

Effective and appropriate care of the fatally ill requires
an awareness of potential sources of distress so that distress can be anticipated and thus be avoided or alleviated.
Of course, distress is not confined to the patient: effective care and support for those who are close to the patient
is merited not only on humanitarian grounds, but also
because of the exacerbation of the patient's suffering that
can result from the distress of relatives and friends. Table
1 summarizes some of the most common sources of distress
for patients and those who are close to them.

The listing contained in table 1 is by no means
exhaustive, but it illustrates a number of points. First,
given some capacity for empathy on the part of the
survivor(s) there is little that the terminally ill person
must endure that the survivor can avoid. This commonality
of the sources of distress argues strongly for the need to
attend to the welfare of survivors before they become
bereaved. Second, it is clear that almost all the potential
sources of distress are psychological in nature. Even some
of the physical symptoms such as incontinence or smells are
distressing because of our values and expectations. Also,
pain itself is an experience that is subject to psychological factors rather than a sensation that is elicited by
an appropriate stimulus.

Although we cannot examine in detail the physical distress of terminal illness, our discussion would be incomplete without a summary of this. Cartwright et al (1973) and
Ward (1974) identified retrospectively the physical symptoms
experienced by their samples of terminal cancer patients,
215 and 264 individuals respectively. These data are
summarized in table 2.

It is striking that the rank order of symptoms is the
same for both samples and a significant proportion of
patients in each sample experienced each of the symptoms
listed. Other common physical symptoms were breathing
difficulties, 52 per cent; coughing, 48 per cent (Ward); and
sleeplessness, 17 per cent (Cartwright et al).

Distress and coping

An examination of tables 1 and 2 points to a number of
psychological processes that predispose people to react with
depression and anxiety during a terminal illness. Current
approaches to depression emphasize the role of loss and
helplessness as aetiological factors. Loss refers to the
real or imagined loss of a valued object, role, activity,
relationship, etc. The individual relevance of the concept
of loss lies in the individual differences of our value
systems. For example, a person who highly values physical
abilities, physical appearance, etc., is likely to be more
at risk for depression as a result of physical debility,
tiredness and deterioration in appearance, than someone for
whom such attributes are low in a hierarchy of values.

Helplessness describes a state that is characterized by
an awareness that one's behaviour is unrelated to the events

Table 1

Common sources of distress

Fatally ill person (P)	Those who love P
Awareness of impending death	Awareness of impending bereavement
Anticipation of loss	Anticipation of loss
Physical sequelae of disease process, e.g. tumours, lesions, nausea, incontinence, breathlessness, unpleasant smells	Empathic concern, aversion, etc.
Frustration and help-lessness as disease progresses	Frustration and help-lessness as disease progresses
Uncertainty about the future welfare of the family	Uncertainty about the future welfare of the family
Anticipation of pain	
Empathic concern	Caring for P, night-sitting, tiredness, etc.
Changes in roles with family, friends, etc.	Changes in roles with family, friends, etc
Changes in abilities as illness progresses	Empathic concern
Changes in appearance as illness progresses	Empathic concern, aversion, etc.
Uncertainties about dying	Empathic concern
Dying	Empathic concern
	Discovery of death, directly or indirectly
	Practicalities, funeral, etc.
	Grief
	Role changes
	Reconstruction of life

Table 2

Symptoms suffered by terminal cancer patients

Symptom	Per cent in sample of Cartwright et al	Per cent in sample of Ward
Pain	87	62
Anorexia	76	61
Vomiting	54	38
Urinary incontinence	38	28
Faecal incontinence	37	20
Bedsores	24	13

---

which impinge upon oneself. When a person is subjected to aversive events whose occurrence, intensity, duration, etc., is quite independent of behaviour, a characteristic state may ensue. This state, which occurs in the majority of subjects tested, is known as learned helplessness. There are individual differences in susceptibility to learned help-lessness, but the more aversive the events and the more frequently they are experienced as independent of behaviour the more likely it is to develop. It is a generalized state characterized by apathy, dysphoric mood, psychomotor retar-dation (i.e. slowness in thought and action), and feelings of hopelessness. Many clinical depressions are explained most fully in terms of the development of helplessness and there is evidence that sudden death is not an uncommon consequence of learned helplessness in laboratory animals. There can be little doubt about the relevance and importance of helplessness to our consideration of the welfare of the terminally ill.

Let us now return to the sources of distress summarized in tables 1 and 2. It is clear that some of these are intrinsically uncontrollable, and others duplicate the procedures that are used in experimental work to induce helplessness in that they are aversive, uncontrollable and repeated: for instance, urinary incontinence and vomiting. Furthermore, many patients undergo physical investigations and treatments that they do not understand, that they find unpleasant or painful and about which they feel they have little choice other than to accept them passively. It is not surprising to find that depression is commonly encountered in the terminally ill. A significant minority of fatally ill people and their next-of-kin become moderately or severely depressed (about one in five people in each group). Those most at risk are adolescents, young parents with dependents, those who have many physical symptoms and those who experience lengthy hospitalization.

The reciprocal interaction of physical and psychological processes must not be overlooked. We have already considered the depressive role of repeated, unpleasant physical symptoms. However, the interaction also proceeds in the other direction: adverse emotional states such as depression and anxiety augment pain and other physical discomforts. The essential point is that pain is not a simple response to an appropriate physical stimulus such as tissue damage: it is an experience that is compounded of the stimulation and the person's response to that stimulation. The motivational and emotional state of the person acts, as it were, to colour the sensation and to produce the experience we call pain. Without such 'colouring' and evaluation the sensation may be perceived but not experienced as painful.

It is the experience of most who work in terminal care that the relief of anxiety or depression through appropriate support, communication and practical help reduces the pain of patients and, not insignificantly, reduces the need for medication. The point is not that attention to the psychological state of the patient removes the need for relevant medication but that it reduces the dosages that may be required to bring relief. There are many obvious advantages that derive from this, not the least of which is the ability to alleviate pain without resorting to medications that render the patient confused, drowsy or comatose.

Anxiety arises when a future event is appraised as threatening. This appraisal is the evaluation of an event in terms of its harmful implications for the individual, harm being the extent to which continued physical and psychological functioning is endangered. Threat appraisal is a highly subjective process that depends upon the subjective likelihood of an event - that is, how probable the person feels the event to be - and the degree of harm that will result, this again being subjectively assessed. So terminally ill people are anxious to the extent that the events that they anticipate are both likely and harmful in their own terms: if events are not perceived as likely or harmful then they will not provoke anxiety.

Anxiety is an essentially adaptive emotion, in that it motivates us to initiate behaviours that prevent the anticipated harm being realized. To the extent that individuals accept that they are dying and are unable to reduce or eliminate the harmful consequences of this process, they are liable to remain anxious. An inspection of tables 1 and 2 reminds us that there are many potential types of harm that the fatally ill person is motivated, by anxiety, to alleviate. It is reassuring to note that the intense panic that is such a common feature of clinical anxiety states occurs rarely in terminal illness except, perhaps, in those who continue to deny the imminence of death as the end approaches and those for whom breathing is difficult. However, moderate anxiety is by no means uncommon in the terminally ill. This is not only an extra burden of suffering for the person but it also exacerbates other discomforts including pain.

There are few systematic reports of anxiety in terminal illness but from the data that do exist it is clear that moderate anxiety is experienced by between one-quarter and one-half of patients. The anxiety may be readily discerned in those people who are able to verbalize their fears, and who are given the opportunity to do so, but it may be less obvious in those who communicate less well verbally. However, the physiological and behavioural concomitants of anxiety are good indicators of the presence of unspoken fear. Often it is difficult to distinguish between physiological signs of anxiety such as gastric upset, nausea, diarrhoea, muscular pains, etc., and symptoms of the disease process or side effects of treatment. Nevertheless, the possibility that a patient might be persistently anxious should not be overlooked.

Given the subjective nature of threat appraisal, the causes of an individual's anxiety can be surprisingly idiosyncratic, but there are a few consistencies that may provide some clues. Younger adults expect to be distressed by pain and parting from the people they love, whereas the elderly fear becoming dependent and losing control of bowel and bladder functioning. Hinton (1972) reports that almost two-thirds of his patients who died aged 50 years or less were clearly anxious but this was true of only one-third of those aged 60 years and over. There is a clear and understandable trend for young parents of dependent children to be more anxious than other groups. Perhaps it is not insignificant that younger patients also tend to experience more physical discomfort during their terminal illnesses.

According to Hinton (1963), anxiety is more common in people with a lengthy terminal illness. He found more than 50 per cent of those who had been ill for more than one year to be clearly anxious, but only 20 per cent of those who had been ill for less than three months showed similar levels of anxiety. Although anxiety levels fluctuate during a patient's terminal illness, there is no general trend for anxiety to increase as the person draws closer to death. Some people become more apprehensive as their illnesses progress, but others become more calm during the last stages of their lives.

Some specific experiences of illness may be potent sources of anxiety. Prior episodes of intolerable pain can provoke great anxiety when they are recalled or when their return is anticipated. Difficulties in breathing are commonly associated with anxiety and a tendency to panic. Also, in the context of a mortal illness there are a number of sources of distress that are intrinsically uncontrollable and uncertain, such as the final process of dying, death and the nature of the world in which one's dependent survivors

will be living. When anticipated harm remains and individuals perceive it as beyond their ability to influence, they
become liable to the state of helplessness. If this is
severe they may become depressed, as we have discussed: if
less severe, then they may exhibit the resignation that has
been termed 'acceptance' (Kubler-Ross, 1969). If they
persist in their attempts to control and influence events
that are beyond their reach they are likely to remain
anxious and even to become more anxious as they approach
death.

For the fatally ill child under five or six years of
age, anxiety takes the form of separation anxiety, loneliness and fears of being abandoned. The young child does
not appear to fear death and its implications, but fears are
aroused by those aspects of illness and hospitalization
which elicit fear in most ill children who require hospital
treatment.

Between the ages of six and ten or eleven years, separation fears persist, but the child is increasingly prone to
anxiety over painful treatments and bodily intrusions. Such
fears of mutilation and physical harm are intensified in the
absence of familiar, trusted adults. Some children in this
age group, because of differing prior experiences or more
advanced cognitive development, are also aware of the
cessation of awareness and bodily functioning consequent
upon death.

Although there is some dispute as to whether the child
under ten years of age can be aware of impending death at a
conceptual level, there is little doubt that many young
children perceive that their illness is no ordinary illness. This is a frequent clinical observation and there is
a good deal of evidence that it is so whether or not the
diagnosis is discussed with the child (Spinetta, 1974). Of
course there are many cues that may indicate to the child
that something very serious and threatening is happening,
quite apart from the numerous tests, treatments and visits
to hospital. Most children are finely tuned to detect
meaningful and subtle signs in the verbal and non-verbal
behaviour of adults: the things that are not talked about,
tone of voice, eye contact, posture, etc. Also, there are
many cues that the child would find it hard to overlook:
whispered conversations, unusually frequent and intense
bodily contact, unusual generosity and freedom of choice
with regard to presents and treats, and so on.

Parents and others usually begin to grieve for the
fatally ill child soon after they accept the prognosis.
Their ability to cope with this grief is an important
determinant of their effectiveness in supporting the child.
Since familiar adults and siblings are likely to be the
child's greatest potential source of comfort and reassurance, it is important that time and attention is devoted to
these significant others for the sake of the child's welfare. There are indications of a high incidence of psychological difficulties in family members, particularly

siblings, during the terminal illness of a child. Clearly parents, who are themselves struggling with their own emotions, may have difficulty sustaining the other children in the family, let alone in providing comfort and reassurance to the one who is ill.

Adolescents and some younger children will be aware of the finality of death. Although dependent upon adults in a functional sense, they may perceive themselves as having important roles to play in the welfare of others and thus be subject to fears for the well-being of their survivors in much the same way as adults with dependents. Very young children may endure a terminal illness with striking calmness and acceptance of their lot, provided that their separation fears are allayed, but once they are past the age of six or seven years they become prone to a wide range of fears that exceed those of their 'normally ill' counterparts with severe, chronic, but non-fatal illness. Although children may be reluctant to express their fears, or may express them unclearly and indirectly, they should be anticipated in all aspects of care.

We have examined the range of potential sources of distress in terminal illness and the most common types of distress that result from these. Pain, anxiety and depression are sufficiently frequent and severe to merit attention when services are being planned and delivered. However, a majority of fatally ill people do not become severely anxious, deeply depressed or suffer from unrelieved pain. This does not minimize the awful suffering of the large minority or the pressing need for improvements in care to which this suffering testifies. It indicates only that, with whatever help they receive, most people who endure a terminal illness cope reasonably well, keeping their levels of distress within limits that are acceptable to themselves and to those who care for them.

The responses of people who are faced with impending death show sufficient uniformity to enable observers to write of stages, phases and patterns of coping (e.g. Kubler-Ross, 1969; Falek and Britton, 1974). Quite apart from doubts about the uniformity and progressive nature of stages of coping in terminal illness (e.g. Schulz and Aderman, 1974), it cannot be assumed that any particular individual needs to negotiate these stages in order to cope most effectively with impending death. The emotional responses and their dependent behaviours are indicators of the difficulties, and triumphs, experienced by people in their attempts to cope. The absence of a specific emotion does not mean that the person has omitted a necessary stage of the 'normal' coping pattern and that this omission detracts from the person's adjustment. Provided we do not equate 'typical' with 'ideal' or 'necessary', an awareness of the emotional stages or phases that are commonly encountered in terminal patients can help us to understand the problems they face, to provide the types of help and support that might be beneficial and to improve our ability to cope with the emotions that their behaviours arouse in relatives and in ourselves.

However, there are a number of general points that can be made about a stage model of terminal illness. The responses delineated, including denial, anger, bargaining, depression and acceptance (Kubler-Ross, 1969), are not specific to people who are facing death; they have been observed in many other stressful situations that involve loss and uncontrollable harm, such as bereavement, amputation and imprisonment. The generality evidenced by these observations does not confirm the progression of the stage model: it highlights the normality of disbelief, anger, sadness, etc., in the face of irretrievable and severe loss.

Often it is difficult to decide which stage or phase a person is in. Without reasonable certainty in the identification of stages, the predictive value of a stage model is severely impaired. This predictive aspect of the model is also reduced if the stages are not ubiquitous and if they are not successive. Clinical observation suggests that the emotion displayed by a person is responsive to many internal and external events. Perhaps all that can be said with any certainty is that some responses, when they occur, are likely to predominate earlier in a terminal illness, for example denial, and some are more likely to appear later, for example depression and acceptance.

We must take care not to lose sight of the individual in anticipating responses to a terminal illness. Fatally ill people bring with them their own particular views of themselves, their families, their futures, doctors, death, etc. The importance of individual differences during the terminal phase of life is well illustrated by the work of Kastenbaum and Weisman (1972). They found that their patients could be divided into two broad groups, both of which were aware of the imminence of death but which differed markedly in their behavioural styles. One group gradually withdrew from their usual activities and social contacts, remaining inactive until their final illness. The other group was characterized by involvement: patients in this group remained busily engaged in everyday activities until death occurred as an interruption in their living.

Dying

The relationship between a patient's reactions to a terminal illness and dying is not only that these are the psychological context within which the final process occurs, but also there are increasing indications that they influence the timing of death (see Achterberg and Lawlis, 1977). Whereas blood chemistries reflect on-going or current disease status, psychological factors are predictive of subsequent disease status and longevity. Poorer prognosis and shorter survival occurs in patients who, typically, show great dependence upon others, who deny the severity of their conditions, who have a history of poor social relationships and who do not have access to, or do not utilize, supportive social relationships during their illnesses. These patients tend to become more withdrawn, pessimistic and depressed as their illness progresses. Longer survival is associated with patients who maintain good personal and social relationships in the context of an existing network of such relationships. They can be assertive without hostility, asking for and receiving much medical and emotional support. They may be concerned about dying alone and seek to deter others from withdrawing from them without their needs being met. These patients also experience less pain, or at least complain less about pain and discomfort.

Dying is a process rather than an event that occurs at one point in time. This final process that constitutes the transition from life to death is usually of short duration, a matter of hours or days. For the vast majority of people it is not dramatic. Most people, both ill and well, express a desire to die peacefully or to die in their sleep. There is little doubt that this wish is fulfilled in most cases. Although there are a few people for whom pain or breathlessness may increase near the end, most slip knowingly or unawares into the unconsciousness that continues until their dying is finished.

After a terminal illness lasting some months, most patients are tired and wearied by their experiences. During their last days, apart from having their needs tended, patients may wish to be alone or to avoid news and problems of the 'outside world'. They may well become less talkative and prefer shorter visits. Communication tends to shift increasingly towards the non-verbal. In terms of interaction they may want little more than somebody to sit with them in silence, perhaps holding hands. It is clear from those who wish to talk briefly in their last hours of life that there is an experience of 'distance' from life. As Saunders (1978) so aptly puts it, 'They were not frightened nor unwilling to go, for by then they were too far away to want to come back. They were conscious of leaving weakness and exhaustion rather than life and its activities. They rarely had any pain but felt intensely weary. They wanted to say good-bye to those they loved but were not torn with longing to stay with them.'

Euthanasia

Euthanasia, meaning a gentle and easy death and the act of bringing this about, has been a source of discussion and controversy for many years. The level of current interest is evidenced by the large number of recent publications on the topic in the professional literature and the increasing support of the public for such organizations as the Voluntary Euthanasia Society in the UK and the Euthanasia Education Council in the USA.

The public support for euthanasia is probably based upon an expectation that death will come as a result of a lengthy illness, an illness that may well be prolonged unduly by the application of current medical knowledge and techniques. It is based upon fears of the physical and psychological incompetence, dependence, indignity and pain that may result from a chronic or terminal illness. Even those professionals who oppose euthanasia on ethical, religious or practical grounds readily concede that such fears are not unjustified for many people. We have already examined the potential distress of terminal illness but, for many people, support for euthanasia is prompted by thoughts of an unwanted, useless existence where biological life is maintained artificially and against their wishes in a hospital, nursing home or geriatric ward. Sadly, such thoughts are all too often reinforced by cases that Saunders (1977) rightly describes as 'truly horrendous'. As a society we cannot escape the reality that far too many elderly people end their days in loneliness, isolation and degradation. Even when the physical care provided is good, the psychological distress can be great. The prima facie case for euthanasia appears to be strong.

The many logical, philosophical and ethical arguments relating to the legalization of voluntary euthanasia, both active and passive, have been well stated several times (e.g. Rachels, 1975; Foot, 1978), and space precludes their consideration here. However, these arguments frequently take little account of relevant practical and psychological issues. In drawing up the necessary guidelines for the legalization of voluntary euthanasia there are major problems in guarding against error and potential abuse, both by relatives and professionals. Nevertheless, many of these problems could be surmounted by the use and recognition of the Living Will. This document, as distributed by the Euthanasia Educational Council, is signed and witnessed when the person is in good health. Its aim is to avoid an existence in dependence, deterioration, indignity and hopeless pain.

Doctors spend their lives preserving the lives of others and alleviating their suffering. It can be argued that, in recent years, the pendulum has swung too far in the direction of the maintenance of life at the expense of the relief of distress, but the activities of doctors make demands upon their energies and their personal time that few other professions would tolerate. This degree of commitment is consistent with, and continually reinforces, a value system that places a very high priority upon the preservation of life and actions that serve this end. For individuals in whom such values relate closely to their self-concepts, the active termination of life may be damaging to their self-regard and to their concept of their own worth as individuals. Although there is little difference between active and passive euthanasia on moral and logical grounds, for individual doctors the difference may be vast and unbridgeable in terms of their own psychology. It would be quite unjustifiable to place such men in a position where society expected them to implement active euthanasia.

From the patient's point of view, the availability of euthanasia has a wider potential than the avoidance of further suffering. People who are given control over aversive and painful stimulation, by having the facility to terminate, reduce or avoid it in some way, are better able to cope with the experience. Even though the available control is rarely exercised, the aversive stimulation is better tolerated and provokes less distress. Provided that patients are quite sure that their lives can be terminated when they wish, and only when they wish, they are likely to cope better with the effects of their illness or condition and to be less distressed.

To allow patients to die in order to release them from hopelessness and irreducible suffering, while continuing to treat their current distress, is thoroughly compatible with the humanitarian principle of care. Whether or not one wishes to describe this as passive, voluntary euthanasia is a matter of personal choice. There are grounds for a more widespread recognition of this compatibility and for more weight to be given to the wishes of patients and their families. Of course, the same grounds demand that more effort, time and resources should be devoted to improving the quality of care that is offered. All such improvements weaken the case for regarding death as a desirable release from suffering, as a release that is needed so frequently that its use should be regularized. In the long term, and certainly in the shorter term, there are likely to be some people for whom death is the preferred option. It is a problem that will become more acute as our society continues to age and as the life-preserving techniques of medicine continue to develop.

Bereavement

Bereavement is a state characterized by loss. The main focus of interest is upon the loss occasioned by the death of a significant person but people are bereaved by other losses such as loss of role, loss of status, separation and amputation. The state of loss serves as the stimulus for the bereavement response, a response that is manifested culturally and individually. The cultural response constitutes mourning and is a pattern of behaviour that is learned from and supported by one's immediate culture as appropriate following bereavement. Grief is the individual response and is the main area of concern for researchers and clinicians alike. In that grief typically follows a reasonably consistent course over time, ending ultimately in its resolution, it can be regarded as an individual process that occurs in response to individual loss.

The nature of grief

Although the major features of grief are known to most of us either intuitively or through personal experience, the chief findings of the many descriptive studies can be summarized broadly as follows:

* grief is a complex but stereotyped response pattern that includes such physical and psychological 'symptoms' as

withdrawal, fatigue, sleep disturbance, anxiety and loss
of appetite;
* it is elicited by a rather well-defined stimulus
situation, namely the real or imagined loss of a valued
object or role, and it is resolved when new object
relations are established;
* it is a ubiquitous phenomenon among human beings and
appears in other social species, especially higher
primates;
* it is an extremely stressful response both physically
and psychologically, but grief-related behaviour is
often antithetical to the establishment of new object
relations and hence to the alleviation of the stress.
For example, fatigue and withdrawal make it much more
difficult for the bereaved person to develop new roles
and new personal relationships in place of those lost
through bereavement.

The complexity and stress of grief is readily appreciated
when the number and nature of its components are considered. Hinton's (1972) description of grief adumbrates the
most commonly observed characteristics: shock, denial,
anxiety, depression, guilt, anger and a wide variety of
somatic signs of anxiety. Other components include searching
behaviour, suicidal thoughts, idealization of the lost person, panic, a heightened vulnerability to physical illness
and to psychological disorders.

The nature of grief as a process is emphasized by the
designation of stages by many observers and authors. Although there is a sequential character to the process it
would be incorrect to anticipate an orderly progression
through the stages in all people. As with the notion of
stages in dying that was discussed earlier, the component
responses of the various stages overlap and merge into one
another. Also, there are frequent 'regressions' to earlier
stages. Again, it is better to think in terms of components,
some of which will predominate earlier in the process and
others that will predominate later. In general, three stages
or phases have been delineated and labelled according to
inclination: perhaps the best descriptive labels are shock,
despair and recovery.

Initially there may be a period of numbness and detachment depending, to some extent, on the unexpectedness of
the news of the death. During this immediate response
people may appear stoical and calm. Normal routines may
be maintained especially where domestic or other factors
structure the situation. Alternatively, people may appear
dazed and quite unable to comprehend the reality of the
news; they may be unresponsive to their environment and in
need of care and support during this period. Whatever the
specific initial reaction in a particular instance, it can
last from a few minutes to two weeks or so, with the stoical reaction being the more likely to persist longer. The
bereaved person is less able than the terminally ill to deny

successfully the reality of the situation: sooner or later, and in many different ways, powerful and pointed signs of the reality of loss occur, such as the empty place at table, the empty bed or chair, the funeral or the silent house when friends and relatives depart. As with the news of terminal diagnosis, people need time to assimilate and to accommodate to a new state of the world. Whether the period of shock and disbelief is long or short, a sense of unreality or even disbelief is likely to return periodically for several months.

As awareness of the loss develops people may express anger at themselves, at staff or at God for not preventing the death. Whether or not anger is present, the phase of acute grieving or despair is the most painful. Lindemann (1944), in his pioneering study of bereavement, observed the following 'symptoms' as common to all individuals suffering acute grief: somatic distress lasting between 20 minutes and one hour at a time, feelings of tightness in the throat, choking with shortness of breath, muscular weakness and intense subjective distress described as tension or psychological pain. This specific response, which appears to be unique to bereavement, occurs against a background of stress, anxiety and sadness or depression, together with the somatic concomitants of these emotions.

Behaviourally, grieving persons may be unable to maintain goal-directed activity, appearing disorganized and unable to make plans. They may be restless, moving about in an aimless fashion and constantly searching for something to do. They may find themselves going, unwittingly, to the places where the dead person might be found if still alive. A preoccupation with the lost person creates a perceptual set that leads to misinterpretations of ambiguous sights and sounds as indicative of his being alive. Some grieving people report seeing the dead person with a clarity that goes beyond illusion and misperception. Such experiences can occur long after the phase of acute grieving is past. Obviously, the physical and psychological demands of this period are heavy and it is not surprising that irritability is common, especially when the person is eating and sleeping poorly. Anger, frustration and resentment may be directed at friends and neighbours irrespective of merit. Such feelings may also be directed against the dead person for abandoning the survivor.

The intense anguish of the despair phase can be unremitting, rising to peaks of distress with thoughts of the loved one who has died. Most bereaved people seem unable to prevent themselves from thinking and talking about the one who has died even though this usually exacerbates their distress. Whether this is conceptualized as 'grief-work' or as repeated exposure leading to habituation, it appears to be necessary to recovery from grief. A reduction in the frequency and intensity of periods of peak distress may be the first sign that the process of recovery is beginning. Although estimates vary, the acute despair phase of grief typically lasts for three to ten weeks.

The process of recovery from grief is a process of reconstruction. Although some aspects of the person's private and public 'self' may survive bereavement relatively unchanged, it is necessary to develop new roles, new behaviours and new relationships with others. Whatever else may or may not be changed by bereavement, the survivor must live without one important and potentially crucial personal relationship that had existed previously: the loss of this relationship is the loss of the psychological and practical advantages, and disadvantages, that it conferred. Socially, the survivor is now a widow or a widower rather than one of a married couple: he is now a boy without a father, or she is now a mother without a child, etc. Apart from the direct, personal impact of such changes, they also influence the way survivors are viewed and treated socially. The bereaved person has to develop a new private and public self that enables him to live in a changed world.

Although a reduction in the frequency and intensity of periods of extreme distress may herald the process of recovery, it cannot begin in earnest until there are periods in which the person is not overwhelmed with despair nor preoccupied with thoughts of the one who has died. Many bereaved people recall with clarity the moment when they realized that they had not been preoccupied with their loss: when, for a brief period at least, their thoughts had been directed elsewhere and their emotions had been less negative, even positive. These moments of 'spontaneous forgetting', together with improvements in sleeping and appetite, provide people with some opportunity to reconstrue and to reconstruct themselves and their futures. With less exhaustion and a lightening of mood, decisions and actions become more feasible and people can begin the active process of reviving previous relationships and activities, perhaps in a modified form, and of developing new ones. This period of active readjustment may never be complete, especially in the elderly, but it usually lasts for between six and 18 months after the phase of acute grief and despair.

Determinants of grief

Strictly speaking, it is inaccurate to talk of determinants of grief for the available data do not allow us to identify the causative factors that lead to variations in the response to bereavement. However, it makes intuitive sense to talk of determinants and is in keeping with other literature on the topic. Parkes (1972) groups the factors of potential importance according to their temporal relationship to the event of death, that is, antecedent, concurrent and subsequent determinants. Among antecedent factors, the most influential appear to be life stresses prior to bereavement, relationship with the deceased and mode of death. On the whole, an atypical grief response with associated psychological problems is more likely when bereavement occurs as one of a series of life crises, when the death is sudden, unanticipated and untimely, and when the relationship with the deceased had been one of strong attachment, reliance or ambivalence.

A number of demographic variables (concurrent) relate to the nature of grief. In particular, being young, female and married to the deceased increases the likelihood of problems arising after bereavement. Of course, these factors are not unrelated to such antecedent factors as strong attachment, reliance and untimely death. Other concurrent factors with adverse implications are susceptibility to grief, as evidenced by previous episodes of depression, an inability to express emotions, lower socio-economic status and the absence of a genuine religious faith.

The presence of religious faith might be placed more appropriately with subsequent determinants, for its role is likely to be one of supporting the bereaved person during the stressful period of grief. Also, someone with an active belief system probably will be associated with a supportive social group, and there is little doubt that a network of supportive social relationships is the most advantageous of the subsequent determinants. Other subsequent factors that have positive implications are the absence of secondary stresses during the period of grief and the development of new life opportunities at work and in interpersonal relationships, for instance. Again, these are more probable when a good network of supportive social relationships exists. It is worth recalling our earlier conclusion about the value of such relationships in a person's adjustment to impending death.

Among the wide range of factors that have implications for a person's reaction to bereavement, there is most controversy about the importance of anticipatory grief. As the term implies, this refers to grief that occurs in anticipation of an expected death, particularly the death of a child or a spouse. Overall, it can be concluded that younger widows experience more intense grief, with associated problems, than those aged 46 years or over. Sudden death exacerbates the severity of the grief response for young widows but not for the middle-aged or the elderly. For the latter two groups there appears to be a small effect in the opposite direction: that is, some symptoms of grief, especially irritability, are greater after a prolonged illness prior to death. It should be noted that the potentially beneficial effects of anticipatory grief are not confined to conjugal bereavement but also mitigate the response to other losses, such as that of a child. Also, it seems possible that there is an optimum period for the anticipation of death, perhaps up to six months, after which the lengthy duration of illness may increase stress and exhaustion and increase the likelihood of adverse reactions in subsequent grief.

Illness and death after bereavement

There are clear data that reveal an elevated mortality risk after bereavement. At all ages, bereaved persons experience a higher risk of dying than married people of corresponding sex and age. The increase in risk is greater for bereaved males than females, and for both sexes, the increase is greater at younger ages.

The elevated risk of death is concentrated particularly in the first six months after bereavement especially for widowers, with a further rise in the second year for widows. The predominant causes of death are coronary thrombosis and other arteriosclerotic or degenerative heart diseases. Most of these causes can be seen as a result of continued stress and a lack of self-care. In general, when the data from replicated studies in the UK and the USA are taken together, the risk of dying is at least doubled for widows and widowers at all ages for a great variety of diseases.

Having briefly examined the possible psychological and physical consequences of bereavement, and having considered relevant predictive factors, it is important to remember that we are talking only of probabilities. A person may be at great risk of problems following bereavement, in the statistical sense, and yet survive the experience well. Another person with only favourable indicators may suffer badly and experience severe physical or psychological problems.

The vast majority of bereaved people, with a little help from their friends, cope well with the experience and reconstruct lives that are worth while in their own terms. There are no persuasive grounds for considering the provision of professional services for the bereaved. The most useful strategy is to maintain some form of non-intrusive follow-up after bereavement with ready access to an informal support group if this should be necessary. The bereaved need somebody who will listen when they want to talk, somebody who will not try to push them into things before they are ready: somebody who will support them emotionally and practically when appropriate and just by showing that they care. This demands an informal response rather than a professional one. However, professional care and concern should not end with the death of a patient: the newly bereaved person still has a long way to go and every effort should be made to ensure that they will have access to whatever social support may be needed.

References

Achterberg, J. and Lawlis, G.F. (1977)
Psychological factors and blood chemistries as disease outcome predictors for cancer patients. Multivariate Experimental Clinical Research, 3, 107-122.

Cartwright, A., Hockey, L. and Anderson, J.L. (1973)
Life Before Death. London: Routledge & Kegan Paul.

Falek, A. and Britton, S. (1974)
Phases in coping: the hypothesis and its implications. Social Biology, 21, 1-7.

Foot, P. (1978)
Euthanasia. In E. McMullin (ed.), Death and Decision. Boulder, Co: Westview Press.

Gerle, B., Lunden, G. and Sandblow, P. (1960)
The patient with inoperable cancer from the psychiatric and social standpoints. Cancer, 13, 1206-1211.

Hinton, J.M. (1963)
The physical and mental distress of the dying. Quarterly Journal of Medicine, 32, 1-21.

Hinton, J.M. (1972)
Dying. Harmondsworth: Penguin.

Kastenbaum, R. and Weisman, A.D. (1972)
The psychological autopsy as a research procedure in gerontology. In D.P. Kent, R. Kastenbaum and S. Sherwood (eds), Research Planning and Action for the Elderly. New York: Behavioral Publications.

Kubler-Ross, E. (1969)
On Death and Dying. London: Tavistock.

Lindemann, E. (1944)
Symptomatology and management of acute grief. American Journal of Psychiatry, 101, 141-148.

Office of Population Censuses and Surveys (1979)
Mortality Statistics. London: HMSO.

Parkes, C.M. (1972)
Bereavement. London: Tavistock.

Rachels, J. (1975)
Active and passive euthanasia. New England Journal of Medicine, 292, 78-80.

Saunders, C. (1977)
Dying they live. In H. Feifel (ed.), New Meanings of Death. New York: McGraw-Hill.

Saunders, C. (1978)
Care of the dying. In V. Carver and P. Liddiard (eds), An Ageing Population. Sevenoaks: Hodder & Stoughton.

Schulz, R. and Aderman, D. (1974)
Clinical research and the stages of dying. Omega, 5, 137-143.

Spinetta, J.J. (1974)
The dying child's awareness of death. Psychological Bulletin, 81, 256-260.

Ward, A.W.M. (1974)
Telling the patient. Journal of the Royal College of General Practitioners, 24, 465-468.

Questions

1. How has the pattern of dying changed in the UK since the turn of the century? What has caused these changes and what are their consequences?
2. Who should be informed of a patient's fatal prognosis? Give reasons for your answer.
3. Summarize the most common sources of distress of the terminally ill and their families: what are the implications of these?
4. Why do terminally ill people become depressed and how large a problem is this?
5. How common is anxiety in terminal illness and why does it arise?

6. What psychological problems might arise for a fatally ill six-year-old child and his family? What steps could be taken to mitigate these problems?
7. Why should there be growing public support for the legalization of voluntary euthanasia and why is this not reflected in professional attitudes?
8. What is the bereavement response and what causes it?
9. What factors are important in influencing the nature of grief?
10. Construct a stereotypic, but detailed, character sketch of the person most likely to cope badly with a terminal illness: do the same for the person most likely to cope well. Justify your answer.

Annotated reading

Doyle, D. (ed.) (1979) Terminal Care. Edinburgh: Churchill-Livingstone.

This is a collection of papers arising from a multi-disciplinary conference. Accordingly, it provides useful reading for a wide range of health-care professionals including nurses, social workers and ministers of religion. In addition to examining the roles of different professions there are chapters on grief, domiciliary care and primary care.

Glover, J. (1977) Causing Death and Saving Lives. Harmondsworth: Penguin.

This is a clear and concise consideration of the ethical and practical problems associated with most aspects of taking life, from abortion to euthanasia. For those who want a brief but careful consideration of euthanasia and those who are seeking to place euthanasia in a wider context, this is a most valuable book.

Hinton, J. (1972) Dying. Harmondsworth: Penguin.

This is an eminently readable book by a psychiatrist with much practical experience of caring for the terminally ill and the dying. This experience enables Hinton to write with some authority on practical considerations and to place research findings in perspective. Relevant data are cited appropriately throughout the text and the book contains a good deal of useful information. The best sections are upon dying and the care of the dying and there is a concluding section on bereavement.

Kastenbaum, R.J. (1977) Death, Society and Human Experience. St Louis, Mo.: Mosby.

Written by a psychologist, but for a general readership, this book provides broad coverage of the psychological and social aspects of death at a level that is readily understood, without being unduly simplistic. Relevant data are cited together with many illustrative examples. A good deal of space is given to concepts of death, from childhood to old age, and there are sections on bereavement and suicide. A few exercises for students are also included.

Parkes, C.M. (1972) Bereavement. London: Tavistock.
This volume appeared in Pelican Books in 1975 and, although it is now beginning to age, it is probably the best single source of information on bereavement. The reader is taken progressively through the response to bereavement in its many manifestations and is provided with a clear account of grief, the factors that influence this and the nature of recovery. Illustrative examples and research findings are used throughout the text and the book concludes with a substantial section on helping the bereaved.

Russell, R.O. (1977) Freedom to Die. New York: Human Sciences Press.
Although the author examines arguments for and against the legalization of voluntary euthanasia, the tone of the volume is clearly in favour of this. The value of the book lies in its uncomplicated style, broad coverage and extensive appendices. In addition to examining the relevant arguments, the author traces the development of public awareness of euthanasia and attempts that have been made to promote the practice. The appendices include an example of the Living Will and various legislative proposals and bills that have been proposed in the UK and USA.

Smith, K. (1978) Helping the Bereaved. London: Duckworth.
This is a short and unpretentious book aimed at a general readership. It is valuable for its reliance on the statements of bereaved people to convey powerfully the experience of grief and the range of emotions and events that commonly occur. The examples help one more accurately to empathize with the bereaved.

8

Interviewing: the social psychology of the interview
Robert Farr

Opening remarks
FAY FRANSELLA

Interviewing is involved in every single one of your roles described in this book and probably many more besides. In the home and the ward you will be interviewing children, the ageing, the dying, the bereaved and the psychologically disturbed. You obviously have to do this before you can formulate any treatment programme. You have to discover their motivation or willingness to get well, their degree of pain, their interest and so on. You may interview in the process of carrying out research or in making a psychometric assessment; you will interview new students coming into your department, potential new staff members, other members of the therapeutic team and those to do with hospital administration; and, most importantly, you will conduct many interviews in your role as psychological therapist.

Although not mentioned in that long list, you 'as a person' are of vital importance in determining whether or not your interview will be successful. This chapter is central to virtually all the work that you do and you may therefore find Farr's account disquieting to begin with, showing as it does how much more there is to it than there appears to be at first sight. But I do recommend that you study it long and hard.

Introduction
ROBERT FARR

Interviewing is an everyday social phenomenon as well as being a widely used technique for gathering data both in professional practice and in social research. It is essentially a technique or method for establishing or discovering that there are perspectives or viewpoints on events other than those of the person initiating the interview. Those who work professionally in the media are accustomed to conducting interviews in the course of a day's work. Many thousands more listen to, view, or read about these self-same interviews. The interview is thus a common event, though many participate only vicariously in such encounters.

An interview is a social encounter between two or more individuals with words as the main medium of exchange. It is, in short, a peculiar form of conversation in which the ritual of turn-taking is more formalized than in the commoner and more informal encounters of everyday life. A conversation or interview is a co-operative venture. Despite the common assumptions that make conversations or talks possible, the interface between the individuals involved is always potentially present. When talks break down or conversation proves difficult this highlights the interface which is always potentially present within the inter-view. Conversations are embryonic interviews even though the participants might not so conceive of them. This general approach is compatible with the viewpoint adopted by Gorden (1975): 'I consider as an interviewer any person who uses conversation as a means of obtaining information from another person.'

The distinctive approach of this chapter

This chapter is intended to be an introduction to the social psychology of the inter-view. As such, it is a modest contribution to the development of a theory appropriate to the practice and conduct of interviews. There is, at present, no adequate theory in psychology of direct relevance to the practice of interviewing. This may surprise the reader. There is much advice offered and many guides are to be found in the literature as to how best to conduct interviews. There is also much research relevant to certain aspects of the interview, such as research in cognitive psychology on how we perceive persons (inspired by Heider's seminal work) and purely behavioural research on various aspects of non-verbal communication, etc. There is, however, no overall framework within which these theoretically opposed areas of research could be integrated with one another and made relevant to the practice of interviewing. We need theory in order to understand what goes on in the interview situation.

Any purely psychological theory is likely to be inadequate as the interview is so obviously a social encounter. Any adequate social psychology of the interview must enable us to account for the actions and experience both of the person being interviewed and of the person conducting the interview. Any theory of the interview which was not also at one and the same time a theory of the human self would be inadequate to the task in hand. Any theory which failed to account for states of awareness or consciousness in the parties to the interaction would similarly be inappropriate. We have sought to keep salient the inherently social nature of the interview by the simple expedient of using a hyphen: that is, by talking about inter-views rather than interviews, and similarly, inter-face and inter-action.

In devising an appropriate theory for the understanding of the interview we have drawn on Heider's psychology of interpersonal relations; on Goffman's work in sociology on the presentation of self in everyday life; on the work of Freud, in psychiatry, in devising a psychology based on listening rather than one based exclusively on visual observation; and on the philosophy of George Herbert Mead. While the influences derive from a number of disciplines the theory is an explicitly social psychological one. We have also found it convenient to adopt and adapt the divergence in perspective between actors and observers first noted by Jones and Nisbett in 1971. We have been impressed by the advantages which Becker and Geer (1957) claim for participant observation as a methodology over an exclusive reliance upon the interview alone. We have sought to include in this approach to the inter-view some of the advantages which Becker and Geer claim for participant observation. In our approach to the inter-view we are, therefore, influenced by the experience of social anthropologists and of sociologists.

The psychology of inter-personal relations

There is much that psychologists can learn from a study of the social psychology of everyday life. This is the viewpoint taken by the psychologist Fritz Heider (1958). He was particularly interested in how we perceive other persons and the evidence we use when we make inferences as to what is going on in the minds of those with whom we inter-act. He referred to the perceiver as P and the person whom he observes as O (i.e. the 'other'). The man-in-the-street does not hesitate to infer the attitudes, hopes, fears, motives, opinions, intentions, etc., of those with whom he inter-acts. Indeed, he is only intermittently aware that most of what he 'knows' about others is highly conjectural. The professional psychologist, however, is more acutely aware of the extent to which our knowledge of the minds of others involves our going beyond the information available; that is, it is based on inference rather than strictly on observation. We cannot directly 'observe' another's motives, intentions, aspirations, attitudes, and so on.

Heider's psychology of inter-personal relations is highly relevant to the inter-view situation. While Man is seldom aware that most of his knowledge of others is based on conjecture, he is sometimes acutely aware that what others know about him is highly conjectural. This is particularly true in the inter-view situation. The persons being interviewed (i.e. the interviewees) are only too well aware that the other (i.e. the interviewer) is likely to be making inferences concerning their motives, intentions, etc., on the basis of what they say and do in the interview.

Heider was primarily concerned with how P perceives O. In common with many other psychologists Heider's primary interest was in what we can learn about others by observing them from the outside. O, however, need not remain silent in the presence of P. O can talk about, or 'reveal', opinions, attitudes, aspirations, motives, hopes, fears and so on. The interview is the technique par excellence for eliciting such self-reports. When O speaks, a perspective other than that of P is revealed. P and O engage in conversation while the unique perspective of each is retained. This difference in perspective between them helps to produce an inter-view in the literal sense of that term.

An interview is also a form of social encounter between persons. Heider set out to devise a psychology of interpersonal relations. It is worth reflecting briefly on what we understand by the word 'person'. The philosopher Strawson considered it to be a characteristic of persons that they can monitor their own actions and give an 'account' of them (see Harré and Secord, 1972). We are accustomed in everyday life to accounting for our actions. Persons have names. When we know people's names we can address them as individuals rather than needing to hail them as strangers. They are 'accountable' and normally 'respond' when others address them. In the technical literature relating to the interview as a research tool in social science, the person being interviewed is normally referred to as the 'respondent'. Persons readily respond to being inter viewed because it is a constituent part of their everyday social experience. It is not an alien or obtrusive mode of investigation.

The divergence in perspective between actors and observers

Heider introduced us to the perspective of P, the observer or perceiver. An actor is any person whose behaviour is currently the focus of attention. In the language of drama which suffuses the writing of Goffman, the actor is the person who is currently 'on stage'. Jones and Nisbett (1971) note an important divergence in perspective between actors and observers: 'There is a pervasive tendency for actors to attribute their actions to situational requirements, whereas observers tend to attribute the same actions to stable personal dispositions' (Jones and Nisbett, 1971). Actors are more likely to consider their actions to be situationally appropriate whilst observers are more likely to make inferences about the sort of person an actor is on the basis of observable actions.

The awareness of actors that they are objects in the social worlds of others leads them to become 'apprehensive' as to how those others might evaluate them. The actors are here clearly aware of the divergence in perspective between themselves and the observing others. Too acute an awareness of this may cause an inter-viewee to perform poorly. For the chronically shy this is likely to be a particular problem. A certain measure of self-confidence is necessary if a person is to create a favourable impression in the inter-view situation. In his description of the art of impression management, Goffman (1959) makes telling use of the metaphor of the theatre. In his everyday presentation of himself, Man as an actor is putting on a 'performance' for a particular audience. The audience may be the 'other' with whom he is inter-acting. This obviously is the case in the typical inter-view. Goffman describes action in terms of its relation to the observing and listening other: that is, his conception of the audience is critical to his portrayal of action. This is why he is so much more genuinely socio-psychological in his approach than any mere psychologist could be. This is an important contribution to an understanding of the dynamics of the inter-view.

Goffman notes that the mirror is one of the most useful devices to be found backstage in any theatre. The mirror enables an actor to become an object to himself before he goes 'on stage' and becomes an object to others. In preparing for inter-views candidates often find mirrors to be similarly useful. The work of Goffman beautifully illustrates why a theory of the human self is necessary in order to understand what occurs in the inter-view. We also believe that an adequate analysis of the nature of human consciousness is an essential ingredient in any theory which purports to shed significant light on what occurs in the course of an inter-view. Mead's theory of action provides us with the necessary theory both of human consciousness and of the human self.

We have drawn on the work of Goffman for an account of human action and for his portrayal of Man as agent or actor; and on the work of Heider for his delineation of the perspective of Man as an observer of others. We are indebted to Jones and Nisbett for suggesting that these two perspectives might be different. It is worth considering how we might apply their distinction to accounting for differing views of the same actions. In a series of experimental studies, Milgram (1974) obtained high levels of obedience to an experimental request to administer what the subject believed to be high levels of electric shock to a fellow subject. Those who complied with the experimental request regarded their actions as being entirely appropriate in the particular experimental setting in which they occurred. This is the perspective of Jones and Nisbett's 'actor'.

The majority of subjects in Milgram's experiment would reject the inference which any who observed their acts of obedience might have made about them as persons on the basis of their actions. That this is so is revealed in an interesting variation on his main theme which Milgram later introduced. He described his experiment to a number of subjects whom he then invited to respond by saying how they would act in this situation. This is more akin to the hypothetical questions which persons being inter-viewed are often invited to consider. Indeed, this particular study was an inter-view rather than being an experiment in any strict sense of the term. The actual task in the original experiment involved increasing the level of shock administered, by way of punishment, to a subject in a learning task each time he made a mistake. Few subjects in this hypothetical situation saw themselves as advancing much beyond the earlier low levels of shock on the generator. It was almost as if there were different 'selves' for each button on the shock generator. In considering how they would act, subjects were able to reject the selves corresponding to the buttons at the 'high shock' end of the generator. They were thus able to consider what they would think of themselves if they were to press each of these buttons. This 'pause for reflection' enabled subjects to adopt the perspective of being an observer of their own hypothetical actions. They were thus able to inter-act with themselves. This is a process which the philosopher, G. H. Mead, called thinking.

In the analysis of Jones and Nisbett, actor and observer are two different persons. The actual face-to-face encounter of the inter-view, however, produces social states of awareness which are infinitely more complex and subtle than those envisaged by Jones and Nisbett. These more complex states of awareness arise because each of the interactants in an inter-view is both an actor and an observer and each is capable of alternating between these two perspectives.

The demise of the interview as a way of assessing persons and the rise of the psychological test: a brief historical note

Humans are liable to 'react' to the knowledge that their actions are being observed. If the very act of investigating behaviour alters what is there to be observed, then the techniques of investigation used can be described as 'reactive' (Webb, Campbell, Schwartz and Sechrest, 1966). The interview is clearly a highly 'reactive' way of appraising people. The inter-view, as proposed in this chapter, is even more explicitly 'reactive' than the commoner and more conventional varieties of the same species. Psychologists, early in the history of their discipline, rejected the interview as a valid way of assessing either the intelligence of children or the suitability of adults for jobs. At the time this rejection was hailed as an important scientific advance. It is worth briefly considering why this was so.

The amount of information potentially present in the face-to-face encounter of an interview is liable to overwhelm even the most experienced of interviewers. Different interviewers sample from the available evidence differently. They use and combine the information they do select in highly impressionistic or subjective ways. Psychologists were quick to prove their worth by reducing the amount of 'noise' (i.e. irrelevant information) present in the appraisal setting. Rather than ranging over the whole gamut of information potentially available they instead preferred to 'tune in' to information transmitted on much narrower wavebands. This information could be collected under quite rigorously controlled conditions. The psychological test yielded much more precise information and this information could be combined objectively in ways which research had demonstrated to be valid. This is how the psychological test - or rather a battery of such tests - came to supersede the interview as the preferred way of assessing persons.

It is worth briefly noting certain aspects of this early critique of the interview. The origins of the doubts which still linger on in the minds of psychologists concerning the validity of the interview can be found in the very success of this early critique. This is one reason why psychologists so far have done so little to improve the interview as a method of investigation. Eysenck (1953) presents a convenient account:

One of the earliest investigations of the interview is reported by Binet, the creator of modern intelligence tests. Three teachers interviewed the same children and estimated the intelligence of each. These estimates were based on the results of an interview conducted by each teacher as he saw fit. Binet reports two outcomes of this experiment which have since been verified over and over again. Each interviewer was confident that his judgement was right. Each interviewer disagreed almost completely with the judgement of the other interviewers.

This was the kind of evidence which highlighted, at an early stage, the unreliability of the interview as an appraisal device. The failure amongst interviewers to agree in their judgements led to the development of standardized tests. Here psychologists were quite consciously adopting a scientific perspective: that of being the detached observer of others. In commenting on the significance of Binet's first conclusion concerning the confidence with which each interviewer held his judgement, Eysenck notes that this 'explains why, in spite of all the factual information regarding its inadequacy, the interview has remained the firm favourite of most people who have to select personnel for industrial and other purposes' (Eysenck, 1953). Here interviewers are behaving like Jones and Nisbett's 'actors': that is, they see their actions as being situationally appropriate. Eysenck neatly captures the difference in perspective noted above between the 'actor' (i.e. the interviewer as agent) and the 'observer' (i.e. the scientist who 'validates' the predictive accuracy of the interviewer's judgements).

Interviewers, naturally, feel that their actions are justifiable and so seek to maintain their autonomy even in the face of scientific evidence:

> Time and time again does one encounter the individual who admits all the evidence about the inadequacy of the interview but stoutly maintains that he or she is the one outstanding exception to this general rule, and that his or her opinions are almost invariably correct. (Needless to say, experimental studies of such individuals fail to disclose any greater ability to forecast success and failure among them than is found among other people) (Eysenck, 1953).

This very human tendency to consider oneself to be an exception may derive from the unique perspective of the 'actor'. Kay (1971) has noted a similar tendency with respect to the occurrence of accidents. Individuals find it difficult to conceive of themselves as having an accident. However, scientists, as observers of others, can afford from the greater distance of their own quite different perspectives to be more sceptical. From this perspective, accidents do not just 'happen': they are caused.

The early pioneers of psychological tests who so readily dismissed the interview as a valid way of assessing people were bewitched by the magic of measurement. Their perspective was that of being a scientific observer of others. Their basic strategy was to standardize the conditions under which they made their observations and then to attribute all of the variance in observed performance to the existence of individual differences. In so doing, they unwittingly adopted the perspective of Jones and Nisbett's 'observer': that is, on the basis of test scores they inferred the existence of 'traits', 'abilities', 'attitudes', etc., as relatively permanent dispositions in those whom they observed or tested.

The social antecedents of mind and self: the philosophy of G. H. Mead

Our sense of our own 'selfhood' has its origin in the experience of interacting with others within the framework of a shared culture and of a common language. This was the viewpoint of the American philosopher, G. H. Mead, who developed a form of social behaviourism at Chicago in the opening decades of the present century (Mead, 1934). Mead understood the symbolic nature of language and its key role in the development and creation of 'mind' in Man.

The model of Man which emerges from the writings of Mead is one of Man as being both speaker and listener. The social behaviourism of Mead is thus more directly relevant to an understanding of the dynamics of inter-viewing than are any of the forms of behaviourism which developed within psychology. Our own approach in this chapter to the dynamics of inter-viewing is much influenced by the work of Mead. Man, according to Mead, is self-reflexive; that is, he is self-aware as distinct from being merely conscious. Consciousness is something which Man shares with other species. Self-consciousness is a distinctly human state of mind. Man is unique as a species in that he can act towards himself as an object. He can do so because he is an object in the social world of those others with whom he interacts. By 'assuming the role of the other' (Mead) with respect to himself, he becomes an 'other' to himself. Man can thus engage himself in inter-action. When he does so we refer to this activity as thinking. Thinking, for Mead, was a kind of internalized dialogue between 'I' and various 'me's. We have already noted above how some of the subjects in Milgram's experiment engaged in such internalized dialogues.

A theory of the human self is needed if we are to understand the dynamics of the inter-view. The meaning of an act for Mead was to be found in the response which it elicits from observing others. Man not only acts but also re-acts to his own actions. He reacts to his own behaviour on the basis of the actual or anticipated reactions of others.

These processes of action and of reaction are highly characteristic of what happens in the course of an interview. Individuals will often anticipate in imagination a formal interview, in the outcome of which they have a personal stake. They may rehearse what they intend to say and do and they may anticipate likely questions which might be asked. After the event they are also likely to 're-enact' what actually occurred in the course of the interview. Sometimes these re-enactments are purely 'private' ones which they carry out solely for their own benefit. Sometimes they are more explicitly social in that they are 'accounts' which the individual provides for others as to what occurred in the course of the interview. Without an adequate theory of the human self the psychologist could not possibly give a coherent account of these important mental events which both precede and follow the interview proper. These fairly familiar experiences can be accounted for, given a theory of the inherently social nature of the mind of Man. Mead provides just such a theory.

Mead developed a purely behavioural account of the origins of mind in Man: a theory of the human self. He also shed important new light on the social nature of 'perspectives'. As children develop, according to Mead, they learn to 'assume the role of the other' with respect to themselves. These social skills are first acquired in role-playing and are then further developed in the playing of games. Commercial transactions, such as those which were of interest to Adam Smith, depend for their success on the reciprocal ability of buyer and seller to assume each other's role. Those who excel in interviewing, either as interviewers or as interviewees, are adept at assuming each other's role in the interview situation.

In his later writings, Mead was much influenced by Einstein. He preferred to talk of 'assuming the perspective' of the other instead of his earlier preference for 'assuming the role' of the other. For Mead these 'perspectives' were objectively real: that is, they represented points in space/time from which one could view events. It was, therefore, entirely possible to change one's perspective by the simple expedient of changing one's position in space/time. It is thus possible both literally and metaphorically to 'turn the tables' and for interviewers and interviewees to 'exchange places'. Successful interviewees already do this mentally in preparing themselves for an interview. Poor interviewers may experience much difficulty in imagining such an exchange of roles or places. Role-playing exercises and the techniques of self-confrontation (e.g. where interviewers watch a videotape of themselves actually conducting an interview) are now increasingly used in the training of interviewers. If the theoretical approach developed in the present chapter is a sound one then such training devices are well-founded.

Observing, questioning and listening: interpreting what we see and hear

Goffman belonged to that important tradition of social psychological thought at Chicago which drew at least some of its inspiration from the work of Mead. In referring to the social interactions of everyday life, Goffman had this to say: 'Many crucial facts lie beyond the time and place of interaction, or lie concealed within it' (1959). This is particularly true of the interview. One fails to grasp the significance of what is happening in an interview if one's attention is confined, in the interest of science, only to what can be directly observed from the outside.

Psychologists, when they accepted behaviourism, came to value what they could see and measure over what they could hear. It was only too easy to overlook the significance of something as invisible to the human eye as speech. In their attempts to make psychology a branch of natural science, the early pioneers stressed the physical rather than the symbolic nature of stimuli. Speech was thought of in terms of sound waves: as changes in the patterns of energy impinging on the human ear. The outcome of collaboration between psychologists and telecommunications engineers was the development within psychology of information theory as a specialism. To reduce language to 'information' as the human engineer uses that term is to destroy something distinctly human. In order properly to appreciate the significance of speech in human development it would first have been necessary to understand the symbolic nature of language. Only a philosopher like Mead would be likely to ask such a preliminary question.

If, instead of observing the actions of others one listens to them talking, one arrives at a totally different type of psychology. Freud established a whole new psychology based entirely upon listening. It is called psychoanalysis. As a theory about human behaviour, psychoanalysis was born and developed within the context of the clinical interview. Rather than visually exploring the natural world as a research physiologist, which was Freud's early training, he became instead, reluctantly, a practising clinician. He spent hours listening to his clients talking about themselves and their problems.

The difference in perspective between speaker and listener in Freud's consulting room gave birth to a psychology of the unconsciousness. There were aspects of the analysand's 'account' of his own actions which were more apparent to the listener than to the speaker. Listener and speaker were here two separate persons. Speakers are less likely to be aware of the non-verbal aspects of their own accounts than listeners. 'Actors' generally are unaware of their own non-verbal behaviour. Non-verbal cues are more salient to the observers/listeners than they are to the actors themselves. The study of non-verbal behaviour is a significant contribution to an understanding of the interview which flows from the perspective of the behaviourist as an observer of others. Behaviourists tend to note or record this behaviour rather than to 'interpret' it. It is worth quoting Freud (1905) on this issue:

> When I set myself the task of bringing to light what human beings keep hidden within them, not by the compelling power of hypnosis, but by observing what they say and what they show I thought the task was a harder one than it really is. He that has eyes to see and ears to hear may convince himself that no mortal can keep a

secret. If the lips are silent, he chatters with his finger tips; betrayal oozes out of him at every pore. And thus the task of making conscious the most hidden recesses of the mind is one which it is quite possible to accomplish.

The difference in perspective between analyst and analysand (i.e. the person undergoing analysis) may have important therapeutic implications. It corresponds to the difference in perspective between actors and observers previously noted. In seeking therapy the analysand might consider himself to be the victim of circumstances; for instance, as being, like King Lear, 'more sinned against than sinning'. The therapist, however, may not accept this 'account'. Therapists usually make the opposite attributional assumption: that is, they see the analysand as being the cause of their own problems. It is possible to consider psychoanalysis as a protracted negotiation of the analysand's original account by two persons who initially make opposite attributional assumptions.

Psychoanalysis, however, is not held in high esteem within scientific circles. As a science based on listening rather than one founded on observation, it is highly marginal within the context of natural science. It is, at one and the same time, both an odd kind of psychology and an odd kind of medicine. Its oddity in both respects may reflect, in part, a strong preference for vision over hearing as the preferred modality of research in both psychology and medicine.

Within psychology, behaviourists sought to make their discipline a branch of natural science by concentrating on what they could observe rather than by striving to understand what they could hear. Watson and Skinner typify this general strategy while Freud remains a striking, but solitary, example of someone who chose the latter alternative. There could scarcely be a more marked contrast than the one between behaviourism and psychoanalysis. This contrast is further mirrored in the differences between behaviour therapy and psychotherapy. In the former one 'treats' people, whilst in the latter one interviews them. In the former one removes 'symptoms', whilst in the latter one 'interprets' them.

The question of interpretation is an important one for the professional interviewer. Freud, in his early clinical interviews, listened to his clients relating how, as young girls, they had been seduced by their own fathers. He was inclined, at first, to believe in the truth of these accounts. When the number of such incidents, of which he had heard tell, came to greatly exceed his own prior expectations concerning the likelihood of such events occurring in Viennese society, he dramatically changed his interpretation of these 'accounts'. His decision to interpret these accounts as fantasy rather than as reflecting reality had dramatic consequences for the subsequent development of psychoanalysis. He was forced to distinguish between fantasy and reality and to oppose the pleasure to the reality principle. This was how he resolved his obligations as an interviewer to indicate the level of reality to which his observations referred.

There are two opposing dangers which threaten to ensnare the unwary social scientist. The first is to believe that he does not need to ask questions in order to establish the veracity of what he can observe for himself. The asking of questions helps to establish the existence of perspectives other than that of the investigator who has initiated the study. This leads to the establishment of an inter-view. There are a number of professional groups whose work directly involves them in observing and recording behaviour, yet who only rarely conduct interviews in the conventional sense of the term, such as nurses and classroom teachers. The written reports of these professional groups, summarizing their observations of behaviour on the wards or in the classroom, are often included as background information on the basis of which others, elsewhere in the organization, conduct clinical or educational interviews. However, persons in the higher reaches of these professions (nursing and teaching) almost certainly spend a great deal of their time interviewing in the more conventional sense of the term. This is probably true of almost anyone in a position of managerial responsibility. When a nurse on the ward, or a teacher in the classroom, asks questions in order to clarify or to verify what they observe, they are engaging in the process of inter-viewing as that term is used in this chapter. This is also true of the manager or supervisor in industry. The process of inter-viewing as outlined here is just such a process of checking on the veracity of one's observations. It is, therefore, a wider process of research than the interview as conventionally conceived. Failure to supplement and verify what one can observe by the asking of questions results in one type of error: that is, the limitations and biasses inherent in one's perspective as an observer are not subject to any process of cross-checking and hence one remains blind to them. A different sort of error arises if one accepts at face value the 'accounts' one elicits. In relation to the work of Herzlich on people's conceptions of health and illness (Herzlich, 1973) and of Herzberg on the nature of work motivation, Farr has identified some of the consequences that can flow from a too uncritical acceptance of what people say in the course of an unstructured or semi-structured research interview (Farr, 1977a,b).

Harré and Secord (1972) advocate the collection of 'accounts' as a brave new methodology for research in psychology. They base their case on Strawson's criterion of a person as being someone who can monitor his own behaviour and give an account of it. Collecting 'accounts' is thus equivalent to treating people as people. 'In order to be able to treat people as if they were human beings it must be possible to accept their commentaries upon their actions as authentic, though revisable, reports of phenomena, subject to empirical criticism' (Harré and Secord, 1972). If their plea were heeded then the interview would become the privileged mode of research in psychology, much as the experiment has been in the past and is still currently. The inter-view, as outlined here, might be more defensible from a scientific point of view, as it highlights the fact that the perspectives of researcher and informant are different and so sensitizes one to the possibility that important consequences might flow from this divergence in perspective.

Harré and Secord's proposal is not a particularly revolutionary one. Social psychologists traditionally have relied upon the collection of just such self-reports. This reflects the influence of Gestalt psychologists on the historical development of social psychology. Gestalt psychologists were interested in the study of perception. In order to explain a person's behaviour it was first necessary, in the opinion of Gestalt psychologists, to understand how that person perceived the world. The best way of finding out about a person's unique perspective, of course, is to invite him to tell you about it. You can best establish that his perspective is different from your own by means of an interview. Behaviourists, by directly relating aspects of the physical environment to observable responses, had completely by-passed perception as an important field of study.

In the study of attitudes the 'view of the world' approach which stems from Gestalt psychology came to prevail over the 'consistency of response' approach associated with behaviourism (see Campbell, 1963). To date, in the history of psychology, either the one or the other of these two perspectives has prevailed. How to inter-relate two such contrasting perspectives is perhaps the most interesting single problem which psychologists now face. By studying attitudes, social psychologists had hoped to avoid the laborious task of noting consistencies in a person's response to his social environment. The relationships between what people say and what they do turn out to be rather tenuous. These findings continue to pose problems for the social psychologist (see Deutscher, 1973). They also pose problems for the professional interviewer. Can one accept at face value what people say? Or does one have to 'interpret' what they tell you? Can one accept oral accounts obtained in interviews as a basis for predicting behaviour in contexts other that that of the interview? Can a knowledge of a person's 'attitudes' help us to predict his behaviour?

Harré and Secord contend that one does not have to accept 'accounts' at face value. They can be 'negotiated'. Here the inter-face within the inter-view enables one to question the face validity of any particular account. The co-existence of more than one perspective helps to ensure that work gets done in the course of the inter-view. The perspective of the interviewer is always different from that of the interviewee. This divergence in perspective is an adequate basis on which to negotiate. Work on inter-views needs to be integrated with work on inter-actions. We have noted above, more than once, how rarely an actor's view of his own

actions corresponds to an observer's view of those same
actions. Individuals may remain blissfully unaware of all
that they communicate in the course of an interview. Goffma:
observed that impressions are 'given off' as well as 'managed'. One could view psychoanalytic theory as an elaborate
set of rules for 'interpreting' the significance of a person's words and actions, especially those which occur in
the course of therapy. Whilst most interviewers would agree
with the truth of Goffman's observation, quoted earlier,
that 'many crucial facts lie beyond the time and place of
interaction, or lie concealed within it', few have need to
draw on 'depth' psychologies such as psychoanalysis in order
to interpret what they hear and observe. Good interviewers,
however, listen not only to what persons choose to talk
about but also to what they may not want to talk about or
cannot say without help.

The recent explosion of research on non-verbal behaviour
is of considerable relevance to the practice of interviewing
(e.g. Weitz, 1974; Argyle, 1975; Ekman and Friesen, 1975).
It accurately reflects the perspective of the outside observer on the behaviour of others. Much of the classic literature on interviewing is highly 'cognitive' in tone and is
now rather dated (Cannell and Kahn, 1968). It tends to
reflect the perspective of the interviewer as 'actor': that
is, presenting the rationale for conducting interviews in
particular ways. Having to sample, in the writing of this
chapter, from two such separate, but unrelated, literatures
has not been an easy task. The fact that the two literatures
are unrelated testifies to the absence of a relevant theory
on the basis of which they might be integrated. Much recent
research of a purely behavioural nature (e.g. on non-verbal
aspects of social interaction), while highly relevant to
the practice of interviewing, has not yet been satisfactorily integrated into the literature on interviewing. We
would claim that this failure in integration reflects the
absence of an appropriate theory of the interview. It is
highly artificial, in practice, to distinguish between
inter-views and inter-actions. For the theory and practice
of inter-viewing it is necessary to understand both: hence
the priority we accord in this chapter to the development of
suitable theory. My approach to theory is a very Lewinian
one; there is nothing so practical as a good theory.

The model of the observer favoured in psychological
circles is that of the detached and objective scientist.
The role of psychologists in relation to selection is often
of this nature: they are usually to be found at several
removes from the face-to-face encounter between assessors
and candidates at the point of selection. There are, of
course, important exceptions such as Civil Service Selection
Boards, where psychologists are actively involved in conducting interviews. The model of the observer which pre-
vails more widely in social science is a more active one;
the researcher is often a participant observer. Becker and
Geer (1957), in what is now a classic paper, argue that

participant observation is a more complete method of research than the interview used alone: 'Participant observation can thus provide us with a yardstick against which to measure the completeness of data gathered in other ways, a model which can serve to let us know what orders of information escape us when we use other methods' (Becker and Geer, 1957).

By participant observation Becker and Geer mean 'that method in which the observer participates in the daily life of the people under study, either openly in the role of researcher or covertly in some disguised role, observing things that happen, listening to what is said, and questioning people, over some length of time'. Inter-viewing as outlined in this chapter is virtually synonymous with Becker and Geer's characterization of participant observation.

This wider conception of the inter-view enables us to encompass professional groups who rarely interview in the conventional sense: for instance, classroom teachers, nurses, supervisors in industry, etc. The skills involved in participant observation are akin to those which a social anthropologist might employ. The seminal work of Goffman, which is highly relevant to an understanding of the dynamics of inter-viewing, is largely based on participant observation; for example, his studies of the under-life of mental institutions (Goffman, 1961) or his study of life in the Hebrides (Goffman, 1959). One can observe and ask questions about what one has observed. One can test out that one has correctly learnt the native language by trying it out in the presence of skilled users of that language. This is synonymous with the process of inter-viewing as outlined here.

We have previously noted the distinction which Jones and Nisbett make between the perspective of the actor and the perspective of the observer. Participant observation preserves both perspectives within the one methodology, as does inter-viewing. The observer is an actor in so far as he is also a participant in the scene he observes. In inter-viewing the participants alternate between the roles of actor and of observer, of speaker and of listener. Observers and inter-viewers, if they are to be effective, need to be conscious of their own actions and of the effects of these on those whom they are observing or interviewing. This awareness of being an 'object' in the social world of the 'other' is enhanced by the face-to-face nature of the inter-view situation. The mechanisms of gaze and mutual gaze help to maintain this duality of awareness in being both observer and observed (Argyle and Cook, 1976). This social psychology of the inter-view applies equally well both to inter-viewers and to inter-viewees.

It is easy to be aware of one's 'other-ness' when the person whom one is observing or inter-viewing comes from a different culture from one's own. This is the typical experience of the social anthropologist. Becker and Geer trenchantly note that persons within the one culture often inhabit

different social worlds but that this is not always recognized. There is much merit, in their eyes, in approaching
the social worlds of others in much the same way as a social
anthropologist approaches a strange culture.

> In interviewing members of groups other than our own,
> then, we are in somewhat the same position as the
> anthropologist who must learn a primitive language, with
> the important difference that, as Ichheiser has put it,
> we often do not understand that we do not understand and
> are thus likely to make errors in interpreting what is
> said to us (Becker and Geer, 1957).

This inter-face is more explicitly recognized in the literature on participant observation than it is in the literature
on interviewing. We have tried to introduce into the literature on interviewing some of the advantages of participant
observation by choosing, on occasion, to distinguish between
inter-viewing and interviewing.
Becker and Geer are critical of the interview 'when it
is used as a source of information about events that have
occurred elsewhere and are described to us by informants'.
We noted above the problems Freud faced in regard to esti-
mating the likely incidence of incest in Viennese society.
Becker and Geer continue:

> In working with interviews, we must necessarily infer a
> great many things we could have observed had we only
> been in a position to do so. We add to the accuracy of
> our data when we substitute observable fact for
> inference. More important, we open the way for the
> discovery of new hypotheses for the fact we observe may
> not be the fact we expected to observe.

It may be that it is only through the process of inter-
viewing that Man develops an awareness of the social world
of others. It is only through Piaget's brilliant use of the
inter-view that we are today as aware of just how different
the world of the child is from the world of the adult (Farr,
1982). Adults often falsely assume, because they were children once themselves, that they therefore understand the
world of a child. By the simple device of inter-viewing
Piaget made quite explicit the many different ways in which
the world of the child and the world of the adult failed to
coincide. Thanks to Piaget, many teachers-in-training become
sensitive to such differences before they encounter children
face-to-face in the classroom.

**Postscript on industrial
psychology**

A good deal is known in industrial psychology about the
behaviour of candidates in selection contexts and the
experience of assessors, for example, advice concerning how
best to conduct interviews, etc. Here again, there is the
same dichotomy between the perspective of the observer and
the perspective of the 'actor'. The time is now ripe to

redress this imbalance in our current knowledge by studying the behaviour of assessors and sampling the experience of candidates within selection contexts. Such additional information could significantly contribute to the emergence of a social psychology of selection which would be highly compatible with the dynamics of inter-viewing as outlined in this chapter. The recognition of the existence of more than one viewpoint or perspective is quite explicit in the notion of the inter-view. At present we know very little about the perspective of candidates within selection contexts.

The classic approach in selection is to collect standardized data about candidates by means of psychological tests, the results of which are then entered into a decision formula based on a regression analysis. The outcome is an 'institutional' decision. The candidate either is or is not offered a job. Such 'objective' test data could, however, be analysed in relation to the candidate's own response to the system either at the time of selection or subsequently on receiving a job offer. Are the inferences that candidates might make about their suitability for a particular job radically different from those which the organization might make concerning their suitability? This is a question which only research can resolve. We have presented evidence elsewhere on the possible use of self-appraisal within a selection context (Downs, Farr and Colebeck, 1978).

References

Argyle, M. (1975)
Bodily Communications. London: Methuen.
Argyle, M. and Cook, M. (1976)
Gaze and Mutual Gaze. Cambridge: Cambridge University Press.
Becker, H.S. and Geer, B. (1957)
Participant observation and interviewing: a comparison. Human Organization, 16, 28-32. Reprinted in G. McCall and J. Simmons (eds), Issues in Participant Observation: A text and readings. Reading, Mass.: Addison-Wesley.
Campbell, D.T. (1963)
Social attitudes and other acquired behavioral dispositions. In S. Koch (ed.), Psychology: A study of a science, Volume 6. New York: McGraw-Hill.
Cannell, C.F. and Kahn, R.L. (1968)
Interviewing. In G. Lindzey and E. Aronson (eds), Handbook of Social Psychology (2nd edn), Volume 2. Reading, Mass.: Addison-Wesley.
Deutscher, I. (1973)
What we say/What we do: Sentiments and acts. Glenview, Ill.: Scott, Foresman & Co.
Downs, S., Farr, R.M. and Colebeck, L. (1978)
Self-appraisal: A convergence of selection and guidance. Journal of Occupational Psychology, 51, 271-278.
Ekman, P. and Friesen, W.V. (1975)
Unmasking the Face: A guide to recognizing emotions from facial clues. Englewood Cliffs, NJ: Prentice-Hall.

Eysenck, H.J. (1953)
Uses and Abuses of Psychology. Harmondsworth: Penguin.

Farr, R.M. (1977a)
Heider, Harré and Herzlich on health and illness: some observations on the structure of 'représentations collectives'. European Journal of Social Psychology, 7, 491-504.

Farr, R.M. (1977b)
On the nature of attributional artifacts in qualitative research: Herzberg's two-factor theory of work motivation. Journal of Occupational Psychology, 50, 3-14.

Farr, R.M. (1982)
Social worlds of childhood. In V. Greaney (ed.), The Rights of Children. New York: Irvington Publications.

Freud, S. (1905)
Fragments of an analysis of a case of hysteria. In The Standard Edition of the Complete Psychological Works of Sigmund Freud (1953), Volume 7. London: Hogarth Press.

Goffman, E. (1959)
The Presentation of Self in Everyday Life. New York: Doubleday.

Goffman. E. (1961)
Asylums: Essays on the social situations of mental patients and other inmates. New York: Anchor Books.

Gorden, R.L. (1975)
Interviewing: Strategy, techniques and tactics (revised edition). Homewood, Ill.: The Dorsey Press.

Harré, R. and Secord, P.F. (1972)
The Explanation of Social Behaviour. Oxford: Blackwell.

Heider, F. (1958)
The Psychology of Interpersonal Relations. New York: Wiley.

Herzlich, C. (1973)
Health and Illness: A social-psychological analysis. European Monographs in Social Psychology, No. 5. London: Academic Press.

Jones, E.E. and Nisbett, R.E. (1971)
The actor and the observer: divergent perspectives of the causes of behavior. In E.E. Jones, D.E. Kanouse, H.H. Kelly, R.E. Nisbett, S. Valins and B. Weiner (eds), Attribution: Perceiving the causes of behavior. Morristown, NJ: General Learning Press.

Kay, H. (1971)
Accidents: some facts and theories. In P.B. Warr (ed.), Psychology at Work. Harmondsworth: Penguin.

Mead, G.H. (1934)
Mind, Self and Society: From the standpoint of a social behaviorist. Edited and introduced by C.W. Morris. Chicago: University of Chicago Press.

Milgram, S. (1974)
Obedience to Authority: An experimental view. London: Tavistock.

Weitz, S. (ed.) (1974)
   Non-verbal Communication: Readings with commentary. New
   York: Oxford University Press.
**Webb, E.J., Campbell, D.T.M, Schwartz, R.D. and Sechrest,
L.** (1966)
   Unobtrusive Measures. Nonreactive research in the social
   sciences. Chicago: Rand McNally.

Questions

1. Why might a theory of the human self be a necessary
   prerequisite to understanding the social psychology of
   the interview?
2. What are the dangers of relying exclusively on the
   interview as a source of information in social
   research?
3. What are the inadequacies of the interview as a way
   of appraising a person's fitness for a particular job?
4. Discuss the similarities and differences between
   interviewing and participant observation as techniques
   of research in social science.
5. 'Many crucial facts lie beyond the time and place of
   interaction, or lie concealed within it' (Goffman).
   Discuss with reference to the interview.
6. Can one accept at face value what people say in an
   interview or does one have to 'interpret' what one
   hears? If you advocate the first strategy, are there any
   qualifications to your acceptance? If you advocate the
   latter strategy, suggest the guidelines you might use in
   making your interpretations.
7. What are the problems of inter-relating what one hears
   in an interview with what one observes?
8. Compare and contrast interviews with conversations.
9. 'It is crucial to an understanding of the interview
   situation to appreciate that more than one perspective
   is involved.' Discuss.
10. Discuss the strengths and weaknesses of behavioural
    approaches to the study of interviews.

Annotated reading

Argyle, M. (1975) Bodily Communication. London: Methuen.
   A popular account of different aspects of non-verbal
   behaviour. Compare and contrast this approach with
   Goffman. Goffman is much more 'cognitive', whilst Argyle
   is more 'behavioural'. Is there scope for both
   approaches?

Goffman, E. (1959) The Presentation of Self in Everyday
Life. Harmondsworth: Penguin.
   Based on astute observations of everyday life. It is
   essentially a theory of action in relation to the
   observing and listening other (i.e. his conception of
   the audience is critical to his portrayal of action).
   Consider the relevance of this book to the problems

faced by the interviewee as he prepares for an interview.

Kahn, R.L. and Cannell, C.F. (1957) The Dynamics of Interviewing: Theory, technique and cases. New York: Wiley. Available in paperback. This has been the standard work for over 20 years. Presents a group dynamic approach to the interview. Concerned with the events of feedback as a way of improving interviewing skills, for example, such self-confrontation devices as tape-recorders. Needs to be up-dated to include video-feedback. Basically very sound.

9

Psychopathology
D. A. Shapiro

Opening remarks
FAY FRANSELLA

This chapter is included in this part of the book for two reasons. First, most of you will be interacting with people in authority who are medically qualified, most often with those who have specialized in psychiatry. Whether or not you agree that those with psychological problems should be classified in medical illness terms or not, this is the language system they will use. As well as giving an outline of the main categories into which the psychiatric patient can be slotted, Shapiro shows the alternatives to this type of classification. Whoever you work with, good communication can only be established if you have an understanding of the other's language system.

The second reason for its inclusion here is that how you decide to view your patients will in many ways determine how you behave in relation to them. If you think a person who is behaving oddly is suffering from some disease you may behave differently towards them from how you would if you considered their problem to be solely psychological. In the former case, the diagnosis will indicate the treatment; in the latter, the way to help will be first to understand what the problem is as THEY see it. I have chosen to elaborate on this slightly by saying something about Laing and how he seeks to understand schizophrenia from the patient's point of view (p. 183). I also take a brief look at a sociological view of depression (p. 184), since so many of the psychiatric patients with whom you come into contact will be depressed, and the great majority of these will be women. In the discussion of Brown and Harris' work on depression in working-class women (1978), there is a mention of 'life events'. This is an interesting area of work that has arisen out of psychiatry. Holmes and Rahe (1967) developed a social 'readjustment rating scale' in which certain common events were given scores according to the degree to which they are expected to cause us stress. If you are interested in this way of thinking about stress, Rahe has two articles in the Journal of Human Stress (1978, 1979) which give up-to-date accounts of the work using this scale.

There is very little in this chapter specifically on psychological disorders, apart from those I have just mentioned, since it is to do with the models people have used to conceptualize the disorders. However, you will find it not only of use in aiding communication with psychiatrists and your own understanding of psychologically disturbed patients, but also when you come to study the subject of psychiatry itself.

**Introduction
D. A. SHAPIRO**

'Psychopathology', literally defined, is the study of disease of the mind. Our society entrusts most of the care of individuals whose behaviour and experience are problematic or distressing to medical specialists (psychiatrists). Being medically trained, psychiatrists see their work as requiring diagnosis and treatment of 'patients'. Psychologists, on the other hand, have sought alternative means of understanding abnormal behaviour, and the aim of this chapter is to outline the progress that has been made in this direction.

The varieties of psychopathology

A good way to appreciate the great variety of problems we are concerned with is to examine the system of classification used by psychiatrists, summarized in table 1. Readers requiring more detailed descriptions of these should consult a psychiatric textbook. In the NEUROSES, the personality and perception of reality are fundamentally intact, although emotional disturbances of one kind or another, usually involving anxiety or its presumed effects, can make life very difficult for the individual. The PSYCHOSES, on the other hand, are characterized by gross impairments in perception, memory, thinking and language functions, and the individual is fundamentally disorganized, rather than merely emotionally disturbed. However, there is no clear-cut brain disease, and so the disorder cannot be explained in purely biomedical terms. The layman's conception of 'madness' is based on the symptoms of schizophrenia, including delusions (unshakeable, false beliefs), hallucinations (such as hearing 'voices') and thought disorder (manifested in 'garbled' speech). The third category of table 1, personality disorders, comprises deeply ingrained, motivational and social maladjustments. Table 1 also includes organic syndromes, which are behaviour disorders associated with identified brain disease. Not included in the table are the important group of psychosomatic illnesses. These are characterized by physical symptoms whose origins are in part psychological (emotional). They include asthma, high blood pressure, gastric and duodenal ulcers. More generally, psychological stress is increasingly implicated in many physical illnesses.

The medical model of psychopathology

Before describing psychological approaches to behaviour disorder, it is necessary to examine critically the predominant medical approach. This makes three major assumptions, which are considered in turn.

Table 1

Major category	Neuroses (milder disturbances)				
Illustrative syndromes	Anxiety state	Obsessive-compulsive disorders	Phobias	Conversion reactions	Neurotic depression
Characteristic symptoms	Palpitation, tires easily, breathlessness, nervousness anxiety	Intrusive thoughts, urges to acts or rituals	Irrational fears of specific objects or situations	Physical symptoms, lacking organic cause	Hopelessness dejection

Major category	Psychoses (severe Non-organic disturbances)		Personality disorders (antisocial disturbances)	Organic syndromes		
Illustrative syndromes	Affective disorders	Schizophrenia	Psychopathic personality	Alcoholism and drug dependence	Epilepsy	Severe mental handicap
Characteristic symptoms	Disturbances of mood, energy and activity patterns	Reality distortion, social withdrawal, disorganization of thought, perception and emotion	Lack of conscience	Physical or psychological dependence	Increased susceptibility to convulsions	Extremely low intelligence, social impairments

The diagnostic system

The first assumption of the medical model is that the various kinds of abnormal behaviour can be classified, by diagnosis, into syndromes, or constellations of symptoms regularly occurring together. This diagnostic system has already been summarized in table 1. It has a number of disadvantages. First, some disorders appear to cut across the boundaries of the system. Thus an individual whose severe anxiety is associated with fears of delusional intensity may defy classification as 'neurotic' or 'psychotic'. Second, scientific studies of the ability of psychiatrists to agree on the diagnosis of individuals have suggested that the process is rather unreliable, with agreement ranging from about 50 per cent to 80 per cent depending upon the circumstances (Beck, Ward, Mendelson, Mock and Erlbaugh, 1962). Third, research also suggests that the diagnosis given to an individual may bear little relationship to the symptoms the individual has (Zigler and Philips, 1961). Fourth, the diagnosis of psychiatric disorder is much more subjective and reflective of cultural attitudes than is the diagnosis of physical illness; one culture's schizophrenic might be another's shaman; similar acts of violence might be deemed heroic in battle but psychopathic in peacetime. Careful comparisons of American and British psychiatrists have shown that the two groups use different diagnostic criteria and hence classify patients differently.

Despite these limitations, the psychiatric classification persists. This is largely because no better descriptive system has been developed, whilst improvements have been obtained in the usefulness of the system by refining it in the light of earlier criticisms. For example, agreement between psychiatrists has been improved by standardization of the questions asked in diagnostic interviews and the use of standard decision-rules for assigning diagnoses to constellations of symptoms. But it is still necessary to bear in mind that the diagnostic system is not infallible and the 'labels' it gives individuals should not be uncritically accepted.

Physiological basis of psychopathology
The second assumption of the medical model is that the symptoms reflect an underlying disease process, physiological in nature like those involved in all illnesses, causing the symptoms. Three kinds of evidence are offered in support of this. First, the influence of hereditary factors has been assessed by examining the rates of disorder among the relatives of sufferers. To the extent that a disorder is heritable, its origins are considered biological in nature. For example, comparison between the dizygotic (non-identical) and monozygotic (identical) twins of sufferers suggests that there is some hereditary involvement in schizophrenia, anxiety-related disorders, depression and antisocial disorders, with the evidence strongest in the case of schizophrenia (Gottesman and Shields, 1973). Studies of children adopted at birth also suggest that the offspring of schizophrenic parents are more liable to suffer from schizophrenia than other adopted children, despite having no contact with the biological parent. On the other hand, the evidence also shows that hereditary factors alone cannot fully account for schizophrenia or any other psychological disorder. Even amongst the identical twins of schizophrenics, many do not develop the disorder. Both hereditary and environmental influences are important.

The second line of evidence for a 'disease' basis of psychopathology concerns the biochemistry of the brain. This is a vastly complex subject, and one whose present methods of investigation are almost certainly too crude to give other than an approximate picture of what is going on. Over the years, a succession of biochemical factors have been suggested as causes for different forms of psychopathology. Unfortunately, the evidence is not conclusive, as biochemical factors found in sufferers may be consequences rather than causes. Hospital diets, activity patterns or characteristic emotional responses may influence the brain biochemistry of disordered individuals.

Despite these problems, there are some promising lines of biochemical research. For example, it has been suggested that schizophrenia may be caused by excess activity of dopamine, one of the neurotransmitters (substances with which neurons stimulate one another: see Snyder, Banerjee, Yamamura and Greenberg, 1974). This suggestion is supported by the similarity in molecular structure between dopamine and the phenothiazine drugs which are used to alleviate schizophrenia, suggesting that these drugs block the reception of dopamine by taking its place at receptors which normally receive it. These drugs also cause side effects resembling the symptoms of Parkinson's disease, which is associated with dopamine deficiency. Although this and other evidence support the dopamine theory of schizophrenia, some research has failed to support it, and so the theory has yet to be universally accepted. In sum, biochemical evidence is suggestive, and consistent with presumed physiological origins of psychopathology, but it is not conclusive, nor can such evidence make a psychological explanation redundant. It is best seen as an important part of our understanding of psychopathology, whose causal significance varies from one disorder to another.

The third line of evidence for the physiological basis of psychopathology concerns disorders with clear organic causes. Disease or damage to the brain can result in severe disturbance of behaviour. A classic example of this is 'general paresis of the insane', whose widespread physical and mental impairments were discovered in the last century to be due to the syphilis spirochete. This discovery encouraged medical scientists to seek clear-cut organic causes for other psychological abnormalities. A large number of organic brain syndromes have been established, in which widespread cognitive and emotional deficits are associated with damage to the brain by disease, infection, or injury. Epilepsy, in which the individual is unusually susceptible to seizures or convulsions, is associated with abnormal patterns of brain activity measured by the electroencephalogram (EEG) even between seizures. Many individuals with severe mental handicap (cf. Clarke and Clarke, 1974), who attain very low scores on tests of general intelligence and show minimal adaptation to social requirements and expectations, suffer from clear-cut organic pathology, often accompanied by severe physical abnormalities.

On the other hand, all of these disorders are affected by the person's individuality, experience and environment. For example, similar brain injuries result in very different symptoms in different individuals. Those suffering from epileptic seizures can make use of their past experience to avoid circumstances (including diet and environmental stimuli) which tend to trigger their convulsions. Most mentally handicapped people do not have clearly identifiable organic illnesses. Even amongst those who do, the environment can make a big difference to the person's ability to learn the skills of everyday living. Psychologists have found that special training can help mentally handicapped people who might otherwise appear incapable of learning.

Medical treatment of psychopathology

The third assumption of the medical model concerns how psychopathology should be managed. Physical treatments are offered in hospitals and clinics to persons designated 'patients'. It is beyond our present scope to describe the extensive evidence supporting the effectiveness of drugs and electro-convulsive therapy (ECT), the major physical treatments currently employed. However, there are several reason why psychologists are often inclined to question the support this evidence gives to the medical model. First, individuals differ in their responsiveness to physical treatments, and nobody really understands why some individuals are not helped. Second, the fact that abnormal behaviour can be controlled by physical means does not prove that its origins are physical. Third, the physical treatments often lack a convincing scientific rationale to explain their effects.

The medical model: conclusions

In sum, the medical model gains some support from the evidence, but is sufficiently defective and incomplete to warrant the development of alternative and complementary approaches. Although the diagnostic system is of some value, it must be used with caution. Although hereditary influences, biochemical abnormalities and organic pathology have a part to play in our understanding of psychopathology, they cannot explain its origins without reference to environmental and psychological factors. The apparent efficacy of physical treatment does not establish the physical origins of what they treat. The remainder of this chapter is concerned with five alternative approaches developed by psychologists and social scientists, and assesses their contribution with respect to some of the most important kinds of psychopathology. The evidence presented is, of necessity, very selective, and a full appreciation of these approaches can only follow more extensive study. It should also be borne in mind that the present emphasis on origins of disorder entails a relative neglect of research on treatment.

The statistical model

The statistical model identifies individuals whose behaviour or reported experience is sufficiently unusual to warrant attention on that basis alone. Abnormal individuals are those who greatly differ from the average with respect to some attribute (such as intelligence or amount of subjective anxiety experienced). For example, according to Eysenck (1970), people who score highly on dimensions known as 'neuroticism' (very readily roused to emotion) and 'introversion' (quick in learning conditioned responses and associations) are likely to show what the psychiatrist calls 'anxiety neurosis'. Although this approach is commendably objective, it is not very helpful alone. Not all unusual behaviour is regarded as pathological. Exceptionally gifted people are an obvious case in point. Some statistically abnormal behaviours are obviously more relevant to psychopathology than are others, and we need more than a statistical theory to tell us which to consider, and why. But the model is of value for its suggestion that 'normal' and 'abnormal' behaviour may differ only in degree, in contrast to the medical model's implication of a sharp division between them.

The psychodynamic model

The psychodynamic model is very difficult to summarize, based as it is on theories developed early in the century by Freud, and revised and elaborated by him and subsequent workers within a broad tradition (Ellenberger, 1970). Like the medical model, it seeks an underlying cause for psychopathology, but this is a psychological cause, namely, unconscious conflicts arising from childhood experiences. Freudians have developed a general theory of personality from their study of psychopathology. Freud viewed the personality as comprising the conscious ego, the unconscious id (source of primitive impulses) and partly conscious, partly unconscious super-ego (conscience). The ego is held to protect itself from threat by several defence mechanisms. These are a commonplace feature of everyone's adjustment, but are used in an exaggerated or excessively rigid manner by neurotic individuals, and are overstretched to the point of collapse in the case of psychotic individuals.

For example, neurotic anxiety is learnt by a child punished for being impulsive, whereupon the conflict between wanting something and fearing the consequences of that desire is driven from consciousness (this is an example of the defence mechanism known as repression). According to this theory, pervasive anxiety is due to fear of the person's ever-present id impulses, and phobic objects, such as insects or animals, are seen as symbolic representations of objects of the repressed id impulses. Dynamic theory views depression as a reaction to loss in individuals who are excessively dependent upon other people for the maintenance of self-esteem. The loss may be actual (as in bereavement) or symbolic (as in the misinterpretation of a rejection as a total loss of love). The depressed person expresses a child-like need for approval and affection to restore self-esteem. In psychotic disorders such as schizophrenia, the collapse of the defence mechanisms leads to the predominance of primitive 'primary process' thinking.

Despite its considerable impact upon the ways in which we understand human motivation and psychopathology, psycho dynamic theory has remained controversial. Most of the evidence in its favour comes from clinical case material, as recounted by practising psychoanalysts, whose work is based on the belief that unconscious conflicts must be brought to the surface for the patient to recover from the symptoms they have engendered. Whilst this method often yields compelling material which is difficult to explain in other terms (Malan, 1979), it is open to criticism as insufficiently objective to yield scientific evidence. It is all too easy for the psychoanalyst unwittingly to influence material produced by the patient, and the essential distinction between observations and the investigator's interpretations of them is difficult to sustain in the psychoanalytic consulting-room. The abstract and complex formulations of psychodynamic theory are difficult to prove or disprove by the clear-cut scientific methods favoured by psychologists, and the patients studied, whether in Freud's Vienna or present-day London or New York, are somewhat unrepresentative.

There is some scientific evidence which is broadly consistent with psychodynamic theory; for example, the defects in thinking found in schizophrenia are compatible with the dynamic concept of ego impairment, and loss events of the kind implicated by dynamic theory are associated with the onset of depression. Although psychologists hostile to dynamic theory can explain these findings in other terms, there is little doubt that the theory has been fruitful, contributing to psychology such essential concepts as unconscious conflict and defence mechanism.

The learning model

The learning model views psychopathology as arising from faulty learning in early life, and conceptualizes this process in terms of principles of learning drawn from laboratory studies of animals and humans. The most basic principles are those of Pavlovian or 'classical' conditioning (in which two stimuli are presented together until the response to one stimulus is also evoked by the other), and 'operant' conditioning (whereby behaviour with favourable consequences becomes more frequent). According to proponents of the learning model, the symptoms of psychopathology are nothing more than faulty habits acquired through these two types of learning. The 'underlying pathology' posited by the medical and psychodynamic models is dismissed as unfounded myth.

For example, it is suggested that phobias are acquired by a two-stage learning process; first, fear is aroused in response to a previously neutral stimulus when this stimulus occurs in conjunction with an unpleasant stimulus; then the person learns to avoid the situation evoking the fear, because behaviour taking the person away from the situation is rewarded by a reduction in fear. Another learning theory is that schizophrenic patients receive more attention and other rewards from other people, such as hospital staff, when they behave in 'crazy' ways, thereby increasing the frequency of this behaviour. Again, depressed people are seen as failing to exercise sufficient skill and effort to 'earn' rewards from situations and from other people; a vicious circle develops and activity reduces still further in the absence of such rewards.

In general, the learning model provides a powerful set of principles governing the acquisition of problem behaviour. But it has severe limitations. For example, the fact that fears and phobias can be established by processes of conditioning in the laboratory does not prove that this is how they come about naturally. The theory cannot readily explain how people acquire behaviours which lead to such distress (it is hardly 'rewarding' to suffer the agonies of depression or anxiety, and learning theorists acknowledge their difficulty over this fact by referring to it as the 'neurotic paradox'). Recently, learning theorists have examined the important process of imitative learning or modelling, whereby the behaviour of observers is influenced by another's actions and their consequences. Fear and aggression can be aroused in this way, with obvious implications for the transmission of psychopathology from one person (such as a parent) to another. But human thinking is considered by many psychologists too complex to be understood in terms of these relatively simple learning theories. Hence the development of the cognitive approach, to which we now turn.

The cognitive model

The cognitive model focusses upon thinking processes and their possible dysfunctions. 'Neurotic' problems are seen as due to relatively minor errors in reasoning processes, whilst 'psychotic' disorders are held to reflect profound disturbances in cognitive function and organization.

For example, it is well known that depressed people hold negative attitudes towards themselves, their experiences and their future. According to cognitive theory, these attitudes give rise to the feelings of depression (Beck, 1967). Although an episode of depression may be triggered by external events, it is the person's perception of the event which makes it set off depressed feelings. Experiments in which negative beliefs about the self are induced in non-depressed subjects have shown that a depressed mood does indeed follow. But whether similar processes account for the more severe and lasting depressive feelings of clinical patients is another matter, although the promising results of 'cognitive therapy', in which the attitudes of depressed patients are modified directly, may be taken as indirect evidence for the theory.

Cognitive theory also embraces people's beliefs about the causation of events (known as attributions). For example, it has been suggested that the attributions one makes concerning unpleasant experiences will determine the impact of those experiences upon one's subsequent beliefs about oneself; thus, if a woman is rejected by a man, this is much more damaging to her self-esteem if she believes that the main cause of the event is her own inadequacy, than if she attributes the event to the man's own passing mood. An attributional approach suggests that failure experiences are most damaging if individuals attribute them to wide-ranging and enduring factors within themselves. Consistent with this, depressed people have been found to attribute bad outcomes to wide-ranging and enduring factors within themselves, whilst they attribute good outcomes to changeable factors outside their control.

Psychologists have devoted considerable efforts to precise descriptions of the cognitive deficits of schizophrenic patients through controlled laboratory experiments. For example, schizophrenics have difficulty performing tasks requiring selective attention to relevant information and the exclusion from attention of irrelevant information. Schizophrenics are highly distractable. This may help to explain how irrelevant features of a situation acquire disproportionate importance and become interpreted as part of their delusional systems of false beliefs, or how speech is disorganized by the shifting of attention to irrelevant thoughts and mental images which other people manage to ignore.

The cognitive approach is of great interest because it combines the systematic and objective methods of experimental psychology with a thoroughgoing interest in an important aspect of human mentality. It is a very active 'growth area' of current research, and shows considerable promise. It is perhaps too soon to evaluate many of its specific theories, however, and it does carry the risk of neglecting other aspects of human behaviour.

The socio-cultural model

The final model to be considered attributes psychopathology to social and cultural factors. It focusses upon malfunctioning of the social or cultural group rather than of an individual within that group.

In terms of the socio-cultural model schizophrenia, for example, has been considered both in relation to the quality of family life and to larger socio-economic forces. Within the family, behaviour labelled schizophrenic is seen as a response to self-contradictory emotional demands ('double binds') from other family members, notably parents, to which no sane response is possible. Although graphic accounts have been offered of such patterns in the family life of schizophrenic patients, there is no evidence that these are peculiar to such families. If anything, the research evidence suggests that abnormalities of communication within the families of schizophrenics arise in response to the behaviour of the patient, rather than causing the disorder. Looking beyond the family, the higher incidence of schizophrenia amongst the lowest socio-economic class, especially in inner city areas, is attributed to the multiple deprivations suffered by this group. Episodes of schizophrenia are triggered by stressful life events, some of which are more common, or less offset by social and material supports, amongst lower-class people. On the other hand, cause and effect could be the other way round, with persons developing schizophrenia 'drifting' into poverty-ridden areas of the city. Indeed, schizophrenic patients tend to achieve a lower socio-economic status than did their parents.

The socio-cultural approach is of undoubted value as a critical challenge to orthodox views, and has generated useful research into social and cultural factors in psychopathology. Its proponents have also made valuable contributions by bringing a greater humanistic respect for the personal predicament of troubled individuals, and to the development of 'therapeutic communities' and family therapy as alternatives to individually-centred treatments. However, many of its propositions concerning cause-effect relationships have not stood the test of empirical research.

The psychology of illness

It is well known that certain physical illnesses are related to psychological factors. These 'psychosomatic disorders' include ulcerative colitis, bronchial asthma and hypertension. It is not so widely appreciated, however, that psychological factors may be involved in any physical illness. This is because the physiological changes associated with stress (for instance, the release of the 'stress hormones' such as adrenalin) can suppress immune responses and so increase the individual's susceptibility to many diseases, ranging from the common cold to cancer (Rogers, Dubey and Reich, 1979). Many aspects of a person's life have been implicated in ill-health, presumably because of their effects on such physiological mechanisms. These include physical stresses such as noise, highly demanding and/or repetitive jobs (whether physical or mental), catastrophic life events (such as accidents, illness or bereavement) and major emotional difficulties (such as marital discord).

However, for physical illness as for psychopathology, the cause-effect relationship is not simple. Some individuals are more constitutionally stress-prone than others, it appears. Some people live in congenial and supportive surroundings, enabling them to withstand pressures which might otherwise lead to illness. Most of the events implicated in psychological distress and ill-health are in part the results of the individual's own state and behaviour. For example, marital conflict may reflect prior strains felt by the individuals involved. Furthermore, the impact of a stressful event or circumstance depends on the individual's appraisal of it. For example, noise is less distressing if we know we can silence it should it become unbearable. Thus consideration of psychological factors in ill-health demonstrates clearly the interaction between features of individuals and of their surroundings. For physical illness as for psychopathology, we must realize that there are many interacting causes rather than imagine that any one factor is alone responsible for the problem at issue.

Conclusions

Each of the approaches surveyed has contributed to our understanding of psychopathology. The evidence presented for each can only illustrate the massive amounts of research which have been carried out. Nonetheless, several clear themes emerge which have profound implications for our present and future knowledge of psychopathology.

First, the system of classification is inadequate, and research shows that different people within the same broad diagnostic group (such as schizophrenia) behave very differently; it therefore follows that different causes may be found for the difficulties experienced by these sub-groups of people.

Second, the different approaches could profitably be integrated rather more than they have been in the past. For example, elements of the medical, statistical, sociocultural and cognitive approaches have been combined in recent work on schizophrenia, in which the vulnerability of an individual to the disorder is seen as reflecting both heredity and environment; this vulnerability determines whether or not a person experiences schizophrenia when faced with stresses which are too much to cope with (Zubin and Spring, 1977). The fact that psychopathology generally has multiple causes lends particular urgency to the need to construct broad theories incorporating the facts which were hitherto regarded as supporting one or another of the competing approaches.

Third, the different approaches have more in common than is often acknowledged. In relation to schizophrenia, for example, the breakdown of ego functioning described by psychodynamic theory resembles the inability to process information identified by cognitive theory.

Fourth, the limitations of existing models have encouraged the growth of alternative approaches. For example, the 'transactional' approach emphasizes the importance of the individual's active part in bringing about apparently external stressful events and pressures (Cox, 1978). This approach views the individual as neither a passive victim of circumstances, nor as irrevocably programmed from birth to respond in a particular way. Person and environment are seen as in continuous interaction, so that one-way cause-effect analysis is inappropriate. For example, harassed executives and mothers of small children bring some of the stress they suffer upon themselves as they respond sharply to colleagues or children and thus contribute to a climate of irritation or conflict. Research using this approach has only recently begun, but it holds considerable hope for the future.

Finally, what can this psychological study of psychopathology offer the professional? There are as yet no certain answers to such simple questions as 'What causes schizophrenia?' or 'Why does Mrs Jones stay indoors all the time?' If and when such answers become available, they will not be simple. They will involve many interacting factors. Meanwhile, the psychological approach teaches us a healthy respect for the complexity of the human predicament, and is a valuable corrective to any tendency to offer simplistic or unsympathetic explanations of human distress. Furthermore, professionals will often find it illuminating to apply some of the approaches outlined here to help understand distressed individuals they encounter in their daily work.

Ronald D. Laing
FAY FRANSELLA

Laing is a rebel. He rebels against the medical establishment, particularly as it relates to psychiatry. He argues that in psychiatry the clinician is not usually relating to the person as a person but rather as an object of fascinating complexity; an object, the parts of which are not working properly; an object which has to be diagnosed in order to be put to rights.

Laing says that although we would agree that our bodies and our brains are physiological mechanisms we, as people, are not those mechanisms; we have our own identity and our own personal experience. For an alternative model he suggests that we should take the other person's experience seriously and listen carefully so as to understand what the other is experiencing: what the experience of being schizoid is like, and so on. In one book he draws a portrait of a schizophrenic person called David:

> The boy was a most fantastic looking character - an adolescent Kirkegaard played by Danny Kaye. The hair was too long, the collar too large, the trousers too short, the shoes too big, and withall, his second-hand theatre cape and cane! He was not simply eccentric. I could not escape the impression that this young man was playing at being eccentric ... He was indeed quite a practised actor, for he has been playing one part or another since his mother's death ... his idea was NEVER TO GIVE HIMSELF AWAY TO OTHERS. Consequently, he practised the most tortuous equivocation towards others in the parts he played (Laing, 1960).

Instead of trying to categorize David as suffering from a psychosis and so treat him as medically sick, Laing says we should own our involvement with him and others like him and try to discover what they are trying to tell us. In a study carried out with Esterson, he elaborates further on the nature of schizophrenia (1964). Their book details a number of studies of families which include a member who has at one time been diagnosed as having schizophrenia. On the basis of extensive interviews, Laing and Esterson mapped out the context in which each schizophrenic person had lived. They then argued that what these people thought was going on was not intrinsically a 'mad' interpretation but an understandable response to a chaotic and confusing world as they saw it. In 1970 Esterson wrote a very detailed account of one of these families and described more fully the methods used.

These studies prove nothing in themselves. But they do indicate an alternative way of thinking about – and so behaving towards – someone called 'psychotic' within the existing medical model. Laing is important if for no other reason than that he arose out of psychiatry and called into question well-established ways of conceptualizing mental illness. And the repercussions of this have yet to die down.

Depression and the female sex role

There is no disputing the evidence now available that depression is more common in women than in men. Why should this be? Some say that it is to do with women's physiology since depression is particularly common at childbirth and at the menopause. But it equally could be that mothers, particularly working-class mothers, find they cannot cope with the abrupt change of role within the family and society at these times. Many find they cannot deal with this bawling bundle of humanity, alone with it in the house all day. Or, at the time of the menopause, they suddenly find there is no role for them within the family, since 'the family' has now grown up and the members have gone their respective ways.

But not all working-class women become depressed and that is where the Brown and Harris VULNERABILITY FACTORS are useful. These factors are loss of mother in childhood, three or more children under the age of 14 living at home, lack of an intimate relationship with someone, and lack of a full- or part-time job. Interest and involvement with one or more people, both inside and outside the family, seem to reduce a woman's susceptibility to depression. Depression is also found to be much more common among the working-class family than it is among the middle class, and the working-class woman is less likely to seek psychiatric help.

It is when a stressful 'life event' occurs in the life of a 'vulnerable' woman that depression is most likely. It seems that death of a parent in childhood is particularly important. In a more recent study, Brown, Harris and Copeland (1979) looked at the effects of various types of loss within the family, be it by death, divorce or separation. They found that it was only loss of a mother before the age of 11 that was associated with greater risk of depression in women. There was no greater risk associated with early death of a father or siblings.

Perhaps it is that women who have lost their mothers at an early age are generally less able to deal with adult stresses. If we consider childbearing and the menopause to be psychological stressors, then increased depression at such times is more comprehensible. It may not be necessary to put the blame on female biology after all.

References

Beck, A.T. (1967)
Depression: Clinical, experimental and theoretical aspects. New York: Harper & Row.

Beck, A.T., Ward, C.H., Mendleson, M., Mock, J.E. and Erlbaugh, J. (1962)
Reliability of psychiatric diagnosis II: a study of consistency of clinical judgments and ratings. American Journal of Psychiatry, 119, 351–357.

Brown, G.W. and Harris, T. (1978)
Social Origins of Depression. London: Tavistock.

Brown, G.W., Harris, T. and Copeland, J.R. (1979)
Depression and loss. In P. Williams and A. Clare (eds), Psychosocial Disorders in General Practice. London: Academic Press.

Clarke, A.M. and Clarke, A.D.B. (1974)
Mental Deficiency: The changing outlook (3rd edn). London: Methuen.

Cox, T. (1978)
Stress. London: Macmillan.

Ellenberger, H.F. (1970)
The Discovery of the Unconscious. London: Allen Lane/ Penguin.

Esterson, A. (1970)
The Leaves of Spring: A study in dialectics of madness. Harmondsworth: Penguin.

Eysenck, H.J. (1970)
The Structure of Human Personality. London: Methuen.

Gottesman, I.I. and Shields, J. (1973)
Genetic theorising and schizophrenia. British Journal of Psychiatry, 122, 15–30.

Holmes, T.H. and Rahe, R.H. (1967)
The social readjustment rating scale. Journal of Psycho-somatic Research, 11, 213–218.

Laing, R.D. (1960)
The Divided Self. Harmondsworth: Penguin.

Laing, R.D. and Esterson, A. (1964)
Sanity, Madness and the Family. Harmondsworth: Penguin.

Malan, D.H. (1979)
Individual Psychotherapy and the Science of Psychodynamics. London: Tavistock.

Rahe, R.H. (1978)
Life change measurement clarification. Psychosomatic Medicine, 40, 95–97.

Rahe, R.H. (1979)
Life change events and mental illness: an overview. Journal of Human Stress, 5, 2–10.

Rogers, M.P., Dubey, D. and Reich, P. (1979)
The influence of the psyche and the brain on immunity

and disease susceptibility: a critical review.
Psychosomatic Medicine, 41, 147-164.

Snyder, S.H., Banerjee, S.P., Yamamura, H.I. and Greenberg, D. (1974)
Drugs, neurotransmitters and schizophrenia. Science, 184, 1243-1253.

Zigler, E. and Philips, L. (1961)
Psychiatric diagnosis and symptomalogy. Journal of Abnormal and Social Psychology, 63, 69-75.

Zubin, J. and Spring, B. (1977)
Vulnerability - a new view of schizophrenia. Journal of Abnormal Psychology, 86, 103-126.

Questions

1. What problems are raised by the diagnostic system used by psychiatrists? Can it be improved?
2. What can the study of twins tell us about psychopathology?
3. Outline the evidence for a biochemical basis for schizophrenia.
4. How useful is the medical model of psychopathology? Does it have any disadvantages?
5. Outline the statistical approach to psychopathology, indicating its value and limitations.
6. What is wrong with psychoanalysis as a scientific method of investigating psychopathology?
7. Is psychopathology simply behaviour which has been learnt because it produces rewards?
8. Which of the models of psychopathology do you prefer? Give your reasons.
9. How can psychological factors affect susceptibility to physical illness?
10. Which forms of psychopathology would be particularly disabling to a person employed in your profession, and why?
11. Discuss the view that Laing is a rebel without a cause.
12. Write an essay on women's greater vulnerability to depression.

Annotated reading

Bannister, D. and Fransella, F. (1980) Inquiring Man (2nd edn). Harmondsworth: Penguin.

A persuasive account of George Kelly's personal construct approach to psychology and psychopathology, written by two of its leading exponents.

Davison, G.C. and Neale, J.M. (1977) Abnormal Psychology: An experimental clinical approach (2nd edn). New York: Wiley.

The present chapter can provide no more than an introduction to psychopathology. This is the best of the textbooks available: it is readable, comprehensive and, in general, accurate. It is useful in teaching, and has been drawn upon extensively for drafting the chapter. If you want to follow up any aspect of the chapter in more detail, look up the topic in the Index of this book.

Hilgard, E.R., Atkinson, R.L. and Atkinson, R.C. (1979) Introduction to Psychology (7th edn). New York: Harcourt Brace Jovanovich (chapters 14, 15 and 16).
Intermediate in length between the present chapter and the Davison and Neale book, this group of chapters gives a good general account. Chapter 14 reviews conflict and stress in terms of both experimental and psychoanalytic work; chapter 15 gives a good outline of much of the ground covered in this chapter; and chapter 16 discusses methods of treatment.

Inechen, B. (1979) Mental Illness. London: Longman.
This reviews the field from a sociological viewpoint, and covers a good deal of research on social factors in psychopathology.

Oatley, K. (1981) The self with others: the person and the interpersonal context in the approaches of C. R. Rogers and R. D. Laing. In F. Fransella (ed.), Personality: Theory, measurement and research. London: Methuen.
A further account of Laing's work and ideas.

Seligman, M.E.P. (1975) Helplessness: On depression, development and death. New York: Freeman.
Seligman presents his theory of learned helplessness in a very stimulating and engaging book. Although the theory was based on laboratory studies with animals, Seligman has injected a great deal of 'human interest' into this account. Students who are especially interested in the theory of depression should note, however, that Seligman's ideas have moved on since the book was written to incorporate attributional concepts.

Spielberger, C. (1979) Understanding Stress and Anxiety. New York: Harper & Row.
A very readable and well-illustrated introduction to experimental and clinical work on stress and anxiety, recommended for the student wishing to look further into these aspects.

Stafford-Clark, D. and Smith, A.C. (1979) Psychiatry for Students (5th edn). London: Allen & Unwin.
The present chapter does not attempt to do full justice to psychiatry. This is the most readable of the general textbooks on psychiatry, written for students rather than practitioners. It is a good source for more details of psychiatric symptoms, disorders and treatments.

Part three

The Occupational Therapist as Teacher

10

Learning, conditioning and skill
Fay Fransella

There are a great many definitions of learning, with most
emphasizing that it is basically a relatively permanent
change in behaviour that occurs as the result of practice.
Within this framework, there are two main divisions: first,
there is CONDITIONING or associative learning. This is
sometimes called 'habit formation' and is 'the acquiring of
a connection between a stimulus and a response that did not
exist before'. Associative learning is sub-divided into the
classical conditioning of Pavlov and the instrumental or
operant conditioning of first Thorndike, then Hull, and
currently Skinner.

The second main division sees learning as a COGNITIVE
PROCESS. Here, particular attention is paid to the role of
cognitive processes such as perception and understanding in
learning. Figure 1 shows the relationship between the two
sub-divisions of conditioning and learning as a cognitive
process with its various sub-branches.

A controversy still exists within psychology as to
whether learning, in its most fundamental form, is best
understood in terms of stimulus-response association or
of cognitive structures. One possible resolution of this
dilemma is to grade it on a crude scale, ranging from the
most automatic kind (best explained as conditioning) at one
end and the most rational (best explained as involving cog-
nition or thinking) at the other. Figure 2 shows such a
scale.

No attempt is made in this chapter to discuss further
the controversy between approaches; it is enough for you to
know that it exists. As an occupational therapist you will
find yourself using both kinds of learning. For instance,
Argyle (see chapter 5) makes the operant conditioning concept of reinforcement central to his work on training people
in social skills. But the other type of learning may also be
used, in that the trainee develops a more effective complex
of actions and ideas through being involved in role-play or
some form of group method. Occupational therapists are becoming increasingly involved both in social skills training
and in behaviour therapy methods, described in Beech's
chapter 18 on creating change (pp. 348-366). There he talks
almost exclusively about the types of therapy based on Pavlovian and Skinnerian principles. So knowledge of concepts
of conditioning is essential not only for you to gain a

Figure 1

Approaches to the study of learning

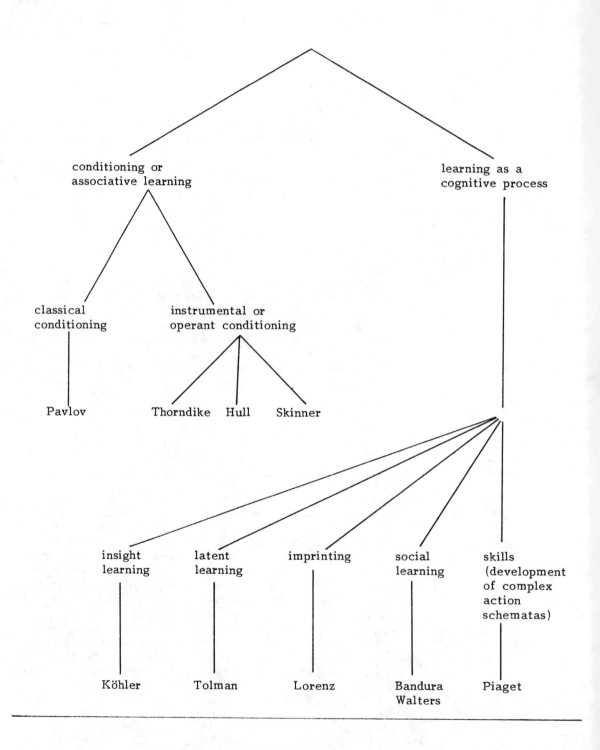

scale of learning from automatic to insightful

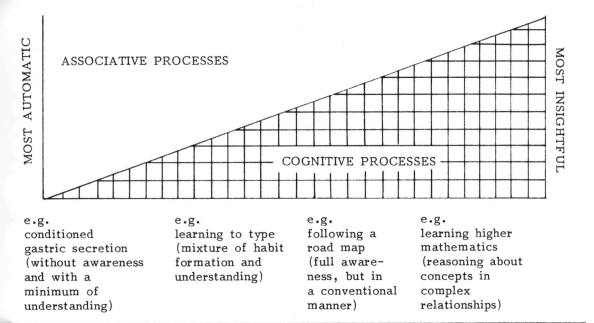

e.g.
conditioned
gastric secretion
(without awareness
and with a
minimum of
understanding)

e.g.
learning to type
(mixture of habit
formation and
understanding)

e.g.
following a
road map
(full aware-
ness, but in
a conventional
manner)

e.g.
learning higher
mathematics
(reasoning about
concepts in
complex
relationships)

fuller understanding of the work and procedures discussed
by Argyle and Beech, but also to enable you to learn to become a skilled social skills trainer and behaviour therapist
yourself.

As you will see in figure 1, the work of Piaget and the
development of schemata can also be included under the
heading of development of skills, and his ideas have already
been discussed in chapter 3. The present chapter ends with a
short account of some of the principles you should bear in
mind when teaching a patient a skill, whether it be weaving,
making a basket or throwing a pot. The chapter therefore
starts with an account of classical and operant conditioning
and then of some of the factors involved in developing a
motor skill.

Classical conditioning

Under natural circumstances the normal animal must
respond not only to stimuli which themselves bring
immediate benefit or harm, but also to other physical or
chemical agencies ... which in themselves only signal
the approach of these stimuli ... The essential feature
of the highest activity of the central nervous system
... consists, not in the fact that innumerable signaling
stimuli do initiate reflex reactions in the animal, but
in the fact that under different conditions these same
stimuli may initiate quite different reflex actions;

and, conversely, the same reactions may be initiated by different stimuli (Pavlov, 1927).

So said the Russian psychologist, Ivan Pavlov (1849-1936), when discussing his important discovery concerning reflex behaviour: that of classical conditioning. He had found that if two stimuli occur together in time, they both come, by association alone, to elicit the same response, although only one of the stimuli did so in the first place. This type of learning could be considered the most automatic that we know about.

Classical conditioning can be defined as the formation of an association between a conditioned stimulus and a response, through repeated presentation of a conditioned stimulus in a controlled relationship with an unconditioned stimulus that normally elicits that response. The terms 'conditional' and 'unconditional' are now regarded as a more accurate translation of Pavlov's writing, but are often used interchangeably with 'conditioned' and 'unconditioned'.

The experimental setting

To start with there was the dog and the bell. Or at least, that is what most people know about conditioning if they have heard of it at all. At that time, Pavlov was, in fact, studying the digestive systems of dogs in his physiology laboratory. During the course of this work he came up against a complication for which he was not prepared. The dogs began to salivate when they were about to be fed as well as when being presented with the food. His dogs had learnt to 'anticipate' the arrival of food. So he set about investigating precisely what the nature of this expectancy might be.

The dogs were placed in harnesses in a soundproofed room under constant illumination. All this was to make sure that no noise or light fluctuation would incidentally affect the experiment. By putting a small tube into the dog's salivary duct in the mouth, he obtained an accurate measure of salivation. The experiment itself consisted of sounding a buzzer and, with the buzzer still sounding, giving food. This sequence was repeated time and time again until, gradually, the amount of saliva secreted increased when the buzzer sounded and before the food was presented.

The important fact is that initially the buzzer had no effect upon salivation, but eventually did so by being paired with a stimulus which invariably elicits the response: food. This sequence depends on the conditional association between the effective and ineffective stimulus. The relationship between the food and the salivation is an unconditional one. We thus have the terminology of unconditional stimulus (UCS), and conditional stimulus (CS). The response produced by presentation of the UCS he called the unconditional response (UCR), and the response produced by presentation of the CS he called the conditional response (CR); this is virtually equivalent to, though measurably distinct from, the UCR. The sequence is shown in schematic terms in figure 3.

Figure 3

Schematic representation of the classical conditioning experimental paradigm

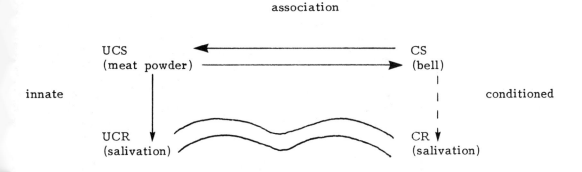

Time relationships between UCS and CS
What has just been described is now called delayed conditioning. That is, the CS begins several seconds before the onset of the UCS and then may continue with it until a response occurs. But there are other types of temporal relationship and these seem to result in differing ability to sustain the conditioned response. A schematic representation of these relationships is given in figure 4.

Figure 4

Schematic representation UCS and CS intervals in classical conditioning

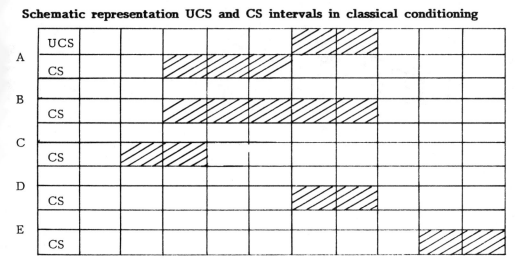

SECONDS

In figure 4, (A) and (B) are the classical delayed conditioning conditions. When the CS is presented before the
UCS starts and is then removed so that only a 'trace' remains, this is called 'trace conditioning' as in (C). Some
experiments suggest that the trace relationship generally
produces the fastest conditioning. When the CS occurs a
fraction of a second before the onset of the UCS and then
continues with it until a response occurs, this is 'simul-
taneous conditioning' as in (D). This exact association
produces almost no conditioning. It is also possible for the
UCS actually to precede the CS, as in (E), and so produce
'backward contitioning'. As might be expected, this is
relatively ineffective.

Features of the classical conditioning process

Terminology and concepts to do with conditioning are important. For instance, a 'trial' refers to each paired presentation of the CS and UCS; and 'acquisition' is that stage
of the conditioning process during which the organism is
learning the association between the conditioned stimulus
and the unconditioned stimulus.

After repeated presentation of the CS and UCS, the CR
begins to appear with increasingly greater strength and
regularity. Eventually a stable level of responding is
reached. This is the asymptote to the curve. After this
further acquisition trials will not result in any greater
strength of responding (see figure 5).

Figure 5

An acquisition learning curve

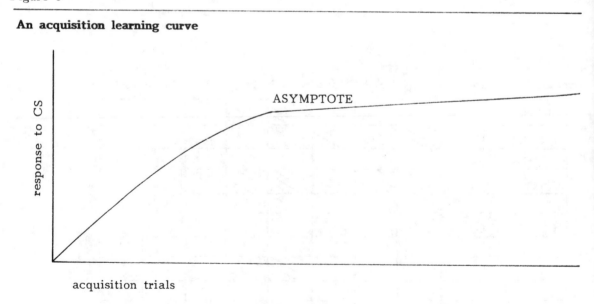

Once established, the conditioned response association can, of course, be weakened. If the CS is continually presented without the UCS there will be a gradual decrease in the CR. This is 'experimental extinction', the curve for which is given in figure 6.

Figure 6

A curve of extinction in conditioning

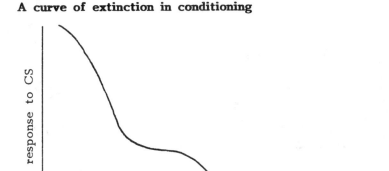

extinction trials

This should not be confused with forgetting. Rather, the response has been inhibited or suppressed. To demonstrate this, numerous studies have shown that future conditioning occurs much more easily in subjects in whom the response has been extinguished than in those who have not previously been conditioned. This return of the conditioned response is called 'spontaneous recovery'. It is particularly important to note that, after a period of rest following extinction, the conditioned response may return partially, even though the UCS has not been presented at all. This is demonstrated in figure 7.

To elicit a conditioned response, the bell, buzzer, light, or whatever the CS is, does not always have to be identical. For instance, if a response has been conditioned to the note middle C, it may also occur in response to D and other notes. But the more nearly alike these are to the original CS, the more completely will they evoke the response. This is the principle of generalization, and the degree of similarity between the original and the new stimuli is called the 'generalization gradient'.

Opposed to the principle of stimulus similarity, there is stimulus differentiation or 'discrimination'. Pavlov found that it was possible to condition a dog to respond to one stimulus and not to another. One of his standard procedures was to introduce a luminous circle as conditioned stimulus, followed by food (the UCS). As soon as a conditioned

Figure 7

The spontaneous recovery of a conditioned response after extinction

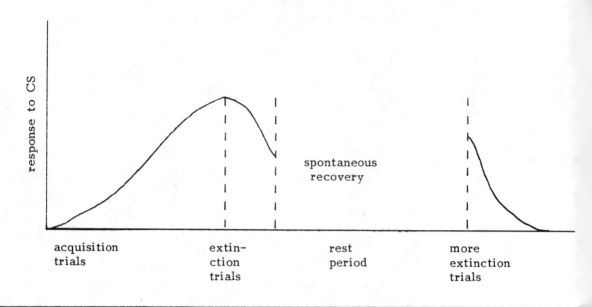

response to the circle has been obtained, Pavlov switched to an ellipse which was not followed by food. Soon the dog salivated only when the circle was presented. Pavlov then began to present an ellipse that was less and less elliptical and more and more circular. Eventually the dog could not make the discrimination. Then Pavlov recorded a remarkable change that came over the dog:

> After three weeks of work on this differentiation not only did the discrimination fail to improve, but it became considerably worse, and finally disappeared altogether. At the same time the whole behaviour of the animal underwent an abrupt change. The hitherto quiet dog began to squeal in its stand, kept wriggling about, tore off with its teeth the apparatus for mechanical stimulation of the skin, and bit through the tube connecting the animal's room with the observer, a behaviour which never happened before. On being taken to the experimental room the dog now barked violently, which was contrary to its usual custom; in short it presented all the symptoms of a condition of acute neurosis. On testing the cruder differentations they were also found to be destroyed (Pavlov, 1927).

Such was the original description of the phenomena of experimental neurosis.

Reinforcement
In instrumental conditioning, the concept of 'reinforcement'

has pride of place. In the classical conditioning paradigm, it simply refers to the pairing of two stimuli (CS and UCS) over time. Reinforcement is empirically defined as 'any event which, when employed appropriately, increases the probability of a particular response recurring in a similar situation'. The association in classical conditioning is therefore a stimulus-stimulus one, and reinforcement is said to have taken place any time they occur together. The reinforcement is, of course, the food (UCS), because any tendency for salivation (UCR) to occur to a bell (CS) is facilitated by its presence. It is important to note that in classical conditioning reinforcement occurs independently of responding; the food follows the bell whether or not the animal has salivated. This is in sharp contrast to the response-dependent situation that exists in instrumental conditioning where the reinforcement only occurs if the animal responds.

Classical conditioning in humans

Classical conditioning in humans is not easy to achieve and is usually limited to such reflex responses as the eye blink. Also, the evidence has not supported Pavlov's belief that 'every imaginable phenomenon of the outer world affecting a specific receptive surface of the body may be converted into a CS'. But such conditioning is often inferred to have taken place in real-life situations; we are 'conditioned' to fear spiders, 'conditioned' to want to work and so forth. It is also the theoretical base on which behaviour therapies such as systematic desensitization are built. Such approaches to treatment are discussed in chapter 18 and should be contrasted with strategies based on other theoretical formulations to describe the same phenomena discussed in chapter 19.

Instrumental or operant conditioning

Even before Pavlov was conducting his experiments that were to influence a generation of psychologists, Thorndike in America was experimenting with hungry animals placed in boxes with food in sight but out of reach. The box was so constructed that the door could be opened if the dog pressed a lever. In due course the dog would press the lever by accident, the door would open, the food would be eaten, and the appetite satisfied. Over time, the animal became quicker and quicker at pressing the lever on being returned to the box, until eventually it would press it at once.

The principle of reinforcement

This is the basic paradigm for operant conditioning. Here the emphasis is on an environmental event and its consequences and not on two environmental events as in classical conditioning. The most important psychological principle is that of reinforcement, and there are two basic types: positive and negative. Positive makes the actions it follows more likely to occur BECAUSE THE GOAL IS ACHIEVED OR THE REWARD OBTAINED; whereas negative REINFORCEMENT

makes the actions MORE likely to occur BECAUSE ESCAPE
FROM AN UNPLEASANT SITUATION HAS BEEN ACHIEVED.
For instance, when a dog leaps through a hoop to escape from
an electric shock coming through the floor of its cage, the
shock is a negative reinforcer, as it increases the likelihood of the response occurring which terminates the aversive
or painful stimulus. Apart from escape training, negative
reinforcement can be used to produce avoidance behaviour.
If the dog jumps quickly enough, it will avoid the painful
stimulus altogether.

Both positive and negative reinforcers increase the
probability of a response occurring. The behaviour can be
said to be strengthened. Negative reinforcement is therefore
different from punishment which weakens or decreases the
likelihood of the behaviour occurring. Behaviour may also be
weakened by the omission of the reinforcer previously present. Omission training leads to the eventual extinction
of the response.

As in classical conditioning, generalization and discrimination also occur. For instance, a pigeon trained to peck
at a blue disc pecks less and less reliably as the colour
fades. And it can be trained to discriminate between blue
and red discs, so that it pecks at blue ones and not at red
ones.

Schedules of reinforcement

Not all reinforcers need be followed by reinforcement every
time for them to be established and maintained. In the laboratory, responses are reinforced by 'schedules of reinforcement'. The four basic schedules are fixed interval (FI),
fixed ratio (FR), variable interval (VI), and variable ratio
(VR).

In 'fixed interval reinforcement', the reinforcement is
administered according to the elapse of a fixed period of
time. For example, if the interval is one minute (FI-1), the
animal that responds once every minute will receive maximum
reinforcement for least effort, since additional responses
will produce no effect.

The effects of different schedules can be demonstrated
by means of a 'cumulative record'. This is a graph which
indicates the 'number of responses' on the vertical axis and
'time' on the horizontal axis. Each response raises the record another step and the width of the step indicates the
time interval between responses. The reinforcements are
shown by a slanted line on the cumulative record curve. As
you will see in figure 8a, fixed interval schedules produce
a typical 'scalloping' effect as each reinforcement is followed by a pause and then an increase in rate of responding
towards the end of the interval. Studying for exams could be
said to follow this pattern. There is little studying after
one exam is over and then the rate gradually increases as
the next exam approaches.

Figure 8

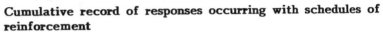

Cumulative record of responses occurring with schedules of reinforcement

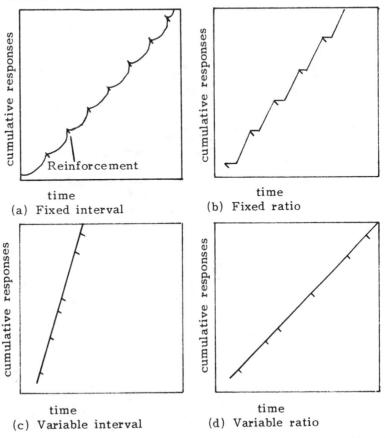

On a fixed ratio schedule, reinforcement occurs after a fixed number of responses has been made. For example, the animal must respond 20 times, say, before obtaining a reward. Figure 8b shows a pause in the response rate after each reinforcement and then a high rate of response. Piece-work in factories could be said to be based on a fixed ratio schedule.

Variable interval schedules involve reinforcing after an average time interval and in variable ratio schedules reinforcement occurs after an average number of responses. A good example of VR is the slot machine, which pays out after a variable number of coins. Figure 8c and figure 8d show the fairly constant rate of responding that variable interval and variable ratio types of reinforcement schedule elicit.

Extinction
With no reinforcement at all, response frequency inevitably decreases until it ceases altogether. But these different

schedules affect the relative resistance of the response to extinction. With continuous reinforcement, extinction is rapid. The change from each response being reinforced to none is a readily discernible one. But extinction after the use of intermittent or 'partial reinforcement' is much less quick. This has important implications for social behaviour. The occupational therapist who occasionally reinforces the disruptive patient by stopping what she is doing and giving the patient her full attention is building up trouble for herself in the future. She is giving positive reinforcement for disruptive behaviour instead of giving partial reinforcement for quiet, concentrated behaviour.

Spontaneous recovery

As with classical conditioning, a response that has been extinguished has not been forgotten. If some days elapse after the apparent complete extinction of a response, and the animal is given the opportunity to perform that response again, it will do so even though there has been no further reinforcement. However, if no reinforcements occur, extinction is more rapid.

Acquisition and shaping

With operant conditioning, as opposed to classical conditioning, the organism can be taught a novel piece of behaviour by the process of 'shaping'. To train a pigeon to turn in a circle, the method of 'successive approximations' can be used. First, the bird is reinforced for any head or body movement in the required direction. When this movement has become established, only half turns will be reinforced, then only full turns. The experimenter is helped in this procedure by the many movements the bird or animal performs when reinforcement is withdrawn, increasing the likelihood of the desired response occurring.

Secondary reinforcement

If tied only to specific reinforcements for behavioural responses, operant conditioning would be severely limited in application. But when the stimuli which are associated with the primary reinforcers themselves come to have reinforcing value, then its range of applicability becomes much wider. In an early experiment by Wolfe (1936), chimpanzees were reinforced with grapes while playing with a vending machine. Wolfe gave poker chips secondary reinforcing value by allowing the chimps to 'buy' grapes by putting poker chips into the machine. After this the chimps would work for the chips themselves on other tasks. It can be argued from this perspective that much human behaviour is the result of such secondary reinforcement. One way of looking at it is to see primary reinforcers as being the more biological ones and secondary reinforcers as the man-made or more artificial ones.

In 1965 Premack suggested discarding such a two-tier system and thinking instead in terms of a single scale of reinforcement value, based on the personal preferences of the individual or the particular animal species. The 'Premack Principle' suggests that activities higher up the scale will reinforce those lower down but not vice versa. For instance, the reinforcement for working overtime is what we want to do with the extra money. A child will do homework because of the increased likelihood of attaining the goal of going to university. By stressing that any activity or set of stimuli can reinforce behaviour, Premack greatly enhanced our ability to understand complex behaviour from a conditioning standpoint.

Learning a motor skill

Motivation and reinforcement
We all have a great deal of personal experience of the rewards and punishments of learning. At times all goes marvellously smoothly and at others we seem beset by difficulties. So it will be with the patient you are helping learn, say, how to do a plaited border on a basket as part of the treatment programme in a psychiatric hospital or to help exercise finger muscles following a stroke. What may patients think of this? They may think the whole exercise a waste of time; they may find it rather uncomfortable or painful; they may believe that to finish the border, and so the basket, will mean that they are on the way to recovery and so to discharge which means facing daily living again for which they do not really feel ready. A vital aspect of any learning situation is how patients construe what you are asking them to do: it depends on their motivation. Some of the things psychologists have to say about motivation will be dealt with in detail in the next chapter and some of the psychological aspects of pain are covered in the chapter after that.

The importance of motivation and the experience of pain cannot be over-emphasized in your role as a teacher, nor can reinforcement. With your patients it will not be necessary to think in terms of food or sweets, but rather in terms of your own words of encouragement and the degree to which they are successful in their own eyes as well as in yours.

Progress in learning
One of the earliest curves showing the process of learning was that produced by Bryan and Harter in 1899. In studying the learning process of students training to be telegraph operators, they found 'plateaux'. Students made steady progress until they had almost reached the minimal standard for receiving signals, and then they remained static for some considerable time. Eventually they started to make progress again and continued to do so well beyond the minimal required level. It is obviously in these plateaux that a person is most likely to lose heart and to need encouragement.

The whole or its parts?
Keeping to the plaited border of a basket as in our example, there is the question of whether you should try to teach

your patients the whole process at once, so that they can get a glimpse of the end result, or whether it is better to break the learning up into specific stages or parts. The advantage of the whole method is that patients do not have to work in ignorance of what they are aiming at and so, if at times they are in doubt, they can picture what the end result looks like and thus perhaps get themselves out of their difficulty. The advantage of the part method is that the procedure can be broken down into relatively easy stages which a patient can master and thereby gain increased confidence.

Which is preferable will depend a great deal on the task, but often it is a good idea to use both approaches. For instance, you could show your patient a basket border that has been finished by another patient and then proceed to teach each of the individual steps, going on to the next when the previous one has been completed. You can use the same method yourself in your own studying. If you have to learn the origins, insertions, nerve supplies and actions of the muscles of the thigh, you can study pictures or models of the thigh and then write the details of each muscle on separate cards. Carry these cards around with you and read them through at bus stops, in trains or in the bath until you can recite them from memory.

The distribution of practice
This raises the issue about the amount of time you should spend learning something at any one sitting. With your patients, it will often be determined by their state of health; some will tire more quickly than others. But supposing fatigue is not a particular problem, there is plenty of evidence to show that spacing your learning out by having brief intervals is more productive than working for long periods at one time. Your patients will learn their basketry better if they are given the opportunity to chat between each of the stages instead of being encouraged to 'keep at it' until the work is completed. Again, the same applies to our own studying. Your coffee breaks may give you a psychological advantage over students who feel they must sit in the library for hours at a time in order to get the most out of their studying.

There is just one exception to the rule that spaced is better than massed practice, and that is when you are doing some creative work. For instance, if you are writing a book, a certain amount of time is necessary each time you start for 'warm-up'. If you try and squeeze writing in between other activities, you start each session 'cold'. In this instance, if you can put aside fairly large chunks of time, much of the time spent on 'warm-ups' will be spent instead on creative work.

Knowledge of results
In learning very complex skills, the units or parts making up the whole are themselves complex; so complex that it is

not possible to see whether one is doing well or not. It follows that information or feedback about how successful one is at a given time (knowledge of results) can have a powerful effect on the ease with which one learns.

Transfer of training

Very often the skills you are teaching your patients will be somewhat similar in nature. Cord knotting spills over into netting; what is learnt in social skills training will transfer to the learning that takes place in a group activity demanding interpersonal co-operation. So transfer of training simply means the carrying over of some aspects of the skill to another activity. However, this transfer can be positive or negative. It is positive when the training in one activity helps the learning of a second activity as between cord knotting and netting; and is negative when the training in one activity inhibits or retards the learning or performance of another. Anyone who has played tennis knows how difficult it is then to play a game of table tennis, and this is a clear example of negative transfer. It can also, of course, be zero when training in one activity has no observed influence on the performance or acquisition of a second.

In conclusion

The different aspects of learning have relevance for different aspects of your work. By and large, the two types of conditioning are particularly relevant in situations in which you are being the psychological therapist, whereas those to do with developing manual skills are more valuable to you when you are playing the role of the teacher. Equally of importance in your work as teacher and therapist are the issues of motivation and psychological aspects of pain which are discussed in the next two chapters.

References

Bryan, W.L. and Harter, N. (1899)
Studies on the telegraphic language: the acquisition of a hierarchy of habits. Psychological Review, 6, 345-375.

Pavlov, I.P. (1927)
Conditioned Reflexes (translated by G.V. Anrep). Oxford: Clarendon Press.

Premack, D. (1965)
Reinforcement theory. In D. Levine (ed.), Nebraska Symposium on Motivation. Nebraska: University of Nebraska Press.

Wolfe, J.B. (1936)
Effectiveness of token-rewards for chimpanzees. Comparative Psychology Monographs, 12, 1-72.

Questions

1. Briefly explain the term 'schedules of reinforcement'. Describe in detail how a schedule of reinforcement may be used to change behaviour.

2. What psychological factors should be borne in mind when teaching a patient a new skill?
3. 'There can be no worthwhile learning without action.' Do you agree with this statement? If so, give your reasons.
4. Define the term 'feedback'. Discuss the importance of different types of feedback in both the teaching and learning of a task.
5. In what ways is 'feedback' or 'knowledge of results' built into any skilled human performance?
6. Distinguish between classical and operant conditioning.
7. Give an account of the role of reinforcement in learning. Illustrate your answer with examples from daily life.
8. Outline the main sources of frustration which adults encounter in learning new skills.
9. Without the development of behaviourism, psychology would have made far greater advances than it has. Discuss this statement.
10. Describe the psychological principles upon which desensitization and 'shaping' procedures are based.

Annotated reading

Gray, J.A. (1979) Pavlov. London: Fontana.
Once again a Fontana book giving a very clear account of Pavlov the man and his ideas as they developed over the years. The only difficulty you may encounter with this book is to prevent negative feelings being built up over the bombardment of UCSs, CSs and UCRs.

Skinner, B.F. (1973) Beyond Freedom and Dignity. Harmondsworth: Penguin.
Skinner's psychology has exerted considerable influence over the way our society works. In this book he sets out his position on the notion of free will and the dignity of Man.

Walker, S. (1975) Learning and Reinforcement. London: Methuen.
This is a paperback giving a straightforward account of the nature of classical and operant conditioning. It is sometimes helpful to have another perspective on the same set of facts.

11

Motivation
Philip D. Evans

Opening remarks
FAY FRANSELLA

You will by now have come across mention of the concept of
motivation in several chapters and here Evans looks at it
in depth. He first outlines the history of the concept and
then discusses it from a present-day standpoint. You may
come to recognize that the history of the concept of motivation is also the history of psychology itself. It starts
with notions of needs and drives stemming from the stimulus-
response behaviourism of Pavlov and others and leads on to
the humanistic psychologists such as Maslow and Rogers.

You may be wondering how the concept of motivation
arose in the first place, since it clearly has developed in
such very different ways. It was all to do with the fact
that the early workers wanted psychology, above all else, to
be a science and some still very strongly support this view
today. The problem stems from the fact that the most basic
of sciences, physics, in those days regarded matter as an
inert substance. Thus, applying the methods of physics to
living organisms was clearly very difficult. Living matter
is not inert: it has the habit of constantly moving and
changing. Some concept had to be introduced to account for
this movement. In physics the concept of force or natural
energy was used to explain why matter moves, so Freud, for
instance, simply translated the notion of physical energy
into psychic energy which he called 'libido'. Many of the
more behaviouristic psychologists did not support this idea
(or any of the ideas of Freud, for that matter) and so in-
voked hypothetical constructs such as 'drives' which were
said to impel the organism to action in order to satisfy
some 'need'.

So the concept of motivation was originally made necessary because of the premise that something must be MAKING
the organism move. But Kelly has argued a contrary view:

> Life itself could be defined as a form of process or
> movement. Thus, in designating man as our object of
> psychological inquiry, we would be taking it for granted
> that movement was an essential property of his being,
> not something that had to be accounted for separately.
> We would be talking about a form of movement - man -
> not something that had to be motivated (1969).

If you conceptualize the person as basically an object to be impelled into action by something, then the concept of motivation is essential; if you regard the person as a living entity and assume that one of the properties of life is that it moves, you will take a quite different viewpoint. This chapter looks at the concept from both angles.

When discussing motivation to achieve in the classroom and at college, Evans mentions 'fear of failure'. Since the majority of occupational therapists are women, and it is likely that more than half your patients will be women, I have included an outline of the work carried out into the opposite concept: 'fear of success' or the 'motive to avoid success'. Fear of failure is thought to occur mainly in men and fear of success mainly in women.

This, of course, is no mere academic question. How do you, yourself, feel about your work? If you are a woman, are you planning to climb the career ladder and strive to get to the top, or are you planning to work only until you find someone 'to take you away from it all'? If you decide to climb the career ladder, you will have less of a problem than do many women because of the sex bias of your profession, but problems do remain. For instance, a report by the Medical Practitioners Union, November 1981, states that women medical students are subjected to unfair pressure. They are expected to be 'flirtatious and feminine' but are criticized if they are. It says, 'If they do behave as expected they will be labelled as unprofessional, and if they don't they will be despised as career women.' The problem continues after qualification. The woman often has to choose between children or a career. If she combines work with child-bearing she is criticized for being a bad mother. This is the layman's attitude in spite of the fact that there is even some evidence to the contrary, as mentioned in chapter 4. The report goes on to say that if she does give up work altogether she is condemned for wasting the investment in her medical education. The Union also says that, to be successful, women are expected to adopt men's attitudes to ambition and success. But these attitudes are inappropriate in medicine. The qualities of a good doctor (and a good occupational therapist) are embodied in women's attitudes to caring and nurturing. The Union advises a woman doctor who wants to combine her career with domestic commitments to 'Decide what you want to do and fight for your right to do it.' I cannot help feeling that what is being said there about women doctors is also very pertinent to women occupational therapists.

Introduction
PHILIP D. EVANS

Poetically speaking, motivation may be considered to be about the 'springs of action'. More prosaically, the motivation theorists ask themselves why any bit of behaviour occurs: what are the necessary and sufficient conditions which make any organism, human or animal, give up one activity and take up another, in the ever-flowing stream that constitutes behaviour?

In everyday life, people answer essentially motivational questions by giving 'reasons' or 'intentions' for their actions, but these are often given after the event and cannot be said to 'explain' behaviour in any scientific fashion. The psychologist is more interested in specifying conditions beforehand which, if they pertain, inevitably lead to a prediction that some behaviour probably will (or will not) occur. Where do we find these all-important conditions? Traditional wisdom, in the case of human behaviour, has until this century always taught us that the answer to questions about why we behave lies inaccessibly in the mind, whatever that may be. The mind wills the body, and since the will is supposedly free, we might as well give up any attempt to predict human behaviour! Fortunately the work of Charles Darwin changed all that and all animal behaviour, including human behaviour, became fair game for systematic and scientific enquiry. Like other areas of psychology, then, empirical research in the field of motivation has been largely a twentieth-century endeavour. First of all, let us briefly sketch in the historical aspects of our subject matter.

Historical perspective

When Ivan Pavlov (1849-1936) discovered the phenomenon of the 'conditioned reflex', the scene appeared to be set for explaining all behaviour as the sum of responses and conditioned responses, which in turn could be traced inexorably back to their controlling stimuli. The answer to the question 'What motivated that particular response?' would simply be: that particular stimulus. This was the revolutionary behaviourism preached in the 1920s by the American psychologist, John B. Watson.

In the 1930s, this strident behaviourism was somewhat moderated by the ideas of Clark Hull, perhaps the most influential theorist of motivation and behaviour right up to the 1950s. Like Watson, Hull believed that all behaviour could be seen as stimulus-response chains. However, he was also influenced by the work of an earlier psychologist, Thorndike, who had shown how animals can learn to solve certain problems by 'trial and error' if successful responses were reliably followed by important consequences such as food for a hungry animal or escape for a confined one. Hull believed that such consequences 'reinforced' a connection between a stimulus and a response and built it into a habit. In trying to define the nature of reinforcement of this kind, Hull committed himself to a belief in internal mediators of behaviour, hidden sources of motivation. Briefly, he believed that physiological needs resulting from deprivation of food, water, etc., brought about a general motivational state within the organism called 'drive' which goaded it into activity. When such activity finally resulted in the animal finding a source of satisfying the need, drive reduction would take place. It was this drive reduction which Hull identified as the basis of reinforcement. Thus, for Hull, the performance of any act was the result of two basic types of variables: the strength of the habit being considered and the motivation, resulting from drive, to perform the habit. The two variables were assumed to act multiplicatively; thus if drive is zero, the animal will not perform the response however well it 'knows' how to perform it: that is, however great the habit strength. Conversely, the animal will not perform the response however great its motivational drive if it does not know how to perform: that is, if habit strength equals zero.

This theoretical approach may seem over-simplified and applicable more to laboratory rats in simple mazes than human beings in more complex situations, but Hull assumed that more complex motives could be acquired by association with more primary ones, through conditioning procedures of a Pavlovian kind.

One of the major embarrassments to Hull's early theory came from findings which suggested that, even in the case of simple animals in mazes, sources of motivation could not be confined to the internal drive variable. It appeared that the reinforcer itself seemed to have incentive properties, which acted to 'pull' the animal towards a goal, as much as the assumed drive force was taken to 'push' it there. An animal's running speed to a goal would reflect, for example, the quantity and quality of the reinforcement given. Hull did not like the mentalistic notion that animals could be motivated by expectations of some future event in the goal box, but he was forced to admit a new motivational term into his theoretical model to account for such incentive motivational effects. The fact that he phrased such incentive effects in mechanistic stimulus-response language reflects only a bias of vocabulary.

The modern era

Hull's intention had been to build up a complex and general model of all motivated behaviour, human and animal. Despite increasing complexity the endeavour failed. Predication on such a grand scale was impossible. The modern trend within psychology as a whole has been to develop mini-theories which can tell us something useful about more limited areas of behaviour, and particularly human behaviour. Whereas Hull had been content to speculate that human motives could be ultimately traced back to biological imperatives shared by all organisms, that formidable task of tracing the development of motives has lost ground to theories which simply assume motives, arising perhaps out of particular human needs, demonstrate that the strength of the motive can be effectively measured, and then propose predictions about how such specified motives interact with an environmental context to produce behaviour related to that motive. The approach is still vaguely Hullian, but by being more narrow in its scope offers greater opportunity for useful application. There are two areas of research which illustrate this. First, work on achievement motivation, that is, striving behaviour in human beings: this is described immediately after a general theory of human needs is outlined. Second, research in the field of anxiety as a motive is examined. The research in both areas has been done with human beings and has scope for application. Lastly, we return to the animal laboratory to show that results from that quarter can themselves be very illuminating when discussed in the context of human problems.

Maslow's theory of human needs

Maslow, like Hull, believed that actions spring from needs but, unlike Hull, was not interested in the derivation of all needs and motives from a few primary biological survival needs. Rather he put forward the interesting idea that the major human needs could be put into a hierarchical order. Having done this, he postulated a theoretical prediction that needs higher up the 'ladder' would only produce striving for fulfilment when those lower down the ladder were satisfied. His category order from lowest to highest was:

* biological survival needs: for example, need for food, water, oxygen, etc.;
* safety needs: for example, need to avoid danger, need for security;
* affiliated needs: for example, love, friendship, acceptance by others;
* self-esteem needs: for example, self-acceptance, success in life;
* self-actualization needs: for example, achievement of one's full potential.

Although Maslow's ideas were not earth shattering, they were put forward at a time (just after the Second World War) when people were becoming receptive. Particularly ready to receive them were the growing number of management training establishments. Managers of industry were of necessity becoming interested in the question of what motivated people to work in modern society where it had to be taken for granted that survival needs would be taken care of by at least a token Welfare State. Nineteenth-century notions of keeping a person at work by keeping the wolf of hunger at the door were no longer practically or ethically possible. Maslow's theory was soon taken up by business schools particularly in the USA, and was used to generate ideas about how work conditions could be arranged to satisfy higher-level needs, rather than just provide a pay-packet at the end of the week. Applied researchers were stimulated to ask whether a particular job allowed affiliative needs to be satisfied; alternatively, did another job foster a sense of personal responsibility which could satisfy self-esteem needs?

Although Maslow's theory could not be said to be predictive of behaviour (it is too general for that), it was generative of much piecemeal research which paid dividends in terms of productivity and job satisfaction. It was also a reference point for later, more specific, theories of work motivation which related performance to an interaction between non-monetary need variables and monetary incentive variables (see Murrell, 1976).

Maslow's views of human motivation have also been taken up in the field of psychotherapy. Traditionally, psycho-therapy has been concerned with resolving, in Maslow's terms, problems with affiliative and self-esteem needs. Maslow's theory, however, hints that people who are reasonably well satisfied with respect to these needs will inevitably turn their attention to satisfying self-actualization needs: that is, fulfilment of full potential. The idea that so-called 'normal' people may seek 'therapy' to help themselves along the road to full growth is no more than a necessary corollary of Maslow's theory. It is less than surprising, therefore, that the human 'growth' movement, with its encounter groups and sensitivity training groups and so on, should have grown up particularly in the rich state of California, where lower-level needs may have been satisfied to a point of boredom!

Achievement motivation

If Maslow's theory of needs lacks predictive power and is instead a useful and productive way of looking at human behaviour, the same is not true of the next motivational theory, which does generate quite specific predictions about how different people react in different situations. In many areas of life one could point to standards which define excellence, achievement, success. A person's motivation to achieve these standards has been called 'need achievement motivation' or nAch for short. One of the pioneers of research in this area, McClelland, was the first to demonstrate that a person's hidden reserves of nAch could reliably be measured by looking at their fantasy life in certain controlled conditions. By using a 'personality test', in which the person invented stories around certain pictures on cards, McClelland found that he could score these stories for the number of achievement-related themes in them. The scores which resulted were reliable enough to differentiate low nAch people and high nAch people. More importantly the scores also had validity: that is, they would to an important degree predict real differences in 'striving' behaviour in real contexts of an achievement kind. In the laboratory, for example, high nAch subjects could be shown to persist longer at some task or other than low nAch subjects. Outside the laboratory, studies have shown that high nAch subjects are more likely to be 'upwardly socially mobile' in terms of changing socio-economic status, whilst low nAch subjects are more likely to stay still, or even move down the scale.

However, it became clear to the early researchers that achievement-related behaviour was powerfully affected by more than just the nAch motive. In particular, certain subjects seemed to behave in such striving situations as if their primary motivation was to avoid failure rather than simply succeed. By using a questionnaire to measure this 'fear of failure' trait, it was possible to make predictions about real achievement behaviour in a more exact fashion. Atkinson, one of the foremost of modern motivation theorists, proposed a modified theory of achievement behaviour, incorporating two major motives, nAch and fear of failure, together with certain contextual variables, notably the perceived probability of success (or failure), and the incentive (or 'negative incentive': 'shame' if you like) associated with success (or failure). The probability variables are related in a complementary way to their respective incentive variables. This is common sense in a way, since if a task is very easy (i.e. the probability of success is very large), then the incentive attached to succeeding is not very high. Conversely, if the task is very difficult (i.e. the probability of success is low) the incentive, or kudos, attached to succeeding is correspondingly high. Now if we look at how the theory works in principle we find that it gives rise to some quite specific predictions. Consider first those individuals whose need to achieve (nAch) is dominant over their fear of failure. Their tendency to approach a task or strive at it is going to be maximized when the probability of success multiplies with the incentive value to give the highest overall result. If, as we have said, probability of success and incentive are intrinsically related and therefore:

Incentive value = (1) - (probability of success)

then it is clear that the multiplicative product of the two variables is at its greatest when probability of success is 0.5 and the incentive is also therefore 0.5 (i.e. 1 - 0.5). All that really needs to be understood is that high nAch subjects, relatively speaking, are predicted to show a real preference for tasks of middling difficulty. Now let us consider the person whose dominating motive is to avoid failure. Where the probability of success is 0.5, so obviously is the probability of failure. Also, if the probability of failure is 0.5, the negative incentive or shame of failing is 0.5 (i.e. 1 minus the probability of failure). Thus the person's avoidance tendency is maximally aroused in exactly the same situation as that which attracted the more nAch-orientated person. Once again, regardless of the mathematics, the prediction is that people whose fear of failure is stronger than their level of nAch will show a preference for either very easy tasks or very difficult ones, but definitely avoid ones of middling difficulty. If the prediction that such a person may seek out very difficult tasks seems to you paradoxical, then just remember that in such tasks the negative incentive or shame of failing is very low; such a person may be considered to have a 'get-out' clause which allows people to say, 'He didn't succeed, but it was very difficult and at least he tried.'

So much for the theory. Are its predictions borne out? In the laboratory, a simple test is to ask subjects to play a hoop-la game of throwing a ring over a peg. In such a situation, the probability of success is clearly largely influenced by how closely one stands to the peg. When given a free choice, dominant nAch subjects showed a much greater propensity to stand a middling distance from the peg than did dominant fear-of-failure subjects. However, Atkinson's theory stands up to examination not just in the laboratory but in the world outside.

Achievement motivation in classroom and college
One of the perennial discussions in education is whether to 'stream' or not. Is mixed ability teaching to be recommended or not? Well, it is not our intention here to give any full answer to the question but it can be shown that Atkinson's theory is of relevance. Let us assume that a child very reasonably gauges the probability of success in academic matters by reference to classroom peers. This means that a child who is in a class of corresponding ability range is more likely to put the probability of success (and probability of failure) not far from 0.5. Our theory predicts that this is ideally motivating for a child whose motivation towards achievement is greater than any fear of failure, but is the worst situation for a child whose two compelling motivations are balanced the other way. In fact, O'Connor tested out the theoretical predictions and largely verified them, both with respect to interest in school work and measures in academic improvement. It should be said that motivational effects of the type of classroom situation are not the only variables which may be important when this controversy is debated; however, anyone's performance is a mixture of ability and motivation, so such motivational factors deserve attention.

Atkinson's theory has also been applied in higher education. Researchers have examined the choice of options that students take in college. Options were first of all classed as easy, middling, or difficult. Students were then measured both in terms of nAch and fear of failure motivation. Once again the predictions were upheld. Students who were relatively high in nAch tended to go for options of middling difficulty, whilst this tendency was not pronounced in the students who were relatively strong on fear-of-failure motivation.

Lastly, some research has been done into how achievement motivation and fear-of-failure motivation influence career choice. Mahone has shown that students whose dominant motivation is nAch are more realistic in their career choices, whilst those students higher in fear-of-failure tend to be unrealistic by going for too easy and unchallenging careers or, alternatively, aiming too high for their abilities.

Can we talk of achieving societies?

The originator of nAch research, McClelland, has tried to investigate this question by examining the literature of different societies and societies at different times with a view to measuring the amount of achievement themes shown, just as for an individual his fantasy stories are examined. Some fascinating results have been reported. Measures of nAch taken from literary sources do predict economic performance. For example, nAch themes in English literature from 1500 to 1800 correspond in their ups and downs very well with economic performance as measured by coal imports into the port of London. In the USA, nAch between 1810 and 1950 rose and fell in tune with the number of patents issued per million of population. Even non-literate societies have been measured for nAch by analysing achievement themes in vase paintings and orally-transmitted folk tales!

The really interesting finding to come out of this work is that changes in nAch typically occur some years before the subsequent change in economic performance. Hence it is possible to make some predictions for the future. According to nAch measures the USA, for example, peaked in nAch around 1945, so the outlook is pretty gloomy for subsequent economic performance! However, all this work is extremely tenuous. The studies are all correlational in nature and difficult to interpret without a degree of arbitrariness. They are crucially dependent on measurement which is difficult to assess in terms of its reliability. And yet it must be said that McClelland's recent work is stimulating, and his statement that scientists should turn away from 'an exclusive concern with the external events of history to the internal psychological concerns that in the long run determine what happens in history' is a statement worthy of consideration.

Anxiety as a motive

We all know individuals who claim to act better when goaded with a bit of 'adrenalin', as the saying goes. Actors claim to give their peak performances when anxiety is there to give them a helping hand. Equally there are many (students taking exams, for example) who claim that anxiety is responsible for poor performance. What then is the truth? To predict the effects of anxiety we have to specify more variables. First, we obviously must take into account the level of anxiety experienced. Second, we must expect that the type of task being considered is important as a variable. Third, whatever the level of anxiety likely in the situation, we should expect some difference in the level experienced by different people: that is, it is to be expected that people have different capacities for being aroused in an anxious way by identical situations.

Let us deal with the simple relationship first between level of anxiety and performance. If we think back to Hull's force of drive, it is clear that we can consider anxiety a source of drive or, some might say, general arousal of the organism. Now there is a long-standing law in psychology

Figure 1
_____

The inverted–U function relating drive to performance

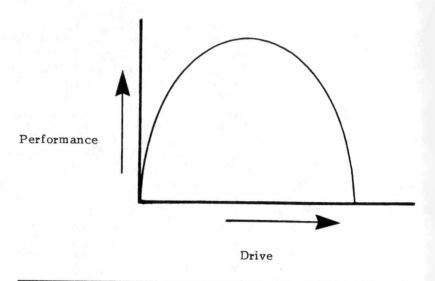

Performance

Drive
_____

which relates drive to performance by a so-called 'inverted-U function'. This is simply illustrated in figure 1.

The predictions that this law makes are equally simple. Other things being equal, performance will be enhanced by increasing drive, but only up to a certain point. Beyond this, further increases in drive will lead to poorer and poorer performance. We can assume anxiety, then, acts broadly in this fashion. However, we should still like to know a bit more. When, for example, is the peak of the inverted U likely to be met? This is where it is important to consider our other factors, such as the nature of the task and the nature of the person. One of the major ways tasks differ is in their difficulty. Spence and Taylor, two psychologists who may be described as latter-day Hullians, did a series of experiments to shed light on how high-anxiety and low-anxiety persons were differentially affected by tasks which were either easy or difficult. Without going into too much theoretical detail, let us say something more about drive. Drive is taken to be a non-directive general pushing force and hence is taken to energize incorrect performance as much as correct performance. The prediction was made, therefore, that in an easy task, where incorrect responses are not much in evidence, high anxiety serves mainly to energize just the correct responses. Therefore Spence and Taylor predicted that high-anxiety subjects would perform such tasks better than low-anxiety subjects. In the case of a difficult task we can assume that incorrect responses are constantly competing with correct ones and that high levels of drive are counter-productive in the sense that they serve only to energize further such incorrect responses. The prediction, therefore, was that low-anxiety subjects would outperform high-anxiety subjects in such tasks. These predictions were in fact upheld in the laboratory tests. Moving outside the laboratory, then, we may speculate that actors may thrive on anxiety because they are performing presumably well-rehearsed material; our exam-taking student is, on the contrary, having to create novel and creative essays by integrating knowledge on the spot, and anxiety here is likely to be disruptive.

Recent trends in 'trait' motive research

Most of the work so far described could be classified as 'trait' motive research. In other words, psychologists have adopted the approach of measuring some assumed stable characteristic of personality, a trait which has motivational properties, such as nAch or anxiety. Within this tradition a large amount of integration is now under way. The work of Spence and Taylor, for example, is considered within the same framework of theory as that of Atkinson. New motives are being measured and entered into ever more complex equations to predict performance with more accuracy, often with the aid of computers.

There is another aspect to the modern trend, however, which needs to be mentioned, and that is the questioning of the unity of these assumed motives. Nowhere is this more in evidence than in the case of 'fear' or 'anxiety' as assumed single entity motives. Motives are usually felt (it is no accident that motivation and emotion share the same Latin root!) and it is when we try to measure that felt emotion or motive at the individual level that we run into difficulties. Clinical psychologists, for example, have learnt a lot recently about phobic reactions and their treatment; and yet, as they find out more, they have increasingly come to question the traditional view that the motive of fear motivates the avoidance behaviour which is the essence of a clinical phobia. The point is that fear is not a 'lump' (see Rachman, 1978); it is divisible. Some people show fear by reporting that they feel afraid, but show no fear in their behaviour. Others show fear by their physiological reactions, such as a pounding heart and clammy hands, but report that they are not feeling fear. There is, in other words, often a non-correspondence between the different measures that we have traditionally conceived as indicating fear. The message, in the case of individuals at any rate, is that the measurement of an assumed single unitary motivational trait is full of pitfalls. This is to some extent, then, a limitation of the type of research strategy that we have been describing so far. Note, however, that we say limitation rather than criticism. To be capable of reasonable prediction of the behaviour of broad types of people in a reasonable variety of situations is no mean achievement. The work described so far has demonstrated that this is possible.

The reinforcement view of motivation: no hidden motives

We promised at the beginning to return to the animal laboratory for an assessment of the relevance of that work to motivational questions. We mentioned then that one of the embarrassing findings for Hull's early theory was that the incentive or reinforcement which followed a response had motivational properties in its own right. The way in which different patterns of responding in an organism can be motivated and maintained by different patterns of reinforcement has been of central interest to that body of researchers who, broadly speaking, have followed in the footsteps of the celebrated psychologist B. F. Skinner. The literature which has accumulated is so vast that we can here do no more than give one or two examples and refer interested readers elsewhere, if they like the flavour of what they read.

Let us dive straight in with an example of a problem which might be faced by any marketing man. You have a product called 'Superchoc' which you want to promote. You devise a traditional promotion campaign which requires your young consumers to collect 20 wrappers, send them in, and be reinforced by the gift of a Superchoc plastic space-ship. Can this basic strategy be improved upon? Let us look at the animal laboratory. Your technique so far resembles that in which a rat is trained to press a bar 20 times for one sugar-pellet reward. The ratio of responses to reinforcement is fixed at 20 to 1; that is, in psychologists' terms, the rat is on a fixed-ratio 20 schedule of reinforcement. Now we know that all organisms respond in the same sort of way on a fixed-ratio schedule. The pattern of cumulative responding is given below in figure 2.

Note that after each reinforcement the organism takes a break; there is a lull in responding shown by a scallop on the graph. In terms of your marketing problem, these scallops represent unprofitable periods which you could do without. Now there are easy ways of removing scallops by making the reinforcement come after a varying amount of responses, but this method is not applicable in this case, nor would it motivate more vigorous (buying) behaviour overall. Let us then adopt a different method. Let us redefine the problem by considering it in terms of two schedules, one superimposed on the other. First we say that one response is going to be made up of five of our previous responses, and that the organism has to make four of these larger unit responses in order to get the reinforcement. In terms of the rat in the laboratory, what we do is to give it some sort of signal, perhaps a tone or a light, after each five bar-presses which signals that it has made one composite response; when it has made four composite responses it gets its food pellet. In the case of the marketing problem, we say that five wrappers get a certificate and that four certificates earn a space-ship. Well, you might say, nothing has really been changed: the same number of wrappers are finally exchanged for the same amount of reinforcement. That may be so, but the two methods of going about the exercise

Figure 2

The typical scalloped record of cumulative responding obtained on a fixed-ratio schedule. The schedule is FR20, and instances of reinforcement are shown by slashes.

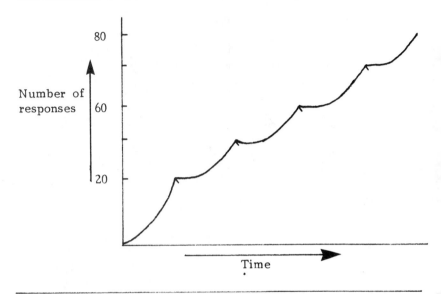

motivate very different patterns of performance and in the case of the second method, the lull that we talked about is shortened and performance as a whole is more vigorous; a worth-while thing to know in applied contexts.

Note that this area of research is not concerned with 'hidden motives'. It is solely interested in how behaviour patterns can be predicted from a knowledge of the way behaviour is externally reinforced. It must be said that individual differences are largely ignored, which is the very opposite of the 'trait' motive research that we have previously dealt with. On the other hand, when one is interested in motivating behaviour of large numbers of people, on the average so to speak, it is perfectly possible to ignore individual differences in the certain knowledge that one's reinforcement contingencies will by and large have the predicted results.

The reader who wishes to explore further this entire area, known as the experimental analysis of behaviour, should consult any major text such as Rachlin (1976).

Conclusions

Let us try now to pull together some theoretical strands. Motivation is a potentially vast and wide-ranging area of psychology. Traditionally it has been about the causes of action. There are two traditions which have defined the major approaches to the study of motivation. One sees action as a result of an interaction between current environmental variables - the context of the act, if you like - and a motivational tendency within the organism. Such a tendency may be considered a convenient fiction since no one supposes that motives are real things like tables and chairs; to talk of a motive is to use a kind of shorthand for referring to a relatively stable propensity for engaging in certain acts.

The other broad tradition is the Skinnerian approach mentioned latterly and perforce briefly since it takes motivation into almost a new field altogether. If we think of behaviour as output, the Skinnerian would have us believe that all output can in principle be predicted from a knowledge of input in terms of environmental observables, with no necessity to ask what goes on inside the organism. Motivation as traditionally conceived is rather redundant. Motivation becomes at once everything and nothing.

The former approach which does allow for the term 'motive' stems directly from the Hullian tradition. Note how similar Atkinson's theory is to Hull's. Probability of success is like habit strength and both reflect the capability of the organism; nAch is like drive and reflects the motivational push to perform; finally, both admit an incentive variable which also motivates the organism towards a goal. All three variables interact in both systems in a broadly multiplicative fashion.

Both approaches have proven to be useful and lastly we should perhaps point out that in certain areas, notably choice of behaviour where an organism has a choice of activities, it is becoming evident that their predictions are essentially the same (see Atkinson and Birch, 1979). Perhaps, like so many differences of approach and theory, eventually our two traditions described here will be seen to differ solely in their vocabulary, terms, and ways of putting the argument.

Fear of success and under-achievement
FAY FRANSELLA

Fear of success

As mentioned above, McClelland's early work on achievement motivation was carried out using the Thematic Apperception Test (TAT). In this test, people are asked to tell a story about a series of pictures. Although McClelland's work showed that scores on the TAT were related to desire for achievement for men, this was not the case for women. In many studies there was no relationship at all, for women, between the number of 'achievement themes' and their performance in a test situation; nor did the measures predict how hard they would try.

Stein and Bailey published a comprehensive review of this literature in 1973 and suggested a reason for the inconclusive results. It is not that women are simply less interested in achieving for its own sake than are men, but that women want to achieve and be successful in different ways from men. Stein and Bailey argue that women want to achieve in interpersonal relationships and social skills, and are less interested in academic success. This, they say, results from a culture which defines social success as appropriate for women, whereas academic success is not. They cite a study in support of this theory in which American college women, who valued 'traditional' roles, increased their 'achievement imagery' scores after being told that they were to complete a 'test of social skills' which predicts how successful people are likely to be both socially and in their marriages.

But, as so often in psychology, there is an alternative theory. Horner (1970, 1972) says that many women do want to achieve but are afraid of success because they see it as having undesirable consequences. She tested this hypothesis in a very simple way. She asked 90 women college students to complete a story which begins 'At the end of term finals, Anne finds herself at the top of her medical school class ...'. Eighty-eight male students were also asked to complete the story but had the name John substituted for the name Anne.

These stories were scored according to whether or not they contained statements suggesting conflict about the success; the presence or anticipation of negative consequences because of the success; denial of effort or responsibility for attaining the success; denial of the success itself; or some other bizarre or inappropriate response to the success. The results of this analysis showed that 65 per cent of the women wrote stories containing statements showing fear of success, whereas only eight of the 88 men did so. Horner gave the following as an example of a typical series of statements: 'Anne deliberately lowers her academic standing next term, and does all she can to help Carl, whose grades come up. She soon drops out of med-school, they marry, and Carl goes on in school while she raises their family.' Ninety per cent of the men, on the other hand, showed confidence and pleasure at the success. Horner concludes that the overall picture is one of women seeing unusual excellence as clearly associated with loss of femininity, social rejection, personal or social destruction, or a combination of these, whereas the men seemed just out and out pleased at John's success and saw him going on to have a very happy and successful life (see Medrick, Tangri and Hoffman, 1975).

However, in 1974, Feather and Raphelson suggested a somewhat different interpretation of Horner's results. They argued that the results did not indicate that the women were expressing their fear of success but indicated straightforward sex-role stereotyping. This basically says that it is not socially appropriate for women to succeed academically: or at least to be better than men. If this were so, then men should express negative attitudes about success when writing about Anne, and women should express no such negative consequences when writing about John.

To test this, Feather and Raphelson studied 126 men and 88 women Australian students and 88 men and 113 women American students. Half the men and half the women wrote stories about John and the others wrote about Anne. Their prediction was found to be correct for the men from both countries: there were significantly more 'fear of success' stories when writing about Anne than about John. But this was not so for the women. The Australian women were like the men in seeing Anne in 'fear of success' terms, but the American women produced similar amounts of fear of success for both Anne and John.

Thus, the Australians, men and women, supported the idea that it was sex-role stereotypes that were being measured and not specifically fear of success in women. But American women did not use the stereotype in this way. This could reflect cultural differences and the effects of the women's movements in America. Of course, the fact that the American women gave no more negative consequences to Anne for being a success compared with John does not mean that they themselves do not actually fear the social consequences of being a success. What we say we believe in relation to others does not always reflect what we believe or want for ourselves.

Yet there is evidence from many other studies that men do show as much fear of success in the stories they write as do women. Hoffman (1974) pointed out that the negative consequences of success for men and women may be different, just as the goals for achievement differ. Women most commonly told stories about Anne that indicated social rejection. 'She had no social life and therefore had spent all first semester studying. She was always a good student. Lonely but good.' By contrast, the most common theme for men seems to be one in which the whole value of achievement is questioned. 'John graduated with honours and hates being a doctor. He wonders what it was all about.'

In the summary to our chapter on fear of success in 'On Being a Woman', Frost and I say:

> The difference in the ways that men and women value themselves fits in very well with their notions of the different life roles expected of them. But which comes first? Very likely this is not a sensible question.
> Girls and women learn at one and the same time, that they are supposed to have certain qualities, that this is what is expected of wives and mothers, and that wives and mothers they are going to be. All this would be fine and good. But they also learn that they are not supposed to have qualities which belong to roles they are not intended to have. Without these qualities they are disabled in academic and working life. Yet when they do possess them, they experience conflict and anxiety (Fransella and Frost, 1977).

This subject continues to be studied in psychology and has clear social importance. It seems highly unlikely that women's failure to be represented in the 'top jobs' and in certain professions is solely to do with male prejudice. It is indeed not unknown for certain important posts to be specifically designated for a woman so that the organization can be seen to be satisfying the demand for equality, and yet be unable to find an applicant.

Under-achievement

In the context of motivation it is useful to look at those who do not demonstrate their predicted potential; those who under-achieve as well as those who do achieve. The question to be asked is 'Do women shy away from success and, if so, when does it start?' A study by Shaw and McCuen (1960) suggests that the rot sets in early. They checked up on 168 children who had been given an IQ test when they were in the eighth grade (aged about 12) and who were now in the eleventh and twelfth grades (aged about 15 and 16). The children were grouped into 'achievers' and 'under-achievers' and their academic records studied from the time they were in the first grade. The curves for the boys and girls were different. Boys who started under-achieving in the first grade continued to do so. The girls, however, did not seriously start to under-achieve until the sixth grade or around puberty.

Horner has suggested that women may be in conflict because they see being successful as being unfeminine. If there is something in this idea, then it could well be expected to begin to take effect at puberty: certainly in the 1960s.

Others have pointed out how women will adopt submissive roles on purpose, so as to avoid being threatening to men. John Coleman (1961) studied the self-evaluations of boys and girls and how these change over time. He says: 'Boys and girls start very close to the same point, but then diverge, the best girl students becoming less likely over the four years to want to be remembered in this way.' However, it is interesting to note that in the ten schools that were studied, the girls consistently got higher marks than did the boys. Coleman continues:

> The double constraints on girls (to do well but not to be brilliant) are evident in other ways as well. For many a girl, the solution to the dilemma of 'good but not aggressively brilliant' is an ingenious one; she gets good grades, but she is never extremely outstanding. She is neither better than the best boy student nor poorer than the worst. Her grades are 'compressed' by the double constraints of conforming to the two norms. As a result, the grades of a girl are more nearly alike from course to course than those of a boy, and the within-girl variance in grades is less than for boys. If a girl has a B average, she has more Bs and fewer Cs than does a boy with a B average (Coleman, 1961).

Like so many seemingly straightforward issues concerning how human beings go about making sense of themselves and life, the concept of motivation is a very complex one.

References

Atkinson, J.W. and Birch, D. (1979)
An Introduction to Motivation. Princeton, NJ: Van Nostrand.

Coleman, J. (1961)
The Adolescent Society. Glencoe, Ill: Free Press.

Feather, N. and Raphelson, A. (1974)
Fear of success in Australian and American student groups: motive or sex-role stereotype? Journal of Personality, 42, 190-201.

Fransella, F. and Frost, K. (1977)
On Being a Woman. London: Tavistock Publications.

Horner, M. (1970)
Femininity and successful achievement: a basic inconsistency. In J. Bardwick, E. Douvan, M. Horner and D. Gutman (eds), Feminine Personality and Conflict. Belmont, Ca: Brooks-Cole.

Horner, M. (1972)
Toward an understanding of achievement-related conflicts in women. Journal of Social Issues, 28, 157-175.

Hoffman, L. (1974)
Fear of success in males and females: 1965 and 1971. Journal of Consulting and Clinical Psychology, 42, 353-358.

Kelly, G.A. (1969)
Man's construction of his alternatives. In B. Maher (ed.), Clinical Psychology and Personality: The selected papers of George Kelly. New York: Krieger.

Medrick, M.T.S., Tangri, S.S. and Hoffman, L.W. (eds) (1975)
Women and Achievement: Social and motivational analysis. New York: Halsted Press.

Murrell, H. (1976)
Motivation at Work. London: Methuen.

Rachlin, H. (1976)
Introduction to Modern Behaviorism. San Francisco: Freeman.

Rachman, S.J. (1978)
Fear and Courage. San Francisco: Freeman.

Shaw, M. and McCuen, J. (1960)
The onset of academic under-achievement in bright children. Journal of Educational Psychology, 51, 103-108.

Stein, A. and Bailey, M. (1973)
The socialization of achievement orientation in females. Psychological Bulletin, 80, 345-366.

Questions

1. What do you understand by the term 'drive' as used by psychologists? Discuss its merits and demerits.
2. We have to 'interpret' a stimulus before we react to it as that particular stimulus. Do we have to interpret our motives before we act on the basis of that particular motive?

3. How do nAch and fear of failure work together in determining the extent to which different people approach achievement-orientated situations?
4. Write an essay on the motivational properties of reinforcers and 'secondary' reinforcers.
5. What can psychologists working in the animal behaviour laboratory tell us about motivating changes in behaviour patterns in individuals and groups of individuals by the operation of reinforcement principles?
6. Are some societies more 'motivated' to achieve than others?
7. Examine the proposition that motives can be measured by looking at fantasy themes.
8. Why might anxiety give the edge to one person's performance and take the edge off another's?
9. What human needs underlie the motivation of human behaviour?
10. Is fear a unitary motive?
11. To what extent do you consider that career women have conflict of roles in present-day society? Illustrate your answer with research evidence.
12. When we ask 'Is he motivated?', what do we mean? Discuss in relation to any two approaches to the study of motivation.

Annotated reading

Atkinson, J.W. and Birch, D. (1979) Introduction to Motivation. Princeton, NJ: Van Nostrand.
> This book covers the area of human motivation well from the point of view of internal trait motives interacting with environmental contingencies. It fills in the details of recent research in achievement motivation and allied topics. At times the mathematical statements of theory might be too much for certain arts-biassed students, but the essential logic - all that is needed for an introductory appreciation - is clear.

Evans, P. (1975) Motivation. London: Methuen.
> This is a short book which should not present the reader with any difficulty. It is very much a theoretical-cum-historical overview of approaches to the study of motivation, leaving it to other texts, such as the one above, to fill in details of particular approaches. It also has chapters on instinct and on biologically based motivations such as hunger, thirst, sex, and sleep. This might interest a student who wishes to extend the chapter's coverage at a still introductory level.

Medrick, M.T.S., Tangri, S.S. and Hoffman, L.W. (eds) (1975) Women and Achievement: Social and motivational analysis. New York: Halsted Press.
> A collection of previously published papers, many in obscure journals. As in other contexts, it is often

rewarding to read what a much-quoted author actually did say. In particular you will find Horner's early paper on fear of success.

Rachlin, H. (1976) Introduction to Modern Behaviorism. San Francisco: Freeman.
This is the best introductory book for the student who is interested in following up the idea mentioned in the chapter that 'Motivation = Reinforcement'. In line with that view, it is no surprise that the word 'motivation' does not occur in the index! (Reinforcement, however, does.

Ward, C. (1979) Is there a motive in women to avoid success? In O. Harenett, G. Boden and M. Fuller (eds), Women: Sex-role stereotyping. London: Tavistock Publications.
This is an up-to-date account of the work on the topic.

12
Pain
C. Ray

Opening remarks
FAY FRANSELLA

The work of the occupational therapist often necessitates increasing a person's pain or discomfort in order to widen the range of movement in a joint, prevent the formation of adhesions after surgery or the limitation of movement as the result of formation of scar tissue. It will be part of your task to encourage the patient to persist in the activity in spite of the pain. To begin with you may find this personally distressing but, as with so many things, an understanding of some of the psychological aspects of pain can be a great help in handling your own distress.

At first thought, you may even be surprised that there is anything at all to talk about on a subject that manifests itself so clearly, that is so familiar to us all, and which we take as part of the business of living life. But in this chapter you will learn that people from different cultures respond differently to pain, and personality seems to be implicated as well, particularly the measures of neuroticism and extraversion which were mentioned in chapter 2. Ray also describes how it is possible to bring the level of pain experienced under control using reinforcement techniques. You will be advised to have your neuroanatomy book handy so that you can trace the neural pathways it is suggested may be involved in pain experience. But bear in mind that there are still very few hard facts about pain, our present state of knowledge being nicely summed up by the title of Melzack's book 'The Puzzle of Pain'.

Introduction
COLETTE RAY

Pain may be defined as an unpleasant sensation which is focussed upon the body, and is often but not always associated with tissue damage. While it may be generally true that physical injury produces pain and that pain occurs as a result of injury, this is by no means always the case. There are many syndromes for which a somatic explanation is not easily available, and the source of the disorder can be attributed either to an abnormality in the way in which normal sensory inputs are processed or to psychological factors. Similarly, people may meet with injury but fail to experience pain as a consequence. This will sometimes happen if the damage occurs suddenly in a compelling situation, such as in battle or on the sportsfield, where attention and emotions are directed elsewhere. It is difficult, therefore, to determine in a priori terms when pain should and should not be experienced, and we must rely primarily upon the individual's own self-report to indicate whether it is present or absent and the intensity of his feelings. Given a similar degree of pain, however, any two people will react to this in different ways. They may vary in their evaluation of the symptom's significance; in their emotional reactions and expression of these; in the extent to which they complain verbally about the pain and the kinds of remedies they seek; and in the effect that the pain has upon their family, occupational and social activities. Such reactions to symptoms are distinct from the symptoms themselves and are generally referred to as 'illness behaviour' (Mechanic and Volkart, 1960). A number of factors will influence these behaviours, including the individual's personality and cultural background and the rewards and expectations associated with pain.

Personality and culture

It has been widely argued that pain will in some cases have a psychodynamic significance: that is, a psychological meaning and function. Freud regarded it as a common conversion syndrome, representing the transformation of a repressed drive into physical symptoms; the pain need not be created to achieve this end, but may be selected from a background of 'possible' pain as that which best fulfils a specific symbolic function. A state of emotional disturbance can also influence pain in a less specific way, if the person fails to recognize the true nature of the disturbance and seeks instead an explanation in terms of everyday physical symptoms which might otherwise be ignored. An individual who is generally over-preoccupied with physical concerns would be most likely to misattribute psychological distress to somatic symptoms in this manner. Engel (1959) has suggested that there is a 'pain prone personality', characterized by feelings of guilt which can be in part relieved by pain; other relevant characteristics he lists are a family history of violence and punishment, a personal history of suffering and defeat, a state of anger and hostility which is turned inwards rather than outwards and conflict over sexual impulses. The immediate 'trigger' for pain in the case of such a personality may be the loss of someone valued, and several writers have seen physical pain as a symbol of real or imagined loss.

People show consistency in their response to pain over time, while there are distinct differences between people. Generally speaking, women are more responsive than men, and the young more than the old. The relationship between pain responses and personality traits has been extensively studied, particularly with respect to neuroticism and extraversion. There is some tendency for the former to be related to pain proneness, but many inconsistent findings have been obtained both in the laboratory and in natural settings. Extraverts under some conditions tolerate pain better than introverts, but may in some situations report more pain because of a greater readiness to brave the possibility of social disapproval. Many studies have looked at pain in psychiatric patients, and at the personality profiles of pain patients compared with those of control samples. A relatively high incidence of pain is found in psychiatric groups and pain patients have a more 'neurotic' profile than control groups (see Sternbach, 1974). It is, however, unclear to what extent personality disturbance predisposes to pain and to what extent the experience of pain causes emotional difficulties. The relative importance of these two different effects will depend upon whether the context is that of psychiatric patients who experience pain, or pain patients without a psychiatric history; in the former case maladjustment is likely to give rise to physical pain rather than the reverse, while in the latter emotional difficulties will generally be a consequence, rather than a cause, of pain.

Responses to pain differ not only between individuals and groups within a society, but also between cultures. All groups develop norms or expectations of how one should perceive and react to any particular situation, and individuals will adopt these to the extent that they are part of or identify with the group. Some norms are prescriptive: that is, there is a certain pressure upon the individual to conform with expectations in this respect, and deviation will meet with disapproval. An example of such a norm relevant to pain behaviour would be the expectation that one should not evade one's obligations by faking or 'malingering'. Descriptive norms, in contrast, do not imply an obligation to conform, but merely describe the behaviour which is characteristic or typical of the group. Cultural stereotypes suggest the existence of differences between nationalities in their expression of pain, and there is empirical evidence for such differences. Zborowski (1969) studied a group of American male patients and compared reactions for those of Jewish, Irish, Italian and Old American descent. Both Old Americans and Irish Americans were inhibited in the expression of pain, while the Italians and Jewish patients were more reactive. These latter groups both sought to draw attention to their pain by this expressive behaviour, but their underlying aims were different. The Italians were primarily concerned with obtaining relief from pain, while for the Jewish patients the primary concern was to discover the cause of the symptom. These cultural differences appear quite reliable, since Zborowski's findings were supported by those of a study in which the responses of similar groups were compared, but in a very different laboratory setting (Sternbach and Tursky, 1965).

Rewards and expectations   Learning theorists make a distinction between a respondent behaviour which is closely linked with the occurrence of a particular stimulus or situation and does not require any other support for its establishment or maintenance, and an operant behaviour which is not directly elicited by the stimulus but can become associated with it given appropriate conditions of reinforcement. Reinforcement is defined as any event which strengthens a behaviour; rewards will generally operate as reinforcers, as will the termination of an aversive stimulus, while punishment generally weakens behaviour. This kind of analysis may be applied to pain behaviour (Fordyce, Fowler, Lehmann and de Lateur, 1968). We can assume that certain responses to pain will be directly elicited by the experience, withdrawal or crying for example, while others may be prompted by the experience but depend effectively upon the outcomes which they produce. An individual may thus adopt and maintain a number of pain behaviours because they bring rewards such as sympathy and nurturance, and enable him to avoid activities or obligations which he finds unpleasant.

Behaviour will not only be influenced by the rewards associated with different kinds of response, but also by an awareness of how other people react in a similar situation. The experience of pain may involve considerable uncertainty, and when faced with uncertainty people often look to others as guides to determine both how the experience should be interpreted and the norms governing behaviour in that situation. This process has been described as one of 'social comparison' (Festinger, 1954). We compare our own interpretations and reactions with those of others to decide whether or not they are valid or appropriate in the circumstances, and may seek a lead from another before making our own interpretation and response. Thus the presence of a calm individual to act as a model may reduce the response to a painful stimulus, and the presence of one who appears distressed may intensify the response. Such effects have been demonstrated in the laboratory, in studies where the experimenter recruits a confederate who supposedly undergoes electric shocks similar to those to which the subject is indeed exposed, and instructs him to react to these with or without expression of pain and distress. Both 'tolerant' and 'intolerant' models in such studies can change subjects' reports of the intensity of the pain they experience and their willingness to tolerate shocks of various intensities. Similar effects can be observed in clinical settings; patients with problems or treatments in common will observe each other, develop expectations about pain intensity and the course of recovery, and learn the norms of pain expression within that group. Modelling processes will occur within the family but over a longer period of time. Children's reactions to pain will be influenced by their observations of their parents' behaviour, and the child whose parents focus upon his or their own pain symptoms and react strongly to these may come to react in the same way. This effect would initially operate with respect to specific situations but could then generalize to pain behaviour in general.

Theory and research

Early theories regarded pain as arising from the relatively direct transmission of signals from 'nociceptors' to pain centres in the brain, and the receptors, pathways and centres involved were thought to be specific to pain. The assumption of specificity does not, however, seem justified, and this simple model cannot account for many common pain phenomena, including the known effects of psychological factors such as experience, motivation, attention and emotionality. A recent theory which has attracted much interest is the gate-control theory (see Melzack, 1973). The gate referred to is a hypothetical mechanism at the level of the spinal cord, which is assumed to modulate signals from the periphery before they are centrally processed. It is suggested that this mechanism is situated in the substantia gelatinosa and has its effect by inhibiting or facilitating the transmission of signals from the dorsal horns to the adrenolateral pathways of the spinal cord. Activity in peripheral fibres will not only influence the transmission of pain signals directly but also affects the operation of the gate, as can central brain processes. Three distinct psychological dimensions of the pain experience have been related to these neurophysiological concepts. These are the sensory-discriminative, the motivational-affective and the cognitive-evaluative dimensions respectively. The first is associated with the rapidly conducting spinal systems projecting to the thalamus, the second with reticular and limbic structures, and the third with neocortical processes. The model is a complex and dynamic one, and can hence explain many diverse phenomena.

Some areas of research focus upon physiological aspects of pain, while others are more directly concerned with identifying those factors which can modify the experience. These investigations are carried out both in laboratory and in clinical settings. Experimental laboratory studies may be criticized on the grounds that the kinds of pain that can be induced and the conditions in which it is experienced are rather different from those that apply under natural conditions. They do, however, allow the researcher to control and monitor carefully the variables under study. Various methods of inducing pain have been developed for this purpose. These include application of heat or pressure; administration of electric shocks; the cold pressor test for which the subject has to immerse his hand in ice-cold water; and the submaximal tourniquet technique which produces ischaemic pain. Using such methods experimenters can study the effects of various manipulations upon pain measures such as the threshold, or the point at which the subject first reports pain, and tolerance level or the point at which he requests that the painful stimulus be terminated. Threshold and tolerance levels are not appropriate for use in the context of naturally occurring pain, and measures in clinical situations are primarily concerned with the assessment of subjective intensity. Estimates of this may be obtained by asking the patient to rate the symptom on a scale which is gradated by numbers or by verbal descriptions representing different levels of pain from mild to severe. The experience of pain does, however, vary in quality as well as in degree. Melzack and Torgerson (1971) have thus developed a questionnaire which enables patients to describe their symptoms in terms of a wide range of adjectives such as sharp, tugging, aching, piercing, nagging and so on. These descriptions can be related to the three dimensions of pain described earlier.

Somatic therapies

The chemical agents used in the treatment of pain are numerous and varied in their nature. They include, first, narcotic drugs such as opium, morphine and their derivatives; these act centrally and produce both pain relief and a state of tranquillity. There is, however, a risk of establishing a dependency and this obviously places constraints on the way in which they may be employed. A second category comprises the psychotropic drugs or minor tranquillizers and anti-depressants; these are directed at the reduction of emotional distress rather than the pain experience per se. Third, there are agents which act peripherally and not centrally; examples are the salicyclates and analine derivatives, including aspirin and phenacetin. These have antipyretic and anti-inflammatory properties which can reduce pain, although not as effectively as the narcotic agents. They can have physical side effects if taken in large quantities or over long periods of time. Recent developments in the study of the brain's chemistry may provide new directions in the psychopharmacological treatment of pain. Opiate-binding sites have been discovered in the dorsal horns and in the central nervous system, and there is much interest currently in substances such as encephalin and the endomorphins which are naturally occurring morphine-like peptides. It seems that morphine and similar substances may produce their effects by mimicking the action of these endogenous peptides. However, we are still far from fully understanding the properties of these compounds and the way in which they interact with the complex anatomical structures involved in the transmission of pain.

In many cases chemical therapies provide insufficient relief, or cannot be used in the quantities required for adequate relief because of their side effects, and other forms of physical treatment may then be demanded. Surgical procedures designed to interrupt the nervous system's transmission of pain signals have been carried out at many different sites from the periphery to the centre, but the general effectiveness of such procedures is disappointing. There have been some encouraging results, but in many cases where relief is obtained it may only be temporary. This outcome, in the context of the irreversibility of the procedures employed, has focussed attention on less drastic forms of treatment. One of these is to 'block' sensory input by injecting alcohol or a local anaesthetic agent such as procaine into the nerve root. Another is to increase this input by peripheral stimulation. This practice is conceptually similar to the 'counter-irritation techniques' that have been commonly used throughout history. These have included hot fomentations, vigorous massage, and the raising of blisters and dry cupping. For the latter a cupping glass, with the air partly withdrawn from it by means of an air pump or flame, was drawn across the skin, thus raising a painful red weal. Both nerve blocks and peripheral stimulation can be very effective in the treatment of appropriate syndromes. Not only may they have an immediate effect through restoring normal sensory inputs, but they can disrupt abnormal patterns of central nervous system activity and thus permanently affect the way in which pain is processed.

A method that may comprise important psychological as well as physical factors is acupuncture. This has only recently been applied to the control of pain and is most often used in the context of surgery. The procedure involves inserting needles into one or several skin areas, and these needles are then stimulated either manually or electrically. The successes claimed may be in part attributable to effects associated with peripheral stimulation, but Chaves and Barber (1974) have proposed a number of psychological bases for its apparent efficacy. These include the fact that a low level of anxiety is looked for in those selected for treatment by this method; the expectation among these patients that the experience will be pain free; a thorough preparation before surgery with a strong suggestion of pain relief, and exposure to models who have successfully undergone the experience; and the distractions associated with the general procedure which should draw attention away from the operation itself. These authors also suggest that the pain of surgery may be generally exaggerated, and point out that acupuncture is not generally used in isolation but in combination with sedatives and analgesics. The apparent success of acupuncture may then depend upon the existence of such physical and psychological supports, but as yet the relative contribution of these factors and of any direct somatic effects of the technique is unknown.

Psychological approaches to therapy

We cannot have direct access to another's experience and must make inferences about this on the basis of overt behaviours, such as motor activity, autonomic reactions, verbal descriptions, and so forth. Some psychologists argue from this that any distinction between experience and behaviour will be unproductive, and that the psychological analysis of pain and treatments for its relief should be directed at the behavioural level (Fordyce, Fowler, Lehmann, de Lateur, Sand and Trieschmann, 1973). With respect to therapy, typical goals would then be the reduction of help-seeking and dependent behaviour, a decrease in the medications taken, and an increase in physical and social activity. The therapist would first identify those behaviours thought to be undesirable within this framework, and would then seek the co-operation of the individual's family and friends in withdrawing the presumably rewarding conditions which serve to maintain these. For example, they might be advised to meet unreasonable requests for assistance with disapproval and reluctance, and to respond to legitimate demands or complaints helpfully but without the accompanying expressions of sympathy and concern which serve to reinforce these. At the same time, alternative desirable behaviours would be met with attention, approval and encouragement. This approach is most obviously appropriate where changes have occurred as a response to suffering, and have been maintained in spite of the removal of the pain source because they are found to fulfil other needs. It may also help in cases where the underlying condition cannot be alleviated, in this context by motivating the individual to lead as normal a life as possible in the circumstances, and to avoid the temptation of making a 'career of suffering'. A behavioural approach may not alter the intensity of the pain experienced, and pain may even intensify during therapy as physical activity increases. Nevertheless, a change at this level can have a positive impact on emotional adjustment and can improve the general quality of life for both the individual and his family.

Other psychological therapies attempt to modify the underlying experience of pain rather than the behaviours associated with this. One such approach is to provide training in the use of cognitive strategies which either direct attention away from pain or restructure the experience so that it is no longer distressing. The sufferer may be instructed to counter the pain when it occurs by attending to distractions in the environment rather than to his sensations, or by constructing fantasies and concentrating on thoughts which are incompatible with these. He may, alternatively, be advised to acknowledge the painful sensations but to reinterpret them in imagination as something less worrying or take a 'clinical' attitude which distances him emotionally. There have been many attempts to study the effectiveness of these strategies in laboratory experiments, but with suprisingly inconsistent results. One reason for the failure of some studies to demonstrate a positive effect may be the difficulty of ensuring that subjects follow the instructions faithfully. Those in the experimental group will sometimes reject the strategy suggested to them and substitute their own, while the control group may spontaneously employ strategies even though not instructed to do so (Scott, 1978). The very nature of the problem suggests that cognitive strategies in general play an important role in coping with pain, but it presents considerable methodological difficulties in establishing the effectiveness of a given strategy, either in absolute terms or in comparison with another strategy.

A third clearly psychological approach to pain therapy is that of hypnosis. Here the aim is to manipulate the experience directly by means of suggestion. There has been much discussion about the nature of hypnosis. Some have thought of it as a special state of consciousness or trance which is distinct from other experiences, but others have argued that it is an example of complete or almost complete absorption in a particular role and conformity with the expectations associated with this (Sarbin and Anderson, 1964). The subject has faith in the hypnotist's power to influence him, and is prepared to accept such influence to the extent that not only his outward behaviour but also his subjective experience will be modified. Hypnotic suggestion has been used for pain relief in surgery, dentistry, terminal care and obstetrics (Hilgard and Hilgard, 1975). Verbal reports of pain are affected by hypnosis, but involuntary physiological responses such as heart rate or galvanic skin responses are not generally affected. This indicates that there is still some sense in which the pain is present, and it has been suggested that the absence of the subjective experience of pain under hypnosis is a form of dissociation, with pain being processed at a preconscious, but not at a conscious, level. In one study subjects were trained to make two reports of pain simultaneously, one using a key press and another by verbal description, and the results supported the dissociation hypothesis. The key press response indicated more pain than the verbal report, although less pain than that reported verbally under comparable conditions but in a normal 'waking' state.

Hypnosis is not itself a means of preventing or alleviating pain, but a method for increasing the potency of the suggestion of analgesia made to the subject while in this state. Suggestion can have a powerful effect outside the context of hypnosis merely by creating the expectation of pain relief, and this is the basis of the well-known placebo effect. A placebo drug is a neutral substance which has a positive influence because of the expectations created by the context in which it is administered, and all treatments can be assumed to have some placebo element given that the subject is aware of their intended purpose. Substances which are known to be pharmacologically inert are thus used for comparison purposes in drug trials, rather than no treatment, in order to control for the anticipation of relief and provide a true baseline for evaluating the active and specific influence of the drug on trial. It is estimated that placebo treatments can alleviate surgical pain in about one-third of patients; laboratory studies produce lower estimates, but a significant proportion of subjects are still found to benefit. The effectiveness of a placebo will vary with the situation in which it is administered and with the status and manner of the person who administers it, since effectiveness will depend on expectations and the latter will be influenced by these factors. It will vary also with the individual to whom it is administered, and people can be grouped as either 'reactors' or 'nonreactors'; the former are not only more responsive to placebos, but are less differentially responsive to active drugs. While from a methodological viewpoint placebo effects may often be regarded as 'mock' effects for which controls must be introduced, from an applied perspective it is evident that the patient's expectations can be construed as powerful and legitimate agents of change. Their general influence will be added to that produced by the specific nature of any physical or psychological manipulation which is, with the patient's awareness, diverted at the treatment of pain, and can significantly enhance the therapeutic impact of these.

Psychological preparation for pain

The occurrence of pain may sometimes be anticipated before the event: for example, if a patient is scheduled for an unpleasant medical examination. Many of the treatments referred to earlier may be used as a form of preparation for a painful experience as distinct from an agent for relief once pain has occurred, but particular attention has recently been given to psychological preparation with an emphasis on those forms which enhance 'cognitive control'. These involve the provision of information which enables the individual to predict accurately what will happen in the situation and the nature of his experience, and instructions in strategies which may be employed to maximize the chances of successful coping. A number of laboratory studies have investigated the effect of the former, 'informational control', and have found that the stressfulness of electric shock and similarly noxious stimuli is reduced if subjects are made aware in advance of the timing and intensity of these and the fact that there is no danger of actual injury. The potential of the second kind of manipulation, 'strategic control', is demonstrated by the work of Turk (1978) who has developed a procedure for enhancing subjects' ability to control their response to painful stimuli, hence increasing their resistance to stress and tolerance for pain. The training procedure is quite complex. First, the subjects are given general instruction in the nature of pain; it is not considered essential that the explanation should be theoretically valid, but merely that it should provide a framework within which the experience may be conceptualized and the recommendations for coping presented. In the second stage of the procedure the subjects are trained to relax physically and mentally, and are provided with a selection of varied cognitive strategies with which to confront and control the pain. These strategies are similar to those described earlier, comprising methods both for redirecting attention and reinterpreting the experience. In this context, however, they are presented as a 'package' from which the subjects will select those suited to their personal needs. At this stage they will also be asked to generate feedback statements that can later be used to foster a feeling of control while in the painful situation and provide self-reinforcement. The final stage is that of rehearsal, where the subjects imagine the painful situation and their reactions, and subsequently play the role of a teacher instructing someone else in the procedure. This training has been found to increase pain endurance considerably in a cold pressor task. Subjects were able to extend the time during which they kept their hand in ice-cold water by 75 per cent, from before to after training, and this compared with a 10 per cent improvement for a 'placebo' group who had been given attention and encouragement but no instruction in specific cognitive techniques. The experimental group also showed a significant decrease in pain ratings.

It might be argued that many of the laboratory studies that have investigated informational control have involved highly structured and artificial tasks, and that the results might not be applicable to patients' experiences in clinical settings. It might also be pointed out that the cognitive training described above is highly complex; it has several components and stages and is orientated towards the particular personality and needs of each individual. It thus requires some investment of time and effort on the part of both the trainer and trainee, and such elaborate procedures might not be practicable in most naturally occurring situations. Similar, positive effects of preparation have, however, been found both under hospital conditions and in laboratory studies which have simulated these closely in terms of the nature of the painful procedures employed and the complexity of the preparation attempted.

Some of the most influential studies carried out in this area have been those conducted by Johnson and her colleagues (Johnson, 1975). In one of the first of these, male subjects were exposed to ischaemic pain in the laboratory and were either told what physical sensations they might expect as a result of the procedure, or the procedure itself was described without elaborating the sensations associated with it. It was found that the former preparation reduced distress, but the latter was ineffective in comparison with a control group. The intensity of the sensations experienced by the two information groups was the same, and the results could not be accounted for by group differences in either the degree of attention paid to these sensations or the anticipation of possible harm. It seemed, then, that this effect must have been due to the expectations held by subjects about what they were to experience, with more accurate expectations being associated with lower levels of distress. Further studies have used patients undergoing a variety of stressful medical examinations or treatments, including gastroendoscopy, cast removal and gynaecological examination. These too point to the conclusion that providing information about what to expect reduces stress and unpleasantness, especially if this focusses upon what the subject will experience rather than the objective nature of the procedure.

The effects of psychological preparation have also been extensively studied within the context of surgery. This will be a stressful experience for most patients, and the anticipation and experience of pain will contribute to this distress. The kinds of preparation attempted in these studies have varied quite widely. Most have taken a broad approach, providing information about procedures and sensations, offering reassurance and emotional support and advising on how to cope with physical discomfort and difficulty. The effects of these interventions are consistently positive, with both reductions in subjective distress and improvement in post-operative measures of recovery. Two such studies which have focussed on pain are those of Egbert, Battit, Welch and Bartlett (1964) and Hayward (1975). Wherever preparation comprises a number of different components it is difficult to determine which of these are responsible or necessary for the effectiveness of the whole. Some research has thus attempted to isolate and compare different kinds of preparation. It seems, for example, that providing instructions on how to cope with physical difficulties is not in itself very helpful, but is beneficial when presented against a background of accurate expectations (Johnson, Rice, Fuller and Endress, 1978). Only one study has attempted any detailed training in cognitive strategies and looked systematically at the impact of this training. Langer, Janis and Wolfer (1975) encouraged the development of coping devices, such as the reappraisal of threatening events, reassuring self-talk and selective attention, and showed a significant and independent effect of this instruction.

There is, then, evidence from a number of studies that the distress associated with an unpleasant procedure can be reduced by making the individual aware of what this involves from his point of view. It is, however, important to recognize that such information can only be expected to have a beneficial effect if it is presented in a reassuring way: creating an expectation of pain, whether accurate or not, can of course alarm the patient and counteract any positive effects of informational control. Instructions or training which help the individual to cope with physical or psychological stresses also have a role in the preparation for pain, and will enhance the effects of accurate expectations.

Final comments

The experience of pain depends upon a complex signalling system whose functions are determined by neurophysiological and biochemical influences which are not yet understood but are acted upon by physical and psychological factors of which we have some knowledge. These influences are many and varied, and provide a relatively broad scope for treatment. Some cases may call for one form of therapy rather than another, but for many a combination of physical and psychological approaches will present the most productive strategy.

A number of writers have called attention to the importance of the doctor-patient relationship in the treatment of pain. Szasz (1968) and Sternbach (1974) have pointed to motives which can cause the latter to resist abandoning his

symptoms, and show how the physician may play a complementary role which facilitates these efforts: the patient
who wishes to maintain his invalid status will have this
claim effectively legitimized by the doctor who continues to
treat him as though he were ill. Another common theme of
doctor-patient interaction is an attempt by the patient to
place responsibility for the outcome of treatment on the
physician's shoulders, with the latter accepting this responsibility because of an eagerness to help and a reluctance to admit to the limitations of his professional skill.
Such attitudes have been criticized as maladaptive. It has
been argued that doctors should discourage passivity and
helplessness, and cultivate a co-operative and problem-
orientated relationship in which the patient takes an active
role. This will involve confronting any undesirable attitudes he holds towards the pain, and emphasizing that the
outcome of treatment will be determined as much by his
own efforts as by what can be done for him. Sympathy and
reassurance can reinforce pain behaviour and can foster a
dependency which discourages self-help and the development
of strategies for coping.

On the other hand, the total care of the pain patient
should be concerned not only with the relief of pain but
also with the psychological stress to which this suffering
can give rise. The danger of emotionally isolating the
patient is as real as that of over-protecting him. The
attitude of family, friends and even professional helpers
may be complex and emotionally charged, reflecting both an
altruistic concern for the victim's welfare and personal
fears and conflicts associated with suffering. The distress
of the person in pain will in itself be distressing, particularly where it seems that there is little hope of providing immediate relief, and this can prompt either physical
withdrawal or psychological distancing to prevent or defend
against emotional upset. Moreover, pain is greatly feared,
both for its own sake and because of its association with
illness, injury and death, and contact with suffering can
elicit anxiety about one's own vulnerability in this respect. This, too, can lead to avoidance or a reluctance to
become practically and emotionally involved. Finally, while
suffering is often unmerited, the recognition of this is
disquieting, since it reminds us of the injustice of the
world and our powerlessness in the face of events. Experimental studies have found that blameless victims are sometimes perceived as responsible for their fate, or are
derogated so that this fate appears to be less unjust. We
can predict from these studies that feelings towards the
pain victim in real life might sometimes have a hostile
element, and bear the implication that he is in some way to
blame for his situation whether or not this is the case.

Few would dispute the importance of emotional support
in alleviating immediate distress, and the availability of
social support is a key factor in protecting an individual

under stress from long-term maladjustment. It is therefore important to adopt a balanced approach in the care and management of the person in pain, helping him to help himself while at the same time providing the sympathy and reassurance to reduce anxiety and prevent despair.

References

Chaves, J.F. and Barber, T.X. (1974)
Acupuncture analgesia: a six-factor theory. Psychoenergetic Systems, 1, 11-21.

Egbert, L.D., Battit, G.E., Welch, C.E. and Bartlett, M.K. (1964)
Reduction of post-operative pain by encouragement and instruction of patients. New England Journal of Medicine, 270, 825-827.

Engel, G.L. (1959)
'Psychogenic pain' and the pain prone patient. American Journal of Medicine, 26, 899-918.

Festinger, L.A. (1954)
Theory of social comparison processes. Human Relations, 7, 117-140.

Fordyce, W.E., Fowler, R.S. Jr, Lehmann, J.F. and de Lateur, B.J. (1968)
Some implications of learning in problems of chronic pain. Journal of Chronic Diseases, 21, 179-190.

Fordyce, W.E., Fowler, R.S. Jr, Lehmann, J.F., de Lateur, B.J., Sand, P.L. and Trieschmann, R.B. (1973)
Operant conditioning in the treatment of chronic pain. Archives of Physical Medicine and Rehabilitation, 54, 399-408.

Hayward, J.C. (1975)
Information: A prescription against pain. London: Royal College of Nursing.

Hilgard, E.L. and Hilgard, J.R. (1975)
Hypnosis in the Relief of Pain. Los Altos: Kaufmann.

Johnson, J.E. (1975)
Stress reduction through sensation information. In I. G. Sarason and C.D. Spielberger (eds), Stress and Anxiety: Volume II. Washington, DC: Hemisphere.

Johnson, J.E., Rice, V.H., Fuller, S.S. and Endress, M.P. (1978)
Sensory information, instruction in a coping strategy, and recovery from surgery. Research in Nursing and Health, 1, 4-17.

Langer, E.L., Janis, I.J. and Wolfer, J.A. (1975)
Reduction of psychological stress in surgical patients. Journal of Experimental Social Psychology, 11, 155-165.

Mechanic, D. and Volkart, E.H. (1960)
Illness behavior and medical diagnosis. Journal of Health and Human Behavior, 1, 86-94.

Melzack, R. (1973)
The Puzzle of Pain. Harmondsworth: Penguin.

Melzack, R. and Torgerson, W.S. (1971)
On the language of pain. Anaesthesiology, 34, 50-59.

Sarbin, T.R. and Anderson, M.L. (1964)

Role-theoretical analysis of hypnotic behavior. In J.
Gordon (ed.), Handbook of Hypnosis. New York:
Macmillan.

Scott, D.S. (1978)
Experimenter-suggested cognitions and pain control:
problem of spontaneous strategies. Psychological
Reports, 43, 156-158.

Sternbach, R.A. (1974)
Pain Patients: Traits and treatment. New York: Academic
Press.

Sternbach, R.A. and Tursky, B. (1965)
Ethnic differences among housewives in psychophysical
and skin potential responses to electric shock.
Psychophysiology, 1, 241-246.

Szasz, T.S. (1968)
The psychology of persistent pain: a portrait of l'homme
douloureux. In A. Soulairac, J. Cahn and J. Charpentier
(eds), Pain. New York: Academic Press.

Turk, D.C. (1978)
Application of coping-skills training to the treatment
of pain. In I.G. Sarason and C.D. Spielberger (eds),
Stress and Anxiety: Volume V. Washington, DC:
Hemisphere.

Zborowski, M. (1969)
People in Pain. San Francisco: Jossey-Bass.

Questions

1. What cues might we use in determining whether a person is in pain and the degree of pain experienced?
2. Describe the range of chemical and physical therapies available for the treatment of pain.
3. Can pain be treated using psychological methods alone?
4. Write a short essay on the use of hypnosis and acupuncture in the treatment of pain.
5. What is a placebo effect? What role can it play in the treatment of pain?
6. How do factors such as personality and culture influence pain behaviour, and in what sense can it be said that pain is 'learnt'?
7. What criteria might be employed in selecting one form of pain treatment rather than another?
8. What psychological preparation would you recommend for an adult who has to undergo an unpleasant medical examination or treatment?
9. What psychological preparation would you recommend for a child who has to undergo an unpleasant medical examination or treatment?
10. Discuss the possible disadvantages of being either too 'soft' or too 'hard' in one's attitude toward the pain patient.

Annotated reading

Fagerhaugh, S. and Strauss, A. (1977) Pain Management:
Staff-patient interaction. Reading, Mass.: Addison-Wesley.

Hayward, J.C. (1975) Information: A prescription against pain. Royal College of Nursing.

McCaffery, M. (1972) Nursing Management of the Patient with Pain. Philadelphia: Lippincott.
> These three books focus applied aspects on pain, relating theoretical knowledge to problems of patient care. The text by J. C. Hayward describes a study concerned with the psychological preparation of surgical patients.

Melzack, R. (1973) The Puzzle of Pain. Harmondsworth: Penguin.

Sternbach, R.A. (1974) Pain Patients: Traits and treatment. New York: Academic Press.
> Both of these books provide a broad introduction to physiological, psychological and social aspects of pain and its treatment.

Sternbach, R.A. (ed.) (1976) The Psychology of Pain. New York: Raven.

Weisenberg, M. and Tursky, B. (eds) (1976) Pain: New perspectives in therapy and research. London: Plenum.
> These are collections of papers, recommended for students who wish to consider issues and controversies within the area in greater detail than that provided by the introductory texts.

Part four

The Occupational Therapist as Scientist

13

How do you know? Psychology and scientific method
David Legge

Opening remarks
FAY FRANSELLA

Wherever I put this chapter it seemed out of place. If at the beginning, I thought it might put you off reading any more; at the end, it was incongruous because so much of psychology is based in experiment and research. So here it is in the middle.

Why should I think you might be put off? Many occupational therapists tell me that theirs is an art and not a science, so let us leave science to the scientists. Many say they are no good at mathematics and so it is no use their even thinking of reading about research, let alone doing it. Many think that, as so little has been done in the field, it cannot really be of much value. I believe all these reasons are incorrect or based on false premises. Art can be looked at scientifically, just as science can be looked at in, say, a philosophical way; anyone who has been accepted for an occupational therapy training course can master statistics: all you really need is enough understanding of the language to know what the statistician is trying to tell you. The fact that so little research has been done is a reflection of the difficulty of the task and not the fact that it is not worth doing.

I would argue that research is one of the most fascinating of professional enterprises. It is about asking simple questions and then trying to see what the answer is. Over 20 years ago, I asked a simple question when I was an occupational therapist in a psychiatric hospital. The question was, 'How do I know that what I am doing is any use?' Hundreds of patients would attend the departments every day; it seemed to be useful, but how could I know? I was helped to find the answer by the clinical psychologist at the hospital. I learnt how to define my problem more precisely; what 'double blind' experiments were; what unexpected things could happen in spite of the most careful planning and, most importantly, I learnt that the occupational therapy programme we had designed had a more beneficial effect than drugs in the long run. As a result, I learnt the pleasure (and some of the pains) of publishing when I wrote this research up for the Occupational Therapy Journal in 1960.

I was so fascinated by this research that it was a major factor in my decision to become a psychologist. Nowadays I would not have to take that drastic step because, although research projects in occupational therapy cannot be said to be numerous, they are beginning to happen. This is because students are being taught about scientific enquiry. I would, therefore, ask you to read this chapter with the idea that it is relevant to your future work and that research will indeed make your work more interesting and more effective. Forget the hang-ups about statistics; those will take care of themselves.

Introduction
DAVID LEGGE

Of all the lessons that one might learn at school, probably the most important is how to find out. Systematic changes in the school curriculum and in methods of teaching have given pupils today arguably the soundest preparation they have ever had and the best foundation for intellectual independence.

There is a basic dilemma in education: on the one hand there is the plethora of facts unearthed and polished by our predecessors, and on the other is the need to prepare pupils to find out for themselves and to develop sufficient confidence to question academic authority. It would be a denial of the principal benefits of a literate culture to withhold the hard-won knowledge received from earlier generations: we have the advantage of standing on the shoulders of those who have gone before. But too great a dependence on received wisdom could over-emphasize the value of current knowledge, hiding the real possibility that it is wrong, misunderstood or out of its relevant context.

The introduction of discovery learning methods in schools has tended to strike a better balance between these two sources of knowledge than faced earlier generations of pupils. In a previous time 'experiment' was used loosely as a label to refer to a wide variety of practical demonstrations and enquiries. At the worst it was used about practical work that was designed to bring about a particular specified outcome. If that outcome was not achieved the 'experiment' might even be said to have failed. This is a travesty. An experiment cannot fail. It may give rise to unexpected results, it may be poorly designed and the desired experimental conditions may not be achieved, but it cannot fail. In contrast, an attempt to demonstrate a phenomenon can fail. The difference is that the experiment is a special procedure for finding out. It gives rise to knowledge. What the knowledge is about depends upon the design of the experiment.

Discovery learning is a rather slow way of becoming better informed. It would be many thousands of times quicker to learn chemistry from textbooks than by repeating centuries of experimentation and building up the same body of knowledge from one's own painstaking experimentation. Didactic instruction is undoubtedly quicker, but knowledge acquired from an authority may be received as if impressed on tablets of stone. It may be depended upon as if it were inviolable and unquestionably reliable. Few scientists have such a view about the original knowledge that they have personally discovered. Truth is a relative concept and the 'facts' of today may be exploded as myths tomorrow. It is important to be just a little sceptical of received wisdom lest it be elevated to the status of dogma. It is important to find out, and it is important to know how you know.

Making a mental model of the world

Few of our school experiences prepare us for a view of science that identifies a reality outside ourselves which we seek to describe by our scientific theories. That reality is not open to us. We have to build a model of it for ourselves, and that model is our scientific knowledge. In general, the model is simpler than reality, and it has the massive advantage that since we have built the model, we can understand it. Reality is a different order of problem. If the model is a sufficiently good one, it will behave like reality. It will give us a way of understanding reality because we understand our model.

For example, Newton developed his celebrated laws of motion. They describe how bodies move in space as a function of the forces bearing upon them. They are precisely formulated as mathematical equations and offer a basis for predicting the movements of physical bodies. They are not, however, correct under all circumstances. In particular they break down at extremes of velocity and distance. But on an earthly and human scale Newton's model is immensely valuable because it works. The model describes closely enough how certain aspects of the world work.

Acquiring knowledge

How do you know? The simplest way is by deduction from a set of assumptions or premises. Provided the assumptions are true and the logic is sound, knowledge flows unremittingly. This is knowledge that depends upon the existence of a developed model that is relevant to the issue. Sometimes such models relate to only part of the real world and we then extend them beyond their domain of relevance and validity at our peril. Scale models offer some assistance to design engineers but only as analogies. It could be disastrous to assume that the load-bearing characteristics of a model bridge would be reflected in comparable scale in the full-grown version.

Another way of finding out is to ask. Asking another person, or his writings, is a way of seeking human authority. The success of this approach depends upon the question being well phrased so that it is understood; and likewise the answer. It also depends upon the questioner choosing an authority who knows the answer! The main problem with this approach is that a critical evaluation of answers can only be attempted where several authorities can be approached. Several versions of the same basic authority should not mislead us into believing that such consensus guarantees truth. Reference to an authority does have one cardinal virtue, however, and that is its convenience and speed. No other way of getting answers can be accomplished so quickly.

Empirical enquiries

The best way of finding out about the real world, however, is to ask a question directly of that world rather than of its interpreters. If you have a question about the motion of moving bodies (like billiard balls) the best way of finding an answer is to study the motion of, say, billiard balls. It is more direct and less likely to be distorted than asking a snooker-player his opinion. It may even be better than asking a physicist. This reference of questions to the world to which they refer is the essence of empiricism. It is the foundation upon which all science is based. Science has as its principal aim the description of the world in sufficient detail that at least it will be possible to predict its behaviour.

The physical sciences were the first to break away from natural philosophy as a methodology developed that allowed these empirical questions to be posed. Chemistry and physics were born. Somewhat later biology established itself as well. At the same time it became clear that there were relatively good ways of asking empirical questions that led to unambiguous answers, and there were also less satisfactory ways.

Causal explanations

A prominent feature of the physical sciences was the success of explanations couched in causal terms. The concept was that a particular act or condition would unerringly be followed by another, much as a billiard ball will move predictably (by Newton's Laws more or less!) when struck by another. The causational concept is a very attractive one because it offers a very compact basis for description, but even more so because it provides an obvious basis for prediction. It also identifies strongly the sort of observation that should be made in order to test the prediction, and hence to test that particular model of the world.

Once a phenomenon of some kind has been identified an obvious first question is 'What causes it?' What set of conditions willl guarantee its occurrence? For example, what are the critical factors which determine photosynthesis? It is fairly obvious that one way of getting an answer to this sort of question is to vary conditions and observe what happens. It would quite quickly become clear that one of the main features of an efficient procedure is the unambiguous determination of the relation between the factor being manipulated (the independent variable) and the factor being observed (the dependent variable).

Attributing effects

Perhaps the strongest, and therefore most sought after, evidence in science is the kind that leads to 'unequivocal attribution of effect': in simpler language, 'we know what caused it'. It establishes that two variables should be considered and connected, perhaps by a causal chain. It may also establish the nature of that connection, perhaps in sufficient detail to admit a mathematical definition of the relationship.

The simplest way of achieving this desirable unequivocal attribution is to demonstrate that introduction of a factor is associated with the appearance of a phenomenon and removal of that factor with its disappearance. If no other factor affects the phenomenon, one would be likely to feel confident in asserting that the factor caused the phenomenon. An investigation in which a factor is carefully manipulated and the effects of such manipulation are carefully monitored is an experiment. The key feature of the experiment is the manipulation of some factor, which must not be left to vary by chance or by association with some other uncontrolled factor. Sometimes the term controlled experiment is used to stress the fact that close control of the conditions of observation is essential. The controlled experiment produces the best evidence there can be leading to unequivocal attribution of effect.

The importance of the experiment as a method of finding out becomes more obvious when one compares it with other techniques that might be used instead. For example, let us consider the problem of isolating factors that lead to the development of lung cancer. A number of studies of the incidence of lung cancer (and also bronchitis and other chest diseases) revealed that cigarette smokers seemed to be more likely to develop lung cancer than non-smokers. The data were not absolute, of course, so that many smokers died of 'natural causes' without ever developing cancer and some lung cancer victims had never smoked. The next problem is to discover just what this statistical association between smoking and cancer means.

A number of substances are known to be carcinogenic. For example, certain coal tar compounds applied to the skin of mice have been shown to produce tumours. Though in much reduced concentrations, similar compounds are produced in burning tobacco, so the suggestion that tobacco smoke might produce tumours in the respiratory tract is not a far-fetched one. At least some of the intermediate links in a causal chain already exist. On the other hand, the fact that many smokers manage to avoid lung cancer shows that the story is not a very simple one. Smoking is clearly not the only factor and, indeed, it may very well not be the most significant one.

More sophisticated studies have contrasted the morbidity of smokers in rural and urban areas, of different ages and socio-economic groups. There have also been national comparisons. One of the most interesting findings is that smokers who give up the habit have a smaller chance of developing lung cancer than those who do not, though a higher chance than abstainers. This sort of study focusses on smoking and cancer rather than on the general problem of the aetiology of cancer. Decades of studies searching for a single cause have left researchers sceptical of finding such a solution and, instead, the prevailing expectation is that a cluster of factors will together determine the onset of the disease. At most, smoking could be identified as one of those causal factors. Its status might be a major factor, or subsidiary; it might have a primary or a contextual role to play. Either way, if causal, its influence would be relatively direct.

The principal limitation of the studies of associated incidence such as that described above is that one cannot be sure how whatever was observed happened. The effect cannot be unequivocally attributed to particular prior events and conditions. In the case of smoking and cancer the group of smokers differs from the group of non-smokers by more than just the breathing in of tobacco smoke. For instance, they comprise different individuals. This might not be a serious difficulty, provided that the people in one group do not share a common feature other than smoking. Unfortunately, they probably do. Why do the smokers smoke? Is it perhaps because they have some characteristic, no matter whether it be psychological (such as anxiety) or physiological (such as nicotine dependence)? If so, then smokers differ from non-smokers, not only in what they do (that is, smoke) but also in their constitution. Logically we are now incapable of separating two hypotheses about where the association between smoking and cancer comes from. On the one hand is the causal relationship, on the other the possibility that a tendency to smoke is due to some internal characteristic which is also a predetermining factor influencing the development of cancer.

One might argue that this confusion would be removed by observing that smokers who become abstainers have a reduced morbidity. Unfortunately, and this is borne out by the experiences of smokers who attempt to give up, some smokers find it relatively easy to give up, some difficult, and some try but never succeed. This variation between individuals could reflect a variation in the power of the internal factor. A weak factor would allow a smoker to give up easily but would also mean a relatively weak tendency to develop cancer. Studying the morbidity of smokers who become non-smokers voluntarily would tell nothing about the direct-ness of the link between smoking and cancer. Smoking might still be no more than an index of an individual's morbidity.

The only way of settling this question is to gain control of the main variable that has hitherto been left uncontrolled: that is, the question of who smokes. If the experimenter chooses who smokes, instead of allowing the subjects to choose, he can effectively separate the act of smoking from the predilection to smoke. In practice this means either forcing non-smokers to smoke and smokers to stop smoking or both. The decision of who is treated in this way has to be unrelated to any other relevant factor and a random decision is usually found to be the best way of achieving this.

Ethical considerations make it unthinkable to carry out this experiment on human beings. Clearly it would be unacceptable to force on people a treatment - smoking - that was thought might very well induce a fatal disease. Forcing people to give up a potentially dangerous habit is less of an ethical problem than a problem of practicability. It is doubtful whether sufficient control over other people's lives can be exerted outside a prison or similar institution. Animals have, however, been subjected to enforced smoking and a sufficient proportion have developed tumours to lend very powerful weight to the hypothesis that tobacco smoking is a primary causative agent in the development of lung cancer. It is not a necessary cause, since non-smokers may also develop cancer. Nor is it a sufficient cause because by no means all smokers will succumb. It is, however, a very significant factor, and a very substantial improvement in health could be achieved if tobacco smoking were to become an extinct behaviour pattern.

When experiments may not be used

The logical preference for using experiments to ask questions is, perhaps, an obvious one. The reasons for not using experiments are less obvious in the abstract, although when one is plunged into the actuality of doing research they become overwhelmingly real. We have mentioned one or two reasons in discussing the cancer example above. There are some things that it is generally agreed one should not do to one's fellow man. There are ethical constraints to our research. This difficulty is an intrinsic feature of social science or medical research, but it very seldom impinges upon research in the physical sciences. In general, we have little compunction about subjecting concrete beams to sufficient forces to destroy them, or stretching wires to the point that they cannot recover their previous form. Inanimate subject matter does not require much, if any, consideration. We see below that there are other advantages, too, that physical scientists enjoy and, perhaps, sometimes take for granted.

In the cancer example we saw how the ethical boundaries which would have prevented an experiment being carried out were circumvented by using animal subjects in place of the ethically unacceptable human ones. This is a partial solution in some instances. The limiting circumstances are, first, that there are ethical reservations about using animals (and there is increasing concern about the extent to which Man exploits sub-human species who have generally no way of lodging their objections) and, second, whether they really possess those essential characteristics which would permit the results of the experiment to be generalized to human beings. Animals may be invaluable in testing new drugs and pharmaceutical preparations that are intended for use with humans. The bulk of animal experiments are toxicity studies on new chemicals. It is reasonable to expect that substances which poison animals will probably poison Man, and vice versa. On the other hand, an experiment concerning

251

feelings will inevitably have to be conducted on human subjects. Even if animals have feelings, they do not have the power to communicate them and this severely limits their usefulness. In consequence, it may be that no experiment could be done at all, in which case the only source of knowledge would be non-experimental.

In practice, surrendering the use of the experiment is seldom the result of ethical constraints. More often it is simply because the control necessary to do an experiment is not available. The resources required may exceed those that can be afforded. In some cases control is lacking on logical grounds. The missing resource may be knowledge rather than cash.

The classic example of resource limitations prohibiting experimentation is in astronomy. Observing the heavens from earth can lead to a plethora of hypotheses about the universe, its contents and how they relate to one another. Theories of planetary motion would be easiest to test if one could carry out experiments by, for example, moving planets about, extracting them from their orbits and so on. Failing the power to do that, astronomers have had to use other means of finding out. A considerable portion of social science research is like astronomy. The researcher lacks the power necessary to manipulate variables to the extent necessary to carry out an experiment.

The third main reason for not carrying out an experiment stems from the conclusions one would want to draw from its results. In order to effect the degree of control necessary to achieve experimental manipulations and make precise, preferably quantifiable, measurements, laboratory conditions are often preferred. In the physical sciences this is nothing but an advantage. It is of no concern to a concrete beam whether it is subjected to forces in a laboratory or in a tower block of flats. It is the forces, its composition and age, the prevailing temperature, humidity and to some extent, its past history that determines its behaviour.

Human subjects play a rather more active role in experiments than do concrete beams and they tend to be very well aware of the difference between the reality of their normal life and the unreality of the 'games' which they are invited to play in laboratories. Even without that awareness of context, it may be that the version of a task which is devised and enacted in the laboratory is critically different from the real-life situation it was designed to simulate. For example, one cannot be absolutely certain that the speed of reaction in a real-life emergency which arrives without warning will be accurately mimicked by a reaction-time experiment conducted in a laboratory where the 'unexpectedness' of the emergency is at best relative. The problem is to determine the 'ecological validity' of the simulation. It is really the old problem of what degree of generalization is permissible from the observations that have been made. Essentially the same questions have to be asked about the concrete beam. Its characteristics in a warm, dry laboratory might be radically different at the bottom of the North Sea. But it is generally true that there is more likely to be limited generalization in the social sciences.

This problem has led many researchers to maximize the reality value of their research situations and to minimize the use of laboratory-based research. They feel that the potentially misleading quality of laboratory research is so serious a problem that they prefer to make their observations in more realistic circumstances, accepting the severe restrictions placed on the manipulation and control of experimental variables. It is a dilemma. Should one conduct relatively well-controlled experiments (which allow quite precise attribution of experimental effects) but which have limited relevance to natural behaviour, or use real-life (ecologically valid) situations which frequently leave considerable uncertainty about what induced whatever was observed? There is likely to be room for both kinds of research, and there are probably persisting differences in preference between researchers. This underlines the importance of discovering the strengths and weaknesses of the non-experimental and quasi-experimental methods that have been devised as alternatives to experiments.

Alternatives to experimentation

One of the great advantages in doing experiments is that the conditions under which the observations are made are very carefully designed to provide information about particular questions. In other circumstances one has to make the most of whatever information is available. Returning for a moment to the example of astronomy, the researcher has available to him only the options of looking in different directions at different times. His difficulty is to relate the information he gathers to his developing model of the universe. In these circumstances, since there is no way of knowing what particular aspects of what could be recorded might be relevant at some time and from some particular perspective, there is considerable pressure to record observations in as objective a way as possible. There is also a premium on precise description.

Non-experimental studies are usually either descriptive or correlational. In the former an attempt is made to record what is or what happens, without (necessarily) giving reasons or accounts of what causes what. Studies of this kind are potentially of immense value since they can define the general arena in which detailed accounts of what leads to what must be placed. They are also useful in relating the development of theoretical models to the reality of a life-situation. They are, however, very difficult to do because of the virtually infinite variety of things that could be relevant to record, so that even the most objective recorder would find it necessary to make some selection. The appropriateness of that selection is what makes the results of such a study valuable or worthless.

Correlational studies come in various forms, varying as to the restrictiveness of the set of variables that can be intercorrelated after the data have been collected. In essence, correlation is a statistical technique which measures the closeness of an association between two or more variables. Associations may vary from perfect correlation in which any change in one variable is reflected by a change in the other, to a much looser relationship marked by a mere tendency for changes in the two variables to go together. Correlational studies may involve selecting what to observe, and that is certainly the case when specialized instruments are used to make the observations (mental tests, for example), but they do not intervene in ways that are necessary in an experiment which depends upon manipulating and controlling variables, as well as accurate observation and recording. Studies of this kind can reveal what variables tend to change together, but they cannot reveal why. As we saw above, statistical studies of the incidence of lung cancer and smoking reveal that the disease is significantly correlated with the behaviour. They cannot lead to the inescapable conclusion that the one causes the other. If two variables are causally related there must be a correlation between them, but the reverse is not true.

One-subject studies

A particularly difficult set of problems surrounds asking questions about a particular individual. For example, if a young man visits a hypnotist before taking a driving test and subseqently passes it, what can be said about the effect of the hypnotist's treatment on his success? The answer is very little, with confidence. Clearly the hypnotist may have helped: there are several reports available of people believing that their test anxiety was reduced in this way. But our particular young man may not be exactly the same as other people so grouping him together with them may not be appropriate. One basic difficulty is that we cannot set up a control. We cannot discover how our examinee would have fared without hypnotism. Once he has taken the test and passed it, no fair comparison could be made by subsequently testing him again without a visit to his hypnotist. Though in some studies it makes sense to use a subject as his own control, in many others it does not. The subject is likely to be affected to a significant extent by one experience, so that he is not going to behave in a comparable manner if that experience is repeated. From the research point of view this raises almost insurmountable problems. There is no way in which one can achieve an unequivocal picture of what causes a particular individual to behave in a particular way, without either assuming that his behaviour patterns will be very similar to those of other people, or that he will be unaffected by his experience. Neither assumption will ever be wholly true, and the advances that can be made in understanding him will depend upon how true these assumptions are for particular aspects of his behaviour.

On theories and data

One of the reasons why it is important to be careful about collecting data in attempting to find out why something happens is that of the difficulty in spotting when an answer is a true one.

Many people have been taught that one of the most important aspects of science is that its theories are disciplined by data. They are kept in touch with the real world they seek to describe. If the theory says one thing and the data say something else, then the theory must change to accommodate the data.

Two schemes of investigation have been described as representing two distinct ideals. Inductive research involves making unselected observations of phenomena followed by ordering and categorizing them, from which a theoretical structure may emerge. Linnaeus' development of a taxonomy of plants is often held up as an example of inductive research. The alternative scheme is hypothetico-deductive research which progresses by a series of two-phase investigations. The first step involves establishing an hypothesis. Following that, a prediction is derived which can be tested directly against data collected for the purpose.

It is most unlikely that either of these schemes is actually used in its pure form. It is inconceivable that Linnaeus never developed any ideas about relevant dimensions of this taxonomy until all the observations had been made, and that his later observations were uninfluenced by his earlier ones. Likewise, the hypothetico-deductive method cannot be used unless there is a pre-existing theory, which is likely to have benefitted at some stage from random, if not comprehensive, unselected observations of phenomenon under investigation.

This contrast focusses on the relative roles of theory and data. Ideally theory suggests relevant observations. Data indicate how satisfactory existing theories are and may point to how they should be modified to become more satisfactory. Having got an enquiry off the ground, progress ought to be orderly. In fact it very seldom is. The most basic problem is that human nature seems to abhor a theoretical vacuum. Almost any theory is better than none at all. Perhaps this explains why magical explanations are preferred to a simple state of ignorance. It is almost as if man needs to have the sense of power that 'knowing how it works' confers. Whatever the reason, however, an embarrassing piece of data is unlikely to result in the only available theory being jettisoned. If there are two or more competing theories, however, data appear to be more powerful and the relative credibility of different theories may very well be adjusted accordingly.

The unexpected weakness of data is not completely accounted for by the need to maintain at least one theory. No theory is likely to survive when faced with strong data that are incompatible with it. The problem is that many data are just not that strong. There is residual doubt about just what the observations from a particular study really mean for that particular theory.

This undesirable state of affairs can arise most easily if the theory has been only poorly defined and, especially, if the rules of correspondence between the elements of the theory and observable aspects of the real world have been omitted or only ambiguously specified. But even when the rules of correspondence are clear, the status of data can be diminished if the data collection scheme has been a rather haphazard one, and particularly if the attribution of any effects observed remains equivocal. A fair conclusion is that a poorly defined theory that seems to explain phenomena which otherwise defy explanation, and an area of enquiry that precludes, or makes very difficult, experimental research, has a very good chance of surviving for a long time irrespective of its actual validity.

Progress without experiment

Much of the foregoing might seem to be pointing in a rather unpromising direction. In order to establish unambiguously that a particular variable reliably produces a particular effect, the experiment is not only the best available research design, it is also irreplaceable. As the advertisements used to say, 'accept no imitations'. However, it would be wrong to conclude that experiments are inevitably effective, as our brief consideration of the relationship between theory and data reveals.

Research is basically a slow business in which researchers inch towards some better appreciation of the world they study. They develop their models, making them increasingly sophisticated as they make progress. The barriers to progress are many and varied including their own mental limitations and the pressures upon them from the prevailing intellectual atmosphere. Experiments can be done which shed no light at all on the question at issue. Many experiments promise more than they deliver once the post mortem has been completed. In this climate of imperfection the fact that experiment may be precluded is disappointing but not, relatively speaking, a disaster.

The development of models of the world is not as neat and tidy a process as, perhaps, we should wish. The prevailing model is the one that seems best able to cope with all that is known (or, better, all that we believe) to be true about the phenomenon we seek to understand. Provided that enough different snapshots from different vantage points can be correlated it is quite possible that ultimately the same model will arise as would have come from direct experimentation. It will almost certainly take longer, but the same end-point may well be reached. This optimism is supported by the progress made in astronomy where experimentation is virtually prohibited. Since the system under investigation is in motion, successive observations provided different but complementary information. As a result Man has managed to navigate unmanned space ships to the outer parts of the solar system and successfully explored the moon.

In many areas of social science, experimentation is either very difficult or unlikely to provide what is needed. In such circumstances correlational studies and descriptive studies of one kind or another are the only sources of information available. Perhaps this will mean slow progress, but there is little doubt that our curiosity about ourselves will be a sufficient motive for the questions to be pressed, and eventually useful answers will emerge. It matters not at all that they should emerge untidily, only that they turn out to be effective aids to our understanding.

Research and common sense

Doing research is essentially detective work, but often with an all-important difference. Police detectives cannot ask questions in the same way that the experimental scientist can. Instead they have to hope that the (probably incomplete) set of data which they collect will distinguish between the competing theories they hold about the crime under investigation. Some science is also like that, and social science especially. Maybe scientists have one major advantage in that their antagonist is nature, which may not be co-operative but is most unlikely deliberately to confuse and deceive.

Just as police detective work has a list of dos and don'ts to guide it into a successful path, so there are good and bad ways of doing science. Most of this chapter is about using common sense in finding out. There are no magical methods and the main thing to remember is to avoid ambiguity. Before starting an investigation, be absolutely clear about what the question is. It will only get more confused later if it is not clear at the start. The study itself needs to yield data that can be interpreted. Ideally, any effect observed should be unequivocally attributable to a particular variable or set or variables. Whatever scheme seems likely to achieve these goals will be worth using. A scheme that will not may well not be worth the effort of putting into practice.

Unfortunately, while much of the physical sciences allow these guidelines to be followed closely, the social sciences are more difficult to tame. Unequivocal attribution is difficult to ensure, and easiest when dealing with laboratory behaviour: a version of behaviour which may not be identical with that in real life. Often compromise is necessary, and progress is painfully slow.

Statistics

There are relatively few special tools available to the researcher corresponding to the finger-print kit of the detective. One of the principal ones, however, is statistics, a branch of mathematics concerned with the determination of the likelihood of events occurring. It is a particularly useful tool in those areas of study which are not very clearly determinate. It was originally developed to help analyse various questions in agriculture which are made difficult by the fact that plant growth is affected by a vast number of factors, some intrinsic to the plant, some extrinsic. This situation is not unlike that in human behaviour and it is no surprise that psychologists have taken up statistics enthusiastically and developed specialized procedures for their own use.

The main advantages that statistics confer are schemes for summarizing data and making them easier to remember and communicate, schemes for measuring the relatedness of two or more variables (correlation) and schemes for aiding decision making. They are important for deciding whether any effects have been netted in the data, and that is a precondition for determining what caused them. In conjunction with experiments, statistics make it possible to face psychological research with some confidence. However, the techniques, though not particularly difficulty to use, are specialist and study in some depth is recommended before trying to use them. It is best to practise under the guidance of an expert first, before launching oneself into research.

Further study

It has only been possible to mention a few basic ideas in this brief introduction to psychological discovery. The interested reader will, we hope, feel an urge to plunge deeper into the jungle. There are an ever-increasing number of texts to guide the way. The next stage in that journey may be aided by three slim volumes out of the Essential Psychology series published by Methuen. They are:

Gardiner, J.M. and Kaminska, K. (1975)
First Experiments in Psychology. London: Methuen.
Legge, D. (1975)
An Introduction to Psychological Science. London: Methuen.
Miller, S.H. (1976)
Experimental Design and Statistics. London: Methuen.

Reference

Fransella, F. (1960)
The treatment of chronic schizophrenia: intensive occupational therapy with and without chlorpromazine. Occupational Therapy Journal, 23.

Questions

1. Write a short essay on the function of theory in psychological research.
2. What are the principal advantages of experimental enquiries? Are there any disadvantages?

3. 'One can never step into the same stream twice.' Discuss in relation to the problems of conducting psychological research.
4. Statistics developed in order to clarify the results of agricultural research. Why should they have been applied so enthusiastically to psychological research?
5. Discuss how theoretical generalizations might inform enquiries about a particular individual.
6. The two main methods of obtaining data about the development of processes and behaviour are longitudinal and cross-sectional. Discuss the advantages and disadvantages of each.
7. 'Quasi-experiments are merely poor experiments.' Discuss.
8. Some researchers argue that if the research method and the task for the subject have been properly designed, statistics are redundant. What does that say for the widespread use of statistics in psychology?
9. Discuss, with particular reference to intelligence, the use of tests to explore personal psychological characteristics.
10. Laboratories permit more exact control over experiments but may condition the results that are obtained. Is there a resolution of this dilemma?

Annotated reading

Cook, T.D. and Campbell, D.T. (1979) Quasi-experimentation: Design and analysis issues for field settings. Chicago: Rand McNally.
   Describes techniques that may be available when experiments cannot be used.

Barber, T.X. (1977) Pitfalls in Human Research. Oxford: Pergamon Press.

Jung, J. (1971) The Experimenter's Dilemma. New York: Harper & Row.
   Some books have analysed the sources of difficulty in finding out; these are two useful ones.

Meddis, R. (1973) Elementary Analysis of Variance for the Behavioural Sciences. London: McGraw-Hill.
   The student can acquire more advanced treatments for complex experiments from this text.

Miller, S.H. (1976) Experimental Design and Statistics. London: Methuen.

Robson, C. (1973) Experiment, Design and Statistics in Psychology. Harmondsworth: Penguin.
   Two relatively simple and accessible paperback volumes which act as starter texts in psychological statistics.

Siegel, S. (1956) Nonparametric Statistics for the Behavioral Sciences. New York: McGraw-Hill.

The 'bible' of the non-parametric techniques that has proved indispensable to psychologists.

Snodgrass, J.G. (1977) The Numbers Game: Statistics for psychology. London: Oxford University Press.
The student who masters the first two may want to go further. This should provide some help to that progress.

Acknowledgements

I am most grateful for the assistance received from Dr Hilary Klee who offered much constructive criticism and Ms Christine Harrison who painstakingly translated my early manuscript into a readable form.

14

The measurement of psychological characteristics
Fay Fransella

Designing tests

It is not totally unknown for an occupational therapist to feel the need to assess, say, memory in a patient and to 'make up' a test. A case in point would be when a number of items are presented to a patient on a tray for a few moments; the tray is then taken away, and the patient is asked to name as many items as possible. This is not a valid procedure. Such 'tests' should never be used unless the aim is solely to obtain a very general notion of what the person can do at that point in time. To be a proper test you need to know, for example, what scores people of a comparable age, intelligence and culture would obtain; and whether you are actually measuring a person's memory and not anxiety or something else. You also need to know if the same individual would get the same score on two separate occasions. You will also have to ensure that the items are shown for precisely the same amount of time, and that the people are given precisely the same instructions and so on. The standardization of a test, and demonstrations of its reliability and validity, are complex and time-consuming matters.

Having said all that, the occupational therapist is continually finding herself in the position of wanting to assess a patient's performance or wanting to get some more detailed ideas about their interests and attitudes. There are thus times when you will have to play the role of psychometrician.

Reliability
A thermometer gives the same reading for the same amount of heat at all times. In just the same way your test must give the same scores for the same person on different occasions. Unfortunately, people are not so consistent in their behaviour as is mercury, but you must design your test to be as consistent as possible. The easiest way of doing this is to give your test to the same group of people on two separate occasions and then to correlate the two sets of scores.

Legge talked in chapter 13 about correlations and so here are a few details. Supposing you were interested in checking your observation that Mrs Jones was not progressing well at her basketry because she was having difficulties in 'remembering' the stages as she was taught them. (I have put remembering in inverted commas because testing memory in people is fraught with many difficulties.) Let us suppose you have worked out details of the 'Tray Test' such that it is always the same tray, the items on it are always the same and are placed in similar positions; the tray is always presented to the patient in the same setting and the instructions given are the same; in other words, the tray is presented to patients in as identical a way as possible. Over a few weeks you have seen a number of patients like Mrs Jones and have given, say, 20 such patients the Tray Test, each on two consecutive days. You thus have two sets of 20 scores. The first operation you can do on the scores is to plot a scattergram (figure 1) which will give you a rough idea of what is happening.

Figure 1

Positive correlation between scores on Occasion 1 and Occasion 2

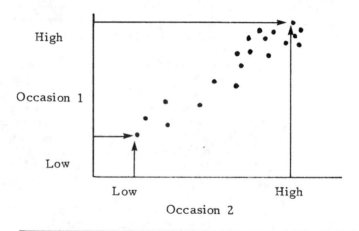

You will see that there is a considerable relationship between the two sets of scores. People who do badly on one occasion are likely to do badly on the second occasion. This would yield a fairly high positive correlation between the two sets of scores, reflecting the fact that, given one score, you can predict what the second score would be. The correlation would be approaching +1.00. However, you can see from the next scattergram (figure 2) that you would not be able to predict a person's score at all on the second occasion knowing the score on the first. The correlation would be approaching zero.

A third possibility would be that you could predict your patient's second score from knowledge of the first score, but it would be in the opposite direction. This would occur if the patients obtained low scores on the first occasion and high scores on the second. This would be a very interesting finding and give you considerable cause for thought. The correlation here would be approaching -1.00 (figure 3).

Figure 2

Zero correlation between scores on Occasion 1 and Occasion 2

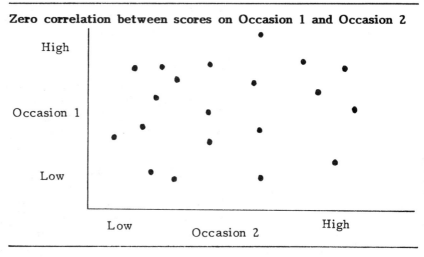

Figure 3

Negative correlation between scores on Occasion 1 and Occasion 2

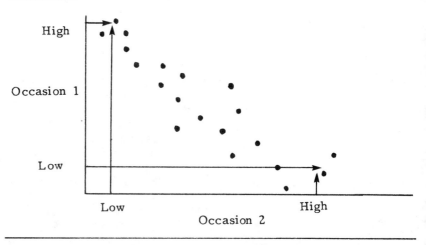

As you can now see, a correlation (usually represented by the letter 'r') ranges from +1.00 through 0.00 to -1.00. Another way of understanding a correlation is to square it and multiply it by 100 ($r^2 \times 100$). For instance, a correlation of 0.80 would become 64. This means that 64 per cent of whatever your two variables are measuring (in this case people's ability to remember items on a tray on two occasions) is shared. A correlation of 0.90 means the scores on the two occasions have 81 per cent of their variance in common. Clearly 1.00 squared times 100 means 100 per cent of the variance is shared; the scores are identical in their relative positions one to the other; and you will be 100 per cent correct in your prediction of a second score with knowledge only of the first. You would always hope to find a reliability coefficient of more than 0.75. To learn exactly how to calculate a correlation you have to go to a book on statistics; some are mentioned at the end of chapter 13.

It is important to realize that scores on two test occasions do not have to be identical in order for you to obtain a high test-retest correlation. They only have to retain the same relative positions one to the other. If everyone increases their score on a second occasion by the same amount this will still result in a high reliability coefficient.

There is another form of reliability that does not really apply to the Tray Test: this is when the scoring is not easy. For instance, you can fairly easily get agreement between two of you on how many items your patient has remembered on the Tray Test, but when a person's description of something has to be scored, as with many of the projective techniques (e.g. the Rorschach), scorer reliability measures the degree to which two or more scorers will give the same scores to the patients' data.

Validity
You may find that your Tray Test gives you very satisfactory test-retest reliability, but that does not mean you are measuring what you think you are measuring; for that you have to establish validity.

There are several types of validity to be considered.

* FACE VALIDITY. Do the items in a 'friendliness' questionnaire seem as if they are dealing with friendliness? The Tray Test has validity, in that it looks as if it is measuring something to do with a person's ability to remember things. But face validity does not tell you whether a person really is 'friendly' or really has a 'poor memory'; for that you need criterion validity.
* CRITERION VALIDITY. You might use teachers' ratings of friendliness or psychiatrists' ratings of memory for the patients. This is CONCURRENT validity in that the test is validated against some criterion that is available at the same time. PREDICTIVE validity is a particularly powerful method since you measure the validity of your test against some criterion in the future. If you have a measure of a patient's speed of putting pegs into holes, its predictive validity might be assessed by the number of people scoring highly on your test who made successful returns to work.

    There is one important aspect of criterion validity: there must be good reason for supposing that the criterion measure itself is valid. Are teachers indeed good judges of friendliness in the classroom, or are psychiatrists expert at assessing memory?

Different types of test

There are two very different approaches to psychological measurement. This concerns whether you should attempt to assess one person in particular or many people in general. This is the IDIOGRAPHY versus NOMOTHESIS controversy.

The term idiography is derived from the Greek word 'idio', meaning own, personal, private. When used in psychology it means that one is interested in studying the individual person or the single event. The opposite of this, nomothesis, refers to the study of a number of individuals or events. Du Mas (1955) defined idiography as 'that method of science which studies and analyses data obtained from an individual'.

There has, until recently, been a tendency to regard one or other camp as wholly good or wholly bad depending on one's own personal choice. As long ago as 1937, Gordon Allport stirred the psychological pot by remarking that nomothetic methods:

> seek only general laws and employ only those procedures admitted by the exact sciences. Psychology in the main has been striving to make of itself a completely nomothetic discipline. The idiographic sciences, such as history, biography and literature, on the other hand, endeavour to understand some PARTICULAR event in nature or in society. A psychology of individuality would be essentially idiographic (Allport, 1937).

In its extreme form, the idiographic supporter would argue that in order to understand the richness of human nature, each one of us must be studied individually so as to gain access to our uniqueness; whereas the nomothetic supporter would claim that the uniqueness of individuals is of no concern to the psychologist. This, they say, should be left to the poets and novelists: scientists should concern themselves with the findings of general laws that can be applied to all people. Eysenck sums up the issue by saying 'Science is not interested in the unique event, the unique belongs to history, not to science.'

The nomothetic investigator thus hopes that general laws will be discovered, so enabling you and I to predict each other's behaviour more and more accurately, and thinks that studying large groups of us will do the trick. But there is considerable evidence to suggest that it is quite difficult to predict the actions or responses of any one individual from group data. This was even suggested as long ago as 1934 from within the inner sanctum of scientific psychology: the rat laboratory. Tryon (1934) made this comment about rat research:

> The intensive study of the average behaviour of a species ... generally leads the ... psychologist to ignore the more interesting and important differences between individuals from whom the 'average individual' is abstracted. The 'average individual' is, in fact, a man-made fiction, and the behaviour of a species can properly be understood only by considering the variations in behaviour of all (or a random sample of) the individuals who are classed in it.

In relation to humans, to quote from Allport once again:
'The chances of a hypothetical average man for survival or
death are all the insurance business wants to know. Whether
Bill himself will be one of the fatal cases it cannot tell -
and this is what Bill wants to know.'

Some nomothetic measures

In fact most tests that you come across will fall into this
category. They will be tests administered to a large sample
of people for which the test is intended and so norms are
established. Your patient's score is then compared with
these norms and is therefore average, low or high in relation to them.

The most common tests in this category are the tests of
intelligence and the personality questionnaires. There are
also tests that measure interests, abilities and moods. And
last, but not least important, are those tests called 'projective' techniques. Here, instead of having a set list of
questions or items to respond to, you usually have pictures
of various degrees of ambiguity. You may know the Rorschach
by its more common name of 'The Ink-Blot Test'.

This is not the place to give you a blow-by-blow account
of what all these tests are like and how you should use
them, because there are very few to which you will have
access. You cannot just go into a shop and buy any test you
want. Organizations which sell tests, such as the Test Department of the National Foundation for Educational Research
(NFER), have clear criteria about which tests can be sold
to whom. For instance, attainment tests (Level A) which include some tests for reading and vocabulary, are 'available
to responsible people who have some experience of testing',
whereas personality questionnaires (Level Q) 'require a
thorough knowledge of the principles underlying testing and
which pre-suppose fairly wide practical experience in addition to specific training in the type of test ordered';
special clinical instruments, such as memory tests, 'are
issued only to persons who have a specific training in the
use and application of the instruments'.

If you are interested in knowing more about what tests
are available, perhaps with a view to obtaining some training in their use, I have given some reference sources at the
end of the chapter; otherwise it will be best if you seek
the advice of one of the clinical psychologists in your District should you have some reason for wanting to know the
IQ scores or degree of neuroticism and extraversion in your
patient. But this is not so much of a problem with idiographic techniques, which may explain why occupational
therapists are becoming increasingly interested in their
use.

Idiographic techniques

By far the most commonly used is the repertory grid (Kelly,
1955). This is essentially a way in which you can get a
person to 'tell' you how he or she sees particular aspects

of their personal world. When used in this way, no attempt is made to relate how person A sees the world with how persons B to Z see it. It is designed specifically for the individual and enables you to monitor change in that one person's world-view if you should so wish.

The most usual procedure for eliciting constructs is to ask the person to name some people they know and like, and some they know and do not like: perhaps six of each. These names (elements) are then written on small cards, one name per card, and presented to the person three at a time with the question, 'Is there any important way in which two of these three people are alike and thereby different from the third?' You are looking for personality descriptions or character traits rather than more concrete answers such as 'Two are dark-haired and the other fair'. There are many variations on this theme. For instance, it is often useful to have the person as one of the three, so that the person construes him or herself along with the two others. This was Kelly's original Role Construct Repertory Test.

A method for eliciting further, more abstract, constructs from a person is called 'laddering'. Not only can this provide more information to help understand another person, but the person being 'laddered' often gains considerable insight into the workings of his or her own construct system. All you do is ask the person to say by which pole of an elicited construct he or she would prefer to be described. For instance, would she prefer to be the sort of person who is GENTLE or AGGRESSIVE? She may say 'gentle'. She is then asked why she made that choice; why would she prefer to be the sort of person who is gentle rather than aggressive? She may reply that to be gentle is preferable because 'people are more likely to be nice to you'. So again the question 'why'; why does she want to be the sort of person people are nice to? The questioning is continued until the person calls a halt, perhaps because some very superordinate construct has been elicited, such as 'It is important to strive to reach your full potential', or 'We are in the world to help others', and then there is nowhere further to go.

Kelly decided that it was useful to go beyond the simple eliciting of constructs and described how it was possible to establish the relationships between constructs mathematically. With elements describing the rows of a matrix and constructs the columns (or vice versa), the person is able to indicate by a tick or a blank in the matrix whether or not a particular element is described by a particular construct. This matrix he called a REPERTORY GRID. The assumption is that when elements are given similar ratings on two constructs, the high correlation between the ratings will reflect psychological similarity for that person. For example, if your ratings of fellow students (elements) on the construct 'Likely to be a good OT'-'Not likely to be a good OT' are very similar to those for the construct 'Like psychology'-'Do not like psychology', then it is assumed that you see people who are likely to be good OTs as liking psychology. Whether this is so or not is a question of validity.

Although the rated grid is the most commonly used form today, there are several others, and for all forms there are various ways in which the grid matrix can be analysed statistically. Although computer programmes are available, such complex analyses need not be used. For instance, correlations can be run between ratings for each of the constructs, or the ratings can be transposed to '1's and 'O's, and the degree of matching between the constructs can then be calculated.

The most comprehensive source describing the various forms of grid, and giving worked examples, is Fransella and Bannister (1977). A shorter account can be found in Fransella (1981).

I want to end by saying a word about the concept of reliability in relation to repertory grids. The whole concept may have to be re-thought when used in relation to such measuring devices. The repertory grid arose directly from Kelly's personal construct psychology in which 'the person is a form of motion'. Grids will therefore be dealing, to some extent at least, with the process of change. If that is so, then assessing reliability in order to indicate a test's resistance to change is a contradiction in terms. Since grids are usually concerned with the construing of individuals rather than groups of individuals, it is as pointless to talk about THE reliability of THE repertory grid as it is to talk about THE reliability of THE conversation. One immediately wants to ask which conversation, between whom, what was the subject matter, and so forth. And, of course, we would be puzzled by the question, since we would know that one conversation on a subject would influence a following conversation on the same subject. It may be more useful, therefore (certainly with grids), to say where one would expect there to be stability between sets of constructs within a particular grid and where one should expect change. The notion of reliability in this context is thus a complex matter and one to which you might well give some thought.

Conclusions

The best way to understand more about existing nomothetic psychological tests is to ask your clinical psychologist to investigate a particular problem you have with a patient. You can ask for an explanation as to why particular tests or methods were used. There is only one way to learn about repertory grid technique and that is to design one for yourself and one or more for friends. This will show you the sort of information they produce which, in turn, will give you an idea of whether the method will answer the question you have in mind.

References

Allport, G.W. (1937)
Personality: A psychological interpretation. New York:
Holt, Rinehart & Winston.

Du Mas, F.M. (1955)
Science and the single case. Psychological Reports, 1,
65-75.

Fransella, F. (1981)
Repertory grid technique. In F. Fransella (ed.), Per-
sonality: Theory, measurement and research. London:
Methuen.

Fransella, F. and Bannister, D. (1977)
Manual for Repertory Grid Technique. London: Academic
Press.

Kelly, G.A. (1955)
The Psychology of Personal Constructs, Volumes I and
II. New York: Norton.

Tryon, R.C. (1934)
Individual differences. In F.A. Moss (ed.), Comparative
Psychology. New York: Prentice-Hall.

Questions

1. Discuss the differences between nomothetic and idiographic tests.
2. Discuss the concept of reliability.
3. What is the relationship between reliability and
validity?
4. What are some of the advantages of using psychological
tests instead of personal impressions?
5. Compare the use of interviews with psychological tests
to assess personality.
6. Outline some of the types of repertory grid in current
use. Give examples of their use.
7. Design a repertory grid to investigate an obese woman's
attitude to weight in general and her own weight in
particular.
8. Under what circumstances is it permissible for an occupational therapist to use psychological tests? Discuss
your views on the limitations.
9. Design a test to assess a patient's ability to concentrate.
10. What is the difference between allowing people to produce their own constructs and requiring them to rate
elements as constructs you have devised?

Annotated reading

Semeonoff, B. (1976) Projective Techniques. Chichester:
Wiley.
This is a comprehensive account of projective techniques
and should be referred to if you wish to learn about
them in some depth.

Semeonoff, B. (1981) Projective Techniques. In F. Fransella
(ed.), Personality: Theory, measurement and research.
London: Methuen.

A short overview of the main techniques with some discussion of measures and uses.

Questionnaires

Kline, P. (1981) Personality Questionnaires. In F. Fransella (ed.), Personality: Theory, measurement and research. London: Methuen.

A short concise account of some of the better known questionnaires and the pitfalls of questionnaire construction.

Repertory grid techniques

See references.

Part five

The Occupational Therapist as Manager

15

Organizational behaviour
R. Payne

Opening remarks
FAY FRANSELLA

Whether you like it or not, and many people do not, as you climb the professional ladder you will become more and more involved with management issues. Up until quite recently, professionals working within government organizations had no training or teaching whatsoever on how to manage their respective departments, how these departments interwove with other departments, how to deal with trade union matters, or generally on what happens to people once they are involved in large organizations and institutions. These next two chapters are therefore directed at you in the role of manager.

In this chapter Payne describes how you, as a member of a professional organization, fit into the whole, and the various lines of communication that are available to you. At one point he presents a diagram (p. 283) to show how a senior occupational therapist may fit into the organization structure in a psychiatric day hospital.

In the next chapter Orford talks specifically about the institution in which many of you will work, and particularly about the large psychiatric institution. He ranges from seeing the institution as a total therapeutic enterprise, to the power an institution can have in controlling not only the way patients lead their whole lives and the effect this has on their personal integrity, but also the effects it can have on the staff. I think you will find Orford's discussion provides much food for thought. For instance, you will often hear an occupational therapist, as well as others, call an old person (or a person who has been in a psychiatric hospital a considerable time), 'dear'. Now this sounds very friendly and cosy. But if you think about it for a moment, it de-individualizes the person. If all are 'dears' then no one can be 'Annie'. Watch for this type of behaviour in yourself and ask whether it is not better to take the trouble to learn the patient's name and then use it. Ask yourself what effect it would have on you if everyone started calling you 'dear' and never gave you personal recognition by using your name. Orford deals with such issues.

Organizational behaviour
ROY PAYNE

Organizational behaviour is concerned with refining our knowledge about the behaviour of individuals and groups in organizations and their role in the growth, development and decline of organizations. These various outcomes are also determined by the financial, political and technological environment in which the organization functions, so researchers in 'organizational behaviour' also study these organization-environment relations and their impact on the behaviour of individuals and groups. It is a multi-disciplinary enterprise involving economics, politics, engineering, management science, systems theory, industrial relations, sociology and psychology.

What are organizations like?

As with men an organization is:

> Like all other organizations
> Like some other organizations
> Like no other organizations.

In any professional work role one will encounter a unique organization, like no other organization. In this chapter we will deal with the ways in which organizations are the same as each other and the ways in which groups of organizations are similar to each other, but different from other types of organizations. Apart from its intrinsic interest such information will enable you to appreciate the ways in which your own organization is unique, and also help you understand something about why it is the way it is.

We are concerned with work organizations so part of our definition must be that an organization exists in order to get work done. They differ in the way they achieve this and two of the major reasons for the differences are (i) the way the organization divides its work into different tasks and (ii) how it co-ordinates those tasks. Most organizations contain several or many people but according to the present definition an organization could consist of only one person. Two different silversmiths may divide the different parts of their work in different ways and co-ordinate the tasks differently. One of them might choose to design and make one complete article at a time. The other might make bowls one week, handles the next week, assemble them the next week and then polish and finish them.

They represent two different organizational structures. Similarly, seven people may work together and agree that each is capable of doing all the tasks that are required to get the work done and the co-ordination of these tasks will be left to the whim of the individuals on a day-to-day basis. Another seven people might have six people each doing different tasks with one person left to co-ordinate the work they do. One thing that is well proven is that once the work of the organization requires more than just a handful of people there is a strong preference for dividing work into different tasks and giving some people (managers) responsibility for supervising and co-ordinating them.

Mintzberg (1979) describes five main ways in which organizations achieve co-ordination amongst people doing different tasks. They are:

* mutual adjustment which relies on informal, day-to-day, communication and agreements. Small companies of professionals operate in this way, such as architects, consulting engineers or small builders;
* direct supervision where one person takes the responsibility for ensuring that other people satisfactorily complete the tasks they have been allocated. The typical factory with its hierarchy of charge hands, supervisors and managers exemplifies this type of co-ordination;
* standardization of work processes refers to the situation where work has been carefully designed from the outset so that the system or technology determines what work gets done. As they say in the car industry, 'The track is the boss'. That is, the operator's work is so organized that he can only screw nuts on wheels, or only place the front seat in the car, or only spray the right side, etc.;
* standardization of work outputs achieves co-ordination by specifying the nature and quality of the completed task. The salesman must take X orders, the craftsman make so many articles. How they do it is not specified, but what they must achieve is;
* standardization of skills is what has produced professions. Doctors, lawyers, teachers and engineers are replaceable parts. In theory anyone with the correct training can be substituted for any other without creating major difficulties of co-ordination. This substitutability is captured in the colloquialism, 'He's a real pro!'

Mintzberg proposes that the major functional parts of more complex organizations can be divided into five broad categories. At the top of the organization there are people whose main role is to determine the goals and policies of the company. These occupy the 'strategic apex'. Below them are the managers and supervisors who have the responsibility of ensuring that policies and procedures are followed: 'the middle line'. They manage the people who work most directly on the outputs or services of the organization and these Mintzberg describes as the 'operating core'. To the right and left of the middle line, and subordinate to the strategic apex, there are people supporting the main workflow of the organization. There are those in the 'technostructure' whose job is to assist the middle line and the operating core by analysing problems and providing solutions and systems for monitoring and implementing them. They include professional workers such as work study analysts, planning and systems analysts, accountants and personnel analysts. The latter assist this analysing and control process by standardizing skills and rewards. The 'support staff' are not directly connected to the main workflow of the organization but they provide services enabling the rest of the organization to function. They include staff handling the payroll, mailroom, cafeteria, reception, legal advice and

research and development. In large organizations any one of
these departments may be large enough to have the same five-
fold structure so that one gets organizations within
organizations.

This very general model is most easily recognized in
production organizations but it can also describe the
structure of schools, universities or hospitals. In a
hospital, however, professionals are the operating core: the
doctors, nurses, physiotherapists, occupational therapists
and radiologists who provide the treatment and care. Other
professionals, such as planners and trainers, are in the
technostructure and basic research scientists or laboratory
staff will be in the support staff. Thus professionals
serve different functions within the same organization.
Figure 1 presents a conventional tree diagram of a secondary
school structure with Mintzberg's concepts overlaid. Note
the small technostructure which is provided mainly by the
local authority and the inspectorate. They are, strictly
speaking, outside the school and this is indicated by a
dotted line.

Building on these two sets of concepts and reviewing a
large body of literature Mintzberg concludes there are five
basic types of organizations. They are theoretical abstractions but some organizations approximate to the pure types
and many larger organizations are hybrids of the types or
contain examples of more than one pure type within them.
Mintzberg continues his fascination with the number five by
offering a pentagon model of the pure types. A simplified
version appears in figure 2.

The different forms of co-ordination pull the organization towards different structures. The strategic apex pulls
the organization structure upwards to centralized decision
making and direct supervision. The name for this type is
'simple structure' and some of the organizations that
frequently take this form are newer, smaller, autocratic
organizations. The technostructure's function is to
standardize and control the work processes so it pulls in
that direction. Mintzberg mixes two metaphors to describe
the resulting structure as a 'machine bureaucracy'. The
bureaucratic element in the metaphor conveys the written
procedures and documents designed to prescribe and control
the system, and the machine element conveys the rationality,
predictability and reliability of the design that has gone
into it. A car or television assembly line plant are good
examples.

The third pull is that exercised by professionals. They
wish to exercise the skills their training has provided and
argue the case for the quality of what they do within the
discretion of their professionalism. This striving for
autonomy is reflected in the small technostructure that
these 'professional bureaucracies' have (see figure 1 for
the school example). Note they are still bureaucratic. Despite their professionalism, organizational size leads to
greater complexity which requires records to be kept,

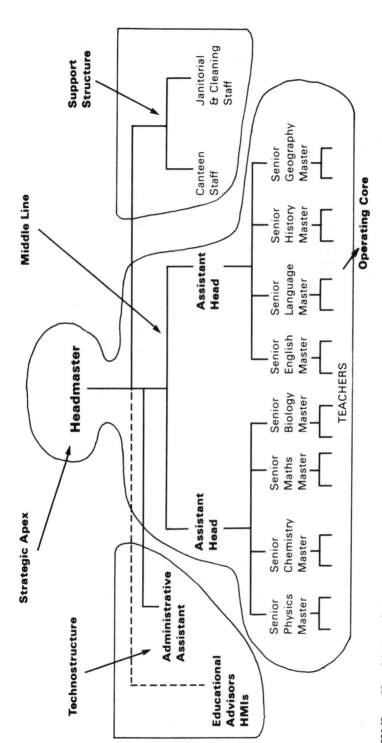

Strategic Apex

Technostructure

Middle Line

Support
Structure

Headmaster

Administrative
Assistant

Educational
Advisors
HMIs

Assistant
Head

Assistant
Head

Senior
Physics
Master

Senior
Chemistry
Master

Senior
Maths
Master

Senior
Biology
Master

Senior
English
Master

Senior
Language
Master

Senior
History
Master

Senior
Geography
Master

TEACHERS

Canteen
Staff

Janitorial
& Cleaning
Staff

Operating Core

HMIs = Her Majesty's Inspectorates

Figure 1

A tree diagram of a school with Mintzberg's elements of structure superimposed

Figure 2

Mintzberg's Pentagon

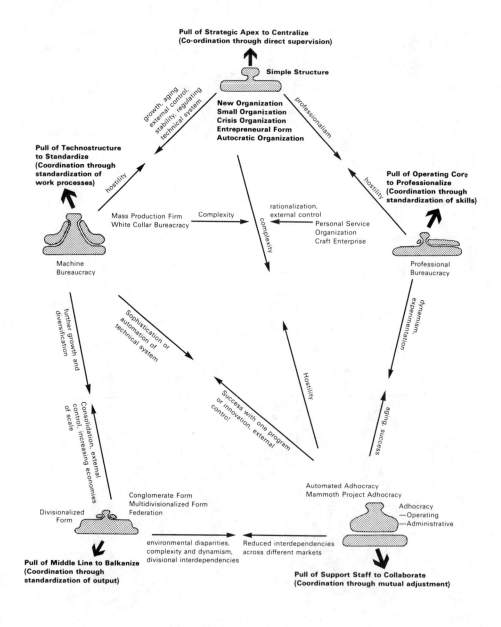

minutes taken, standard procedures followed, and professional standards maintained. Hospitals, universities and craft organizations tend towards this form because the services they supply need people with complex skills and professional training. Since they employ so many professionals it is not surprising that their needs and values influence the way the organization functions.

The fourth group to bid for influence in the design of the organization is the middle management. They too wish to be regarded as professionals and have the responsibility for their production/workflow units. They achieve this autonomy only by agreeing to conform to set standards in the production of the output or service: that is, standardization of outputs. The strategic apex co-ordinates the different units and supplies financial and technical resources, but each unit acquires reasonable autonomy to create the 'divisionalized structure'. This is common in conglomerates such as Imperial Chemical Industries which has separate divisions dealing with organic chemicals, agriculture, fibres and plastics. Within each autonomous division, of course, one may find a different structure: the 'machine bureaucracy' is prevalent, but if a separate research division exists it may be a 'professional bureaucracy' or 'adhocracy'.

The support staff represent the final force. Their preference is to co-ordinate by mutual adjustment and they are frequently supported in this by the 'operating core'. This would be the case in the Research Division just mentioned since the operating core would be scientists who are imbued with values of freedom and innovation. This produces a structure which Mintzberg calls 'adhocracy'. The title attempts to convey the fact that there are limited formal structures and that action and responsibility are defined by the current problem rather than past precedents or personal prestige. Large research and development projects sometimes take this form, as do smaller groups of professionals, such as advertising organizations. It can also serve the needs of the automated factory. Since automation itself controls and monitors the workflow process, the executives and their technical staff can concentrate on designing new products and the processes to market, produce and distribute them.

Mintzberg's thesis is that all organizations experience these five forces and that in a search for harmony one of the forces becomes dominant at any particular point in the organization's history. The dominant force pulls towards one of the five configurations. As circumstances change, however, the dominant forces change.

The arrows in figure 2 indicate the main forces acting on each type trying to move it towards another type. The results of these forces are the myriad of organizational forms we actually find in the world.

In summary, the very essence of organization is the co-ordination of activities. There appear to be a limited number of ways in which co-ordination is achievable. They are co-ordination by mutual adjustment, direct supervision, standardization of work procedures, standardization of work outputs and standardization of inputs or skills. If any of these forms of co-ordination dominate in an organization they tend to lead to a structure of a particular type. Thus co-ordination by mutual adjustment tends to produce an 'adhocracy'. Direct supervision leads to 'simple structure', whilst standardization of work processes tends to produce the pure 'machine bureaucracy'. The 'divisionalized structure' arises from a desire to co-ordinate by standardizing the quantity and quality of work outputs, whilst standardizing inputs (skills) results in a 'professional bureaucracy'. These are 'pure' types and most organizations contain elements of more than one. We now consider some of the factors that produce these hybrids.

Why are organizations the way they are?

Organizations are as they are because people choose, with more or less awareness, to make them that way. It is only too easy to start talking as if organizations make choices, but it is the men and women in them who determine their nature. This is not to say these decision makers are totally unconstrained. The fundamental purpose of the organization sets contraints, though organizations doing the same things may organize very differently to do them. A basic distinction is whether the organization manufactures things or provides a service. The latter could include providing treatment, providing education, selling goods or doing research. One reason that this is such a basic choice is that the decision to manufacture almost certainly involves the use of energy, tools and technology to a much greater degree than is likely in providing a service. This area of organizational theory has become known as the 'technological imperative' implying that certain forms of technology force certain kinds of organizational structure (see Woodward, 1965).

External influences on structure
The external ones include the market/clients the organization is trying to serve; the knowledge/technical change that is occurring in the world; the economic situation resulting from changes in the availability of resources such as raw materials and finance; and the political changes resulting from government legislation. Space prevents a separate discussion of these but together they may be construed as factors which create environmental uncertainty or turbulence (Metcalfe and McQuillan, 1977). To cope successfully with such turbulence requires different structures from those required to survive and develop in a stable and benign environment. One strategy large corporations adopt is to buy out the suppliers or competitors who may be causing uncertainty. This diversification also increases the complexity of the organization so that the divisionalized structure tends to emerge. One of the general principles for dealing with environmental complexity is the 'Law of Requisite Variety' (Ashby, 1956). This states that

the variety/complexity inside a system must be sufficient to match the variety/complexity of the environment outside the system. Thus the diversification strategy not only reduces uncertainty but increases intra-organizational variety which also aids in coping with turbulence. Less rich organizations cope by relying much more on their own flexibility and ability to respond to the uncertainty with new strategies and behaviour. One way they achieve this flexibility and responsiveness is by employing a variety of professional, technical and scientific people, each of whom participates intimately in the decision taken within the company. Such organizations have few rules and regulations. This internal diversity, however, creates problems of communication and integration. To achieve co-ordination and integration special groups are sometimes formed to ensure that the necessary communication takes place. These liaison roles (Lawrence and Lorsch, 1967; Chandler and Sayles, 1971) come to demand special skills and qualities of their own.

A structure specially designed to facilitate co-ordination in such situations is the 'matrix structure'. This structure was developed and extensively used by NASA to complete the US lunar programme. Problems of this scale do not come neatly packaged by function or department, so 'project groups' were formed which combined specialists from different functions (e.g. engineering, human factors, physics, finance). The structure is decribed as a matrix because the groups were formed by project and held responsible to the project leader (see table 1), but each member was also responsible to the head of a functional department. It is this dual membership which provides the expert back-up of the function combined with the good communication and involvement of belonging to a project team. These two responses, the liaison group and the matrix structure, are variations of the Mintzberg 'adhocracy'. The existence of these two structures implies that co-ordination by mutual adjustment sometimes needs some structural support if it is to succeed in complex environments.

Internal influences on structure
If we turn to Mintzberg's pentagon in figure 2 we can see some of the forces within the organization which may influence its structure. These consist of the tensions between the major groups in the organization: the top managers and/or owners, the professionals in the technostructure and the support structure, and the middle and lower parts of the workflow, the middle line and the operating core (figure 1). Those in the strategic apex want to maintain as much control as they can, but the technocrats, the middle managers and the professionals in the support structure, fight to increase their autonomy and influence. The technocrats wish to consolidate and automate the successes of the creative research staff, but the latter prefer to continue creating new products and processes. The operating core strive to professionalize their skills and provide better products/services

Table 1

The matrix structure

		Functional departments			
		Engineering Head + 7 subs*	Physics Head + 5 subs	Finance Head + 2 subs	Maths Head + 4 subs
	A. leader + 4 members	2		1	1
Project Groups	B. leader + 8 members	2	3	1	2
	C. leader + 8 members	1	3	1	3
	D. leader + 6 members	4	1	1	

* A member of a functional department may be a member of more than one project group.

to their clients, but the technocrats wish to rationalize and improve what already exists. As Mintzberg says, at any one time there may be harmony among these forces, but if the external environment changes then the internal environment must respond to it or the organization as a whole will fail. The internal tensions arise again and a new stability emerges through death, amputation, amalgamation or reconciliation.

Professionals can now see how they may be caught in any of these cross-fires. Accountants, for example, can find themselves attached to the apex, the technostructure, the operating core or the middle line. In a hospital the nurses may be in the technostructure, the middle line, the operating core or the support staff. Doctors are trained to diagnose and treat illnesses, teachers to instruct and educate and each progresses in their profession on the basis of their ability in these specific skills. Eventually, however, they become managers, administrators and policy makers with little formal training in these skills. No wonder hierarchical organizations have been accused of promoting people to the point where they reach their level of incompetence (Peter, 1969). This only goes to emphasize the flexibility required of professionals in complex organizations, for the roles they create extend far beyond those for which the professional was originally trained. Indeed, roles provide the link between the broad abstractions so far discussed and the actual behaviour of people at work.

Roles in organizations

The term structure refers to the pattern of offices or positions existing in an organization, and to the nature of the behaviour required of the people filling each of the offices. It is this dramaturgical aspect of structure, the definition of the parts to be played, that leads to the use of role as the central concept. In their work on organizational structure the Aston group (Pugh and Hickson, 1976) relied heavily on the concept in constructing their major measures, 'role specialization' and 'role formalization', and it is important in other concepts such as 'standardization of procedures' (for roles) and 'configuration' (distribution of roles). A major research project which utilized the concept contains some useful definitions and distinctions (Kahn, Wolfe, Quinn, Snoek and Rosenthal, 1964) and these are outlined below.

ROLE: the activities and patterns of behaviour that should be performed by the occupant of an office: for example, the nurse must administer drugs and follow the correct procedures in doing so.

ROLE-SET: all other office holders who interact with another office holder, the latter being designated the focal role. Figure 3 illustrates the role-set of a senior occupational therapist in a psychiatric day hospital.

ROLE EXPECTATIONS: the attitudes and beliefs that members of a social system have about what the occupant of any office ought to do; for example, as well as doing their job, teachers are expected to be honest, moral, dedicated to children.

SENT ROLE: the expectations sent to individual office holders by other members of the role-set; for example, a head of a department presses a scientist for more research, whilst colleagues expect that scientist to be a creative theoretician.

RECEIVED ROLE: the role as understood by individual occupants based on the expectations sent to them by their role-set; for example, the scientist just mentioned interprets the message to mean, 'publish as much as you can'.

There may well be a difference between the sent role and the received role. This may be partly due to inadequate information/communication, but will also occur because the receiver, consciously or unconsciously, wishes to see the world in a way which is found comfortable and acceptable. Cognitive dissonance and perceptual defence are terms used to describe these distorting processes. The disparity may also occur because the role is not clearly specified: small, expanding organizations have often not stopped to clarify who does what and have never written role specifications. Large organizations are sometimes called bureaucracies

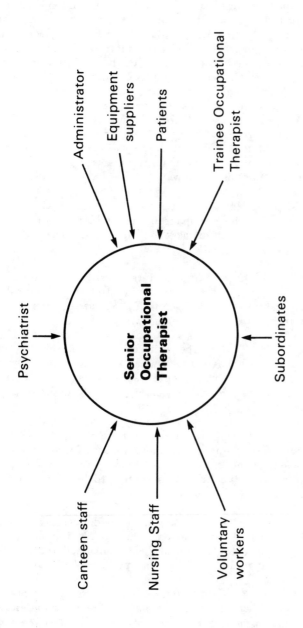

Figure 3

The role-set of a senior occupational therapist in a psychiatric day hospital

because they do write rules and specifications for jobs and they are kept in a 'bureau'. The written word is being used here to delineate the role. We can see from the role-set in figure 3, however, that the senior occupational therapist is at the focus of a disparate set of expectations. Even if all expectations are transmitted accurately (low role ambiguity) they are likely to be in conflict. The psychiatrist may want more group work, but the nurses and trainees more individual treatment. Kahn et al defined a number of types of role conflict.

INTER-SENDER CONFLICT: the expectations of two or more role senders are incompatible.

INTER-ROLE CONFLICT: two or more of the roles we occupy are in conflict; for example, manager and trade union representative; worker and father.

INTRA-SENDER CONFLICT: the same role sender has conflicting expectations; for example, increase output and improve quality.

ROLE OVERLOAD: simply means being unable to meet the legitimate expectations of role-senders.

The fact is, of course, that role-senders also develop illegitimate expectations. This is partly because individuals in organizations are not only concerned with meeting the organization's needs; many are more concerned with meeting their own needs. Ambitious managers may develop all sorts of illegitimate ways round the rules to improve the performance of a department so that they get promotion and leave the clearing up to somebody else! On the other hand, we (as the general public) know from bitter personal experience that 'working to rule', the organization's carefully thought out, written down, legalized prescriptions, means inefficiency and frustrations for all. That is, some bending of the rules is actually highly functional for the organization. The universality of this slip between what is and what is supposed to be has been recognized by the concept of 'the informal organization'. The concept of role enables us to see how and why the slippage occurs. More generally the concepts relating to role enable the occupants of an office to analyse why their roles are the way they are, and why they are not what they expected!

The informal organization

In work organizations role-sets do not occur randomly. They arise from the tasks to be done. In figure 3 we depicted one based on the senior occupational therapist. If we were to search for others in the hospital setting we would find them centred on the surgeon's 'firm', on the portering staff, on the accident department, on the administrative office, on the junior doctors and so on. Within each of these role-sets there would be frequent face-to-face interaction and high levels of communication. Relationships between them, however, would be much less clear-cut. In the current jargon whereas within a role-set it would be a 'tightly-coupled' system. It is also obvious that members of one role-set are often members of another. The surgeon's 'firm' will contain some of the junior doctors. The surgeon will be on committees guiding policy-making which will also contain members of the administration. These formally required interactions open up informal communication channels. It is much quicker, and perhaps more revealing, to make a direct informal approach to another department than to work through the formal channels where the information has to go up, along, back, along and then down. It is faster, and perhaps more satisfying, to take the organizational hypotenuse than the organizational right angle. The fact that many people in organizations do prefer them is confirmed by studies of how managers spend their time. About 45 per cent of their time in communication is spent communicating outside the formal chain of authority.

These informal 'grapevines' appear everywhere and are very vigorous. Caplow (1966) studied rumours in wartime conditions and found they travelled surprisingly quickly and were often surprisingly accurate. Davis (1953) studied an organization of 600 people and traced the pattern of various decisions. For one letter from a customer he found that 68 per cent of the executives received the information but only three out of the 14 communications passed through the formal chain of command. Getting things done at all, and certainly getting them done quickly, depends heavily on knowing and understanding the nature of the informal organization. It seems impossible to regulate the behaviour of human beings by fiat and authority alone. Professional, ideological and social interests cross the formally defined boundaries and these reciprocal relationships very quickly begin to twine themselves around the organization's neatly designed trunk and branches. As with vines they provide extra support and bear rich fruits but they sometimes need pruning, or re-planting. And if they are accidently uprooted they can leave the ground exposed, as it may be if a consultant recommends and installs a different, perhaps more clearly prescribed structure, but one which breaks up established relationships. An organization risks relying too heavily on the informal system which is why formalization and bureau-cratization are utilized in the first place, but there is danger in trying to eliminate it altogether. Farris (1979) contrasts the formal with the informal as in table 2 and it shows clearly how the informal relies heavily on expecta-tions rather than rules. He quotes several examples of how the formal organization, or at least the managers repre-senting it, can make use of the informal organization to better achieve its purposes; for example, they place new-comers with people at crucial cross-over points in the informal network in order to teach them quickly how the

Table 2

Some contrasts between formal and informal organizations
From Farris (1979): reprinted with permission.

Element	Organization	
	Formal	Informal
Salient goals	Organization's	Individual's
Structural units	Offices/positions	Individual roles
Basis for communication	Offices formally related	Proximity: physical, professional, task social, formal
Basis for power	Legitimate authority	Capacity to satisfy individuals' needs (often through expert or referent power)
Control mechanisms	Rules	Norms (expectations)
Type of hierarchy	Vertical	Lateral

system really works. Effective organizations then allow the formal and informal to work symbiotically: to sustain and support each other. Less effective ones fight a battle for the dominance of one over the other. We can see from Farris' table that the informal is, in fact, very similar to the co-ordination principle of mutual adjustment. As Mintzberg's model indicated, all organizations face the problem of resolving the tensions between the five co-ordinating mechanisms. From the universality of the informal organization it seems that adhocracy is never completely defeated.

This incipient victory of adhocracy has an influence on managerial behaviour as we see in the next section.

The nature of managerial work

The difference between what is specified in a job (role) description and what actually happens can also be illus-trated by the study of how managers actually spend their time. The classical description of management is that it involves planning, organizing, co-ordinating and finally controlling systems and people in order to achieve the goals outlined in the plans. A relatively small number of re-searchers have actually studied what managers do and one of

the most influential of these pieces of research has again
been done by Mintzberg (1973). In 1975 Mintzberg compared
folk-lore to fact. The first element of folk-lore he
discussed was that the manager is a reflective, systematic
planner.

His own intensive study of five chief executives showed
that only one out of 368 verbal contacts was unrelated to a
specific issue and could be called general planning. A diary
study of 160 British top and middle managers found they
worked for a half-hour or more without interruption only
once every two days (Stewart, 1967). Mintzberg concludes
that not only is a manager's work characterized by brevity,
variety and discontinuity but that they actually prefer
action to reflection. Plans, if they exist, are formulated
and re-formulated in the executive's head; they are not
written down and rationally elaborated.

On the other hand, our folk-lore of the modern super-
hero is that the effective executive has no regular duties
to perform. He sits on the Olympian heights, waiting the
calls of us lesser mortals. The facts show that he is down
in the valley dealing with the unexpected directly, encouraging the peasants, negotiating with neighbours, and
even mending the fences.

Executives spend much time meeting important customers,
carrying out regular tours round their organizations, and
officiating at rituals and ceremonies. Much of their time is
spent scanning the environment for information which can
then be passed to their subordinates. This is not 'hard',
easily-available information but 'soft', given in confidence
or as a favour, but which becomes available only as a result
of maintaining regular contact: informal contacts!

A third piece of conventional wisdom is that senior
managers need aggregated information which a formal management information system best provides. Computers have
encouraged this view as they seemed to be able to make such
information up-to-date and easily available. The evidence
suggests that managers do not use the information even if it
is there. They strongly prefer to rely on meetings and
telephone calls. Burns (1954) found managers spent 80 per
cent of their time in verbal communication, and Mintzberg 78
per cent. The latter's five managers produced only 25 pieces
of mail during the 25 days he investigated them. Only 13 per
cent of the mail they received was of specific and immediate
use. Managers appear to operate this way because they are
future orientated and their active scanning for hints and
gossip is felt to be more useful than detailed understanding
of the past. Such behaviour puts a heavy premium on their
personal ability to store and sort information. It also
makes it difficult for them to transfer their personal
images and maps to others in the company.

A related piece of folklore is that management is a
science and a profession. It is true that the technostructure in large organizations uses mathematical modelling and

sophisticated planning and control techniques, but these have little influence on senior managers or even on the managers of the specialists running such facilities. All are still reliant on their intuition and judgement. This is because they manage (i) people and (ii) very complex situations: imagine the problems facing the head of a department of management services in a regional hospital authority who manages 70 professional staff ranging from computer specialists, through work study to behavioural science change agents. That it is correct to give people problems priority over situational problems is reflected in Mintzberg's conclusions about the different roles a manager must perform. These appear diagramatically in figure 4.

Figure 4

The ten roles of the manager
Reprinted by permission of the Harvard Business Review. Exhibit from, 'The Manager's Job: Folklore and fact', by Mintzberg (July-August, 1975). Copyright 1975 by the President and Fellows of Harvard College; all rights reserved.

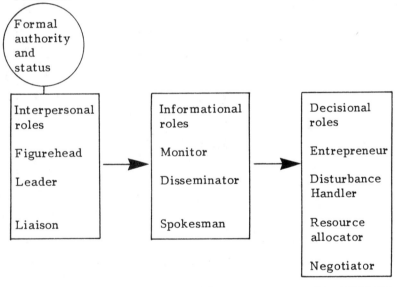

The titles of the ten roles are precise enough not to require further elaboration. The arrows indicate that the organization gives the manager the authority and status to perform the interpersonal roles, that this requirement leads to the performance of the informational roles and that this forces involvement in the decisional roles.

The effective managers are the ones who carry out all ten roles but who do so by finding ways to:

* gain control over their time: they tend to be bombarded by others so they must find ways of using these obligations to others to suit their own ends. Their only other hope is that people do things for them because of personal commitment. In hierarchical and competitive situations this highly desirable state is often lacking. They may have to be political and devious to achieve their goals;

* some of the time thus gained must be used to determine which issues are really important in the overall picture. This ability has been called the 'helicopter capacity';

* to use the rest of their saved time to ensure that they regularly and systematically share with colleagues and subordinates their privileged information and how it fits into the images and plans that are guiding their actions.

With this amount of preparation managers have a good chance of sneaking through the interpersonal barrage that makes up their weekly war. This applies to managers and supervisors at all points in the organization: low, middle or high, in the technostructure or the support structure. For these different positions the task changes in quantity rather than quality, and in the severity of the consequences which result from failure.

References

Ashby, W. (1956)
An Introduction to Cybernetics. London: Chapman & Hall.

Burns, T. (1954)
The directions of activity and communication in a departmental and executive group. Human Relationships, 7, 73-97.

Caplow, T. (1966)
Rumours in War. In A.H. Rubenstein and C.J. Haberstroth (eds), Some Theories of Organization. Homewood, Ill.: Irwin-Dorsey.

Chandler, M.K. and Sayles, L.R. (1971)
Managing Large Systems. New York: Harper & Row.

Davis, K. (1953)
Management communication and the grapevine. Harvard Business Review, Sept.-Oct., 43-49.

Farris, G.F. (1979)
The informal organization in strategic decision-making. International Studies of Management and Organization, 9, No. 4, 131-152.

Kahn, R.L., Wolfe, D.M., Quinn R.P., Snoek, J.D. and Rosenthal, R. A. (1964)
Organizational Stress. New York: Wiley.

Lawrence, P.R. and Lorsch, J.W. (1967)
Organization and Environment. Boston: Harvard Business School.

Metcalfe, L. and McQuillan, W. (1977)
  Managing turbulence. In P.C. Nystrom and W.H. Starbuck, (eds), Prescriptive Models of Organization. Amsterdam: North-Holland.
Mintzberg, H. (1973)
  The Nature of Managerial Work. New York: Harper & Row.
Mintzberg, H. (1975)
  The manager's job: folklore and fact. Harvard Business Review, July-August, 49-61.
Mintzberg, H. (1979)
  The Structuring of Organizations. Englewood Cliffs, NJ: Prentice-Hall.
Peter, L.F. (1969)
  The Peter Principle. New York: William Morrow.
Pugh, D.S. and Hickson, D.J. (eds) (1976)
  Organizational Structure in its Context. Farnham: Saxon House/Teakfield Press.
Stewart, R. (1967)
  Managers and Their Jobs. London: Macmillan.
Woodward, J. (1965)
  Industrial Organization: Theory and practice. Oxford: Oxford University Press.

Questions

1. Describe the different ways by which organizations attempt to achieve co-ordination. Give examples of each.
2. What is a matrix organization? When is it likely to be used?
3. What type of organizational structure(s) would you expect to find in (i) a medium-sized general hospital; (ii) a department store?
4. Illustrate your understanding of the concepts related to role-set by analysing the role of student (or any suitable variation of that).
5. Compare and contrast the formal versus the informal organization. Provide examples from an organization of which you are a member.
6. Why do informal organizations develop?
7. What factors influence the structural characteristics of organizations? Give examples.
8. Compare and contrast stereotypes about managerial roles with what managers actually do.
9. Why might the training of professional workers fail to truly prepare them for a career in a large organization?
10. Which of the main types of organizational structure most appeals to you? Why?
11. Discuss the relevance for occupational therapists of the study of organizations.
12. Because of the varied nature of their work, occupational therapists do not always fit neatly into an organizational structure. Discuss whether or not you think this may be a true statement and, if so, how might you deal with the situation.

Annotated reading

Child, J. (1977) Organization: A guide to problems and practice (paperback). New York: Harper & Row.

A readable and informed account of the meaning of organizational structure. It discusses the choices managers have when faced with designing an organization around the issues of shaping the jobs/roles people do, having tall or flat chains of command, grouping activities by function, product or some mixture, mechanisms for integrating the divisions so created, and how to control the humans working in the system. Child also discusses how to change organizations and the future forms they may need/choose to adopt.

Handy, C. (1976) Understanding Organizations. Harmondsworth Penguin.

This is an extremely well written and lively book, rich with pertinent examples. The first part introduces basic concepts for understanding organizations: motivation, roles, leadership, power and influence, group processes, structure and politics. The second part applies the concepts to problems such as how to design organizations, how to develop and change them and the working of the various aspects of organizations as systems (budgets, communications, computers, bargaining). The last chapter describes what it is like to be a manager and the dilemmas faced. The book has a very useful third section which is a guide to further study for each of the 12 chapters.

Mintzberg's ideas are only available in his 1979 book, 'The Structuring of Organizations'. Englewood Cliffs, NJ: Prentice-Hall.

This is a detailed review and synthesis of a mass of literature on organizations, but the first chapter describes the five co-ordinating mechanisms and the last describes the five types of structures and the pentagon model.

Warr, P.B. (ed) (1978) Psychology at Work (2nd edn). Harmondsworth: Penguin.

This book contains 16 chapters, each written by different authors. It is moderately technical in places, but much of it is quite understandable to the non-psychologist. The chapters cover the following topics: hours of work and the 24-hour cycle, workload and skilled performance, training, the design of machines and systems that optimize human performance, accidents, computers and decision making, selection, interviewing, negotiation and collective bargaining, leadership, attitudes and motives, job redesign and employee participation, work stress, counselling in work settings, how to change organizations and organizational systems as psychological environments.

16

Institutional climates
Jim Orford

A person's behaviour is influenced by the surrounding
environment, as well as by attributes which the person
brings to that environment, such as personality, abilities
and attitudes; behaviour is a function of person and
environment. Many people either live or work in institutions
of one kind or another. For such people, the institution
constitutes an important part of their environment. For some
people it constitutes almost their total environment. Those
who work in an institutional setting cannot fail to notice
how the institution influences its members, either for good
or ill. Many will have felt frustrated by the values which
the institution seems to embody, or by the practices which
are prevalent within it, feeling that members could be
helped more if things were otherwise, or even that members
are being harmed by the institution. The great importance of
these matters has begun to be recognized in psychology and
there is a growing psychological literature on the organization of institutions and how to change them. The study of
institutions holds wider lessons for social psychology too.
An institution is a social psychological laboratory. The
experiments which take place there are naturally occurring
experiments in the psychology of social interaction, social
roles, intergroup attitudes, conflict and cohesiveness. The
study of institutions is of vital significance for both
theoretical and applied psychology.

Much of the literature on the subject concerns health
care or social service institutions such as mental hospitals
and hostels or homes for children, the elderly, or the
disabled. Although many of the examples upon which this
chapter draws are taken from such institutions, the chapter
attempts to build up a general picture of institutional life
which is equally as relevant, for example, to educational
institutions such as schools and colleges, and to penal institutions such as prisons and detention centres. These different institutions have a great deal in common. Each is a
collection of people, gathered together in a special building or group of buildings. These people are not normally
linked by family ties, but are there because of the special
'needs' (for education, care, treatment, rehabilitation, or
punishment) of inmates, users, or 'clients' (pupils, members, patients, residents). It is the responsibility of

another group of people, the staff, to provide for the clients' needs. This they are in a position to do on account of their special training, skills, or occupation (as teacher, prison officer, warden, doctor or nurse). Usually the institution has been set up by, and is part of, a larger organization which is responsible for managing the institution. Penal institutions in Britain are governed by the complex machinery of the Home Office; hospitals by the Department of Health and its network of Regional, Area and District Authorities, each with a complex system of members, officers and management teams; local authority schools and homes by committees and sub-committees of elected and co-opted representatives, the Authority's officers and the institution's committee of governors or managers; and institutions run by voluntary bodies by their trustees and management committees. Institutions are almost always influenced by people, often a large number of them, who have control over the institution but who are not involved in day-to-day work with the institution's clients. It is more than purely academic to consider some of these defining features of human service institutions. They immediately suggest ways in which an institution differs from a person's own home, and hence they indicate where some problems with institutions are to be expected. The small family home provides the clearest contrast to the large residential institution. People are not gathered together in the former on account of their special needs or their special qualifications, there is no demarcation between staff and clients, and the influence of outside organizations is minimal. It is no wonder that a great deal of thought and effort has been devoted to the goal of making institutions as normal and home-like as possible. Many other comparisons and contrasts between organizations and groups could be made, and there is no absolute definition of an institution.

Ideal types: the total institution and the therapeutic community

It is important to be clear what is meant by a 'total institution' and by the term 'therapeutic community'. They are important ideas which have had much influence but as terms they are liable to be used loosely, and hence may obscure rather than reveal the true facts about institutional climates. In a much-read and often-quoted collection of essays, Goffman (1961) noted that it is normal in modern society for people to conduct different aspects of their life, for example sleeping, playing and working, in different places, with different people, and under different authorities. Total institutions, in contrast, are places where these barriers between different spheres of life are broken down. All aspects of life are conducted in the same place and, most importantly, under the same single authority. It is quite likely that activities are tightly scheduled by those in authority in accordance with an overall plan. He noted that many penal and caring institutions were total institutions in this sense. So were a number of places, with which this chapter is less concerned, such as army barracks, ships and monasteries. On the other hand, certain places with which we are concerned, such as day schools and day hospitals or centres, would not qualify as total institutions.

It is also important to recognize the variety of climates which exist even within total institutions. Tizard, Sinclair and Clarke (1975) point out the danger of generalizing from studies of single institutions, such as Goffman's study of an American mental hospital. Used loosely, the expression 'total institution' can give rise to a misleading stereotype. There is now ample evidence, some of which is considered later in this chapter, that institutions vary greatly, and furthermore that individual institutions can be changed.

Nevertheless, the harm that institutions may do has increasingly been recognized. Barton (1959) has gone so far as to say that the symptoms of institutionalization are so well marked that they constitute a disease entity which he called 'institutional neurosis'. He has written:

> Institutional Neurosis is a disease characterized by apathy, lack of initiative, loss of interest ..., submissiveness, and sometimes no expression of feelings of resentment at harsh and unfair orders. There is also lack of interest in the future ..., a deterioration in personal habits ..., a loss of individuality, and a resigned acceptance that things will go on as they are.

The concept of the 'therapeutic community' is an important one because it represents one type of ideal contrasting markedly with the most inhumane or least therapeutic institutional climates. The model therapeutic community was the Henderson Unit at the Belmont Hospital in Surrey. The unit, described by Maxwell Jones (1952) and studied by Rapoport (1960), was principally aimed at helping young adult psychiatric patients, many of whom had problems of repeated antisocial conduct and who were difficult to accommodate elsewhere. Amongst the ideals of the therapeutic community are an emphasis on active rehabilitation as opposed to custodialism; democratization, namely that decision making about the unit's affairs should be shared amongst staff and patients alike; permissiveness, that is, that distressing or deviant behaviour should be tolerated rather than repressed in the interests of institutional conformity; communalism, that is, that the climate should be informal without the development of highly specialized roles, and that relationships should be close but never exclusive; and reality confrontation, that is, that patients should be continually given interpretations of their behaviour as other members of the unit see it. It is important to appreciate that the Henderson model is a very specific one. Structurally it was a total institution and although its climate was undoubtedly in contrast to that of many large impersonal

institutions, in some ways it was rather formal, with a
detailed programme of therapeutic and administrative groups,
work assignments and other activities. Units are often self-
styled 'therapeutic communities', but they are rarely aiming
to recreate the type of therapeutic community unit described
by Jones and Rapoport.

Structural features of institutions

There are many separate features of institutions which
contribute to climate and a number of these are considered
in turn.

Size

There is considerable evidence that people prefer, and are
more active socially in, small units of organization. One
explanation for these findings is based on the idea of
'manning'. Where there are relatively few patients, pupils
or residents, there are relatively many tasks and activities
for them to undertake. There is much scope for involvement
in activity; the setting may be said to be relatively under-
manned. In contrast, settings with relatively many individuals may be over-manned, with relatively less opportunity
for involvement for all.

This is perhaps why efforts are often made to break up
an institution into smaller, more manageable, groups such as
classes, houses or year groups in schools, and wards and
small units within hospitals. Unfortunately, the overall
institution may continue to exercise a strong influence on
the smaller units that comprise it. One recent study
(reported in Canter and Canter, 1979) found that staff
working in institutions for handicapped children adopted
more institution-orientated as opposed to child-orientated
practices in looking after the children when their unit was
part of a larger overall institution. The size of the unit
itself was unimportant. Individual units within institutions
are rarely fully autonomous but continue to be dependent on
the larger institution in many ways. This notion of autonomy is an important one to which this chapter returns.

Location

Location is of both symbolic and concrete significance. The
isolated mental hospital symbolizes community attitudes to
the mentally ill, for example. Other features of institutions may symbolize a similar relationship between institution and community. Prisons are often located in cities
but their isolation is ensured by their high walls and
impenetrable, fortress-like entrances; they are in the
community, but not of it. It is important to consider what
factors are operating to promote closeness of contact
between an institution and its local community, and what
factors are operating to inhibit it. It is interesting to
speculate, for example, on whether a prominent sign
announcing that a house is a home for the elderly eases
visiting by members of the community or makes it more

difficult? Certainly many small residential caring units such as hostels and halfway houses pride themselves on carrying no such institutional signboard.

Ease of access to community facilities may be crucial for those who must remain in an institution for a long time. A lack of interest in, or desire to return to, life outside are considered by Barton and others to be amongst the main features of institutionalization, and he lists loss of contact with the outside world, loss of personal friends, and loss of prospects outside as three of its main causes.

The issue of location illustrates an important point about the psychology of social organizations. The point is that no single variable is independent of others, and consequently it is almost impossible to impute causal significance to single features of institutions. In this case, it is very unlikely that the location of an institution is independent of the philosophy or ideology under which it operates, or the attitudes of staff who work in it. A rehabilitation philosophy is likely to be associated with close community contacts, either because the institution was located close to the community in the first place, or because means had been found to overcome an unsatisfactory location.

Internal design

Large rooms with high ceilings, glossy interior wall paint in drab colours, no change of decor from one area to another, lack of personalization by the use of pictures, photographs and ornaments, lack of privacy, even sometimes extending to a bathroom and toilet, absence of individualized sleeping accommodation, few personal possessions or places to keep them, and generally an absence of opportunity to express individuality; these are amongst the internal design features of an institution which contribute to an institutional as opposed to homely atmosphere.

Once again, however, it is important to avoid over-simple ideas of cause and effect. Two examples from Canter and Canter's book (1979) on the influence of design in institutions illustrate this point. One example concerns the first several years' operation of a purpose-built unit for disturbed children. A number of features, such as outside play facilities, were designed by the architect with the express purpose of reducing institutional climate. Others, such as doors for bedrooms, were strongly advocated by the director and were eventually installed. Observation of the day-to-day life of the unit, however, led to the view that the overwhelming ideology of the unit, which placed emphasis on the children's disturbance and on the need for staff control and surveillance, undermined the use of these design features. Play facilities were rarely spontaneously used, bedroom doors were hardly ever closed, and rooms which were designed for personal use were used as seclusion rooms for punishment. The second example concerns a purpose-built forensic unit where it was possible to show, by a process of behaviour mapping (a procedure whereby a map of who does what and where is produced by observing samples of behaviour in different places at different times), the use to which different spaces were put and the meanings that became attached to them. Certain areas were clearly designated as staff offices, and others as patient lounges. As a result, segregation of staff and patients was the rule rather than the exception.

One small-scale feature of physical layout which is relatively easily manipulated is that of seating arrangement. The terms 'sociopetal' (meaning encouraging interpersonal relationships) and 'sociofugal' (discouraging relationships) have been used to describe possible seating arrangements in institutions. Seats in the lounge areas of old people's homes and other institutions are often arranged around the edge of the room or in some other sociofugal pattern, such as in rows facing a television set. Sociopetal patterns, on the other hand, have been found to lead to more interaction, more multi-person interaction, and more personal conversations. Once again, it is important to appreciate other, more human, aspects of the environment. It is often found, when attempts have been made to rearrange furniture in a more sociopetal fashion, that there is a tendency for the seating to revert to its former arrangement. It is as if the institution has a will of its own and is in some way resistant to change. Exploring how this reversion to type comes about, and making a diagnosis of what is to blame, may provide vital insights into the nature of the institution.

It is worth speculating on the function which may be served by furniture arrangement in different types of institution. For example, why is the seating arrangement of pupils in a primary school often very different from, and usually more sociopetal in design than, that to be found in a secondary school? Is this difference accidental, or does it say something about the expected relationship between teacher and pupils, and perhaps thereby about the whole underlying philosophy of education?

Rules, regulations and routines

Studies of institutional practices

Considerable progress has been made in describing the variety which exists within health and social care residential institutions. Similar variety exists within educational establishments, and within penal settings.

Studies have compared hostels and hospitals for mentally handicapped children, and have found the latter to be much more institutional in their handling of the children: routine is more rigid, children are more likely to be treated en bloc, treatment is less personalized, and social distance between staff and children is greater. Wide variation is found in the degree of 'ward restrictiveness' in adult mental hospitals. Similar variation exists in halfway houses for ex-psychiatric patients. On average, hostels are less institutional than mental hospitals, the former having

between one-half and two-thirds the number of 'restrictive
practices' found in the average hospital ward in one study.
However, considerable variation is found in both types of
facility and there is an overlap between them. Some of the
hostels, whilst being small in size, and designed to provide
a link between the large institution and the community,
nevertheless retain a number of institutional practices. In
one instance a hostel had more institutional practices than
the hospital rehabilitation ward from which most of its
residents came.

A key idea linking these studies is that of clients'
decision making freedom. Table 1 provides an indication
of some of the major areas of decision making considered in
such studies. The list could be expanded greatly to include
a large range of day-to-day activities over which most
people are able to exercise personal choice. Whether an
institution allows this exercise of choice to continue for
its clients or whether these decision-making freedoms are
curtailed is crucial in determining whether an institution
creates a therapeutic climate or institutionalization.

Table 1

**A range of decisions which may be allowed or restricted in
institutions and which are illustrative of those considered
in studies of institutional practices**

What time to get up and go to bed
What to wear
What to eat for breakfast and other meals
Planning future meals
Whether to make a drink or snack
Whether to visit the local shops
Whether to go to work
Whether to go to the pictures
How to spend own money
When to have a bath
When to have a haircut
Whether to have medicine
Deciding arrangement of own room
Deciding decoration of own room
Whether to smoke
Whether to play the radio or TV
When to invite friends in
Whether to have a sexual relationship with a friend
Planning decoration or repair of the place
Deciding how to care for or control other members
Deciding policy

Staff autonomy
Reference has already been made, when considering the size
of an institution, to the importance of a unit's autonomy
within the larger institution. Decision-making freedom may

be limited not only for clients but also for those staff who have the closest dealings with them. The advantages of the informality which can occur in a truly independent small unit are illustrated by an incident which occurred at Woodley House, an American halfway house for the mentally ill. It concerned a dispute between pro- and anti-television factions in the house. The former decided to convert part of the basement of the house for their use, leaving the living room to the others. A staff member took them in her car to buy paint and other materials and later the same day the newly-decorated television room was in use. Such an incident could not easily occur in that way in a larger and more formal institution. There are a number of reasons for this, one being that the staff member at Woodley House was not limited to a prescribed professional role, and there were no other members of staff upon whose role territory she was trespassing.

It is this variable of staff autonomy which Tizard et al (1975) considered to be one of the strongest influences upon the quality of staff-client interaction in an institutional setting. The firmest evidence for this hypothesis is contained in a chapter of their book written by Barbara Tizard. It concerns residential nurseries run by voluntary societies. She observed 13 such units, all of which had been modernized in recent years to provide 'family group' care. Mixed-age groups of six children each had their own suite of rooms and their own nurse and assistant nurse to care for them. Despite this effort at 'de-institutionalizing', marked differences existed in the degree to which nurses were truly independent agents. Nurseries were divided by the research team into three classes on the basis of the amount of unit autonomy. The first group, it was felt, was in effect run centrally by the matron:

> Decisions were made on an entirely routine basis or else referred to the matron. Each day was strictly time-tabled, the matron would make frequent inspections of each group, and freedom of the nurse and child was very limited. The children were moved through the day 'en bloc' ... The nurse had little more autonomy than the children, e.g. she would have to ask permission to take the children for a walk or to turn on the television set. As in hospital each grade of staff wore a special uniform, and had separate living quarters, and the nurse's behaviour when off duty was governed by quite strict rules.

At the other extreme was a group of nurseries which more closely approximated a normal family setting:

> The staff were responsible for shopping, cooking, making excursions with the children and arranging their own day. The children could move freely about the house and garden and the staff rarely referred a decision to the

matron. The nurse-in-charge did not wear uniform, and her off-duty time was not subject to rules. Her role, in fact, approximated more closely to that of a foster-mother. Since she could plan her own day and was not under constant surveillance she could treat the children more flexibly.

A third group of nurseries was intermediate in terms of independence. As predicted, the more autonomous staff were observed to spend more time talking to children, and more time playing, reading and giving information to them. Furthermore, children in units with more autonomous staff had higher scores on a test of verbal comprehension. The difficulty of teasing out what is important in complex social situations, such as those that exist in institutions, is illustrated by Barbara Tizard's findings. Autonomy was correlated with having a relatively favourable staff-to-child ratio and hence we cannot be certain that autonomy is the crucial variable.

Nevertheless, an effect of staff hierarchy was noticed which could explain the apparent importance of autonomy. When two staff were present at once, one was always 'in charge'. This had an inhibiting effect on a nurse's behaviour towards children: she would function in a 'notably restricted way, talking much less and using less "informative talk" than the nurse in charge'. This might explain differences between autonomous and less independent units, as staff in the latter type of unit would be much more likely to feel that someone else was in charge whether that person was present or not.

Flexible use of space, time and objects

Inflexible routine is one of the major charges brought against the institution by such writers as Barton and Goffman. Institutional life can be 'normalized' as much as possible by allowing flexible use of different areas of buildings and grounds, by varying time schedules, and by allowing flexible use of objects such as kitchen and laundry equipment, televisions, radios and record players. Residential institutions usually deprive adult inmates of the opportunity to take part in 'complete activity cycles'. Instead of taking part in a complete cycle of shopping for food, preparing it, eating, clearing away and washing up after it, residents may simply be required to eat what others have purchased and prepared, rather like guests in a hotel.

Staff attitudes and behaviour

Ideology

The influence of an institution's ideology or philosophy is pervasive, although its significance can be missed altogether by those taken up in the day-to-day activities of the place. Many examples could be given. The philosophy of a progressive school such as Summerhill, with its emphasis on personal development, is distinct from that of a regular secondary school with its emphasis on academic learning. The rehabilitation philosophy of Grendon Underwood prison is distinct from that of most closed penal establishments with their emphasis on custody. Many institutions have mixed and competing ideologies. These frequently give rise to conflict within the institution, the different ideologies often being represented by different cadres of staff. For example, educational and child care philosophies compete within institutions for handicapped children, as do educational and disciplinary philosophies within institutions for young delinquents. Important shifts may take place gradually over time. For example, a general shift from a custodial philosophy to a more therapeutic ideology has occurred in mental hospitals over the last several decades. Quite recently some of those working in British prisons have detected a move in the opposite direction in response to the call for tighter security.

Words such as 'open' to describe penal institutions, 'progressive' to describe educational facilities, and expressions such as 'therapeutic community' to describe an institution for residential care, all serve as public announcements of ideology and intended behaviour. However, it has already been noted that terms such as 'therapeutic community' are frequently used loosely, and sufficient is known about the absence of a strong correlation between attitudes and behaviour to make us doubtful that ideal philosophies will always be perfectly borne out in practice.

Staff attitudes
Nevertheless, no one who has worked in an institution for very long can have failed to notice what appear to be marked individual differences in staff attitudes. In the mental hospital setting questionnaires have been devised to detect staff attitudes of 'custodialism' or 'traditionalism'. The matter is by no means simple, however, and attitudes vary along a number of dimensions. For example, one study distinguished between 'restrictive control' and 'protective benevolence'. Staff high on restrictive control tended to be described as 'impatient with others' mistakes' and 'hardboiled and critical', and not 'sensitive and understanding' and 'open and honest with me'. Those high on protective benevolence, on the other hand, were described as 'stays by himself' and 'reserved and cool', and not 'lets patients get to know him' and 'talks about a variety of things'. Staff members high on this attitude scale expressed attitudes that appeared to suggest kindliness towards patients and yet they appear to have been seen by the latter as basically aloof, distant and non-interacting.

A study of hostels for boys on probation also illustrates the complexity of the matter. This study examined the relationship between failure rate, based on the percentage of residents leaving as a result of absconding or being reconvicted, and the attitudes of 16 different wardens. Two components of attitude were identified, each positively associated with success: strictness as opposed to permissiveness; and emotional closeness, which included warmth and willingness to discuss residents' problems with them, versus emotional distance. However, the two components, each separately associated with success, were negatively associated with one another. Hence wardens who displayed more warmth and willingness to discuss problems were also likely to be over-permissive, whilst those who were relatively strict tended to be lacking in emotional closeness. The ideal combination of warmth and firmness was a combination relatively rarely encountered.

Individual staff attitudes can partly be explained in terms of individual differences in general attitudes or personality: members of staff who are more generally authoritarian in personality tend to hold more custodial attitudes. This alone, however, cannot explain differences that are found between different institutions. Although the correspondence is far from complete, it has been found to be the case that where the prevailing policy is custodial, staff subscribe to a custodial view and tend to be generally authoritarian in personality. This raises the fascinating question of how such relative uniformity comes about. It can be presumed that the same three main processes are at work as those that operate to produce consensus and similarity of attitude in any social group or organization. The three processes are (i) selection-in, (ii) selection-out, and (iii) attitude change. Selection of new staff will most likely operate in a way that increases uniformity of attitude, both because certain people are more attracted than others by the prospect of working in a particular institution, and also because certain potential staff members are thought more suitable by those responsible for the selection (selection-in). Staff remain in one place for a variable length of time, and the institution may retain for longer periods those members whose attitudes are in conformity with the prevailing ideology (selection-out).

As social psychological experiments on conformity show so clearly, it is difficult to maintain a non-conformist position in the face of combined opinion, and the third process - attitude change - is likely to be a strong factor.

Staff behaviour and staff-client social distance
Although research leads us to expect none too close a correspondence between attitudes and behaviour, a number of studies in institutions suggest that philosophy and attitudes can be conveyed to residents via staff behaviour. Studies of units for handicapped children, for autistic children, and for the adult mentally ill, suggest that staff behaviour towards clients is more personal, warmer and less rejecting or critical when management practices are more client-orientated and less institution-orientated. Large

differences have also been detected in the amount of time
which staff members in charge of hostel units spend in face-
to-face contact with their residents. Sharing space and
activities together, and spending relatively more time in
contact with one another, may be the most important factors
in reducing social distance.

Social distance between staff and clients was an important concept in Goffman's and Barton's analyses of institutions. Avoidance, or reduced time in contact, is a fairly
universal indication of lack of affection and often of
prejudiced and stereotyped attitudes. There are numerous
means of preserving social distance including designation of
separate spaces, such as staff offices. A clearly designated
staff office makes staff and client separation easier, but
such a space may be used in a variety of different ways. The
door may be kept open, or closed, or even locked with a key
only available to staff.

Controversy often surrounds the wearing of staff uniform
in institutions. There are arguments for and against, but
inevitably the uniform creates or reinforces a distinction
and may therefore increase social distance. A movement away
from the traditional institutional organization is very
frequently accompanied by the abandonment of uniforms where
these previously existed. The use of names and titles in
addressing different members of a community is another
indication of the presence or absence of social distance.
Forms of address are known to be good signs of both soli-
darity and status within social groups. The reciprocal use
of first names is a sign of relative intimacy, and the
reciprocal use of titles (Mr, Mrs, etc.) a sign of distance.
Non-reciprocal forms of address, on the other hand, are
indications of a status difference, with the person of
higher status almost always using the more familiar form of
address (say a first name or nickname) in addressing the
person of lower status, and the latter using title and
surname towards the former, or even a form of address which
clearly indicates the former's superior status (sir, boss,
etc.). If forms of address change as people get to know one
another better, it is usually the person of higher status
who initiates the use of familiar forms of address first.

Hence an examination of a particular institution in
terms of designated spaces for staff and others, uniforms
and other visual indications of role or rank, and of forms
of address, can give useful clues to status divisions and
social distance within the institution. However, it is of
the utmost importance to keep in mind that social distance,
like all of the social psychological features of institutions considered here, is a highly complex matter. It has
been suggested, for example, that there are at least two
distinct forms of social distance, namely status distance
and personal distance. If these aspects of social distance
are relatively independent, as has been suggested, it
follows that status distance need not necessarily preclude
the formation of a personally close relationship.

nstitutions as complex
ystems

The client contribution

Staff may be crucial determinants of climate, particularly
senior staff, but so too are the institution's users or
clients. The climate in an institution is the product of a
bewildering complexity of factors which interact in ways
that are far from straightforward. No simple theory which
attempts to explain what goes on inside an institution in
terms of physical design alone, of the attitudes of senior
staff alone, or of management practices alone, can do
justice to them. It would be as faulty to ignore the personalities, abilities and disabilities of the users as it
would be to ignore the philosophy of the institution or the
design of its buildings. This point is forcefully brought
home in Miller and Gwynne's (1972) account of homes catering
for people with irreversible and severe physical handicaps
where the most likely termination of residence is death.
They contrasted two ideologies which they believed existed
in such institutions: the 'warehousing' philosophy, with its
emphasis upon physical care and the dependence of residents;
and the 'horticultural' philosophy, with its emphasis on the
cultivation of residents' interests and abilities. They
stress that each has dangers - the one of dependence and
institutionalization, the other of unrealistic expectations
being set - and that each is a response to the serious
nature of the residents' handicaps.

There are a number of studies of social behaviour on the
wards of mental hospitals which prove the point that social
climate depends upon the mix of patients who are residing
there. A clear instance was provided by Fairweather's (1964)
study which is described more fully below. Introducing
changes of a progressive nature on a hospital ward increased
the level of social interaction generally but significant
differences between different patient groups still persisted, with non-psychotic patients interacting most, acute
psychotic patients an intermediate amount, and chronic
psychotic patients the least. The mix of clients is especially crucial where group influence is considered to be one
of the principal media of change (whether the change desired
be educational, therapeutic or rehabilitative). Even in the
relatively permissive climate of the Henderson therapeutic
community, those with particularly socially disruptive
personalities cannot be tolerated and, if accidentally
admitted, may have to be discharged.

Under circumstances where group influence operates, it
is particularly important that the client group exerts its
main influence in a manner consistent with the overriding
philosophy espoused by staff. This is always in danger of
going wrong in secondary schools where the 'adolescent sub-
culture' may exert a countervailing force, and in prisons
where the 'inmate code' has to be contended with. In
Canadian schools and centres for juvenile delinquents a
procedure known as the 'Measurement of Treatment Potential'
(MTP) has been in use to assess this aspect of climate.
Where clients choose as liked fellow clients the same

members as those whose behaviour is approved of by staff, then treatment potential is considered to be high. When there is a mismatch between residents' and staff choices, treatment potential is said to be low.

Climate

Many factors contributing to climate have been considered in this chapter and there are many others which it has not been possible to consider. Repeatedly emphasized has been the complex way in which these factors interact to influence the climate of an institutional unit. 'Climate', a word used here to cover any perceptions of, or feelings about, the institution held by those who use it, work in it or observe it, is not the same thing as success, effectiveness, or productivity. However, the latter are notoriously difficult to define, let alone measure, whereas people's perceptions of atmosphere can be collected and their relationships with features of the institution analysed. A massive programme of research along these lines has been conducted by Moos (1974). He has devised a series of questionnaires to tap the perceptions of members of various types of institutions and organizations. The most thoroughly tested of these scales is the Ward Atmosphere Scale (WAS), which assesses perceptions along the ten dimensions shown in table 2. This list was based upon earlier research by others as well as a great deal of preliminary work of Moos' own. He claims that dimensions 1-3 (the relationship dimensions) and 8-10 (the system maintenance and system change dimensions) are equally relevant across a wide range of institutions including schools, universities, hospitals and penal institutions. Dimensions 4-7 (the personal development dimensions), on the other hand, need modification depending upon the setting.

Amongst the many findings from research based upon the WAS and similar scales are the following. First, when staff and patient perceptions are compared in hospital treatment settings, average staff scores are regularly found to be higher on all dimensions except Order and Organization (no difference between staff and patients), and Staff Control (patients scoring higher than staff). Second, when scores are correlated with size of unit and with staff-to-patient ratio, it has been found that Support and Spontaneity are both lower and Staff Control is higher where patient numbers are greater and staff-to-patient ratios are poorer (MTP has also been found to correlate with smallness of size and favourability of staff to pupil ratios). Third, where patients have greater 'adult status' (access to bedrooms, television, unrestricted smoking, less institutional admission procedure, etc.), Spontaneity, Autonomy, Personal Problem Orientation, and Anger and Aggression are all higher and Staff Control is lower. Fourth, all scales correlate positively with ratings of general satisfaction with the ward and with ratings of liking for staff, with the exception of Staff Control which correlates negatively with both.

Table 2

The 10 dimensions measured by Moos' Ward Atmosphere Scale

RELATIONSHIP DIMENSIONS

1. Involvement measures how active and energetic patients are in the day-to-day social functioning of the ward. Attitudes such as pride in the ward, feelings of group spirit, and general enthusiasm are also assessed.

2. Support measures how helpful and supportive patients are towards other patients, how well the staff understand patient needs and are willing to help and encourage patients, and how encouraging and considerate doctors are towards patients.

3. Spontaneity measures the extent to which the environment encourages patients to act openly and to express freely their feelings towards other patients and staff.

PERSONAL DEVELOPMENT DIMENSIONS

4. Autonomy assesses how self-sufficient and independent patients are encouraged to be in their personal affairs and in their relationships with staff, and how much responsibility and self-direction patients are encouraged to exercise.

5. Practical orientation assesses the extent to which the patient's environment orients him towards preparing himself for release from the hospital and for the future.

6. Personal problem orientation measures the extent to which patients are encouraged to be concerned with their feelings and problems and to seek to understand them through openly talking to other patients and staff about themselves and their past.

7. Anger and aggression measures the extent to which a patient is allowed and encouraged to argue with patients and staff, and to become openly angry.

SYSTEM MAINTENANCE AND SYSTEM CHANGE DIMENSIONS

8. Order and organization measures the importance of order on the ward; also measures organization in terms of patients (do they follow a regular schedule and do they have carefully planned activities?) and staff (do they keep appointments and do they help patients follow schedules?)

9. Programme clarity measures the extent to which the patient knows what to expect in the day-to-day routine of the ward and how explicit the ward rules and procedures are.

10. Staff control measures the necessity for the staff to restrict patients: that is, the strictness of rules, schedules and regulations, and measures taken to keep patients under effective control.

Changing institutions   A knowledge of the factors discussed in this chapter should enable those involved in policy, planning and management to generate ideas for constructive change, and those in relatively junior positions to try and bring about change in their practice within the prevailing limits of autonomy. However, major changes may require innovations or interventions from outside and it is these that are now discussed in the remainder of this chapter.

Innovative programmes

One of the best documented programmes of institutional change in the mental health care system is the work reported in a series of publications by Fairweather and his colleagues. The first report (Fairweather, 1964) described dramatic differences in patient social behaviour between an experimental 'small group' ward and a physically identical 'traditional' ward in a mental hospital. In the traditional ward, staff members made final decisions on all important matters. By contrast, on the small group ward it was the responsibility of a group of patients to orient new fellow patients to the ward, to carry out work assignments, to assess patient progress, and to recommend privileges and even final discharge. The total experiment lasted for six months, and staff switched wards halfway through. Social activity was at a much higher level on the small group ward, and the climate in the daily ward meeting was quite different with more silence and staff control on the traditional ward, and more lively discussion, less staff talk, and many more patient remarks directed towards fellow patients on the small group ward. Nursing and other staff evaluated their experience on the small group ward more highly, and patients spent significantly fewer days in hospital.

In a further report, Fairweather, Sanders, Cressler and Maynard (1969) compared the community adjustment of ex-patients who moved together as a group from a small group ward in the hospital to a small hostel unit in the community (the 'lodge'), and others who moved out of the hospital in the normal way. The results were quite dramatic, with the lodge group surviving much better in the community in terms of the prevention of re-admission to hospital, the amount of time in work (much of which was organized by the ex-patient group as a consortium), and residents' morale and self-esteem. This is a particularly good example of the setting-up from scratch of a new small institution designed to avoid many of the most disagreeable features of large institutions.

Changes in the philosophies and modes of practice in institutions mostly take place over a period of years as a result of the slow diffusion of new ideas. A third report by Fairweather, Sanders and Tornatsky (1974) was concerned with this process. Having established the value of the lodge programme, they set out to sell the idea to mental hospitals throughout the USA. They were concerned to know the influence of a number of variables upon the diffusion process, and consequently adopted a rigorous experimental approach. First, they varied the degree of effort required on the part of the hospital contacted in order to accept the initial approach offered. Of 255 hospitals contacted, one-third were merely offered a brochure describing the lodge programme (70 per cent accepted but only 5 per cent finally adopted the lodge programme), one-third were offered a two-hour workshop about the programme (80 per cent accepted and 12 per cent finally adopted), and one-third were offered help with setting up a demonstration small group ward in the hospital for a minimum of 90 days (only 25 per cent accepted but 11 per cent finally adopted the lodge). A second variable was the position in the hospital hierarchy of the person contacted with the initial approach offer. One-fifth of initial contacts were made to hospital superintendents and one-fifth to each of the four professions, psychiatry, psychology, social work and nursing. This variable turned out to be relatively unimportant: contacts were just as likely to result in the adoption of the lodge programme when they were made to people in nursing as to superintendents or those in psychiatry.

Much more important than the status of the person who initiates an idea is, according to Fairweather et al, a high level of involvement across disciplines, professions, and social status levels within the institution. When change did occur there was most likely to exist a multi-disciplinary group which spearheaded the change, led by a person who continuously pushed for change and attempted to keep the group organized and its morale high. The disciplinary group to which this person belonged was of little importance. Nor was change related to financial resources. The need for perseverance is stressed. The need to keep pushing for change despite 'meetings that came to naught, letters that stimulated nothing, telephone calls unreturned, and promises unkept' is a necessary ingredient of institutional change.

Action research
Fairweather's studies concerned the setting-up of new facilities or units. If, on the other hand, constructive change is to be brought about in existing institutions and their units, the total climate of the institution, and particularly the autonomy of the individual staff members, are limiting factors. A number of schemes have been described for providing helpful intervention from outside in the form of a person or team who act as catalysts or change agents. Several of these involve the process known as Action Research. For example, Towell and Harries (1979) have described a number of changes brought about at Fulbourne psychiatric hospital in Cambridgeshire with the help of a specially appointed 'social research adviser'.

The process begins when the interventionist(s) is invited to a particular unit to advise or help. It is stressed that the initiative should come from the unit and not from the interventionist, although it is clearly necessary for the latter to advertise the service being offered, and Moos (1974), for example, has argued that feeding back research data on social climate can itself initiate a change process. After the initial approach there follows a period during

which the action researcher gets to know the unit, usually
by interviewing as many members as possible individually, by
attending unit meetings, and by spending time in the unit
observing. Then follow the stages which give 'action
research' its name. With the help of the action researcher,
members of the unit (usually the staff group collectively)
decide upon a piece of research which can be quickly mounted
and carried through and which is relevant to the matter in
hand. The results of this research are then used to help
decide what changes are necessary. The action researcher
remains involved during these phases and subsequently as
attempts are made to implement changes and to make them
permanent.

For example, one of the Fulbourne projects concerned a
long-stay ward which had adopted an 'open door', no-staff-
uniforms policy and which was designated as suitable for
trainee nurses to gain 'rehabilitation experience'. The
staff, however, felt 'forgotten' at the back of the hospital, felt that scope for patient improvement was not often
realized, and that they were unable to provide the rehabilitation experience intended. The social research adviser
helped the staff devise a simple interview schedule which
focussed on such matters as how patients passed their time,
friendships amongst patients, and feelings patients had
about staff and their work. Each member of staff was responsible for carrying out certain interviews and for writing
them up and presenting them to the group. All reports were
read by all members of staff and discussed at a special
meeting. The group reached a consensus that patients were
insular, took little initiative, expected to be led by
staff, had no idea of 'self-help', saw little treatment
function for the nurses, saw little purposeful nurse-patient
interaction, and had only negative feelings, if any, towards
fellow patients.

Although there were no immediate or dramatic changes,
a slow development over a period of 18 months was reported
in the direction of a much increased 'counselling approach
to care'. The research interview was incorporated into
routine care. This itself involved the setting-up of a
special contact between individual nurse and individual
patient, a factor which is mentioned in other projects
described by Towell and Harries and by many other writers
who have described constructive changes in institutions. At
first the social research adviser took a leading role in
groups in helping to understand the material gathered in
interviews. This role was later taken over by the ward
doctor and later still by a senior member of the nursing staf
At this point the social research adviser withdrew. Later on
patients read back interview reports and there were many
other signs of reduced staff and patient distance. Over the
three-year period during which these changes came about, the
number of patients resettled outside the hospital increased
from two in the first year to eight in the second and eleven
in the third.

It is stressed by those who have described 'action research' and schemes like it, such as 'administrative consultation' and the type of social systems change facilitated by a consultant described by Maxwell Jones (1976), that staff of a unit must be fully involved and identified with any change that is attempted. It is relatively easy to bring about acceptance of change on an attitudinal level, largely through talking, but to produce a behavioural commitment to change is something else. Those who have written of the 'action research' process talk of the importance of 'ownership' of the research activity. The aim is to get the unit's members fully involved and to make them feel the research is theirs.

Resistance to change

We should expect such complex social systems, whose mode of operation must have been arrived at because it serves certain needs or produces certain pay-offs for those involved, to be resistant to change. Particularly should we expect it to be resistant to change when this threatens to involve change in status and role relationships. Unfortunately, it is just such changes for which we so frequently search. The themes of decision-making autonomy and social power have been constant ones throughout this chapter; they lie at the heart of what is wrong with many of the worst institutions. Maxwell Jones (1976) believes it is almost always the required task of the social systems facilitator to 'flatten' the authority hierarchy, and to support lower status members in taking the risks involved in expressing their feelings and opinions, whilst at the same time supporting higher status members in the belief that they can change in the direction of relinquishing some of their authority.

As in most earlier sections of this chapter, examples of attempts to change institutions or parts of institutions have been taken from the mental health field. Nevertheless, the processes and problems involved can be recognized by those whose main concern is with other types of institution such as the educational and penal. In particular, those who have in any way, large or small, attempted to change such institutions can recognize the problem of resistance to change. Nothing illustrates better the need to add to our understanding of how institutions work. In the process of finding out more on this topic we learn more of man in a social context, which is part of the central core of the study of psychology.

References

Barton, R. (1959; 3rd edn, 1976)
Institutional Neurosis. Bristol: Wright.
Canter, D. and Canter, S. (eds) (1979)
Designing for Therapeutic Environments: A review of research. Chichester: Wiley.

Fairweather, G.W. (ed.) (1964)
   Social Psychology in Treating Mental Illness. New York:
   Wiley.
Fairweather, G.W., Sanders, D.H., Cressler, D.L. and Maynard, H. (1969)
   Community Life for the Mentally Ill: An alternative to
   institutional care. Chicago, Ill.: Aldine.
Fairweather, G.W., Sanders, D.H. and Tornatsky, L.G. (1974)
   Creating Change in Mental Health Organizations. New
   York: Pergamon.
Goffman, E. (1961)
   Asylums: Essays on the social situation of mental
   patients and other inmates. New York: Anchor Books,
   Doubleday.
Jones, Maxwell (1952)
   Social Psychiatry: A study of therapeutic communities.
   London: Tavistock. (Published as The Therapeutic
   Community, New York: Basic Books: 1953.)
Jones, Maxwell (1976)
   Maturation of the Therapeutic Community: An organic
   approach to health and mental health. New York: Human
   Sciences Press.
Miller, E.J. and Gwynne, G.V. (1972)
   In Life Apart: A pilot study of residential institutions
   for the physically handicapped and the young chronic
   sick. London: Tavistock.
Moos, R.H. (1974)
   Evaluating Treatment Environments: A social ecological
   approach. New York: Wiley.
Rapoport, R.M. (1960)
   Community as Doctor: New perspectives on a therapeutic
   community. London: Tavistock.
Tizard, J., Sinclair, I. and Clarke, R.V.G. (eds) (1975)
   Varieties of Residential Experience. London: Routledge &
   Kegan Paul.
Towell, D. and Harries, C. (1979)
   Innovations in Patient Care. London: Croom Helm.

Questions

1. Give two different definitions of 'institution' and give
   examples of places which fit both definitions, which fit
   one but not the other, and which fit neither.
2. What do you understand by the term 'total institution'?
   Why is it thought that they may do harm?
3. What principles are embodied in a proper Therapeutic
   Community? Is it possible in your view to say when these
   have been achieved, and when not?
4. What structural features contribute to the climate of an
   institution, and why?
5. How can the internal design of an institutional unit be
   changed to bring about change in the behaviour of those
   who live or work in it?
6. Discuss the proposition that the most important thing to
   change in an institution is staff attitudes.

7. Are staff more important than the users or residents in determining the climate of an institution, and in what ways might social distance between staff and residents of an institution be detected?
8. What formal and informal methods would you use to assess the climate or atmosphere of an institution?
9. What important principles should be kept in mind when trying to change an institution in some way?
10. The only sensible thing to do with institutions is to abolish them altogether. Discuss.

Annotated reading

Barton, R. (1959; 3rd edn, 1976) Institutional Neurosis. Bristol: Wright.
> This is now a classic book, describing institutionalization as a state analogous to a disease. It is written from a medical perspective but is brief, easy to read, describes the effects of institutionalization within a hospital setting, and forcefully makes the point that the state can arise in any institutional setting.

Fairweather, G.W., Sanders, D.H., Cressler, D.L. and Maynard, H. (1969) Community Life for the Mentally Ill: An alternative to institutional care. Chicago: Aldine.
> The main part of this book describes the story of a group of mental hospital patients who left the hospital together and set up home in a 'lodge', living and working productively together. Elsewhere in the book research findings are reported. Those who enjoy reading about research findings may also wish to read Fairweather, G. W. (ed.) (1964), 'Social Psychology in Treating Mental Illness', New York: Wiley.

Goffman, E. (1961) Asylums: Essays on the social situation of mental patients and other inmates. New York: Anchor Books, Doubleday.
> Another classic volume, in which a sociologist describes the events and processes he saw in a large American mental hospital. The book is full of telling sociological insights, but it is important when reading 'Asylums' to have in one's mind the knowledge that not all institutions, not even all mental hospitals, are alike and that there are important differences amongst them.

Jones, Maxwell (1952) Social Psychiatry: A study of therapeutic communities. London: Tavistock. (Published as 'The Therapeutic Community', New York: Basic Books, 1953).
> Again a classic book. The original description of the concept of the Therapeutic Community. Revolutionary in its time and still very well worth reading to understand the basic ideas behind the concept.

King, R.D., Raynes, N.V. and Tizard, J. (1971) Patterns of Residential Care: Sociological studies in institutions for handicapped children. London: Routledge & Kegan Paul.
This book is detailed and has quite a high research content. It is especially useful for the definitions and criteria for assessing institutional practices. Because of this it has been an influential book upon which later research has been based.

King's Fund (undated). Living in Hospital: The social needs of people in long-term care. London: Research Publications Limited.
This is an easy to digest pamphlet designed to be read by people who work in institutions. It poses a number of very detailed questions which readers should ask them-selves about the environments created in their own institutions for those who reside there.

Miller, E.J. and Gwynne, G.V. (1972) A Life Apart: A pilot study of residential institutions for the physically handi-capped and the young chronic sick. London: Tavistock.
This is an account of a study of several homes and hospital units for a very disadvantaged group, most of whom would never leave the institutions in which they were resident. It describes several places in consider-able detail and in the course of so doing raises many of the issues with which the present chapter on institutional climates is concerned.

Otto, S. and Orford, J. (1978) Not Quite Like Home: Small hostels for alcoholics and others. Chichester: Wiley.
This book is in two parts. The first reviews work on institutions and on small hostels for the mentally ill, offenders, and people with drinking problems in particular. The second part describes in detail a research study of two particular hostels for problem drinkers. It covers a great deal of important ground but is probably not so easy to read as some of the other books suggested.

Rutter, M., Maughan, B., Mortimore, P. and Ouston, J. (1979) Fifteen Thousand Hours: Secondary schools and their effects on children. London: Open Books.
Here is a recent account of a detailed research project concerning the organization of a number of London secondary schools and their effect on the pupils' achievement and behaviour. The research is detailed and painstaking and the book is probably not easy to read, but for those who find statistics heavy going it contains some valuable passages about differences in school organization.

Tizard, J., Sinclair, I. and Clarke, R.V.G. (eds) (1975) Varieties of Residential Experience. London: Routledge & Kegan Paul.

This book is an important collection of chapters written by different authors describing a variety of studies of residential institutions of one kind or another, mostly for children or adolescents. Particularly important are the first chapter in which the editors criticize the simplicity of Goffman's approach in 'Asylums', and the chapter by Barbara Tizard in which she shows how residential nurseries can be run in very different ways.

Towell, D. and Harries, C. (1979) Innovations in Patient Care. London: Croom Helm.
These authors describe how changes were brought about in the running of a mental hospital. Particularly inspiring is chapter 2 which describes how significant change was brought about in an acute psychiatric ward and on a long-stay ward.

Walter, J.A. (1978) Sent Away: A study of young offenders in care. Farnborough, Hants.: Teakfield.
Walter's book describes his detailed observations and results of interviews at one Scottish List D school (the equivalent of the English Community Home or, as it used to be called, Approved School). It is a racy, easy to read account, concentrating particularly on the overall ideology or philosophy of the school and its effect upon staff and boys.

Part six

The Occupational Therapist as Psychological Therapist

17

Counselling and helping
Barrie Hopson

From a situation in the mid-1960s when 'counselling' was
seen by many in education as a transatlantic transplant
which hopefully would never 'take', we have today reached
the position of being on board a band-wagon; 'counsellors'
are everywhere: beauty counsellors, tax counsellors,
investment counsellors, even carpet counsellors. There are
'counsellors' in schools, industry, hospitals, the social
services. There is marriage counselling, divorce counselling, parent counselling, bereavement counselling, abortion
counselling, retirement counselling, redundancy counselling,
career counselling, psychosexual counselling, pastoral counselling, student counselling and even disciplinary counselling! Whatever the original purpose for coining the word
'counselling', the coinage has by now certainly been de-
based. One of the unfortunate consequences of the debasing
has been that the word has become mysterious; we cannot
always be sure just what 'counselling' involves. One of the
results of the mystification of language is that we rely on
others to tell us what it is: that is, we assume that we,
the uninitiated, cannot know and understand what it is
really about. That can be a first step to denying ourselves
skills and knowledge we already possess or that we may have
the potential to acquire.

It is vital that we 'de-mystify' counselling, and to do
that we must look at the concept within the broader context
of ways in which people help other people, and we must
analyse it in relation to objectives. 'Counselling' is often
subscribed to as being 'a good thing', but we must ask the
question, 'good for what?'

Ways of helping

'Counselling' is only one form of helping. It is decidedly
not the answer to all human difficulties, though it can be
extremely productive and significant for some people, sometimes. Counselling is one way of working to help people
overcome problems, clarify or achieve personal goals. We can
distinguish between six types of helping strategies (Scally
and Hopson, 1979).

* Giving advice: offering somebody your opinion of what
  would be the best course of action based on your view
  of their situation.

* Giving information: giving a person the information he needs in a particular situation (e.g. about legal rights, the whereabouts of particular agencies, etc.). Lacking information can make one powerless; providing it can be enormously helpful.
* Direct action: doing something on behalf of somebody else or acting to provide for another's immediate needs; for example, providing a meal, lending money, stopping a fight, intervening in a crisis.
* Teaching: helping someone to acquire knowledge and skills; passing on facts and skills which improve somebody's situation.
* Systems change: working to influence and improve systems which are causing difficulty for people; that is, working on organizational development rather than with individuals.
* Counselling: helping someone to explore a problem, clarify conflicting issues and discover alternative ways of dealing with it, so that they can decide what to do about it; that is, helping people to help themselves.

There is no ranking intended in this list. What we do say is that these strategies make up a helper's 'tool-bag'. Each one is a 'piece of equipment' which may be useful in particular helping contexts. What a helper is doing is to choose from available resources whichever approach best fits the situation at the time.

There are some interesting similarities and differences between the strategies. Giving advice, information, direct action, teaching and possibly systems change recognize that the best answers, outcomes, or solutions rely on the expertise of the helper. The 'expert' offers what is felt to be most useful to the one seeking help. Counselling, on the other hand, emphasizes that the person with the difficulty is the one with the resources needed to deal with it. The counsellor provides the relationship which enables the clients to search for their own answers. The 'expert' does not hand out solutions. This does not deny the special skills of the helper, but does imply that having 'expertise' does not make a person an 'expert'. We all have expertise. In counselling, the counsellor is using personal expertise to help to get the clients in touch with their own expertise. Counselling is the only helping strategy which makes no assumption that the person's needs are known.

Teaching, systems change, and counselling are only likely to be effective if the 'helper' has relationship-making skills. Giving advice, information and direct action are likely to be more effective if he has them. Systems change is different in that it emphasizes work with groups, structures, rules and organizations.

The counsellor possibly uses most of the other strategies at some time or other, when they seem more appropriate than counselling. The other strategies would have an element of counselling in them if the 'helper' had the necessary skills. For example, a new student having difficulties making friends at school could lead to a counsellor, in addition to using counselling skills, teaching some relationship-building skills to the student, getting the staff to look at induction provision, making some suggestions to the student, or even taking the student to a lunchtime discotheque in the school club.

Who are the helpers?

Strictly speaking we are all potential helpers and people to be helped, but in this context it may be useful to distinguish between three groups.

Professional helpers

These are people whose full-time occupation is geared towards helping others in a variety of ways. They have usually, but not always, received specialist training. Social workers, doctors, teachers, school counsellors, nurses, careers officers and health visitors are a few examples. They define their own function in terms of one or more of the helping strategies.

Paraprofessional helpers

These people have a clearly defined helping role but it does not constitute the major part of their job specification or represent the dominant part of their lives, such as marriage guidance counsellors, priests, part-time youth workers, personnel officers and some managers. Probably they have received some short in-service training, often on-the-job.

Helpers in general

People who may not have any specially defined helping role but who, because of their occupational or social position or because of their own commitment, find themselves in situations where they can offer help to others, such as shop stewards, school caretakers, undertakers, social security clerks or solicitors. This group is unlikely to have received special training in helping skills. In addition to these groupings there are a variety of unstructured settings within which helping occurs: the family, friendships, and in the community (Brammer, 1973).

What makes people good helpers?

In some ways it is easier to begin with the qualities that quite clearly do not make for good helping. Loughary and Ripley (1979) people their helpers' rogue's gallery with four types of would-be helpers:

* the 'You think you've got a problem! Let me tell you about mine!' type;
* the 'Let me tell you what to do' type;
* the 'I understand because I once had the same problem myself' person;
* the 'I'll take charge and deal with it' type.

The first three approaches have been clearly identified as

being counter-productive (Carkhuff and Berenson, 1976) while the fourth one certainly deals with people's problems but prevents them ever learning skills or concepts to enable them to work through the problem on their own the next time it occurs. The only possible appropriate place for this person is in a crisis intervention. However, even this intervention would need to be followed up with additional counselling help if the needy person were to avoid such crises.

Rogers (1958) came out with clearly testable hypotheses of what constitutes effective helping. He said that helpers must be open and that they should be able to demonstrate the following qualities:

* unconditioned positive regard: acceptance of clients as worth while regardless of who they are or what they say or do;
* congruence: helpers should use their feelings, their verbal and non-verbal behaviour should be open to clients and be consistent;
* genuineness: they should be honest, sincere and without façades;
* empathic: they should be able to let clients know that they understand their frame of reference and can see the world as the client sees it, whilst remaining separate from it.

These qualities must be not only possessed but conveyed: that is, the client must experience them.

Truax and Carkhuff (1967) put these hypotheses to the test and found considerable empirical support for what they identified as the 'core facilitative conditions' of effective helping relationships - empathy, respect and positive regard, genuineness, and concreteness - the ability to be specific and immediate to client statements. They differed from Rogers in that whereas he claimed that the facilitative conditions were necessary and sufficient, they only claimed that they were necessary. Carkhuff has gone on to try to demonstrate (Carkhuff and Berenson, 1976) that they are clearly not sufficient, and that the helper needs to be skilled in teaching a variety of life and coping skills to clients. The other important finding from Truax and Carkhuff was that helpers who do not possess those qualities are not merely ineffective, for they can contribute to people becoming worse than they were prior to helping.

The evidence tends to suggest that the quality of the interpersonal relationship between helper and client is more important than any specific philosophy of helping adhered to by the helper. This has been demonstrated to be the case in counselling, psychotherapy and also teaching (Aspy and Roebuck, 1977). A recent review of the many research studies on this topic would suggest, as one might expect, that things are not quite that simple (Parloff, Waskow, and Wolfe, 1978), but after a reappraisal of the early work of Truax and Carkhuff and a large number of more recent studies, the authors conclude that a relationship between empathy, respect and genuineness with helper effectiveness has been established. They also shed light on a number of other factors which have been discussed periodically as being essential for effective therapists (their focus was therapy, not helping):

* personal psychotherapy has not been demonstrated to be a prerequisite for an effective therapist;
* sex and race are not related to effectiveness;
* the value of therapist experience is highly questionable; that is, someone is not necessarily a better therapist because of greater experience;
* therapists with emotional problems of their own are likely to be less effective;
* there is some support for the suggestion that helpers are more effective when working with clients who hold values similar to their own.

What they do point out is the importance of the match between helper and client. No one is an effective helper with everyone, although we as yet know little as to how to match helpers with clients to gain the greatest benefits.

Helping and human relationships

Carl Rogers states very clearly that psychotherapy is not a 'special kind of relationship, different in kind from all others which occur in everyday life' (1957). A similar approach has been taken by those theorists looking at the broader concept of helping. Brammer (1973) states that 'helping relationships have much in common with friendships, family interactions, and pastoral contacts. They are all aimed at fulfilling basic human needs, and when reduced to their basic components, look much alike'. This is the approach of Egan (1975) in his training programmes for effective interpersonal relating, of Carkhuff and Berenson (1976) who talk of counselling as 'a way of life', of Illich, Zola, McKnight, Kaplan and Sharken (1977) who are concerned with the de-skilling of the population by increasing armies of specialists, and of Scally and Hopson (1979) who emphasize that counselling 'is merely a set of beliefs, values and behaviours to be found in the community at large'. Considerable stress is placed later in this chapter on the trend towards demystifying helping and counselling.

Models of helping

Any person attempting to help another must have some model in mind, however ill-formed, of the process which is about to be undertaken. There will be goals, however hazy, ranging from helping the person to feel better through to helping the person to work through an issue independently. It is essential for helpers to become more aware of the value-roots of their behaviours and the ideological underpinning of their proffered support.

> The helper builds his theory through three overlapping stages. First he reflects on his own experience. He becomes aware of his values, needs, communication style, and their impact on others. He reads widely on the experience of other practitioners who have tried to make sense out of their observations by writing down their ideas into a systematic theory ... Finally the helper forges the first two items together into a unique theory of his own (Brammer, 1973).

Fortunately, in recent years a number of theorists and researchers have begun to define models of helping. This can only assist all helpers to define their own internal models which will then enable them in turn to evaluate their personal, philosophical and empirical bases.

CARKHUFF AND ASSOCIATES: Carkhuff took Rogers' ideas on psychotherapy and expanded on them to helping in general. He has a three-stage model through which the client is helped to (i) explore, (ii) understand and (iii) act. He defines the skills needed by the helper at each stage of the process (Carkhuff, 1974), and has also developed a system for selecting and training prospective helpers to do this. Since the skills he outlines are basically the same skills which anyone needs to live effectively, he suggests that the best way of helping people is to teach them directly and systematically in life, work, learning and relationship-building skills. He states clearly that 'the essential task of helping is to bridge the gap between the helpee's skills level and the helper's skills level' (Carkhuff and Berenson, 1976). For Carkhuff, helping equals teaching, but teaching people the skills to ensure that they can take more control over their own lives.

BRAMMER (1973) has produced an integrated, eclectic developmental model similar to Carkhuff's. He has expanded Carkhuff's three stages into the eight stages of entry, classification, structure, relationship, exploration, consolidation, planning and termination. He has also identified seven clusters of skills to promote 'understanding of self and others'. His list of 46 specific skills is somewhat daunting to a beginner but a rich source of stimulation for the more experienced helper.

IVEY (1971) AND ASSOCIATES have developed a highly systematic model for training helpers under the label 'microcounselling'. Each skill is broken up into its constituent parts and taught via closed-circuit television, modelling and practice.

HACKNEY AND NYE (1973) have described a helping model which they call a 'discrimination' model. It is goal-centred and action-centred and it stresses skills training.

KAGAN, KRATHWOHL (1967) AND ASSOCIATES have also developed a microskills approach to counsellor training which is widely used in the USA. It is called Interpersonal Process Recall which involves an enquiry session in which helper and client explore the experience they have had together in the presence of a mediator.

EGAN (1975) has developed perhaps the next most influential model of helping in the USA after Carkhuff's and, indeed, has been highly influenced by Carkhuff's work. The model begins with a pre-helping phase involving attending skills, to be followed by Stage I: responding and self-exploration; Stage II: integrative understanding and dynamic self-understanding; and Stage III: facilitating action and acting. The first goal labelled at each stage is the helper's goal and the second goal is that of the client.

LOUGHARY AND RIPLEY (1979) approach helping from a different viewpoint, which, unlike the previous theorists, is not simply on the continuum beginning with Rogers and Carkhuff. They have used a demystifying approach aimed at the general population with no training other than what can be gleaned from their book. Their model is shown in figure 1.

Figure 1

Model of helping
From Loughary and Ripley (1979)

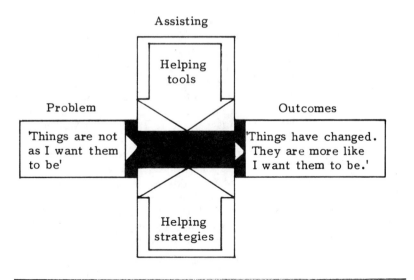

The helping tools include information, ideas, and skills (such as listening and reflecting dealings). The strategies are the plans for using the tools and the first step is always translating the problem into desired outcomes. Their four positive outcomes of helping are: changes in feeling states, increased understanding, decisions, and implementing decisions. Their approach does move away from the counselling-dominated approach of the other models.

HOPSON AND SCALLY: we reproduce our own model in some detail here, partly because it is the model we know best and it has worked very effectively for us and for the 3,000 teachers and youth workers who have been through our counselling skills training courses (Scally and Hopson, 1979), but also because it attempts to look at all the aspects of helping defined at the beginning of this chapter.

Figure 2 outlines three goal areas for helpers, central to their own personal development. It also defines specific helping outcomes. Helpers can only help people to the levels of their own skills and awareness (Aspy and Roebuck, 1977). They need to clarify their own social, economic and cultural values and need to be able to recognize and separate their own needs and problems from those of their clients. Helpers see in others reflections of themselves. To know oneself is to ensure a clarity of distinction between images: to know where one stops and the other begins. We become less helpful as the images blur. To ensure that does not happen, we need constantly to monitor our own development. Self-awareness is not a stage to be reached and then it is over. It is a process which can never stop because we are always changing. By monitoring these changes we simultaneously retain some control of their direction.

From a greater awareness of who we are, our strengths, hindrances, values, needs and prejudices, we can be clearer about skills we wish to develop. The broader the range of skills we acquire, the larger the population group that we can help.

As helpers involved in the act of helping we learn through the process of praxis. We reflect and we act. As we interact with others, we in turn are affected by them and are in some way different from before the interaction. As we attempt to help individuals and influence systems we will learn, change, and develop from the process of interaction, just as those individuals and systems will be affected by us.

Having access to support should be a central concern for anyone regularly involved in helping. Helpers so often are not as skilled as they might be at saying 'no' and looking after themselves.

We would maintain that the ultimate goals of helping are to enable people to become self-empowered and to make systems healthier places in which to live, work and play.

Self-empowerment

There are five dimensions of self-empowerment (Hopson and Scally, 1980a).

* Awareness: without an awareness of ourselves and others we are subject to the slings and arrows of our upbringing, daily events, social changes and crises. Without awareness we can only react, like the pinball in the machine that bounces from one thing to another without having ever provided the energy for its own passage.
* Goals: given awareness we have the potential for taking charge of ourselves and our lives. We take charge by exploring our values, developing commitments, and by

specifying goals with outcomes. We learn to live by the question: 'what do I want now?' We reflect and then act.

* Values: we subscribe to the definition of values put forward by Raths, Harmin and Simon (1964): a value is a belief which has been chosen freely from alternatives after weighing the consequences of each alternative; it is prized and cherished, shared publicly and acted upon repeatedly and consistently. The self-empowered person, by our definition, has values which include recognizing the worth of self and others, of being proactive, working for healthy systems, at home, in employment, in the community and at leisure; helping other people to become more self-empowered.

* Life skills: values are good as far as they go, but it is only by developing skills that we can translate them into action. We may believe that we are responsible for our own destiny, but we require the skills to achieve what we wish for ourselves. In a school setting, for example, we require the skills of goal setting and action-planning, time management, reading, writing and numeracy, study skills, problem-solving skills and how to work in groups. Figure 3 reproduces the list of life skills that we have identified at the Counselling and Career Development Unit (Hopson and Scally, 1980b) as being crucial to personal survival and growth.

* Information: information is the raw material for awareness of self and the surrounding world. It is the fuel for shaping our goals. Information equals power. Without it we are helpless, which is of course why so many people and systems attempt to keep information to themselves. We must realize that information is essential (a concept), that we need to know how to get appropriate information, and from where (a skill).

Healthy systems

Too often counsellors and other helpers have pretended to be value free. Most people now recognize that fiction. Not only is it impossible but it can be dangerous. If we honestly believe that we are capable of being value free, we halt the search for the ways in which our value systems are influencing our behaviour with our clients. If we are encouraging our clients to develop goals, how can we pretend that we do not have them too? Expressing these goals can be the beginning of a contract to work with a client for, like it or not, we each have a concept, however shadowy, for the fully functioning healthy person to which our actions and helping are directed.

As with clients, so too with systems. If we are working towards helping people to become 'better', in whatever way we choose to define that, let us be clear about what changes we are working towards in the systems we try to influence. Figure 2 lists our characteristics of healthy systems. Each of us has our own criteria so let us discover them and bring them into the open. Owning our values is one way of demonstrating our genuineness.

Figure 2

Goals of helping

GOALS OF HELPING

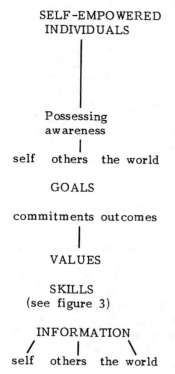

SELF-EMPOWERED
INDIVIDUALS

Possessing
awareness

self   others   the world

GOALS

commitments outcomes

VALUES

SKILLS
(see figure 3)

INFORMATION

self   others   the world

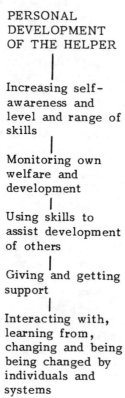

PERSONAL
DEVELOPMENT
OF THE HELPER

Increasing self-
awareness and
level and range of
skills

Monitoring own
welfare and
development

Using skills to
assist development
of others

Giving and getting
support

Interacting with,
learning from,
changing and being
being changed by
individuals and
systems

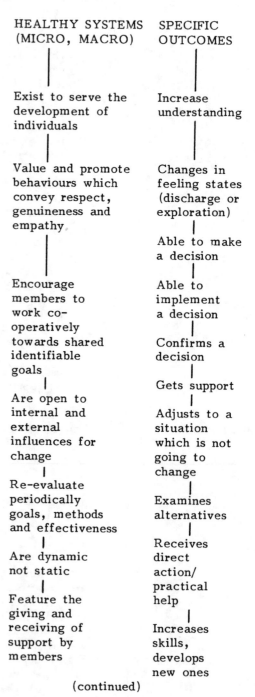

HEALTHY SYSTEMS
(MICRO, MACRO)

Exist to serve the
development of
individuals

Value and promote
behaviours which
convey respect,
genuineness and
empathy.

Encourage
members to
work co-
operatively
towards shared
identifiable
goals

Are open to
internal and
external
influences for
change

Re-evaluate
periodically
goals, methods
and effectiveness

Are dynamic
not static

Feature the
giving and
receiving of
support by
members

SPECIFIC
OUTCOMES

Increase
understanding

Changes in
feeling states
(discharge or
exploration)

Able to make
a decision

Able to
implement
a decision

Confirms a
decision

Gets support

Adjusts to a
situation
which is not
going to
change

Examines
alternatives

Receives
direct
action/
practical
help

Increases
skills,
develops
new ones

(continued)

Focus on
individual's
strengths
|
And builds on
them
|
Use problem
solving strate-
gies rather than
scapegoating,
blaming or focus-
sing on faults
|
Use methods which
are consistent
with goals
|
Encourage power-
sharing and enable
individuals to
pursue their own
direction as a
contribution to
shared goals
|
Monitor their own
performance in a
continuing cycle of
reflection/action
|
Allow people
access to those
whose decisions
have a bearing
on their lives
|
Have effective
and sensitive
lines of
communication
|
Explore differ-
ences openly and
use compromise,
negotiation and
contracting to
achieve a maxi-
mum of win/win
outcomes for all
|
Are always open
to alternatives

Receives
information
|
Reflects on
acts

Figure 3

Lifeskills: taking charge of yourself and your life

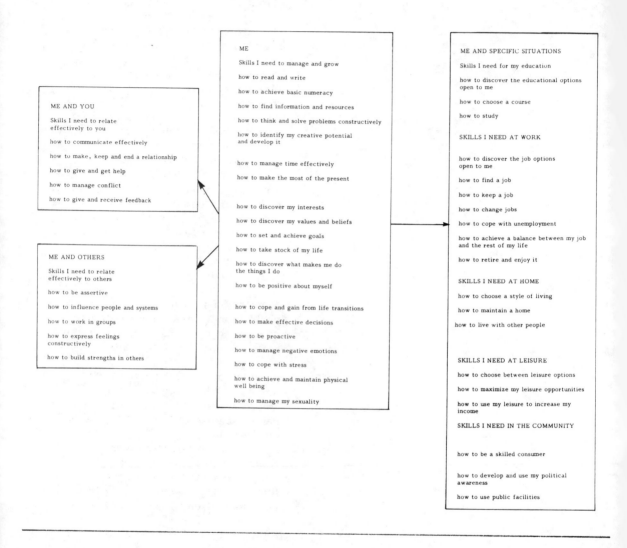

ME

Skills I need to manage and grow

how to read and write

how to achieve basic numeracy

how to find information and resources

how to think and solve problems constructively

how to identify my creative potential and develop it

how to manage time effectively

how to make the most of the present

how to discover my interests

how to discover my values and beliefs

how to set and achieve goals

how to take stock of my life

how to discover what makes me do the things I do

how to be positive about myself

how to cope and gain from life transitions

how to make effective decisions

how to be proactive

how to manage negative emotions

how to cope with stress

how to achieve and maintain physical well being

how to manage my sexuality

ME AND YOU

Skills I need to relate effectively to you

how to communicate effectively

how to make, keep and end a relationship

how to give and get help

how to manage conflict

how to give and receive feedback

ME AND OTHERS

Skills I need to relate effectively to others

how to be assertive

how to influence people and systems

how to work in groups

how to express feelings constructively

how to build strengths in others

ME AND SPECIFIC SITUATIONS

Skills I need for my education

how to discover the educational options open to me

how to choose a course

how to study

SKILLS I NEED AT WORK

how to discover the job options open to me

how to find a job

how to keep a job

how to change jobs

how to cope with unemployment

how to achieve a balance between my job and the rest of my life

how to retire and enjoy it

SKILLS I NEED AT HOME

how to choose a style of living

how to maintain a home

how to live with other people

SKILLS I NEED AT LEISURE

how to choose between leisure options

how to maximize my leisure opportunities

how to use my leisure to increase my income

SKILLS I NEED IN THE COMMUNITY

how to be a skilled consumer

how to develop and use my political awareness

how to use public facilities

What is counselling?

Having identified six common ways of helping people, counselling will now be focussed on more intensively, which immediately gets us into the quagmire of definition.

Anyone reviewing the literature to define counselling will quickly suffer from data-overload. Books, articles, even manifestoes, have been written on the question.

In training courses run from the Counselling and Career Development Unit we tend to opt for the parsimonious definition of 'helping people explore problems so that they can decide what to do about them'.

The demystification of counselling

There is nothing inherently mysterious about counselling. It is merely a set of beliefs, values and behaviours to be found in the community at large. The beliefs include one that says individuals benefit and grow from a particular form of relationship and contact. The values recognize the worth and the significance of each individual and regard personal autonomy and self-direction as desirable. The behaviours cover a combination of listening, conveying warmth, asking open questions, encouraging specificity, concreteness and focussing, balancing support and confrontation, and offering strategies which help to clarify objectives and identify action plans. This terminology is more complex than the process needs to be. The words describe what is essentially a 'non-mystical' way in which some people are able to help other people to help themselves (see figure 4).

Training courses can sometimes encourage the mystification. They talk of 'counselling skills' and may, by implication, suggest that such skills are somehow separate from other human activities, are to be conferred upon those who attend courses, and are probably innovatory. In fact, what 'counselling' has done is to crystallize what we know about how warm, trusting relationships develop between people. It recognizes that:

* relationships develop if one has and conveys respect for another, if one is genuine oneself, if one attempts to see things from the other's point of view (empathizes), and if one endeavours not to pass judgement. Those who operate in this way we describe as having 'relationship-building skills';
* if the relationship is established, an individual will be prepared to talk through and explore thoughts and feelings. What one can do and say which helps that to happen we classify as exploring and clarifying skills (see figure 4);
* through this process individuals become clear about difficulties or uncertainties, and can explore options and alternatives, in terms of what they might do to change what they are not happy about;
* given support, individuals are likely to be prepared to, and are capable of, dealing with difficulties or problems they may face more effectively. They can be helped by somebody who can offer objective setting and action planning skills.

Counselling skills are what people use to help people to help themselves. They are not skills that are exclusive to one group or one activity. It is clear that the behaviours, which we bundle together and identify as skills, are liberally scattered about us in the community. Counselling ideology identifies which behaviours are consistent with its values and its goals, and teaches these as one category of helping skills.

Figure 4

The counselling process

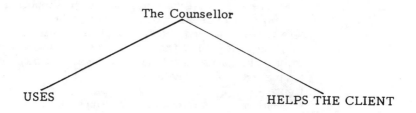

The Counsellor

USES   HELPS THE CLIENT

RELATIONSHIP   respect   to feel valued, understood
BUILDING   genuineness   and prepared to trust the
SKILLS   empathy   counsellor

                contracting   to talk and explore
                open questions   to understand more about
EXPLORING   summarizing   how he feels and why
AND   focussing   to consider options and
CLARIFYING   reflecting   examine alternatives
SKILLS   immediacy   to choose an alternative
                clarifying
                concreteness
                confronting

                objective setting   to develop clear objectives
                action planning   to form specific action
                problem-solving   plans
                strategies   to do, with support, what needs to
                                        be done

COUNSELLING IS HELPING PEOPLE TO HELP THEMSELVES

What may happen, unfortunately, is that the promotion of counselling as a separate training responsibility can increase the mystification. An outcome can be that instead of simply now being people who, compared to the majority, are extra-sensitive listeners, are particularly good at making relationships, and are more effective at helping others to solve problems, they have become 'counsellors' and licensed to help. A licence becomes a danger if:

* those who have it see themselves as qualitatively different from the rest of the population;
* it symbolizes to the non-licensed that they are incapable, or inferior, or calls into question valuable work they may be doing, but are 'unqualified' to do.

It is important to recognize that labelling people can have unfortunate side effects. Let us remember that whatever the nomenclature - counsellor, client or whatever - at a particular time or place, they are just people. All, at some time or other, will be able to give help, at other times will need to seek or receive help. Some are naturally better fitted to help others; some by training can improve their helping skills. All, through increased awareness and skill development, can become more effective helpers than they are now.

Counselling is not only practised by counsellors. It is a widespread activity in the community and appears in several guises. Its constituent skills are described variously as 'talking it over', 'having a friendly chat', 'being a good friend' or simply 'sharing' with somebody. These processes almost certainly include some or all of the skills summarized in figure 4. Often, of course, there are notable exceptions: for instance, we do not listen well; we cannot resist giving our advice, or trying to solve problems for our friends; we find it difficult to drop our façades and roles. Counselling skills training can help reduce our unhelpful behaviours and begin to develop these skills in ourselves, making us more effective counsellors, as well as simply being a good friend. In almost any work involving contact with other people, we would estimate there is a potential counselling component. There is a need for the particular interpersonal skills categorized here as counselling skills to be understood and used by people at large, but particularly by all people who have the welfare of others as part of their occupational roles. Specialist 'counsellors' have an important part to play, but it is not to replace the valuable work that is done by many who would not claim the title. Having said that, people sometimes think they are counselling, but in fact are doing things very far removed: disciplining, persuading people to conform to a system, and so on.

Types of counselling

Developmental versus crisis counselling
Counselling can operate either as a response to a situation

or as a stimulus to help a client develop and grow. In the past, counselling has often been concerned with helping someone with a problem during or after the onset of a crisis point: a widow unable to cope with her grief, the boy leaving school desperate because he has no idea what job to choose, the pregnant woman with no wish to be pregnant. This is a legitimate function of counselling, but if this is all that counselling is, it can only ever be concerned with making the best of the situation in which one finds oneself. How much more ambitious to help people anticipate future problems, to educate them to recognize the cues of oncoming crisis, and to provide them with skills to take charge of it at the outset instead of running behind in an attempt to catch up! This is counselling as a stimulus to growth: developmental as opposed to crisis counselling. All successful counselling entails growth, but the distinction between the two approaches is that the crisis approach generates growth under pressure, and since this is often limited only to the presenting problem, the client's behavioural and conceptual repertoire may remain little affected by the experience. There will always be a need for crisis counselling in a wide variety of settings, but the exciting prospect of developmental counselling for growth and change has only recently begun to be tackled.

Individual counselling
As counselling was rooted in psychotherapy it is hardly surprising that the primary focus has been on the one-to-one relationship. There are a number of essential elements in the process. Clients are to be helped to reach decisions by themselves. This is achieved by establishing a relationship of trust whereby individual clients feel that the counsellor cares about them, is able to empathize with their problems, and is authentic and genuine in relating to them. Counsellors will enter the relationship as persons in their own right, disclosing relevant information about themselves as appropriate, reacting honestly to clients' statements and questions, but at no time imposing their own opinions on the clients. Their task is to facilitate the clients' own abilities and strengths in such a way that clients experience the satisfaction of having defined and solved their problems for themselves. If a client lacks information on special issues, is incapable of generating alternative strategies, or cannot make decisions in a programmatic way, then the counsellor has a function as an educator whose skills are offered to the client. In this way the client is never manipulated. The counsellor is negotiating a contract to use some skills which are possessed by the counsellor, and which can be passed on to the client if the client wishes to make use of them.

Individual counselling has the advantages over group counselling of providing a safer setting for some people to lower their defences, of developing a strong and trusting relationship with the counsellor, and of allowing the client maximum personal contact with the counsellor.

Group counselling

Group counselling involves one or more counsellors operating with a number of clients in a group session. The group size varies from four to sixteen, with eight to ten being the most usual number. The basic objectives of group and individual counselling are similar. Both seek to help the clients achieve self-direction, integration, self-responsibility, self-acceptance, and an understanding of their motivations and patterns of behaviour. In both cases the counsellor needs the skills and attitudes outlined earlier, and both require a confidential relationship. There are, however, some important differences (Hopson, 1977).

*   The group counsellor needs an understanding of group dynamics: communication, decision making, role-playing, sources of power, and perceptual processes in groups.
*   The group situation can provide immediate opportunities to try out ways of relating to individuals, and is an excellent way of providing the experience of intimacy with others. The physical proximity of the clients to one another can be emotionally satisfying and supportive. Clients give a first-hand opportunity to test others' perception of themselves.
*   Clients not only receive help themselves; they also help other clients. In this way helping skills are generated by a larger group of people than is possible in individual counselling.
*   Clients often discover that other people have similar problems, which can at the least be comforting.
*   Clients learn to make effective use of other people, not just professionals, as helping agents. They can set up a mutual support group which is less demanding on the counsellor and likely to be a boost to their self-esteem when they discover they can manage to an increasing extent on their own.

There are many different kinds of group counselling. Some careers services in higher education offer counsellor-led groups as groundwork preparation for career choices; these small groups give older adolescents an opportunity to discuss the inter-relations between their conscious values and preferred life styles and their crystallizing sense of identity. Other groups are provided in schools where young people can discuss with each other and an adult counsellor those relationships with parents and friends which are so important in adolescence. Training groups are held for teaching decision-making skills and assertive skills. There are also groups in which experiences are pooled and mutual help given for the married, for parents, for those bringing up families alone and for those who share a special problem such as having a handicapped child. All these types of groups are usually led by someone who has had training and experience in facilitating them. The word 'facilitating' is used advisedly, for the leader's job is not to conduct a seminar or tutorial, but to establish an atmosphere in which

members of the group can explore the feelings around a
particular stage of development or condition or critical
choice.

Another type of group is not so specifically focussed on
an area of common concern but is set up as a sort of laboratory to learn about the underlying dynamics of how people in
groups function, whatever the group's focus and purpose may
be. These are often referred to as sensitivity training
groups (e.g. Cooper and Mangham, 1971; Smith, 1975). Yet
a third category of group has more therapeutic goals, being
intended to be successive or complementary to, or sometimes
in place of, individual psychotherapy. This type of group
will not usually have a place in work settings, whereas the
other two do have useful applications there. Obvious uses
for this type of group occur in induction procedures, in
preparation for retirement, in relation to job change
arising from promotion, or in relation to redundancy. The
second type of group is employed in training for supervisory
or management posts, though one hears less about their use
in trade unions.

Schools of counselling
Differences in theories of personality, learning and perception are reflected in counselling theory. It is useful to
distinguish between five major schools.

1. Psychoanalytic approaches were historically the first.
Psychoanalysis is a personality theory, a philosophical
system, and a method of psychotherapy. Concentrating on
the past history of a patient, understanding the internal
dynamics of the psyche, and the relationship between the
client and the therapist are all key concerns for psychoanalysis. Key figures include Freud, Jung, Adler, Sullivan,
Horney, Fromm and Erikson.

2. Client-centred approaches are based upon the work of
Rogers, originally as a non-directive therapy developed as a
reaction against psychoanalysis. Founded on a subjective
view of human experiencing, it places more faith in and
gives more responsibility to the client in problem-solving.
The techniques of client-centred counselling have become the
basis for most counselling skills training, following the
empirical evaluations by Truax and Carkhuff (1967).

3. Behavioural approaches arise from attempts to apply
the principles of learning to the resolution of specific
behavioural disorders. Results are subject to continual
experimentation and refinement. Key figures include Wolpe,
Eysenck, Lazarus and Krumboltz.

4. Cognitive approaches include 'rational-emotive therapy'
(Ellis), 'transactional analysis' (Berne) and 'reality
therapy' (Glasser), along with Meichenbaum's work on cognitive rehearsal and inoculation. All have in common the

belief that people's problems are created by how they conceptualize their worlds: change the concepts and feelings will change too.

5. Affective approaches include 'Gestalt therapy' (Perls), 'primal therapy' (Janov), 're-evaluation counselling' (Jackins), and 'bioenergetics' (Lowen). These have in common the belief that pain and distress accumulate and have to be discharged in some way before the person can become whole or think clearly again.

There are many other approaches and orientations. The existential-humanistic school is exemplified by May, Maslow, Frankl and Jourard. Encounter approaches have been developed by Schutz, Bindrim and Ichazo, 'psychosynthesis' by Assagioli, 'morita therapy' by Morita, and 'eclectic psycho-therapy' by Thorne. In the United Kingdom the biggest influence on counsellor training has been from the client-centred school. Behavioural approaches are becoming more common and, to a lesser extent, so are transactional analysis, Gestalt therapy and re-evaluation counselling.

Where does counselling take place?

Until recently counselling was assumed to take place in the confines of a counsellor's office. This is changing rapidly. It is now increasingly accepted that effective counselling, as defined in this chapter, can take place on the shop floor, in the school corridor, even on a bus. The process is not made any easier by difficult surroundings, but when people need help, the helpers are not always in a position to choose from where they would like to administer it. Initial contacts are often made in these kinds of environment, and more intensive counselling can always be scheduled for a later date in a more amenable setting.

What are the goals of counselling?

Counselling is a process through which a person attains a higher stage of personal competence. It is always about change. Katz (1969) has said that counselling is concerned not with helping people to make wise decisions but with helping them to make decisions wisely. It has as its goal self-empowerment: that is, the individual's ability to move through the following stages.

* 'I am not happy with things at the moment'
* 'What I would prefer is ...'
* 'What I need to do to achieve that is ...'
* 'I have changed what I can, and have come to terms, for the moment, with what I cannot achieve'.

Counselling has as an ultimate goal the eventual redundancy of the helper, and the activity should discourage dependency and subjection. It promotes situations in which the person's views and feelings are heard, respected and not judged. It builds personal strength, confidence and invites initiative and growth. It develops the individual and encourages control of self and situations. Counselling obviously works for the formation of more capable and effective individuals, through working with people singly or in groups.

In its goals it stands alongside other approaches concerned with personal and human development. All can see how desirable would be the stage when more competent, 'healthier' individuals would live more positively and more humanly. Counselling may share its goals in terms of what it wants for individuals; where it does differ from other approaches is in its method of achieving that. It concentrates on the individual - alone or in a group - and on one form of helping. Some other approaches would work for the same goals but would advocate different methods of achieving them. It is important to explore the inter-relatedness of counselling and other forms of helping as a way of asking, 'If we are clear about what we want for people, are we being as effective as we could be in achieving it?'

Counselling outcomes

This chapter has defined the ultimate outcome of counselling as 'helping people to help themselves'. A natural question to follow might be, 'to help themselves to do what?' There follows a list of counselling outcomes most frequently asked for by clients:

* increased understanding of oneself or a situation;
* achieving a change in the way one is feeling;
* being able to make a decision;
* confirming a decision;
* getting support for a decision;
* being able to change a situation;
* adjusting to a situation that is not going to change;
* the discharge of feelings;
* examining options and choosing one (Scally and Hopson, 1979).

Clients sometimes want other outcomes which are not those of counselling but stem from one or more of the other forms of helping: information, new skills, or practical help.

All of these outcomes have in common the concept of change. All counselling is about change. Given any issue or problem a person always has four possible strategies to deal with it:

* change the situation;
* change oneself to adapt to the situation;
* exit from it;
* develop ways of living with it.

Is counselling the best way of helping people?

In the quest for more autonomous, more self-competent, self-employed individuals the helper is faced with the question, 'If that is my goal, am I working in the most effective way

towards achieving it?' As much as one believes in the potential of counselling, there are times when one must ask
whether spending time with individuals is the best
investment of one's helping time and effort.

Many counsellors say that time spent in this way is
incredibly valuable; it emphasizes the importance of each
individual, and hence they justify time given to one-to-one
counselling. At the other end of the spectrum there are
those who charge 'counsellors' with:

* being concerned solely with 'casualties', people in
  crisis and in difficulty, and not getting involved with
  organizational questions;
* allowing systems, organizations and structures to
  continue to operate 'unhealthily', by 'treating' these
  'casualties' so effectively.

To reject these charges out-of-hand would be to fail to
recognize the elements of truth they contain. One respects
tremendously the importance that counselling places on the
individual, and this is not an attempt to challenge that.
What it may be relevant to establish is that counselling
should not be seen as a substitute for 'healthy' systems,
which operate in ways which respect individuality, where
relationships are genuine and positive, where communication
is open and problem-solving and participation are worked at
(see figure 2). 'Healthy' systems can be as important to the
welfare of the individual as can one-to-one counselling. It
is unfortunate therefore that 'administrators' can see personal welfare as being the province of 'counselling types',
and the latter are sometimes reluctant to 'contaminate'
their work by getting involved in administrational or
organizational matters. These attitudes can be very detrimental to all involved systems. The viewpoint presented here
is that part of a helper's repertoire of skills in the 'tool-
bag' alongside counselling skills should be willingness, and
the ability, to work for systems change. Some counsellors
obviously do this already in more spontaneous ways; for
example, if one finds oneself counselling truants, it may
become apparent that some absconding is invited by timetable anomalies (French for remedial groups on Friday
afternoons?). The dilemma here is whether one spends
time with a series of individual truants or persuades the
designers of timetables to establish a more aware approach.

One realizes sometimes also that one may, in counselling, be using one's skills in such a way that individuals
accept outcomes which possibly should not be accepted. For
example, unemployment specialists in careers services sometimes see themselves as being used by 'the system' to help
black youths come to terms with being disadvantaged. Such
specialists ask whether this is their role or whether they
should in fact be involved politically and actively in
working for social and economic change.

Resistance to the idea of becoming more involved in
'systems' and 'power structures' may not simply be based

upon a reluctance to take on extra, unattractive work. Some will genuinely feel that this approach is 'political' and therefore somehow tainted and dubious. It is interesting that in the USA during the last five years there has been a significant shift in opinion towards counsellors becoming more ready to accept the need to be involved in influencing systems:

> Their work brings them face to face with the victim of poverty; or racism, sexism, and stigmatization; of political, economic and social systems that allow individuals to feel powerless and helpless; of governing structures that cut off communication and deny the need for responsiveness; of social norms that stifle individuality; of communities that let their members live in isolation from one another. In the face of these realities human service workers have no choice but to blame those victims or to see ways to change the environment (Lewis and Lewis, 1977).

In this country, perhaps a deeper analysis is needed of the 'contexts' in which we work as helpers.

Can counselling be apolitical?

It is very interesting that in his recent book, Carl Rogers (Rogers, 1978) reviewing his own present position vis-à-vis counselling, indicates the revolutionary impact of much of his work as perceived by him in retrospect. Perhaps identifiable as the 'arch-individualist', Rogers signals now that he had not seen the full social impact of the values and the methodology he pioneered. He writes eloquently of his realization that much of his life and work has in fact been political, though previously he had not seen it in those terms. Counselling invites self-empowerment; it invites the individual to become aware and to take more control; it asks 'How would you like things to be?' and 'How will you make them like that?' That process is a very powerful one and has consequences that are likely to involve changing 'status quos'. Clearly processes that are about change, power, and control are 'political' (although not necessarily party political).

From this viewpoint counsellors are involved in politics already. As much as one may like there to be, there can really be no neutral ground. Opting out or not working for change is by definition maintaining the status quo. If the 'status quo' means an organization, systems or relationships which are insensitive, uncaring, manipulative, unjust, divisive, autocratic, or function in any way which damages the potential of the people who are part of them, then one cannot really turn one's back on the task of working for change. 'One is either part of the solution or part of the problem!' We have argued (Scally and Hopson, 1979) that counsellors have much to offer by balancing their one-to-one work with more direct and more skilled involvement in making systems more positive, growthful places in which to live and work.

To counsel or to teach?

Counselling is a process through which a person attains a higher level of personal competence. Recently, attacks have been made on the counselling approach by such widely differing adversaries as Illich (1973) and Carkhuff (Carkhuff and Berenson, 1976). They, and others, question what effect the existence of counsellors and therapists has had on human development as a whole. They maintain that, however benevolent the counselling relationship is felt to be by those involved, there are forces at work overall which are suspect. They suggest:

* that helpers largely answer their own needs, and consciously or unconsciously perpetuate dependency or inadequacy in clients;
* helping can be 'disabling' rather than 'enabling' because it often encourages dependency.

For counsellors to begin to answer such charges requires a self-analysis of their own objectives, methods and motives. They could begin by asking:

* how much of their counselling is done at the 'crisis' or 'problem' stage in their clients' lives?
* how much investment are they putting into 'prevention' rather than 'cure'?

To help somebody in crisis is an obvious task. It is, however, only one counselling option. If 'prevention' is better than 'cure' then maybe that is where the emphasis ought to be. Perhaps never before has there been more reason for individuals to feel 'in crisis'. Toffler (1970) has identified some likely personal and social consequences of living at a time of incredibly rapid change. Many, like Stonier (1979), are forecasting unparalleled technological developments over the next 30 years which will change our lives, especially our work patterns, dramatically. There are so many complex forces at work that it is not surprising that many people are feeling more anxious, unsure, pessimistic, unable to cope, depersonalized, and helpless. Helpers are at risk as much as any, but are likely to be faced with ever-increasing demands on their time and skills. Again, this requires a reassessment of approaches and priorities, which could suggest a greater concentration on the development of personal competence in our systems. We need to develop more 'skilled' (which is not the same as 'informed') individuals and thereby avert more personal difficulties and crisis. One view is that this, the developmental, educational, teaching approach, needs to involve more of those who now spend much time in one-to-one counselling; not to replace that work but to give balance to it.

Personal competence and self-empowerment, which are the 'goals' of counselling, can be understood in many ways. A recent movement has been to see competence as being achievable through skill development. 'Life skills' are becoming as large a band-wagon as counselling has become.

We are producing a series of Lifeskills Teaching Programmes (Hopson and Scally, 1980b) which cover a range of more generic personal skills: for example, 'How to be assertive rather than aggressive', 'How to make, maintain and end relationships', 'How to manage time effectively', 'How to be positive about oneself', 'How to make effective transitions', etc. (figure 3). The programmes attempt to break down the generalization of 'competence' into 'learnable' units, with the overall invitation that, by acquiring these skills, one can 'take charge of oneself and one's life'. We have the advantage, working in a training unit, of being able to work directly with teachers and youth workers on the skills this way. Aspy and Roebuck (1977) have identified that the most effective teachers are those who have, and demonstrate, a high respect for others, who are genuine, and display a high degree of empathy with their students. Many professional counsellors therefore should have the basic qualities required in teaching, and could make appreciable contributions by being involved in programmes in the community which encourage 'coping' and 'growth' skills. More personally skilled individuals could reduce the dependence, inadequacy and crises which are individually and collectively wasteful, and take up so much counselling time.

Towards a 'complete helper'

The argument here is for the development of more complete helpers, more 'all-rounders', with a range of skills and 'tool-bags' full of more varied helping equipment. It is possible to work to increase the level of skill in each particular helping technique and go for 'broader' rather than 'higher' skill development. This diagram (figure 5) could map out for individual helpers how they may want to plan their own development.

On a graph such as this an effective teacher may be placed typically along the line marked 'x'. A full-time counsellor working in a school or workplace may typically be indicated by the line marked 'o'. An organization-change consultant may typically be somewhere along the dotted line.

How much one wants to be involved in helping, at whatever level and in whatever form, obviously depends upon many factors. How much one sees helping as part of the roles one fills; how much helping is part of the job one does; how much one wants to be involved as a part-time activity; how much helping is consistent with one's values, politics and personality; all will have a bearing on where an individual may wish to be placed on the graph. One person may decide to specialize in a particular approach and develop sophisticated skills in that field. Another may go for a broader approach by developing skills from across the range. Yet another may at particular times develop new specialisms as a response to particular situations or as part of a personal career development.

Figure 5

Helpers' skills levels and possible approaches to increasing them
(What skills do I have and in which directions can I develop?)

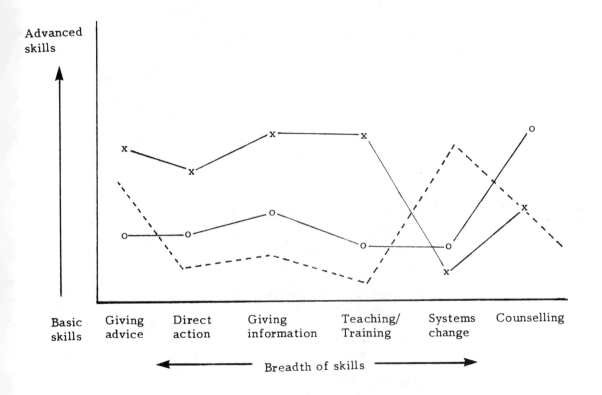

What is advocated here is that basic helping skills can be regarded as essential life skills. These skills can be made available to, and developed very fully in, professional helpers and in those for whom helping is part of their job specification in the workshop, in hospitals, in the social service agencies or in education. They can also be taught to young people in schools and at work.

Counselling in the UK   It is interesting that 'counselling' was a term rarely used in Britain until the mid-1960s. According to Vaughan's analysis (1976),

> three factors gradually tended to focus more attention on this area. One was the emergence throughout this century of a wider band of 'helping' professions, such as the Youth Employment Service, the social work services, and psychotherapy, as well as other 'caring' organizations, such as marriage guidance, and more recently such bodies as the Samaritans and Help the Aged. A second was the development of empirical psychology and sociology, which began to offer specific techniques for the analysis of personal difficulties; and a third was the rapid spread from about the mid-1960s onwards of the concept of counselling as a specific profession derived almost wholly from North America, where it had undergone a long evolution throughout the century from about 1910. Thus today we have a situation comparable in some ways to that of the development of primary education in Britain before the 1870 Act. A new area of specialization seems to be emerging.

It is just because a new area of specialization is developing that people already engaged in, or about to involve themselves in, counselling need to think carefully of where and how they wish to invest their time and resources. Counselling clearly is an important way of helping people, but it is not the only way.

References

Aspy, D.N. and Roebuck, F.N. (1977)
Kids Don't Learn from People They Don't Like. Amherst, Mass.: Human Resource Development Press.

Brammer, L.M. (1973)
The Helping Relationship. Englewood Cliffs, NJ: Prentice-Hall.

Carkhuff, R.R. (1974)
The Art of Helping. Amherst, Mass.: Human Resource Development Press.

Carkhuff, R.R. and Berenson, B.G. (1976)
Teaching As Treatment. Amherst, Mass.: Human Resource Development Press.

Cooper, C.L. and Mangham, I.L. (eds) (1971)
T-Groups: A survey of research. Chichester: Wiley.

Egan, G. (1975)
The Skilled Helper. Monterey, Ca: Brooks/Cole.

Hackney, H.L. and Nye, S. (1973)
Counseling Strategies and Objectives. Englewood Cliffs, NJ: Prentice-Hall.

Hopson, B. (1977)
Techniques and methods of counselling. In A.G. Watts (ed.), Counselling at Work. London: Bedford Square Press.

Hopson, B. and Scally, M. (1980a)
Lifeskills Teaching: Education for self-empowerment.
Maidenhead: McGraw-Hill.

Hopson, B. and Scally, M. (1980b)
Lifeskills Teaching Programmes No. 1. Leeds: Lifeskills
Associates.

Illich, I. (1973)
Tools of Conviviality. London: Calder & Boyars.

**Illich, I., Zola, I.K., McKnight, J., Kaplan, J. and
Sharken, H.** (1977)
The Disabling Professions. London: Marion Boyars.

Ivey, A.E. (1971)
Microcounseling: Innovations in interviewing training.
Springfield, Ill.: Thomas.

Kagan, N., Krathwohl, D.R. et al (1967)
Studies in Human Interaction: Interpersonal process
recall stimulated by videotape. East Lansing, Mich.:
Educational Publication Services, College of Education,
Michigan State University.

Katz, M.R. (1969)
Can computers make guidance decisions for students?
College Board Review, New York, No. 72.

Lewis, J. and Lewis, M. (1977)
Community Counseling: A human services approach. New
York: Wiley.

Loughary, J.W. and Ripley, T.M. (1979)
Helping Others Help Themselves. New York: McGraw-Hill.

Parloff, M.B., Waskow, I.E. and Wolfe, B. (1978)
Research on therapist variables in relation to process
and outcome. In S.L. Garfield and A.E. Bergin (eds),
Handbook of Psychotherapy and Behavior Change: An
empirical analysis (2nd edn). New York: Wiley.

Raths, L., Harmin, M. and Simon, S. (1964)
Values and Teaching. Columbus, Ohio: Merrill.

Rogers, C.R. (1957)
The necessary and sufficient conditions of therapeutic
personality change. Journal of Consulting Psychology,
21, 95-103.

Rogers, C.R. (1958)
The characteristics of a helping relationship. Personnel
and Guidance Journal, 37, 6-16.

Rogers, C.R. (1978)
Carl Rogers on Personal Power. London: Constable.

Scally, M. and Hopson, B. (1979)
A Model of Helping and Counselling: Indications for
training. Leeds: Counselling and Careers Development
Unit, Leeds University.

Smith, P.B. (1975)
Controlled studies of the outcome of sensitivity
training. Psychological Bulletin, 82, 597-622.

Stonier, T. (1979)
On the Future of Employment. N.U.T. guide to careers
work. London: National Union of Teachers.

Toffler, A. (1970)
Future Shock. London: Bodley Head.

Truax, C.B. and Carkhuff, R.R. (1967)
>Toward Effective Counselling and Psychotherapy: Training and practice. Chicago, Ill.: Aldine.

Vaughan, T. (ed.) (1976)
>Concepts of Counselling. London: Bedford Square Press.

Questions

1. Distinguish counselling from other forms of helping.
2. How can counselling and helping be 'demystified'?
3. How large a part do you think counselling does and should play in your work?
4. Distinguish between counselling and counselling skills.
5. Who are 'the helpers'?
6. What makes people effective helpers?
7. Compare and contrast two different models of helping.
8. What in your opinion are the legitimate goals of helping and why?
9. How useful a concept is 'self-empowerment' in the context of helping?
10. What are the advantages and disadvantages of individual and group counselling techniques?

Annotated reading

Corey, G. (1977) Theory and Practice of Counseling and Psychotherapy. Monterey, Ca: Brooks/Cole.
>This contains an excellent review of all the schools of counselling described in the chapter. There is an accompanying workbook designed for students and tutor which gives self-inventories to aid students in identifying their own attitudes and beliefs, overviews of each major theory of counselling, questions for discussion and evaluation, case studies, exercises designed to sharpen specific counselling skills, out-of-class projects, group exercises, examples of client problems, an overview comparision of all models, ethical issues and problems to consider, and issues basic to the therapist's personal development.

Corsini, R. (ed.) (1977) Current Psychotherapies (2nd edn). Itasca, Ill.: Peacock Publications.
>An excellent introduction to the main schools of psychotherapy by leading practitioners who have been bullied to stick to the same format. Covers psychoanalysis, Adlerian, client-centred, analytical, rational-emotive therapy, transactional analysis, Gestalt, behavioural, reality, encounter, experiential and eclectic. Contributors include Carl Rogers, Albert Ellis, William Glasser, Alan Goldstein, Will Schutz and Rudolf Dreikurs.

Egan, G. (1975) The Skilled Helper. Monterey, Ca: Brooks/Cole.
>This text is now widely used in counselling skills training throughout the USA. It aims to teach the skills

of attending, responding, stimulating and helping the
client to act. It emphasizes the importance of teaching
the same skills to clients as to counsellors. There is
an accompanying training manual packed with group
exercises for the tutor to use to teach the skills in
Egan's model.

Vaughan, T.D. (ed.) (1975) Concepts of Counselling. British
Association for Counselling, London: Bedford Square Press.
A guide to the plethora of definitions of counselling.
Uneven, illuminating, with some useful descriptions of
developments in the UK.

18

Creating change
H. R. Beech

Politicians and kings have perhaps made the most distinctive and historically interesting attempts to change the behaviour of those they seek to control. Sometimes this has involved extreme measures, such as torture and execution, sometimes more subtle legal approaches to behaviour control, but these attempts perversely - and to the bafflement of the controller - have often failed to produce the desired outcome. Somehow, it seems, human nature appears to be resistant to change.

Psychologists are disposed to argue that such failures are mainly attributable to two causes. First, until recently, there was an obvious lack of the technology to effect changes with any degree of reliability: the methods which had been used before were both crude and unsystematically applied. Second, sometimes the attempts to effect change involved very fundamental aspects of human functioning and it might not be within the capacity of the species to accomplish them. Indeed, the contention of the behavioural psychologist these days might be that substantial changes can be wrought in carefully selected behaviours where the appropriate techniques can be freely applied. This is not to say, of course, that some psychologists fail to perceive in these strategies a means of acquiring very substantial or near complete control over human nature or, indeed, the means by which the very fabric of society could be altered. Of course, it would be unwise to allow psychologists (even if their techniques did permit such achievements) also to determine the types of change to be brought about. Psychologists are in no better position to decide what kind of society we should live in than is any other group.

For the most part, however, the aims and aspirations of psychologists are generally less ambitious and merely involve the deployment of strategies for change to areas where help is needed and requested. But to understand the origin of these strategies it is first useful to describe the influence exerted by Freud and Pavlov.

Freud's theories (Munroe, 1955) were important because they gave an entirely new interpretation to 'bad', 'wrong' or 'unacceptable' behaviour. Rather than seeing these behaviours as the reflection of something defective in the very substance of man, Freud argued that such conduct arose out of environmental experiences. Indeed, Freud is often thought of as a thoroughgoing psychic determinist, believing that all behaviour is determined by prior experience and, in a very real sense, is programmed to be just the way it is, free will and choice being merely illusory. In short, enormous importance is attached to the influence of the environment as a determinant of what we are.

Pavlov (1927) was also interested in how behaviour became modified (although primarily concerned with how the physiological systems of animals worked) and devised the method of classical conditioning to assist in this endeavour. The definitive experiment carried out in his laboratory was to show that, after training, the sound of a bell could produce salivation in dogs. Clearly the dog does not start life with this capacity and needs to learn this reaction, and it is the process by which such learning takes place that is called 'classical conditioning'. Briefly, the process involves presenting the new stimulus (bell) before the old stimulus (food) to the response (salivation). Repetitions of this arrangement, with only a brief (say half a second) interval between the sound of the bell and pre-sentation of food leads to the new association being formed. Instead of requiring food before salivating, the dog now has come to salivate at the sound of the bell alone.

Perhaps not of itself a particularly compelling piece of learning, but to many psychologists this type of association appeared as one of the fundamental building blocks of learn-ing; such learning could be seen as underpinning all human behaviour.

An early enthusiast of Pavlov's work, Watson, was said to have been so impressed by such demonstrations of condi-tioning that he declared that any American child might be turned into the President using these methods. Whether or not Watson accorded such power to classical conditioning, he was certainly enthusiastic to use it and has achieved an important place in psychological history through his Little Albert experiment (Watson and Rayner, 1920).

In this study Watson's aim was to investigate the acquisition of emotional responses, arguing that they are probably learned by the associative process called condi-tioning. For this demonstration he chose an 11-month-old boy called Albert and set out to create a learned emotional reaction in this child. Watson had observed Albert's fondness for a tame white rat and chose to reverse this feeling by arranging for a loud noise to be made (by crashing two metal plates together behind Albert's head) whenever the child reached out for this pet. After just a few trials of this kind, Albert's fear, occasioned by the sudden loud noise, was transferred to the white rat so that every time this animal appeared Little Albert would whimper and crawl away. Furthermore, it was noted that the new fear reaction had transferred to other objects with some similarity to the rat (e.g. a ball of cotton wool) and it appeared to be enduring over the period of observation.

This latter observation led Watson to speculate upon the fate of a more mature Albert, lying on the psychoanalyst's couch, and vainly trying to understand how he came to worry about white fluffy objects! But the conditioning process might well be the basis for all our irrational (neurotic) fears.

It is important to point out, however, that the environment is not the only contributing factor to learning since, from Pavlov on, it has been observed that not all learning opportunities are realized or, if they are, there are individual differences in the character of the learning which is affected.

The earliest experimental observations of such limitations of a purely environmentalist approach were made by Pavlov. He is said to have first formed this conclusion as a result of flood waters entering his laboratories in Leningrad, finding that this had made some of the animals very disturbed while others appeared to treat the matter with indifference. Later, experiments showed more conclusively that some animals appeared to be susceptible to disturbance and others more phlegmatic, these two types being labelled 'weak' and 'strong' nervous systems respectively. This differentiation has been repeatedly confirmed in the experimental work of other investigators and clearly shows that an opportunity to learn is not all that is involved: a major influence is the basic temperament of the organism which is doing the learning.

Another study which points to this conclusion was conducted by Rachman (1966). The problem posed by the investigator here was that of whether or not fetishistic behaviour (sexual arousal to unusual stimuli) could be acquired by a simple associative process. Briefly, three male volunteers were exposed to conditions in which pictures of boots were linked with pictures of an erotic nature to see if bonding occurred in such a way that the sight of boots alone would produce sexual excitement. Such was in fact found to be the case and establishes that fetishes can come about through associations of this kind. However, the point to be made here is that the subjects took varying numbers of trials to lose such reactions; in short, the disposition of the individual seems to be very much implicated in what we learn and how well such learning is preserved.

Generally these results are thought to reflect some permanent characteristics of the individuals concerned, but it is important to add that even temporary states of the organism can affect learning, a point which has been made by Beech and others (see Vila and Beech, 1978).

Clinical experience would tend to indicate that symptoms of distress (e.g. inability to go out of the house or to meet others socially without feeling anxious) often appear to be preceded by a period of general tension and emotional upset; it is as if such states prepare the ground for certain kinds of learning to take place: as if they put the organism on a defensive footing, ready to react adversely to relatively minor provocation. The kind of disturbance referred to here is quite commonly experienced by women in the few days prior to menstruation and has been given the name of pre-menstrual tension. If this condition is a good parallel to the situation in which abnormal fears can arise, then it should be possible to show a propensity for 'defensive' or adverse learning in pre-menstrual days which is not present at other times in the cycle. This is, in fact, what has been found. The evidence indicates that the state of the organism at the time when some noxious event is present not only determines the speed at which learning takes place but also any tendency for the learning to be preserved over time. One might be tempted to argue that this 'natural' disposition to acquire neurotic symptoms could explain why disproportionately large numbers of women complain of neurotic symptoms.

Another influence to be taken into account as limiting the scope of a purely environmentalist view of human behaviour is that of biological potential for learning. The argument here has been cogently presented by Seligman and Hager (1972), who conclude that all organisms appear to show a great readiness to acquire certain associations while other connections will be made only with difficulty or even not at all. Among the examples cited by Seligman and Hager is that of the dog which can very quickly associate the operation of a latch with its paw to escape from a box, but seems quite unable to learn to effect escape by wagging its tail. It is not that tail-wagging is a difficult action for the dog to perform or even that it is an uncommon reaction; rather it seems that the problem lies in making the connection itself. It is argued that the species has no biological propensity to make such a connection; the evolutionary history of the dog did not prepare the animal for this kind of learning.

It is not yet known to what extent humans are affected by preparedness, although it is obvious that certain connections appear to be 'natural' and made quite easily, while others are not. It has been suggested that a good example of preparedness is to be found in the prevalence of spider and snake phobia found in populations not at all at risk from these creatures. A more purely environmentalist approach might argue that one would need to be bitten by a spider or snake before a phobic reaction could be developed yet, obviously, there seems to be a great readiness in many people to display a wariness about spiders in a country such as England, while no such widespread fear is evoked by horses or hamsters. Somewhere in our evolutionary history, it can be argued, the species has acquired a readiness to respond with fear to potential dangers, including spiders and snakes. Perhaps this is why open spaces present a problem for many people; such 'exposure' was to be avoided in the interests of survival and this potential for acquiring a fear of open spaces is easily tapped.

The thoroughgoing environmentalist would want to argue that man is virtually a blank sheet, a complicated learning machine and, given the appropriate incentives and opportunities, can be moulded to any desired pattern. In the light of the limitations to learning which have been mentioned it is obviously appropriate to take a more moderate view and regard man as a creature highly susceptible to modification through learning, but far from infinitely so. As yet, we do not know quite how far the capacity to learn can take us. Can it, for example, so change human nature that one becomes entirely altruistic, greed, selfishness and other 'human failings' becoming totally alien? There are those, like Dawkins (1978) who would not think this possible but, on the other hand, Skinner (1953) and many others see almost limitless possibilities to behaviour modification with the psycho-technology currently available even now.

For Skinnerians the basic principle of change can be stated quite simply; the consequences of any piece of behaviour affects the future of that behaviour. If the consequence is rewarding then the behaviour is strengthened (i.e. rendered more likely to occur again); if it is punishing, then the same response tends to be weakened. Using this basic proposition, it is argued, far-reaching changes can be made to occur.

Of course, such a view is as profoundly hedonistic as Pavlov's or Freud's, the basic contention being that man is simply a pleasure-maximizing, pain-minimizing organism; this is as much part and parcel of his make-up as any other creature. Changing behaviour, according to this view, depends upon the nature, timing and other attributes of rewards and punishments rather than upon appeals to reason or religious precepts.

There is, understandably, considerable resistance to accepting such a stark view of man's nature; it appears to accord no place at all to free will and choice, nor does it allow man any special place in biological or other terms. Hedonism is the key mechanism in what we are; man can (and does) learn to do and to be anything, providing that the rewards and punishments are there to chart the way.

What we can now do is to examine the achievements to date; to see how far Pavlovian and Skinnerian principles of learning have been effective in producing change. It is anyone's guess how much further it is possible to go.

Aversive learning

Most of us subscribe to the validity of the adages that 'the burnt child dreads the fire' or 'once bitten, twice shy'. These sayings simply embody the importance of pain avoidance in our biological make-up. Clearly, deprived of such protection the species could hardly be expected to survive; we learn pretty quickly and thoroughly if the consequences of some actions are painful. Yet there appear to be some notable exceptions to such a compelling principle; martyrs and heroes often seem to subject themselves to avoidable pain while hard-bitten criminals may appear unaffected by the punishment society metes out to them. Obviously the problem is more complex than at first sight appears. Perhaps one should not be overly influenced by these exceptions, since the rule does seem to hold in general, but it is just as well to begin by recognizing that the results of punishment are unpredictable. For that matter, the outcome of rewarding behaviours shows much the same variability and such findings make fools of those who argue for simple solutions. For example, on the one hand there are those who want to create a better society by wreaking extreme retribution upon all who infringe rules while, on the other, the 'progressives' appear to think that the solution to crime is to remove all sources of discomfort and irritation. Both views, obviously, are patently absurd; crime has persisted in spite of great harshness in past years and, as is now well documented, the rate has risen dramatically as the number of social workers, leisure centres and social welfare has increased.

There are several arguments advanced to explain why punishment fails to achieve good effects in the context under discussion. In the first place it is said that its application is seldom timely: it works very well if immediate, but poorly or not at all if the crime and later court sentence are separated by lengthy intervals of time. Second, it is said that the rate of successful to unsuccessful crime is unfavourable to learning to resist temptation: numerous crimes may be rewarded before one act leads to punishment. A third argument is that the rate of criminal behaviour is inversely related to the strength of punishment, and that deterrents are not nearly strong enough to be effective. Yet another reason is said to be the temperament of the habitual criminal who, it is alleged, does not generate the kind of anxiety which most of us experience when 'wrong doing'. This last point refers to evidence that the nervous systems of individuals appear to extend over a range from the excessive 'jumpiness' of the chronically anxious at one end of the spectrum to those who appear to be 'psychopathically' resistant to showing disturbance to even strong stimulation.

There is probably something to be said for each of these points and, at least, all serve to indicate the complexities which may underlie the application of punishments.

To some extent it is possible to avoid a number of these problems when aversive consequences are part of a treatment programme; here, more of what takes place is under the control of the therapist or experimenter. Perhaps the best-known example of this is to be found in the treatment of alcoholism. With this, an attempt is made to ensure that drinking (and stimulus situations related to it) leads to aversive consequences; a convenient means of achieving this in practice has been to administer an emetic drug and, when this is beginning to take effect, the individual is permitted to sip the alcohol to which he is addicted. Unpleasant feelings of nausea and vomiting will, in this way, become associated with the particular sight, smell and taste involved (Voegtlin and Lemere, 1942).

Of course, it can be argued that simply punishing the 'wrong' response is hardly likely to lead to the adoption of a socially-acceptable reaction. What, for example, can the homosexual do with the sexual impulses he experiences after the usual way in which these are expended have been denied to him by punishment? Accordingly, more sophisticated attempts to help have included not only punishment but also opportunities to escape from punishment. In the context of treating homosexuals, for instance, the individual concerned has been allowed access to slides depicting homosexual activity only at the cost of receiving strong electric shocks, while the rejection of such slides and their substitution by heterosexual material can lead to the avoidance of punishment altogether.

A perennial problem of aversive training has been that of securing appropriate levels of co-operation and motivation and, no doubt, many failures are attributable to this difficulty. A simple example of this clarifies the point in practical terms. The investigation here was of a young boy whose habit of thumb-sucking was to be dealt with by capitalizing upon his enjoyment of cartoons. The therapist arranged for the boy to sit through protracted showings of cartoon films but these showings ceased abruptly if thumb-sucking occurred, and the film would only be continued when this behaviour stopped. It took a relatively short time for the boy to control his bad habit during the film shows but it was noted that the training had no effect upon what happened outside that situation! Indeed, one might reasonably argue that, in this case, the boy had learned how to control the behaviour of the psychologist, rather than the opposite!

Since aversion therapy is given only to those voluntarily submitting themselves to this form of training, one should be able to assume a reasonable level of motivation to change. However, as we all recognize from personal experience, our commitment to change can be quite ephemeral and today's resolution to give up smoking (or whatever) can disappear completely tomorrow. Perhaps this is only another way of saying that the aversive condition has not been applied sufficiently vigorously or intensively to inhibit the temptation: the associative bond between aversive feelings and the 'unwanted' action is insufficiently strongly made. Nevertheless, it is apparent that this problem is a major obstacle to the success of punishment as a means of control.

Systematic desensitization

Few doubt the power of anxiety to alter and disrupt ordinary behaviour patterns; anxiety can handicap our attempts to cope with a whole range of life's problems, it may prevent anything approaching an adjustment to quite ordinary events and it may totally ruin our enjoyment of relationships and circumstances which should be pleasurable. The capacity to deal with and eliminate anxiety can be regarded as of major importance to the effective control of our behaviour since, essentially, anxiety is a disruptive influence which erodes our capacity to control our own thought and action. In short, changing behaviour often seems to involve removing anxiety.

The behavioural strategy to resolve this problem appears to be surprisingly direct and simple. All that is needed is a gradual, step-by-step approach to the feared object or situation together with some means of inhibiting anxiety at each of these stages. The technique for accomplishing this was developed and refined by Wolpe (1969). More than 30 years earlier Mary Cover Jones (1924) had described essentially the same method in successfully eliminating the children's fears and, in a sense, there seems to be nothing particularly remarkable or novel in the method. Nevertheless, Wolpe's standardization of an effective technique for the analysis of anxiety and the application of a treatment strategy was enormously important from both practical and theoretical points of view.

The basic argument is that fear (or anxiety) has inadvertently, through a process of association, become a learned reaction to the presence of certain cues. For example, fear may be triggered by the presence of several people because, at some time in the past, the individual has been made anxious in a social setting; or anxiety is aroused by the sound of quarrelling voices because, at some time, the individual was threatened by the belligerence of others. The task of treatment, therefore, is to sever this connection: to detach anxiety from the innocuous cue.

Some years ago the author was asked for help in removing an extreme fear of spiders in a lady so incapacitated by this anxiety that she was unable to perform household chores. Any article of furniture moved or corner dusted might dislodge one of these alarming creatures and so occasion acute anxiety. Being outdoors clearly also presented problems to this lady, although she recognized that her fear was actually groundless in the sense that none of the spiders she encountered, indoors or out, could actually harm her.

Questioning revealed that the fear she experienced could be broken down into a number of separate components which, in various combinations, could evoke either more or less anxiety. Size, for example, was an important variable: the larger the spider the more fear would be experienced. Similarly, blackness, hairiness, degree of activity, and proximity all affected the amount of fear experienced. It was possible, therefore, to describe 'spider situations' which would produce little by way of upset, and others which would create a good deal. A small, light-coloured, apparently hairless spider, quite dead and at some distance away, would cause only mild apprehension, while an active, large, black and hairy spider, galloping across her body, would produce a sense of panic.

One must begin, in desensitization treatment, with the least anxiety-provoking situation and as each of these ceases to produce anxiety, so one moves on to the next step in the hierarchy. In the spider phobic case quoted, one can obviously begin with exhibiting a small, dead, pale-coloured, hairless spider in one corner of the room, while the patient sits in the opposite corner. When this condition ceases to produce anxiety, then the insect can be moved a little closer or, alternatively, some characteristic can be changed (e.g. substitution of a slightly larger specimen) so that we have moved one notch up the fear hierarchy.

What is notable here is that each step in the hierarchy appears to produce a smaller reaction than was anticipated before treatment; it is as if accomplishing each step has resulted in some small but discernible loss in the total anxiety now experienced. This kind of psychological arithmetic applies with every step taken, so that the total amount of anxiety to be eliminated becomes less and less.

So far so good, but systematic desensitization involves some means of inhibiting anxiety at each stage, for only in this way can the anxiety connection be broken. Each hierarchical step, therefore, must be capable of producing some amount of fear, but this must be sufficiently small to be extinguished by some other feeling state, and the most convenient means of achieving this is to train the individual in muscle relaxation.

It is argued that muscle relaxation is in fact an ideal counter to anxiety feelings, since it is both easy to learn and very effective. In short, there is good evidence that one cannot be anxious and completely relaxed at the same time; relaxation effectively inhibits the experience of fear. Accordingly, such training precedes the hierarchical presentation of fear stimuli; the individual is instructed to remain as relaxed as possible each time the fear-stimulus is presented so that the experience of anxiety is controlled. In this way a new type of association is being learned: that in the presence of certain cues which previously occasioned fear, no such feelings are present.

Understandably, while this method may work quite well it is not one which is easily put into practice in all cases. The various spider specimens needed to form the hierarchy may be easily secured, but in the case of, say, a fear of flying, there are serious practical problems. One could not, for example, easily arrange that the aeroplane merely completes the dash down the runway (as one item on the hierarchy) without actually taking off (which may occupy a very different hierarchical level). The necessary control over the situation here, and in numerous other cases, simply could not be achieved.

This problem is solved by presenting such situations as imagined scenes instead of as real-life experiences. This obviously makes it very much easier to arrange for events to accord precisely with treatment requirements and allows all the refined control over circumstances that one would wish to have. The only question to ask about this solution is that of whether or not dealing with an imagined situation is as beneficial as dealing with the real one. The evidence indicates that it is, although all therapists like to include experience of the real event (the real spider, lift, aeroplane, etc.) as a way of consolidating and affirming the new found absence of fear. Merely learning not to experience anxiety in imagined examples of fear aspects or situations, using the little-by-little approach and suppressing any worry by preserving muscle relaxation, can produce important changes in behaviour.

This approach is widely used in the treatment of major and incapacitating phobias with considerable success, but it is worth pointing out that less extreme conditions, including those commonly found in young children, respond very well to sympathetic handling along these lines. Fear of school, of being left by mother, of playing with strange children, of insects, of the car, and many others respond well to the graduated approach described and, of course, the benefit to behaviour generally of shedding such fears makes the effort well worth while.

Cognitive learning

It will be apparent from the description of the behavioural approaches given so far that they seem to depend upon a rather mechanical conception of learning. Insight, explanation, logic and other ways in which we come to modify or correct our view of things appear to count for nothing: the assumption is that we simply cannot talk anyone out of being alcoholic or experiencing acute anxiety; they must be taught to do so by a painstaking and carefully conceived programme of training which avoids any appeal to the 'mind'. Yet we are aware that cognitive learning does occur since we can behave differently as a result of being told that this or that is the case, or by receiving instructions to do something in a particular way. Indeed, if everything about our behaviour had to be acquired by trial and error or successive approximations, then learning would be tedious, slow and in many cases inefficient.

The charge often levelled at the behavioural approach is that it ignores the conceptual thinking that is so peculiarly and importantly human. But this is to misunderstand the situation since it is apparent that the kind of learning process required to effect change appears to depend upon what it is about our behaviour that we are trying to modify. Furthermore, it has been argued that mental events (cognitions, thoughts) are also behaviours and amenable to the same laws and, to an extent, the same training methods.

A good example is the technique called 'thought stopping'. Essentially this represents the attempt to produce the disruption or inhibition of a mental process in much the same way as some more overt activity might be stopped. It is usual to begin (see Wolpe, 1969) with a demonstration by the therapist that a sudden, unexpected and loud noise (banging the table, for example) can interrupt a particular focus of attention. In the same way, it is pointed out, an unpleasant and persistent idea can be interrupted and, with practice, might become permanently inhibited. By stages, the control of the interruptive signal is transferrred from therapist to patient and then from an external signal (banging on the table) to an internal one (saying 'stop' to oneself).

It is readily apparent that this strategy is direct, simple, and treats ideas or cognitions in much the same way as any reflex or motor action. There is, in the application of this technique, nothing special about mental events: they are simply regarded as internal behaviours.

A rather less rigorous behaviour approach is to be found in Rational Emotive Therapy; indeed, many hard-nosed behaviourists would reject any claim that RET derives from learning or conditioning theories and deny that there is any identifiable trace of the behavioural tradition in RET. Nevertheless, this cognitive approach has features which are 'behavioural' in character; for example, the emphasis upon the here-and-now rather than the influence of early life experiences, the parsimonious theoretical formulations, the implicit and explicit dependence upon reinforcing experiences and the directness of attack upon a clearly-identified source of malfunctioning. The main thrust of the technique (Ellis, 1962) derives from the assumption that faulty thinking is revealed in what people say to themselves; such 'self-talk' influences overt behaviours, so changing the cognitions can influence the way we act and feel.

Part of the immediate appeal of this technique lies in the very obviousness that 'self-talk' is a major preoccupation of us all when we are beset by difficulties. As a simple example, when girl informs boy that their relationship is ended a positive torrent of internal conversations is likely to be triggered: 'I am in a terrible mess ... I can't believe it ... there's no hope ... what can I do, nothing matters any more ...' etc. Such self-talk is likely to be accompanied by observable behaviour such as weeping, not eating or sleeping, refusing to socialize, failing to deal adequately with work assignments, and so on.

RET concentrates attention upon those things which are objectively true (e.g. 'she no longer loves me') and those which are not ('no one cares ... life is over ... there'll never be anyone else for me ...'). It is contended that when one is forced to examine the illogicality of deducing certain conclusions from the premise 'she doesn't love me', then shifts toward more positive emotions and behaviours have to occur. Attention is, of course, directed to all faulty ideas which serve as props for disappointment and disillusion: many of these quite commonplace errors of thinking which we are better rid of. For example, that one must always appear competent and without sign of weakness, that one must always have evidence that one is loved, needed and approved of, or that any adverse comment means that no one is to be trusted.

There is no doubt that this kind of counselling approach can help us to gain a perspective on life's bumps and abrasions and so prevent exaggerated and damaging emotional reactions. Yet there are obviously important limitations to an approach which depends so heavily upon exposing the illogicality of much self-talk; the point about such states of mind, as about prejudices of all kinds, is that they tend to be rather resistant to a logical approach. There is, it often seems, a strong desire to bring ideas into line with the feelings being experienced.

Furthermore, a cognitive strategy tends to pay little attention to the internal alterations of state which can often prompt the appearance of faulty ideas. Anyone with experience of depression will recognize that talking someone out of such a state is not just a tall order but pretty well impossible. No doubt where the pattern of gloomy thoughts and ideas arise out of what may be a purely environmental circumstance - a lost job, a failed exam, a lost love - a logical analysis of thoughts and feelings can be beneficial, but perhaps such circumstances are less common than one might at first suppose. Perhaps in part these environmental traumas are not random events but, to a degree, are visited upon those of us who are already vulnerable to an extent.

A cognitive technique which translates rather better from the traditional areas of behavioural concern to mental events is covert sensitization (Cautela, 1966). Basically, this method represents the application of aversive control to thoughts (as opposed to 'actions' such as drinking alcohol or operating a fruit machine) and involves imagined scenes of the unwanted behaviour followed by imagined noxious consequences. For example, the overweight gluttonous lady may be asked to conjure up images of a table groaning under the weight of delicious food, stuffing herself to bursting with cream cake and other goodies and then to create the mental picture of being sick: vomit spilling out over the table, over her dress, on to the food, and so on. In short, it is hoped to create the cognitive equivalent of real events with the consequences of overeating being highly unpleasant and embarrassing.

Another example comes from Foa (1976), whose male client derived sexual gratification from dressing in woman's clothing. This had brought him to the courts, where he was then referred for treatment. Covert sensitization took the form of requiring the patient to imagine that he was driving along in his car when he saw a clothes line on which desirable articles of clothing were hanging; he stops, gets out and attempts to take these clothes, but as he does so, he is overcome by intense feelings of nausea. He was then required to imagine throwing the clothes away and feeling very much better.

It is worth pointing out that in this case, as in other examples of aversive training, the unwanted habit returned again following an initially successful outcome. Generally, the therapist takes account of the need to deal with this problem by arranging 'booster' courses of treatment as and when the need arises.

Operant training

It is apparent from the accounts given that the behavioural approach to change is strongly hedonistic; organisms learn when rewarded and 'unlearn' when punished. Perhaps more than in any other technique of learning, operant training exemplifies this dependence upon the manipulation of the consequences of behaviour: a consequence which is rewarding (positively reinforcing) will strengthen some reaction or response, while one which is punishing (negatively reinforcing) will weaken and discourage further behaviour of the same kind.

It was not until B. F. Skinner's 1953 publication that there was any systematic account of the circumstances under which rewards and punishments work best. Experimenting with small animals, often rats, Skinner was able to demonstrate convincingly that if some observable piece of behaviour (response) was followed consistently by reward, the chances of the same behaviour occurring in a similar situation on subsequent occasions would increase. Similarly, if a response was punished, it would become less likely to occur. Three very important aspects of the apparently simple relationship between response and consequences arose from these animal studies. First, it is imperative that the reinforcement applied to the subject really is rewarding or punishing for them. A puff at a cigarette is obviously pleasant and rewarding to some humans but would probably prove aversive to most rats, whereas the dry food pellets enjoyed by rats would be of little interest to most humans. The second point was that, at least initially, the reinforcement (reward or punishment) must follow immediately after the target response is performed. If we wish to increase the frequency with which a rat presses a lever, it is no use providing the reward half-an-hour after the response has occurred; the necessary association between lever-pressing and, say, food reward would simply not be made. Third, as well as being immediate, the reinforcement must be applied consistently. Under all but very extreme circumstances, the rat does not learn to press a lever as a result of a single reward for doing so but needs numerous rewarded trials until lever-pressing is acquired. It is best to reward every trial initially, for although learning can take place if rewards (or punishments) are more spread out, it is very much slower. However, once learned, a response may be maintained by occasional reinforcement.

Many psychologists have been attracted by Skinnerian research and have applied the rules to the modification of human behaviour. The degree of success which has been achieved has been surprising in view of the frequent criticisms of Skinner's approach as essentially simplistic and mechanistic. Perhaps the greatest changes that have been made in order to accommodate Skinner's system to work with humans have been in response to the obvious superiority of their thinking, memory and reasoning as well as their capacity to use and to understand language. These skills have had most effect on the second aspect of reinforcement described above. As long as individual persons realize that reinforcement will be contingent upon their behaviour within a reasonable time, it may not be necessary for the reinforcement to be immediate. An individual will be able to think about or anticipate the delayed outcome. When working with children, however, some tangible reminder may be given of the reinforcement to come, such as a gold star immediately on completion of some school work as a token representing, say, extra playtime during the day.

The types of problems to which reinforcement procedures may be applied range from minor irritating habits to major disorders which threaten the well-being or even life of the sufferer. Many examples from the field of child-management may be cited to illustrate the least severe end of this scale.

Many young children go through 'phases' which are both worrying and irritating to their parents but usually not harmful in themselves. An example of this would be the temper tantrums fairly frequently observed in toddlers. In nearly all cases such episodes last a few weeks or at most months and then disappear of their own accord. In a few cases they persist much longer, or with greater severity, and perhaps begin to disrupt family life. Providing the cause is not due to some physical illness, one may attempt to modify the behaviour by applying appropriate reinforcements. Very often it is found that a great deal of attention is given when a child has a tantrum, usually because it is alarming and upsetting to the parents. On the other hand, when the child is occupied and behaving well, the parents, sighing with relief, turn their attention to other things, effectively ignoring good behaviour. Evidently the child is being rewarded for having a tantrum but is punished (as being ignored can be aversive) for being well behaved. With these contingencies it is no wonder that such behaviour becomes more frequent and good behaviour becomes rarer. Tantrums may be modified simply by reversing reward and punishment; parents leave children to their own devices when they have a tantrum but take great care to play with them and talk to them when they are being good. Applied systematically, such a straightforward alteration of reinforcements can have amazingly rapid and beneficial effects.

Even relatively minor behaviour problems in children may have more serious effects on their eventual welfare. One form of difficulty that has been tackled fairly often in this way is disruptive classroom behaviour. Children who are frequently out of their seats, moving around and making a noise, usually benefit less from their schooling than their more appropriately behaved peers and are likely to fall behind with their work. In addition they may become unpopular with their companions as they upset the others' work and interfere with their games. In busy classrooms, such children are often reprimanded by teachers when they are a nuisance but receive very little attention for being 'good' since this occurs infrequently and they rarely produce work of a high enough standard to merit praise. Relatively mild chastisements from the teacher may be more rewarding for th child (being preferred to no attention at all) so the child is rewarded for being disruptive and ignored for practically everything else. As with the younger child, the task is to reverse the contingencies. In this case it may not be possible for the teacher to ignore the bad behaviour entirely but, usually, the amount of time and effort spent in the reprimand can be reduced significantly so that the child receives a minimum of attention for each disruptive act. At the same time reward is given for appropriate behaviour and an acceptable (although possibly lower than average) standard of work. If possible, the reward is given immediately with attention and praise but may be supplemented by the use of stars or marks for good conduct, and these tokens can be exchanged for privileges at the end of the day. Usually the co-operation of not only the teacher and pupil but also of the entire class is required to make this procedure fully effective.

The much-publicized condition of anorexia nervosa is an example of a life-threatening state which may sometimes be ameliorated by the use of reinforcement procedures. Patients suffering from this disorder are most commonly girls in their mid- to late-teens who have begun to diet excessively, and now refuse to eat and sabotage attempts to feed them by hiding the food or vomiting. Many lose so much weight that they must be confined to bed. The main management problem is to reinstate eating.

There is no single acceptable account of why a girl begins to become anorexic but there is commonly evidence of considerable social reinforcement for not eating once serious dieting is under way, since serious weight loss causes friends and relatives to become increasingly concerned and respond to refusals to eat by attention and attempts to coax and persuade, and this attention contributes to the maintenance of not eating. Attempts have been made to make positive reinforcement contingent upon eating rather than not eating and, to do this, the patient has been socially isolated and denied pleasures such as radio and television in order to maximize the rewarding effect of social contact. It has been arranged that a friendly therapist will eat each meal with the patient and converse with her when, and only when, she eats a mouthful of food. Once eating a meal has been established, the reward is made less immediate by allowing the patient to earn time with the therapist or friends after the meal has been eaten. She is also allowed access to television, etc., in the same way. This kind of procedure has been found to produce important weight gain in a number of patients. When described in outline it may appear that the patient is the passive recipient of reinforcement, unaware of the contingencies that have been planned, but this is far from the case, as most patients become involved with the preparation of their programmes, the negotiation of weight targets, amounts to be eaten, planning rewards and agreeing to contingencies.

It is clear that reinforcement contingencies can be applied effectively to a wide range of behaviour problems in humans. As long as the contingencies are appropriately rewarding or punishing, and the consequences fairly immediate and consistent, the reinforcements are likely to be effective, but the chances of success will be increased if the individuals with the problems are involved in the construction and discussion of their own management programmes.

In conclusion

Behavioural approaches to change tend to lack appeal when compared to other methods. We would prefer, for example, to think that we are amenable to logic and reason and that if only the facts are made available to us we could change to be in accord with them. Or, in other contexts, we may find the dramatic aspects of psychoanalysis more compelling, with the eccentricities of human behaviour being explained as the result of mysterious and excitingly interesting forces. Certainly, behavioural approaches stand in sharp contrast and seem to inspire all the excitement of Latin conjugations!

On the other hand, while the techniques admittedly tend to apply about as well to animals as to man, their clarity and simplicity arises from sound experimental work and scientific thought, qualities which in any other context would be thought commendable. It is worth while to offer the example of bedwetting as a means of showing how such thinking offers distinct advantages over a more tortuous and complex account.

Psychoanalysts are inclined to regard bedwetting as merely the external sign of some inner turmoil. It has been regarded, for example, as a substitute for sexual gratification or a means by which a child can express aggression and resentment toward others. The behavioural formulation is starkly simple; individuals learn to be dry at night and some fail to acquire this skill. If the former view is correct, then simply removing the behaviour (bedwetting) would not cure the inner discontent; if the behavioural view is correct, however, then getting rid of the symptom would be a very useful thing.

Mowrer's simple device to unlearn bedwetting (Mowrer and Mowrer, 1938) was in fact highly successful and is very widely used today. It deals directly with the symptom and in most cases bedwetting is eliminated. No evidence exists of any underlying pathological process of the kind postulated by the psychoanalyst.

Naturally one example of a greater claim to effectiveness does not establish the general superiority of the behavioural approach, yet it does seem that such examples can be multiplied many times over. This is, in fact, what one would expect from a model constructed from painstaking laboratory experimental work and scientific formulations.

It is not, of course, that the approach or the techniques deriving from it, some of which have been briefly reviewed here, are either wildly successful or beyond criticism. There are, indeed, numerous difficulties and shortcomings and, as indicated earlier, one of the most serious of these is the partiality of the purely environmentalist viewpoint and the almost complete neglect of genetic/constitutional influences. Nevertheless, behavioural strategies now occupy a position of high importance for psychologists, and the influence of these strategies in many and diverse areas of application is still growing.

References

Cautela, J.B. (1966)
Treatment of compulsive behavior by covert sensitization. The Psychological Record, 16, 33-41.

Dawkins, R. (1978)
The Selfish Gene. Oxford: Oxford University Press.

Ellis, A. (1962)
Reason and Emotion in Psychotherapy. New York: Kyle Stewart.

Foa, E.B. (1976)
Multiple behaviour techniques in the treatment of transvestism. In H.J. Eysenck, Case Studies in Behaviour Therapy. London: Routledge & Kegan Paul.

Jones, M.C. (1924)
The elimination of children's fears. Journal of Experimental Psychology, 7, 383-90.

Mowrer, O.H. and Mowrer, W. (1938)
Enuresis: a method for its study and treatment. American Journal of Orthopsychiatry, 8, 436-59.

Munroe, R.L. (1955)
School of Psychoanalytic Thought. New York: Dryden Press.

Pavlov, I.P. (1927)
Conditioned Reflexes (Transl. Anrep). London: Oxford University Press.

Rachman, S. (1966)
Sexual fetishism: an experimental analogue. The Psychological Record, 16, 293-296.

Seligman, M.E.P. and Hager, J.L. (1972)
Biological Boundaries of Learning. New York: Appleton-Century-Crofts.

Skinner, B.F. (1953)
Science and Human Behavior. New York: Macmillan.

Vila, J. and Beech, H.R. (1978)
Vulnerability and defensive reactions in relation to the human menstrual cycle. British Journal of Social and Clinical Psychology, 17, 93-100.

Voegtlin, W.L. and Lemere, E. (1942)
The treatment of alcohol addiction. Quarterly Journal of Studies on Alcohol, 2, 717-803.

Watson, J.B. and Rayner, R. (1920)
Conditioned emotional reactions. Journal of Experimental Psychology, 3, 1-14.

Wolpe, J. (1969)
The Practice of Behavior Therapy. New York: Pergamon Press.

1. Describe the theoretical underpinnings of systematic desensitization as a treatment strategy to eliminate fear.
2. Drawing upon your personal experience, describe and discuss the incapacitating effect of anxiety on coping with a life problem you have had to face. Outline the behavioural strategies that might be useful in overcoming it.
3. Describe the process of classical conditioning and how this process can account for the development of abnormal fears.
4. What are the implications of classical and operant conditioning for a crime prevention policy?
5. Describe the limitations of using aversive therapy as a means of changing behaviour.
6. What are the basic differences between 'cognitive' and behavioural strategies where behaviour change is concerned?
7. In what sense can the behavioural approach be said to be hedonistic?
8. Responses and consequences are the two basic elements of operant training. What are the basic requirements in providing reinforcement in order to secure effective behaviour change?
9. To what extent do you think that we are affected in real life situations by the operation of reinforcement principles?
10. How could one apply an operant approach in a classroom to deal with disruptive class behaviour?

Annotated reading

Griffiths, D. (1981) Psychology and Medicine. London: Macmillan and the British Psychological Society.
    This is primarily intended for GPs to enable the medical profession to acquire concepts relevant to their work so as to facilitate professional skill and expertise. Many of the topics covered will be of interest to the occupational therapist.

Kanfer, F.H. and Goldstein, A.P. (1975) Helping People Change: A textbook of methods. Oxford: Pergamon Press.
    An account of practical behavioural approaches to change.

Oakley, D. and Platkin, H. (1979) Brain, Behaviour and Evolution. London: Methuen.
    Undergraduate level synthesis of disciplines relevant to psychology. How evolutionary perspective can help our understanding of psychological questions.

Rachman, S. (1971) The Effects of Psychotherapy. Oxford: Pergamon Press.
    An account of the problems associated with psychotherapy and the way in which the behavioural approach deals with issues of treatment and training.

Walker, S. (1976) Learning and Reinforcement. London: Methuen.
Introductory text on key concepts to understanding behavioural approaches to change.

19

The theory and practice of psychotherapy
Fay Fransella

The theory and practice of psychotherapy

It is not by chance that both Hopson's and Beech's chapters avoid using the word 'therapy' in the title. It is part of an attempt by many to move away from the 'medical model' which suggests that people with psychological problems are necessarily 'ill' and so require 'treatment'. Another aspect of this same attempt is the use of the word 'client' instead of 'patient'. That no other more satisfactory word has yet been found indicates something of the hold our language has over our thinking. It was against such a model that the psychiatrist Laing rebelled. The hold is such that I can find no alternative to 'psychotherapy' to use in the title of this chapter so as to distinguish it from counselling on the one hand and behaviour therapy on the other.

The psychoanalysis of Freud

It is difficult to say today exactly what psychoanalysis is because there have been so many developments over the years. All I intend to do is present you with some of the main features that are common to the many psychodynamic approaches to psychotherapy. As was pointed out in chapter 2, Freud's theory actually sprang from the procedure of psychoanalysis itself, and so his theory of personality is really a description of what psychoanalysis is about.

Anxiety
Ideas of repression and anxiety are, for Freud, centrally important in understanding the neuroses. Some of the most vital events to be repressed concern those occurring at the time when the boy has hostility to his father and love for his mother. The id's 'wish' is repressed and made unavailable to consciousness. When the latent stage of development is over and the libido returns, there is a threat that these repressed ideas will return to consciousness. They therefore have to be repressed again.

However, this process fails for the neurotic person. The repressed ideas are expressed but the person is not consciously aware of their meaning. In the case of hysteria, Freud saw the conflict being expressed in bodily form, say, in hysterical paralysis of the arm. Thus, although the neurosis is actually acquired in early childhood, it does not usually make its appearance until many years later. For

Freud the hysterical 'symptom' is a communication to the environment from the unconscious.

The Oedipus complex is not the only cause of repression. Libidinal energy can be fixated at any stage of development. Freud believed that such frustration of the libidinal drive is a basic cause of anxiety. In Freud's view, anxiety is inescapable for all of us and serves to alert the ego to some impending danger. The sources of threat to the ego parallel its three tyrannical masters: the external world, the super-ego and the id. The environment produces REALISTIC anxiety, such as occurs at the time of examinations or confrontations with wild animals. The emotional response resulting from threat of punishment from the super-ego is MORAL anxiety. NEUROTIC anxiety occurs when the ego is threatened with the possibility that impulses from the id will become conscious, over which the ego will have no control.

Defence mechanisms
When the ego is threatened with anxiety it can call upon some defences; repression being the most primary. Among these are some of the best known of Freud's ideas. They are not undesirable nor are they indications of neurotic disorder. In Freud's view, we all make use of them, and they are a simple way of coping with one of the forms of anxiety.

* REPRESSION relates to neurotic anxiety.
* SUBLIMATION is the means whereby we are able to use our dammed-up libidinal energy in a socially creative way. In Freud's view, the diverting of energy in this way is a prime cause of advances in culture and knowledge. Students, artists, teachers, writers, occupational therapists and others are all sublimating their libidinal energy. This is not the sole motivating force for cultural advancement, but it plays a considerable part.
* PROJECTION is said to occur when a personal characteristic arouses anxiety and this is defended against by attributing that characteristic to others.
* RATIONALIZATION occurs when we attempt to make our irrational behaviour appear rational; our mistakes, poor judgements and failures are 'explained away'.
* REACTION FORMATION is the way in which we sometimes defend against a forbidden impulse by consciously expressing its opposite. The mother who hates her child may behave in an over-motherly or 'smothering' way.

These defence mechanisms share two things: they occur at an unconscious level, so that we deceive ourselves, and they distort reality, making the situation less threatening.
Freud thought that we rarely use just one mechanism but choose between the many available, only some of which are given above.

The road to change

Originally Freud thought that personal growth in the neurotic person had been slowed down or stopped altogether, and the only way to help that person was to 'unleash' the libido which was dammed up in the unconscious and which was also being used for defensive purposes. If this energy could be released, it could then be redistributed and made available for more healthy living.

He found dreams to be the 'royal road' to the unconscious and hoped to arrive at the latent content of the dream by the method of FREE ASSOCIATION. By allowing the mind to wander 'freely', the person would become aware of those things which were, in fact, striving for expression. But he later came to see that there was more to it than simply trying to make the unconscious conscious. It was important that the person gained emotional insight into these previously repressed memories.

The aims of psychoanalysis are determined by each person's problems. If the person suffered considerable fixation at an early stage of development, then analysis is aimed at making him or her free to take up their psychological development again; if the main problem is an over-tyrannical id, therapy is directed to making that id conscious and so putting the ego in charge. Freud (1940) says this about his plan of cure:

> The ego has been weakened by the internal conflict; we must come to its aid. The position is like a civil war which can only be decided by the help of an ally from without. The analytical physician and the weakened ego of the patient, basing themselves upon the real external world, are to combine against the enemies, the instinctual demands of the id, and the moral demands of the superego. We form a pact with each other. The patient's sick ego promises us the most candour, promises that is, to put at our disposal all of the material which his self-perception provides; we, on the other hand, assure him of the strictest discretion and put at his service our experience in interpreting material that has been influenced by the unconscious. Our knowledge shall compensate for his ignorance and shall give his ego once more mastery over the lost provinces of his mental life. This pact constitutes the analytic situation.

Transference is the means whereby the person comes to expose the unconscious and gain emotional insight into his or her own nature. The patient transfers to the therapist important feelings and attitudes previously held towards important others in the past. Transference occurs in all therapeutic relationships, but there is an aspect of it that is unique to the psychoanalytic approach: the transference neurosis. This is a replica, in miniature, of the neurotic situation as it originally occurred. The patient tries to get from the analyst and the analytic situation all those things which he or she had to do without in childhood. During analysis, only those events occurring within this artificial situation are considered relevant. One way of ensuring that it is indeed central to the person's life is the frequency and number of meetings: up to five or six per week for a period of several years.

The patient can now deal with the original experiences within the analytic situation. He or she finds that the conflict is less intense than it was originally and, being older and more mature, is able to use parts of the ego which were not available at the original time. These three factors offer the chance of re-learning and gaining insight into old conflicts.

The analytical psychotherapy of Jung

Whereas the ultimate goal of psychoanalysis is reconciliation of the individual with the demands of society, the goal for Jung was INDIVIDUATION. I introduced you to Jung's ideas about the person in chapter 2.

> Individuation means becoming a single, homogeneous being, and, in so far as 'individuality' embraces our innermost, last and incomparable uniqueness, it also implies becoming one's own self. We could therefore translate individuation as 'coming to selfhood' or 'self-realization' (Jung, 1956).

One-sidedness is one reason for the blocking of individuation, and this is the main cause of neurosis. A person may be concentrating on goals which were appropriate in an earlier phase of life, or else a basic attitude or function may be over- or under-developed.

Individuation occurs increasingly as we are able to differentiate our ego, or conscious self, from our unconscious. In so doing, we become increasingly aware of the extent to which our thoughts and motives arise from the COLLECTIVE UNCONSCIOUS. At the same time that differentiation occurs, we must bring about increasing integration of the unconscious and conscious but at a higher level of awareness. Jung felt that the dissatisfactions of modern Man were due to our ignoring the unconscious. 'We should never identify ourselves with reason, for man is not and never will be a creature of reason alone ... The irrational cannot and must not be extirpated' (Jung, 1956). Freud, on the other hand, could not imagine an 'excess' of consciousness. Jung, as always, wanted a balance between the two extremes.

Jungian therapy aims to bring about individuation. First, the person has to realize that society's goals are artificial; while being fulfilled they must also be put into perspective. Next must come the awareness of the shadow: we are basically decent and good, but are also capable of unimaginable crimes. The third and last step in individuation involves coming to terms with the anima or animus: this results in freedom from influences of childhood and the awareness of increased creativity. The one final barrier to selfhood concerns meaning. There must be a personal commitment to a primordial fantasy, which involves the discovery of a religious impulse of some sort. By a personal commitment to some symbol we attain selfhood.

Here we come to the mystical nature of Jung's ideas. With the driving force within us (having the quality of an instinct), thrusting toward selfhood or self-realization, Jung made the archetype of the 'self' paramount. To find the self we have to become aware of the ways in which the conscious and unconscious parts of our psyche complement each other, but:

> There is little hope of our ever being able to reach even approximate consciousness of the self, since however much we make conscious there will always exist an indeterminate and indeterminable amount of unconscious material which belongs to the totality of the self. Hence the self will always remain a superordinate quantity (Jung, 1956).

He called the self 'The God within us'. For Jung, it is possible always for us to grow; at least we have that potential. However, it seems as if he felt we should go along with what society has to offer us (be content to be whatever we are) and to find our true personal meaning of life through the individuation process.

The personal construct psychotherapy of Kelly

Its nature

Using the scientist model, Kelly saw those with psychological problems as people who are unable to test out their personal theories decisively, and so are not able to elaborate their construct systems, their understanding of themselves and of their interpersonal worlds. For instance, their construing may have become circular, so that they are endlessly testing and re-testing the same hypotheses and are unable to accept the implications of the data which they collect; or they may have moved into the kind of chaos where constructions are so vague and loose that they cannot yield expectations that are clear enough to be tested.

Whatever the specific difficulty, psychotherapists do not set out to sell a particular construct system to the client as a pre-digested package. Rather they would seek to help the client tighten, reconstrue or test the validity of the client's own construct system. If successful - that is, if the client's system once again begins to move and elaborate - then the direction in which it goes and the issues it pursues are, in a very definite sense, no longer the psychotherapist's business.

Just as Kelly's view of the person and the theory stem directly from his philosophy of constructive alternativism, so also does it form the basis of psychotherapy. Kelly (1955) states that:

> We take the stand that there are always some alternative constructions available to choose among in dealing with the world. No one needs to paint himself into a corner; no one needs to be completely hemmed in by circumstances; no one needs to be a victim of his biography.

We therefore have a hopeful approach; but it in no way suggests that we each can always find these alternatives. We sometimes need another, or others, to point the way. As do Freud and Jung, Kelly sees the interaction between client and therapist as central for the clinical-psychological enterprise. Psychotherapy is a situation in which one person helps another achieve 'the psychological reconstruction of life'.

The psychotherapeutic relationship

As construed by Kelly, the relationship between client and therapist is much more one of equals, each struggling with the same problem, than one between a knower and an ignoramus. Kelly saw the same struggles going on in psychotherapy as he saw going on between a Ph.D. student and a supervisor. Both patient and student have selected the problem on which they wish to work; both may find themselves 'stuck' during the course of the programme; both may look to their partner in the exercise and seek help in getting their construing disentangled so that they can get on the move again.

The essence of the relationship is one of partnership, in which neither has the final answer; this they seek together. In the metaphorical language of science, therapist and client design new experiments that can be tested out in the protected laboratory, which is the psychotherapy room. Together they take stock of outcomes and revise their common hunches. Neither is boss, nor are they merely well-bred neighbours who keep their distance from unpleasant affairs. It is, as far as they are able to make it so, a partnership' (Kelly, 1969).

Psychological disorder

Kelly describes us as behaving in relation to how we construe the events confronting us, and so redefines all the language to do with patients, symptoms, therapy and so on, in terms of such constructions. Thus Kelly defines psychological disorder as 'any personal construction which is used repeatedly in spite of consistent invalidation'. That is, the person is making poor predictions, the experiments are going wrong, the person is being a poor scientist. The person attempts to re-construe, and so achieve some validatory evidence for the construing, but fails.

Predictions about events are tested against reality by our behaving. The outcome of the behavioural experiment can be vital. The person has to do something when predictions are invalidated. We can be hostile and make sure that our behaviour produces results that validate our construing; or we can loosen our construing and make more tentative hypotheses; or we can repeat the experiment just in case we misread the results. If, in spite of varying our strategies for dealing with invalidation, we still continue to be proved wrong in our expectations, then we may so loosen the ties between our constructs (in order to 'hedge our bets') that we are incapable of drawing the constructs together again. Bannister developed the theory of 'serial invalidation' along these lines to account for the type of thought-disorder found in some schizophrenics. He was at pains to point out that schizophrenic thought-disorder is not, in his view, specific to schizophrenia but one extreme on a continuum.

It should be noted that loosening and tightening are not of themselves pathological reations, but are normal reactions to varying validational fortunes. What is being argued is that the thought-disordered schizophrenic has been driven to loosen beyond the point at which there are enough workable lines of implication between personal constructs for that individual to re-tighten the system. 'He has sawn off the psychological branch on which he was sitting' (Bannister and Fransella, 1980).

Happily, of course, invalidation rarely produces such devastating results. More often, those who are unable to make the necessary psychological adjustments become increasingly aware of the mess into which they are getting themselves. As they fail to reconstrue, their behaviour may become ever more unusual both to themselves and to others and, in the end, they may find a solution; they may develop a symptom.

The symptom

'It is suggested that psychological symptoms may frequently be interpreted as the rationale by which one's chaotic experiences are given a measure of structure and meaning' (Kelly, 1955). Within the illness-model the patient may be seen as coming bearing an offering; the symptom for removal. But when focussing on the person as construer, the emphasis is on exploring, with him or her, the paths along which their current construing of life has resulted in the present impasse and identifying those paths that could be opened up for future exploration.

Rowe (1978) has shown how impossible it was for one depressed woman to improve since, for her, being depressed was 'good' and being well was 'bad'. She also described Rose, for whom cleanliness was of vital importance. Rose needed rest, but was unable to remain quiet. During the course of psychotherapy it transpired she thought it was only possible to face the Day of Judgement if one helped others and was clean. Since one never knows when that Day is coming, it is important always to be ready and clean. Construing life in this way, how could she possibly rest?

It has been argued that some forms of behaviour, established for a long period of time, become so much part of a person's way of life that symptomatic treatment without reconstrual is of little value. This applies equally to the alcoholic, the obese, the stutterer, the agrophobic or the ticquer. In several of these groups, a direct relationship between construing and change in the symptomatic behaviour has been demonstrated (e.g. Fransella, 1972). Therapeutic sessions with such people often quickly move far away from the presenting symptoms. This one would expect if the person does indeed focus on a symptom simply as a means of making sense of the disturbing things that are happening. It is often not the 'real' problem.

Psychotherapeutic procedures

The therapy is conducted according to a complex system of professional constructs which are pitched at a very high level of abstraction. The personal construct therapist is thus able to call upon any technique deemed likely to bring about alternative construing in the client. For example, if the diagnosis is that the person has a system of constructs to do with personal relationships which is so tightly organized that movement is impossible, then some technique for loosening that system might be employed: free association or guided fantasy, for example; if the diagnosis is that the person operates a personal dualism and keeps emotional experience ut of daily life, then some procedure to bring them into contact with that side of themselves might be used, such as some 'pillow-bashing' exercises. Equally, for a person who finds it difficult to express things verbally, a programme of systematic desensitization might be designed (see Beech's chapter, pp. 353-356). From a personal construct standpoint, this means introducing the person, systematically, to a previously avoided situation, and so encouraging reconstruction. Implosion can be seen as having its effect by forcing the person to encounter a situation previously construed as 'impossible', likely to make me 'die', 'cause me to lose total control of myself', and so on.

This is not eclecticism. On the contrary, every course of therapeutic action is directed by a highly explicit set of theoretical constructs. Where the approach is unusual is in having the theoretical constructs defined at such a very high level of abstraction.

Kelly regarded role-playing and enactment as being particularly useful techniques for aiding reconstruing. By enacting a role in the clinical sessions 'as if' you are approaching a problem in a different way, new possibilities may be perceived. The woman who doubts her love for her husband might be asked to play the role of a person who really did not do so. What would be the husband's reactions? How would she behave in the morning, in bed, in the garden, and so forth? What possibilities would 'not loving him' open up for her? To play a role is to submerge oneself in it to see how differently the world looks from that stance.

Very often the client needs to elaborate his or her system of constructs in a controlled way so as to increase self-consistency. Since the way problems are construed is a major determinant of whether or not they can be solved, the task of the therapist is to help the patient formulate testable hypotheses. Intellectualization is no good. At some point in time the patient has to be able and, in particular, willing, to go out into the world of reality and test ideas by behaving. Controlled elaboration helps bring this about, whether it is designed to help verbalize pre-verbal constructs, sort out inconsistencies, or elaborate submerged poles of constructs.

There was only one specific technique described by Kelly which can be used when something is needed to 'trigger off' psychological movement. FIXED ROLE THERAPY embodies and illustrates many of the central ideas in personal construct psychotherapy. In the first instance, the client is asked to write a personal character sketch. The therapist, in conjunction with another therapist, then draws up a portrait of a person who is 'at 90 degrees' to the first. The aim is to portray a person who will suggest new dimensions along which life can be seen. For example, if a woman sees her relationships as about dominance versus submission, then the fixed role sketch might describe a person who is fiercely interested in people but not, thereby, either dominant or submissive.

The client is asked if she finds the person credible. If there are doubts, the sketch is altered until it is acceptable. The woman is then told that she should become this new person for the next week or so. She is to eat the kind of food she thinks this person would eat; wear the kind of clothes she would wear, respond to others as she would, dream the other's dreams: in fact, truly to be that other. She is being forced to experience herself and her behaviour in a different manner. Most important, she may be able to see that a person is self-inventing and that she is not necessarily trapped by her circumstances, by the body in which she lives, or by her autobiography.

One study conducted by Karst and Trexler (1970) examined the efficacy of this approach, together with rational-emotive therapy, and compared a group receiving no treatment. They found that both produced change; but it must be emphasized that fixed role therapy is only suggested by Kelly as one technique that could be used with certain clients in certain circumstances. It is not synonymous with personal construct psychotherapy.

Although Kelly's theoretical approach to psychotherapy has been discussed mostly in the context of the individual, he did provide some guidelines for working with a group. He describes six phases through which the psychotherapy group evolves. Starting with the establishment of mutual support, the group goes through stages of enactment within the group setting and on to the designing of experiments for each other to experiment with outside the group setting.

In summary, personal construct psychotherapy takes as its starting point a personal acceptance by the therapist of the philosophy of constructive alternativism. This is a frame of mind in which the client is seen as someone with a unique way of viewing the world of reality. The therapist's job is to subsume this view of the world as far as possible within his or her own construct system. The more the therapist can stand in the shoes of the client and see the world through the client's eyes, the better able will the therapist be to help that person reconstrue the world and so resolve the dilemma.

Personal construct psychotherapy involves the application of the theoretical constructs which form the psychology of personal constructs. This means that the therapist must have considerable knowledge of the theory in its entirety. Only then can these constructs concerning the psychological workings of us all be applied to the client's system.

Using theoretical constructs about how construct systems work, diagnoses can be made about the problem experienced by a person. The diagnoses having being made, specific techniques may be used to encourage helpful change. Diagnoses are only tentative and so may be changed if proved wrong or when the client moves on to some other aspect of the problem. Personal construct psychotherapy thus has at its disposal as many techniques as have been invented. With the procedures of other therapies becoming techniques, it is possible to start to examine, in a systematic manner, the type of technique that is best suited to particular types of construing. Research is directed to the study of the PROCESS OF CHANGE in construing itself, rather than to different types of therapy in particular.

References

Bannister, D. and Fransella, F. (1980)
Inquiring Man (2nd edn). Harmondsworth: Penguin.
Fransella, F. (1972)
Personal Change and Reconstruction. London: Academic Press.
Freud, S. (1940)
An outline of psychoanalysis. In Standard Edition of the Complete Psychological Works of S. Freud, Volume 23. London: Hogarth Press.
Jung, C.G. (1956)
Two Essays on Analytical Psychology. New York: Meridian Books.
Karst, T.O. and Trexler, L.D. (1970)
Initial study using fixed role and rational-emotive therapy in treating public speaking anxiety. Journal of Consulting and Clinical Psychology, 34, 360-366.
Kelly, G.A. (1955)
The Psychology of Personal Constructs, Volumes I and II. New York: Norton.
Kelly, G.A. (1969)
The psychotherapeutic relationship. In B. Maher (ed.), Clinical Psychology and Personality. New York: Krieger.

Rowe, D. (1978)
The Experience of Depression. Chichester: Wiley.

1. Discuss ways in which a psychotherapeutic relationship differs from other interpersonal relationships.
2. How do Freud, Jung and Kelly differ in the way they view unconscious processes?
3. Occupational therapists have no business attempting to do psychotherapy. Discuss this statement.
4. What are defence mechanisms? Describe ways in which we would be said to use them in daily life.
5. How would you define 'psychotherapy'? Describe some of its main features.
6. Describe the basic similarities and differences between behaviour therapy and psychotherapy.
7. If people have a problem in society today, they think they should lie down and be treated for it, rather than attempt to solve it themselves. Discuss this statement.
8. To what extent will your relationships with clients be affected by what you have read in this book about counselling, helping and the process of psychotherapy?

Annotated reading

Jung, C.G. (1956) Two Essays on Analytical Psychology. New York: Meridian Books.
No writings of Jung are easy, but these will give you the flavour of his work.

Landfield, A.W. and Leitner, L.M. (eds) (1980) Personal Construct Approaches to Psychotherapy and Personality. New York: Wiley.
This book includes an introduction to the field and several chapters on the therapy.

Sandler, J., Dare, C. and Holder, A. (1973) The Patient and the Analyst. London: Allen & Unwin.
An account of the psychoanalytic relationship.

Index

Index

Index

Index

Index